MW01031559

BISON
BOOKS

ART AND POLITICS

Richard Wagner

TRANSLATED BY
William Ashton Ellis

John Michael Cooper
Denton, Texas
30 May 2002

University of Nebraska Press
Lincoln and London

Manufactured in the United States of America

☻ The paper in this book meets the minimum requirements of American National Standard for Information Sciences—Permanence of Paper for Printed Library Materials, ANSI z39.48-1984.

First Bison Books printing: 1995
Most recent printing indicated by the last digit below:
10   9   8   7   6   5   4   3   2   1

Library of Congress Cataloging-in-Publication Data
Wagner, Richard, 1813–1883.
[Literary works. English. Selections]
Arts and politics / Richard Wagner; translated by William Ashton Ellis.
p.   cm.
Originally published: Richard Wagner's prose works. Vol. 4, Art and politics. London: Kegan Paul, Trench, Trübner & Co., 1895.
Includes index.
Contents: To the kingly friend (poem)—On state and religion—German art and German policy—What is German?—A music-school for Munich—Ludwig Schnorr of Carolsfeld—Notices—About conducting—Three poems.
ISBN 0-8032-9774-2 (alk. paper)
1. Wagner, Richard, 1813–1886—Political and social views.
2. Art and state—Germany.   3. Music—Germany—19th century—History and criticism.   I. Title.
ML410.W1A12663   1996
780—dc20
95-24316
CIP
MN

Reprinted from the 1895 translation of volume 4 (*Art and Politics*) of *Richard Wagner's Prose Works*, published by Kegan Paul, Trench, Trübner & Co., Ltd., London.

CONTENTS

TRANSLATOR'S PREFACE.

ITH the present volume we reach a complete turning-point in the author's outer career. At Vienna, where the last essay in Volume III. was written, it appeared as though no hope remained of Richard Wagner's ever being able to bring the works of his artistic maturity before the public; from that city he took refuge with some friends of many years' standing, the Willes, at Zurich; at the end of April 1864 he left them, without a prospect in life and prepared to meet the worst, to abandon his art for which there seemed no haven in this world, perhaps to abandon life itself. No one can ever plumb the depth of his sufferings in those days, sufferings that leap for a moment into lurid light in his private correspondence, revealing glimpses of untold abysms, but are promptly smothered by the convulsive smile of the heroic man who bites his lips to mask his pain. But two days after Wagner had left Mariafeld (the Willes' home) King Ludwig's envoy was sent in search of him, and on the fourth of May occurred the first meeting of the artist and the noble prince who was to rescue him from at least the squalor of a life from hand to mouth and bestow on him a priceless friendship. Much more would Ludwig II. of Bavaria fain have done for the man in whom he recognised the personification of German genius, but the jealousy of courtiers and paltry politicians, of all that swarm of narrow-hearted people who are eternally at war with the world's great sons, very soon succeeded in driving Richard Wagner once again to shake from his feet the dust of crowded cities. A turning-point had arrived, indeed, but no secured position; until quite the close of his life, our author had still to wage a fierce battle with the world; and perhaps the most important outcome of his intercourse with the Bavarian King was the widening of his political horizon, as shewn in the two remarkable essays with which this volume opens—though " widening "

vii

may not be quite the word to express that deeper, clearer insight into human affairs afforded by his proximity to the throne of a high-souled ruler. One cannot but feel that much in *Parsifal* itself may be directly traced to Wagner's having been brought so close to the "fortune and the fate of Kings."

In December 1865 he turned his back on Munich, much against the King's own wish, but in the King's immediate interest. One has only to read the German newspapers of that time, to see how impossible for him was any further sojourn amid such sordid surroundings as those so sedulously heaped up for him by the Munich leaders of "Public Opinion." A letter of his (his only public protest, I believe) will sufficiently clear up the point. In the Augsburg *Allgemeine Zeitung* of February 14, 1865, there appeared an unsigned paragraph : " In the *Neueste Nachrichten* of the 12th inst. a correspondent, evidently inspired by the party concerned, characterises as totally without foundation the very widespread rumour that Richard Wagner has fallen into disgrace with His Majesty the King. I, however, can assure you positively that Richard Wagner has wholly forfeited the favour so richly bestowed upon him by our Monarch, and in such a fashion that it is only to be hoped it may not have awoken in the good and noble heart of our youthful King a distrust of men in general. I hear, moreover, that Herr Wagner has left Munich." To this was appended an editorial footnote : " From other sources we have received accounts in detail, about Richard Wagner and his comrades, that more than justify this decision of the King." The next day (Feb. 15) quite at the end of the literary supplement to the *Allg. Ztg.* there appeared, among the Miscellaneous Items, the following : "Whilst Munich letters, from several different sources, maintain that a serious change has taken place in the personal position of Herr Richard Wagner towards the Royal Court, we are in receipt of the following disclaimer from that gentleman : ' Simply to ease the minds of my friends elsewhere, I declare that the reports about myself and friends here, in a Munich paragraph of yesterday's issue of the *Allg. Ztg.*, are false.—Richard Wagner.'"

In the generality of civilised communities this flat denial would have ended the matter, but not so in Munich, not so with the chief daily paper of all Germany, the Augsburg *Allgemeine Zeitung*. Whether Wagner's enemies believed in the rumours of a rupture between the King and himself, or not, they were determined to do all they could to make such a rupture inevitable; so the Allg. Ztg. of Feb. 19 came out with an article a page and a half long (three broad columns), signed by a mere " ·|·," entitled " Richard Wagner and Public Opinion," and filled with nothing but a collection of the pettiest *on dits*. The tone of this article, in which Richard Wagner is not once accorded the customary "Herr," is most offensive; but the editor deliberately shut his eyes to the spitefulness of its nature, and once more added a footnote: " This article comes to us from a man who does not belong to musical circles, so that there can be no possible question of his taking sides for or against " [a particularly ingenious argument, but in the case of *Wagner's* enemies an absolutely fatuous one]. " His whole position authorises him, however, in a matter that touches such delicate and serious interests, to give an opinion ; which opinion at the same time perfectly agrees with other reports that have reached us. Should an answer be sent us by Herr Richard Wagner or one of his friends, an answer as moderate in its form of expression as this article itself, we shall be most happy to publish it."—How " *moderate* the form of expression " in that article was, will transpire from a few of the details quoted in Wagner's reply. This reply, " In refutation of the article, ' Richard Wagner and Public Opinion ' in No. 50 of the *Allg. Ztg.*" appeared in the supplement of that journal for Feb. 22, 1865, as follows :—

" Summoned to Munich by the generosity of His Majesty the King of Bavaria in order that, after severe struggles and endeavours, I might reap the fruits of a laborious artist-life in the undisturbed enjoyment of peace and leisure for my work; in the greatest retirement, and heeding nothing but the commands of my exalted patron, I suddenly find myself dragged from my retreat by attacks on my person, by a storm of public accusations such as make their way into the papers only in the case of legal proceedings, and even then with a certain traditional reserve.

" In London and Paris, in days gone by, I have had the papers making remorselessly merry over my artistic aims and tendencies, my works trodden in the dust, and hissed upon the stage ; that my person, my private character, my social qualities and domestic habits should be given over in the most dishonouring fashion to public contumely—this I was to experience first where recognition is accorded to my works, where my aims and endeavours are allowed the meed of manly earnestness and high intention. What lesson may be derived from this alas ! by no means rare occurrence among us Germans, I leave to those who feel called to educate and elevate the people. For myself, I must be content for now with recording this mournful experience as gone through in my own person, and with publishing the needful declarations in contradiction of the charges brought against me ; declarations intended for the *tranquillising of Public Opinion* and prompted by regard for the Bavarian nation, in whose midst I suddenly find myself denounced as a public danger.

" Before I descend to the very distasteful task of contradicting my accuser's charges point by point, I believe it my duty, but solely for the aforesaid reason, to furnish a positive statement of the character of my situation here.

" After the generosity of His Majesty the King had provided me with means sufficient to enable me to settle in Munich and devote myself untroubled to my labours—labours reckoned moreover for earning me an income from outside—His Majesty entrusted me last autumn with the special commission of completing the music for my Nibelungen-work, a cycle of four entire musical dramas, each of them equal in compass and importance to one of my earlier operas. This commission necessitating the laying aside for some years of any kind of work * that might have brought me immediate payment through its circulation among the German theatres, in the name of His Majesty and under a definite contract certain grants were made me, not exceeding what Bavarian kings had already made in like cases of commission for works of art and science. As I thus have the right to consider myself no Favourite, but an artist well-paid in direct ratio to his labour, I hold myself unaccountable to anyone for the expenditure of my earnings ; were I to render such an account, it would be tantamount to an apology for having found for my labour the same substantial reward as painters, sculptors, architects, men of learning, and so forth, have repeatedly and often found before me. How high, however, I rate the unexpected fortune of having found precisely here the magnanimous patron to recognise the value of the most daring of my artistic projects, may be gathered from my at once begging His Majesty the King

* *Die Meistersinger von Nürnberg.*—TR.

to grant my naturalisation as a Bavarian, and handing in the necessary papers. Though German Art can never be Bavarian, but simply German, yet Munich is the capital of this German Art; here, under shelter of a Prince who kindles my enthusiasm, to feel myself a native and member of the people was to me the homeless wanderer a deep, a genuine need. Accustomed from of old to the greatest seclusion from public life, mostly ill in health and suffering from the after-effects of many years of trouble, in the first months of my sojourn here I must needs defer for a while the fulfilment of my heartfelt wish to make friends with a larger circle, and thus to fully realise my purposed naturalisation in Bavaria.

"What a mare's-nest has been spun from this my attitude and situation, veraciously described above; what a bugbear has been raised to-day to scare the Opinion of the Public, whilst I was waiting for the natural progress of my resolution, will be evident if I enter more minutely on the charges contained in the article of Herr ·|· of Munich.

"Their refutation I can leave to none of my friends, since the advantage of an anonymous correspondent sailing under the special recommendation of the editorial staff must be met by at least the weight of the name of the accused himself, and on the other hand it was to be feared that any friend of mine would have the effect of his rejoinder weakened in advance by his contemptuous introduction as '*one of my comrades.*'

"First of all, then, I have to tell my unknown accuser that he has written his article not *sine ira*, but *sine studio*. A little diligence would have shewn him the great confusion into which he has fallen, for all his semblance of acumen, in his comparative criticism of the dates of a former report and my 'laconic' reply thereto. He thinks he may reckon that I needed *two whole days* to think over my reply, which appeared in the supplement of this journal for Feb. 15 and referred to a report in the principal sheet of Feb. 14; from this calculation he tries to draw the conclusion that within that period I myself believed in the calamity which fills him with 'moral satisfaction.' To collect further proofs in support of this hypothesis appears to him of special weight. He founds them chiefly on my demeanour during the performance of Tannhäuser (Sunday, Feb. 12th), when, so he says, I 'waited in vain for the King's box to be lit up.' In

his opinion 'the same belief was entertained by that portion or
the audience which, with the manifest purpose of a demonstration,
vociferously called the composer on to the stage at the opera's close.'
One has only to compare herewith the report of the Allg. Ztg.
itself as to the character of this performance and its reception by
the public, there described as warmer than anything ever experienced before; if one passes then to my accuser's subsequent
assertion that the Munich public has greeted 'with a general
feeling of moral satisfaction' the news of my downfall, one will
know how to explain the one statement or the other. As to my
disappointed expectation of the King's box being illuminated, I
feel the great difficulty—not very handsomely taken advantage
of on the other side—of a personal position which makes me
deem it quite impermissible to discuss certain exalted questions
which my opponent handles roughly enough; in this instance,
however, I believe I may state without indiscretion that the
reasons why His Majesty the King attended neither that performance of 'Tannhäuser,' nor the preceding one of the 'Flying
Dutchman,' were known to me beforehand. Perhaps those
reasons may dawn on my accuser too, when he some day hears
under *what* characteristic circumstances His Majesty the King
will distinguish performances of these operas with his presence at
another time.

"Upon that selfsame Sunday my accuser 'was informed in
various quarters' of my disaster. The contradiction of similar
rumours contained in the *Neueste Nachrichten* of that very day
was not regarded by him; had he inquired into the source from
which that contradiction flowed, he would have known that, even
were I previously in doubt, I had not to wait three or four days
from then to be relieved of my uncertainty. Let him go for his
information, however, to that 'informant best-accredited by his
position' who retailed him the fable of the portrait by Pecht, for
which I am said to have handed in [to the King] a bill of 1,000
guldens. I assure my accuser that this gentleman, regarded in
the most favourable light, must have been a self-deceiver; for
there is not *one* word of truth in the whole story, as the court-
officer concerned will himself convince him; the fact, at bottom
of this fiction, is capable of none but an uncommonly honouring
interpretation.

"That my accuser is either ill-informed or intentionally perverts the truth, not only on the points alluded to but on all the rest, is obvious from his statements about my esteemed friend Semper, for instance, whose audience with His Majesty the King during a recent visit to Munich is audaciously denied by the correspondent of the Allg. Ztg. I, on the contrary, can assure him that the plans of His Majesty are as little known to him, in this matter also, as it is unallowable for me to forestall the Monarch's decisions by defining them.

" It quite peculiarly rejoices me to be placed by my accuser in the position of seeing the composer of ' Tannhäuser' and ' Lohengrin' accorded in the Allg. Ztg. a praise more flattering even than my old friend Pecht allòwed himself to bestow in that ' Byzantine' article to which this gentleman alludes : it is regrettable, on the other hand, that, extolling my earnestness as artist, he thinks good to represent me as a frivolous and flighty *man*. In Paris things went otherwise : there my art and its tendences were dubbed ' détestables,' but personally I was pointed to as the model of a man who for sake of his serious artistic convictions, and without a moment's flinching, threw willingly away his immediate and most favourable chances of making a quite remarkable ' fortune' ; a man who thus condemned himself to a lot which so worsened during a three years' entirely helpless sojourn in his German fatherland, that a year ago he was on the point of abandoning all hope of performing his later works, and therewith all hope of further practice of his art itself, and was resolved to completely vanish from the scene.

" Because the generous summons of the magnanimous Prince— whom my accuser now would gladly furnish with annoyances of ' moral indignation'—set free this artist from such a plight and restored him to cheerfulness, to his art, and to his justifiable hopes, that accuser by dint of inflammatory innuendoes exaggerates the royal sacrifice (which, for that matter, was not unconditional, but subject to the stipulation of repayment from the later returns of my labours elsewhere) into liquidation of debts and so on. This friendly style of—insolence comes tripping to his tongue, notwithstanding that in an earlier sentence he himself deplores the ' nonexercise of the beautiful princely privilege' of liberality to artists, whereby ' our greatest German geniuses have so often alas! been forced to suffer bitter want.' I can only assume the insincerity of this lament, for he certainly is more sincere when he expresses his

indignation that an artist, whom he himself rates very high as
such, should be paid for his work sufficiently well to furnish himself a comfortable house.   Instead of procuring himself a little
knowledge and understanding of the special needs of an artist of
my stamp, as here was possible to him through one example, my
accuser prefers to raise what is generally left to idle gossips into a
subject for public impeachment of a man ranked high by him as
earnest artist; and he actually is so fortunate as to win the testi-
mony of the able editoriate of the Allg. Ztg. to his being 'fully
authorised to give an opinion in a matter that touches such delicate
considerations and serious interests.'

"If I can only express my wonder at the total lack of breeding
and propriety in the reproaches laid at my door, I have the more
earnestly to meet the imputation of my contempt for musical
affairs in Munich.   What opinion I have formed of modern *German* musical affairs, the public will shortly have the opportunity
of learning;* what hopes I set on Munich's prime assistance in
their raising, will then transpire as well; and it will be seen how
advantageous I must think the results of our highly estimable
Generalmusikdirektor Franz Lachner's labours, as, not being an
inexperienced phantast, I have based my hopes on just the
groundwork of those same results.†

"Now, what can be the object of these charges, as inconsiderate,
to put it mildly, as easily refuted?   Is it the nominal aim of pre-
venting 'an ever darker cloud from coming between the heartfelt
love of the Bavarian people and the lofty image of its youthful
King' by reason of 'his illustrious name being constantly mixed
up, and in no very worthy fashion, with all these true and lying
rumours'?—But the *true* rumours of my real relations with His
Majesty the King, as my accuser himself admits [by inference],
can only tend to his honour.   Who is it, then, that brings the
lying rumours into unworthy contact with the King's illustrious
name?   Plainly those persons whose eager interest it must be to
cast up dust to form that cloud of darkness.   And what is the
actual effect of this cloud-raising upon the veritable Folk?   If one
subtracts the operations of spite and envy on vulgar natures at all

---

* See the article "A Music-school for Munich," p. 171 et seq.—TR.

† See pp. 181 and 215 ; that Wagner found reason to modify his estimate
of Lachner's work, as may be seen in the article on "Conducting," is due to
later experiences.—TR.

times and under any circumstances, from all circles of society there come to me the most friendly and unprejudiced views of the generosity of His Majesty the King towards myself. If, however, it is the desire of *all* parties to correct the most extravagant rumours of my so-called too great influence with His Majesty, why have I not been interviewed in person? For I could only feel myself injured by such utterly untrue assumptions, and never, never lend colour to the false idea of their being justified. If Public Opinion was being led astray in the foolishest of fashions, why add t ﹀ its misleading by endeavouring to make it believe that this position of Favourite, which never really existed, had suddenly terminated? Why not simply come to me for the true story of my personal relations, both now and from the first, with His Majesty? Why proceed, instead, to public threatenings of woe against the heartily beloved Prince?

   " Not to me, to Public Opinion my accuser owes the answering of these questions.

" Munich, February 20, 1865.   RICHARD WAGNER."

To complete the history of this incident, the editor accompanied the publication of the above letter also with a foot-note : " We give this reply verbatim, leaving further discussion to the author of the first article. At any rate, room is open to him for a reply. Herr Richard Wagner must himself be glad to have a matter capable of so many interpretations removed from the atmosphere of rumours and gossip and brought to speech in such a manner that no impartial person will dispute the good intentions and interest in morals (*Sitte*) and justice which inspired our contributor." The editor having thus revealed his own idea of " impartiality " and " morals and justice," Herr ·|· is allowed a " final answer " of a column and a half, containing not one word of apology, but merely saying that the charges brought by him were matters of common report, and ridiculing the notion of going to Richard Wagner himself for enlightenment upon what is " the talk of the town ; " further, the old cry of Wagner's " belittling his great forerunners " of course resumes its accustomed place.

   And this was the manner in which Richard Wagner was attacked, both overtly and covertly, during the remainder of his stay in Munich ; so that the King at last was obliged to abandon his scheme of building a " Model-theatre " after Wagner's own heart in that city ; an undertaking which Munich *now* would give any-thing to have seen carried out, now that a little town like Bayreuth has shewn it what it has lost—not only in prestige, but also in municipal pocket.

But more than the new theatre was doomed to stay abortive. That Music-school upon whose draft of organisation the master was engaged, by order of the King, at the very time his enemies were spreading every kind of disingenuous rumour,—that Music-school never came to birth, at least never in the sense its promoter had sketched out ; and all Germany thus lost a chance which it has not yet recovered. We know what wonders Richard Wagner worked with the singers at the two Bayreuth Festivals that he himself was spared to see ; most of us are old enough to recognise the change in the whole spirit of " conducting " that arrived with the public appearance of men who had come under his immediate influence, and one at all events—the late Hans von Bülow—under his personal *tuition* : it therefore is indisputable that a Music-school of the kind he suggested, and benefiting by his direct co-operation, would have turned out something very different from even the best German dramatic singers of nowadays. Here is a loss that may never be replaced, whereas the transference of the model-theatre to a far smaller town is quite in accordance with the original intentions of the author of the preface to the *Ring des Nibelungen.*

To return to that letter of Feb. 1865 for a moment, it is pitiable to see a great genius obliged to defend himself against such petty accusations as those he alludes to,—disappointment at the King's absence from the theatre, a portrait (of Wagner) painted by one of Wagner's friends and the bill sent in to the King, his carpets and curtains *et id genus omne* ; but it must not be forgotten that these charges at like time implied a slur on King Ludwig himself, and, even if Richard Wagner was not instructed by the King to reply—as is very probable—it was his obvious duty to contradict slanders involving their mutual relations. As to expressions such as " an artist of my stamp " ("*eines Künstlers gerade meiner Art*"), which will be found here and there in other public utterances of Wagner's—in the later pages of this volume, in fact—some people may consider them egoistic and overbearing ; but, remembering Goethe's "*nur die Lumpe sind bescheiden,*" we must also remember that Wagner had a perfect right to speak of himself in this strain. Who among the creative or administrative artists flourishing in his day can possibly be compared with him? Yet these were asserting an equal, nay, a superior right to authority. It was high time they were taught their place, as taught they were in no mild terms in the "Notices" and the essay on "Conducting." Wagner *as man* was kindness and humility itself—a point on which Mr Houston S. Chamberlain has insisted, upon very good evidence, in his recent splendid volume "*Richard Wagner*"; but he held his art in far too high a reverence to be afraid of appealing to its only living exponent, the one great artist alive,—himself.

Another point of interest in this letter, and one of my main reasons for reproducing it, is the fact that it was a reply to an article entitled "Richard Wagner and *Public Opinion.*" The precise application of this formula in the essay on "State and Religion" becomes evident at once, and I am strongly inclined to believe that the date of that essay, "1864," must therefore not be taken quite too strictly; at least a portion of it must surely have been written after, probably immediately after, this worrying newspaper controversy. In that case we may trace the first 224 pages of the present volume (with the exception of the Vaterlandsverein speech and the letter to Lüttichau) to the year 1865; and when we reflect that Wagner was at the same time preparing for the production of *Tristan und Isolde* (Munich, June 1865), making the rough draft of *Parsifal* (the poem) and working at the music of *Siegfried* and *Die Meistersinger*, we shall have sufficient ground for astonishment not only at his enormous energy, but also at his power of rising above surrounding molestations. True that *German Art and German Policy* did not appear till 1867, but the author's prefatory note to *What is German?* shews that this series of articles was founded on a mass of manuscript from the year 1865. Moreover on turning to the Allgemeine Zeitung for the year last-named, one finds a clue to Wagner's association of ideas; in the shape of reviews of books, we have the following topics touched upon in that journal: Louis Napoleon's *César* and Frantz's *Resurrection of Germany*, March; Grimm's *Book of German words* and Carlyle's *Frederick the Great*, April; Napoleon the Great's letters to his brother, May; R. Huguenin's *Histoire du Royaume Merovingien d'Austrasie*, G. Bornhack's *History of the Franks*, and P. A. J. Gérard's *Histoire des Francs d'Austrasie* (reviewed together), also Dr Ernst Wagner's *On English Schools*. June; further articles deal with the Dante Jubilee and the Spanish Inquisition in May, and with the Peerage question in June. It was almost an accident that I lit upon these reviews &c., in searching through the Allg. Ztg. of 1865 for another purpose, but their occurrence appeared to me to throw no little light on Wagner's train of thought at the time.

As for the actual contents of the present volume, they correspond with those of Vol. viii. of the *Gesammelte Schriften*, with two minor exceptions in the way of omission, and two in the way of addition. The 1869 portion of the *Judaism in Music* essay I had already printed in Vol. III., and the short preface to the second edition of *Oper und Drama* in Vol. II., for obvious reasons. Partly to establish an approximate equality iu the size of my volumes, but chiefly to bring Wagner's more important *national* utterances into the same book, I have taken from vol. x. of the *Ges. Schr.* the article *What is German?* and accompanied it by the Vaterlandsverein speech of 1848—one thus obtains a thirty years' survey of Wagner's thought in the political direction, for the last three pages of *What is German?* were written in 1878. When volume ix. of the *Ges. Schr.* appeared (the last that was published in his lifetime) Richard Wagner had no intention of publishing that article at all, otherwise he would certainly have included it in vol. viii.; further information with regard to its genesis will be found on pages 150 and 151.   As to the Vaterlandsverein speech, it was republished in 1883, very soon after Wagner's death, by one of his really intimate friends, W. Tappert, and we may therefore presume that it was a course he himself would have sanctioned.   Much capital, however, has been made (by, to say the least, a *not* so intimate " friend ") of the non-republication of the speech by Wagner himself; unfortunately the originator of this outcry did not content himself with a merely senseless charge, but embodied in his book of compilations an English so-called translation of the speech.   Now, that translation is so preposterously ' free ' that not only does it entirely destroy the simple eloquence of Wagner's sentences by running them into one another and punctuating at will, but in several places it gives the direct opposite of the author's meaning.   If for this reason alone, then, it was necessary to print a faithful English rendering of the

original.   In verification of my statement I give the following
passage in the original German, followed by Praeger's version
(from *Wagner as I knew him*) :—

"Nein, in dieser Zeit erkennen wir auch die Nothwendigkeit
der Entscheidung : was Lüge ist, kann nicht bestehen, und die
Monarchie, d.h. die *Alleinherrschaft* ist eine Lüge, sie ist es durch
den Constitutionalismus geworden.   Nun, wirft sich der an aller
Aussöhnung Verzweifelnde kühn und trotzig der vollen Republik
in die Arme, der noch hoffende lenkt sein Auge zum letzten Male
prüfend nach den Spitzen des Bestehenden hin.   Er erkennt, dass,
gilt der Kampf der Monarchie, dieser nur in besonderen Fällen
gegen die *Person des Fürsten*, in allen Fällen aber *gegen die Partei*
geführt wird, die eigennützig oder selbstgefällig den Fürsten auf
den Schild erhebt, unter dessen Schatten sie ihren besonderen
Vortheil des Gewinnes oder der Eitelkeit verficht.   Diese *Partei*
also ist die zu besiegende : soll der Kampf ein blutiger sein?   Er
muss es sein, er muss Partei und Fürsten zu gleicher Zeit treffen,
wenn kein Mittel der Versöhnung bleibt.   Als dieses Mittel
erfassen wir aber den Fürsten selbst," &c., &c.—

"No ; at the present moment we clearly perceive the necessity
of distinguishing between truth and falsehood, and monarchy as
the embodiment of autocracy is a falsehood—our constitution has
proved it to be so.

"All who despair of a reconciliation throw yourselves boldly
into the arms of the republic ; those still willing to hope, lift their
eyes for the last time to the points of existing circumstances to
find a solution.   The latter see that if the contest be against
monarchy, it is only in isolated cases against the person of the
prince, whilst everywhere war is being waged against the party
that lifts the monarch on a shield, under the cover of which they
fight for their own selfish ends.   This is the party that has to be
thrown down and conquered, however bloody the fight.   And if
all reconciliation fail, party and prince will simultaneously be hit.
But the means of peace are in the hands of the prince," &c., &c.—

The strictest possible translation of this passage will be found
on page 142 infra ; a comparison with that just given will prove
the truth of my previous assertion.   But a still more flagrant
instance of perversion is presented by the rendering of "Würde
hierdurch nun der Untergang der *Monarchie* herbeigeführt?   Ja!
Aber es würde damit die *Emanzipation des Königthums* ausge-

sprochen" into "Does it appear to you that by this proposition, *monarchy would be altogether abolished? Yes, so it would!* But the kingdom would thereby be emancipated." (Cf. p. 144 infra.) Upon a previous occasion when I pointed out the stultification of Wagner's words effected by this same compiler—to whom I trust I may never need to refer again—the latter's spiritual heirs advanced the ridiculous plea that Wagner employed provincialisms such as would only be understood by a fellow-provincial, the compiler or his recent advocate, in fact; in this instance the "provincialism" plea would fall through once more, for we find "*Königthum*" translated a few sentences later as "royalty." Nor would the argument be worth a moment's notice, were it not that it affords me the opportunity of insisting upon a fact well-known to all students of Wagner's writings in the original, namely that he *never* uses a purely German word in a sense not strictly justified by its etymology; with him the philological sense is acute and ever present, and, though we often meet with a homely metaphor in the midst of a serious disquisition, not once do we meet with a slipshod or "provincial" employment of a native German term.

It will thus be seen that a correct translation of that important speech of Wagner's was an absolute necessity, and nowhere could it more properly be introduced than immediately after a series of articles dealing once again with "Kinghood." To add to it the letter of explanation, addressed to a court official, was a simple corollary that needs no comment saving that I now find (from a facsimile reproduction of the letter, in Mr Chamberlain's German work above referred to) that the allusion to "Austria" on page 148 should read "Berlin," the earlier transcriber, R. Proelss, apparently having altered the text for some reason of international politics.

And now I must leave the volume in my readers' hands, with the one remark that it is wellnigh the most important in the whole series of Wagner's prose-writings.

WM. ASHTON ELLIS.

CHRISTMAS, 1895.

TO THE KINGLY FRIEND.

(Summer, 1864.)

My King, thou rarest shield of this my living !
Of bounteous good, thou overbrimming hoard !
I seek in vain, at goal of all my striving,
To match thy favouring grace with fitting word !
Both tongue and pen are hush'd in sore misgiving,
And yet o'er many a record have I por'd
To find the word, the only word, to bear thee
The thanks that deep within my heart I wear thee.

What thou hast wrought, still fills me with amazement,
When I look back on what I was before.
Erst shone no star but left me in abasement,
No hope's last ray but dwindled evermore :
A prey to all the chance of world's appraisement,
A toy to haggling peddlers given o'er ;
What in me strove for freeborn artist's action,
I saw downtrodden in the rout of faction.

Who once His bishop's wither'd staff commanded
To deck itself with quick'ning leaves of green,
E'en though, bereft of hope, life's vessel stranded,
He bade me yield up all that might have been,
One thing around my inmost heart He banded,
Faith in myself, in what my soul had seen :
And promis'd, if I held that faith unshaken,
So should the wither'd staff once more awaken.

A

What erst in lonely silence I had hidden,
Behold ! it liv'd within another's breast ;
With what the elder's mind so sore was ridden,
Behold ! a young man's heart with joy it bless'd :
And what that youthful heart had sweetly bidden
To move towards a goal all unconfess'd,
The Spring it was, in gladness overpowering,
The Spring that woke our double Faith to flowering.

Thou art the gentle Spring that leaf-bedeck'd me,
That fill'd each branch and twig with quick'ning sap,
Thine was the call that out of darkness beck'd me,
Set free my powers from chill of Winter's lap.
Blest with thy regal promise to protect me,
That scatter'd ev'ry cloud of sorrow's hap,
I tread fresh paths, in pride of lightsome burden,
Through Summer-lands aglow with kingly guerdon.

How could one paltry word contain the measure
Of all the plenitude thou art to me ?
Scarce dare I call my soul my scanty treasure,
Whilst thou art thou and all that hangs from thee.
So comes to blissful rest in thy good pleasure
My round of work fulfill'd and yet to be :
And since no shade of fearing thou hast left me,
The very seed and root of Hope thou'st reft me.

Thus am I poor, with but one sole possession,
The Faith whereto belief of thine is wed :
'Tis that, the bulwark of my proud confession,
'Tis that, whereby my Love is steel'd and fed ;
Yet shared, lo ! mine is but a half-possession,
And wholly lost to me, should thine have fled.
So but from thee my strength to thank is taken,
Through thine own kingly Faith of strength unshaken.

ON STATE AND RELIGION.

Über Staat und Religion.
(1864.)

The article on "State and Religion" *was written at the request of King Ludwig II. of Bavaria, in the same year in which Richard Wagner was summoned to his intimate companionship. It does not appear to have been printed, at least for public circulation, until nine years later (1873), when it was included in Vol. viii. of the* Gesammelte Schriften. *Undoubtedly to its intimate character we owe those deeper glimpses into Wagner's inmost thought, such as we meet so often in his private correspondence.*

TRANSLATOR'S NOTE.

HIGHLY-PRIZED young friend desires me to tell him whether, and if so in what way, my views on *State* and *Religion* have changed since the composition of my art-writings in the years 1849 to 1851.

As a few years ago, at the instigation of a friend in France, I was persuaded to re-survey my views on Music and Poetry, and assemble them in one concise synopsis (namely the preface to a French prose-translation of some of my opera-poems *), so it might not be unwelcome to me to clear and summarise my thoughts upon that other side as well, were it not that precisely here, where everyone considers he has a right to his opinion, a definite utterance becomes more and more difficult the older and more experienced one grows. For here is shewn again what Schiller says: "*ernst ist das Leben, heiter ist die Kunst*" ("Life is earnest, Art is gay"). Perhaps, however, it may be said of me that, having taken Art in such special earnest, I ought to be able to find without much difficulty the proper mood for judging Life. In truth I believe the best way to inform my young friend about myself, will be to draw his foremost notice to the earnestness of my artistic aims; for it was just this earnestness, that once constrained me to enter realms apparently so distant as State and Religion. What there I sought, was really never aught beyond my art—that art which I took so earnestly, that I asked for it a basis and a sanction in Life, in State, and lastly in Religion. That these I could not find in modern life, impelled me to search out the cause in my own fashion; I had to try to make plain to myself the tendence of the State, in order to account for the disdain with which I

* See Volume vii., "Zukunftsmusik."—Richard Wagner.—Volume III. of the present series.—TR.

found my earnest art-ideal regarded everywhere in public life.

But it certainly was characteristic of my inquiry, that it never led me down to the arena of *politics* proper ; that is to say, the politics of the day remained as entirely untouched by me, as, despite the commotion of those times, they never truly touched myself.*   That this or that form of Government, the jurisdiction of this or that party, this or that alteration in the mechanism of our State affairs, could furnish my art-ideal with any veritable furtherance, I never fancied ; therefore whoever has really read my art-writings, must rightly have accounted me unpractical ; but whoever has assigned me the rôle of a political revolutionary, with actual enrolment in the lists of such, manifestly knew nothing at all about me, and judged me by an outer semblance of events which haply might mislead a police-officer, but not a statesman.   Yet this misconstruction of the character of my aims is entangled also with my own mistake : through taking Art in such uncommon earnest, I took Life itself too lightly ; and just as this avenged itself upon my personal fortunes, so my views thereon were soon to be given another tinge.   To put the matter plainly, I had arrived at a reversal of Schiller's saying, and desired to see my earnest art embedded in a gladsome life ; for which Greek life, as we regard it, had thus to serve me as a model.

From all my imaginary provisions for the entry of the Artwork into Public Life, it is evident that I pictured them as a summons to self-collection (*Sammelung*) from amid the distractions of a life which was to be conceived, at bottom, merely as a gladsome occupation (*heitere*

* "Gewiss war es aber für meine Untersuchung charakteristisch, dass ich hierbei nie auf das Gebiet der eigentlichen *Politik* herabstieg, namentlich die Zeitpolitik, wie sie mich trotz der Heftigkeit der Zustände nicht wahrhaft berührte, auch von mir gänzlich unberührt blieb."   In confirmation of this statement, which has been disputed by Wagner's enemies and by one so-called "friend," the late Ferdinand Praeger, I may refer to the facts collected in my little brochure "1849 : A Vindication," published in 1892 by Messrs Kegan Paul & Co.—Tr.

Beschäftigung), and not as a fatiguing toil. Hence the political movements of that time did not attract my serious attention until they touched the purely social sphere, and thus appeared to offer prospects of the realisation of my ideal premises—prospects which, I admit, for some time occupied my earnest thought. The line my fancy followed was an organisation of public life in common, as also of domestic life, such as must lead of itself to a beauteous fashioning of the human race. The calculations of the newer Socialists therefore lost my sympathy from the moment they seemed to end in systems that took at first the repellent aspect of an organisation of Society for no other purpose but an equally-allotted toil.* However, after sharing the horror which this aspect kindled in æsthetically-cultured minds,† a deeper glance into the proposed condition of society made me believe I detected something very different from what had hovered before the fancy of those calcu-lating Socialists themselves. I found to wit that, when equally divided among all, actual *labour*, with its crip-pling burthen and fatigue, would be downright done away with, leaving nothing in its stead but an *occupation*, which necessarily must assume an artistic character of itself. A clue to the character of this occupation, as substitute for actual labour, was offered me by Husbandry, among other things ; this, when plied by every member of the common-

---

* "Nicht eher nahmen daher die politischen Bewegungen jener Zeit meine Aufmerksamkeit ernster in Anspruch, als bis durch den Übertritt derselben auf das rein soziale Gebiet in mir Ideen angeregt wurden, die, weil sie meiner idealen Forderung Nahrung zu geben schienen, mich, wie ich gestehe, eine Zeit lang ernstlich erfüllten. Meine Richtung ging darauf, mir eine Organisa-tion des gemeinsamen öffentlichen, wie des häuslichen Lebens vorzustellen, welche von selbst zu einer schönen Gestaltung des menschlichen Geschlechtes führen müsste. Die Berechnungen der neueren Sozialisten fesselten demnach meine Theilnahme von da ab, wo sie in Systeme auszugehen schienen, welche zunächst nichts Anderes als den widerlichen Anblick einer Organisation der Gesellschaft zu gleichmässig vertheilter Arbeit hervorbrachten." As I have been compelled to slightly paraphrase the first of these sentences, and as there are minor difficulties in the other two, I give all three in the original.—TR.

† Cf. Vol. I., 30-31.—TR.

alty [or "parish"—*Gemeinde*], I conceived as partly developed into more productive tillage of the Garden, partly into joint observances for times and seasons of the day and year, which, looked at closer, would take the character of strengthening exercises,* ay, of recreations and festivities. Whilst trying to work out all the bearings of this transformation of one-sided labour, with its castes in town and country, into a more universal occupation lying at the door of every man,† I became conscious on the other hand that I was meditating nothing so intensely new, but merely pursuing problems akin to those which so dearly had busied our greatest poets themselves, as we may see in "Wilhelm Meister's Wanderjahre." I, too, was therefore picturing to myself a world that I deemed possible, but the purer I imagined it, the more it parted company with the reality of the political tendencies-of-the-day around me; so that I could say to myself, my world will never make its entry until the very moment when the present world has ceased—in other words, where Socialists and Politicians came to end, should *we* commence.‡ I will not deny that this view became with me a positive mood (*Stimmung*): the political relations of the beginning of the bygone 'fifties kept everyone in a state of nervous tension, sufficient to awake in me a certain pleasurable feeling which might rightly seem suspicious to the practical politician.

Now, on thinking back, I believe I may acquit myself of having been sobered from the aforesaid mood—not unlike a spiritual intoxication—first and merely through the turn soon taken by European politics. It is an attribute of the poet, to be riper in his inner intuition (*Anschauung*) of the essence of the world than in his conscious abstract knowledge: precisely at that time I had already sketched, and finally completed, the poem of my "Ring des Nibelungen." With this conception I had unconsciously admitted to my-

---

* Cf. Vol. I., 58.—TR.
† Cf. *Letters to Uhlig*, pp. 81-82, written October 22nd, 1850.—TR.
‡ Cf. Vol. I., 24, and Vol. II., 178.—TR.

self the truth about things human. Here everything is tragic through and through, and the Will, that fain would shape a world according to its wish, at last can reach no greater satisfaction than the breaking of itself in dignified annulment.* It was the time when I returned entirely and exclusively to my artistic plans, and thus, acknowledging Life's earnestness with all my heart, withdrew to where alone can " gladsomeness " abide.—

My youthful friend will surely not expect me to give a categorical account of my later views on Politics and State : under any circumstances they could have no practical importance, and in truth would simply amount to an expression of my horror of concerning myself professionally with matters of the sort. No ; he can merely be wishful to learn how things so remote from its ordinary field of action may shape themselves in the brain of a man like myself, cut out for nothing but an artist, after all that he has gone through and felt. But lest I might appear to have meant the above as a disparagement, I must promptly add that whatever I might have to put forward would strictly and solely be a witness to my having arrived at a full valuation of the great, nay, terrible earnest of the matter. The artist, too, may say of himself : " My kingdom is not of this world ; " and, perhaps more than any artist now living, I may say this of myself, for very reason of the earnestness wherewith I view my art. And that's the hardship of it ; for with this beyond-the-worldly realm of ours we stand amid a world itself so serious and so careworn, that it deems a fleeting dissipation its only fitting refuge, whereas the need for earnest elevation (*Erhebung*) has quite become a stranger to it.—

Life is earnest, and—has always been.

Whoever would wholly clear his mind on this, let him but consider how in every age, and under ever freshly-shaped, but ever self-repeating forms, this life and world

* " Zu schauen kam ich, nicht zu schaffen "—Wotan in *Siegfried*, act ii. —TR.

have spurred great hearts and spacious minds to seek for possibility of its bettering; and how 'twas always just the noblest, the men who cared alone for others' weal and offered willingly their own in pledge, that stayed without the slightest influence on the lasting shape of things. The small success of all such high endeavours would shew him plainly that these world-improvers were victims to a fundamental error, and demanded from the world itself a thing it cannot give. Should it even seem possible that much might be ordered more efficiently in man's affairs, yet the said experiences will teach us that the means and ways of reaching this are never rightly predetermined by the single thinker; never, at least, in a manner enabling him to bring them with success before the knowledge of the mass of men. Upon a closer scrutiny of this relation, we fall into astonishment at the quite incredible pettiness and weakness of the average human intellect, and finally into shamefaced wonder that it should ever have astonished us; for any proper knowledge of the world would have taught us from the outset that blindness is the world's true essence, and not Knowledge prompts its movements, but merely a headlong impulse, a blind impetus of unique weight and violence, which procures itself just so much light and knowledge as will suffice to still the pressing need experienced at the moment. So we recognise that nothing really happens but what has issued from this not far-seeing Will, from this Will that answers merely to the momentarily-experienced need; and thus we see that practical success, throughout all time, has attended only those politicians who took account of nothing but the momentary need, neglecting all remoter, general needs, all needs as yet unfelt to-day, and which therefore appeal so little to the mass of mankind that it is impossible to count on its assistance in their ministration.

Moreover we find personal success and great, if not enduring influence on the outer fashioning of the world allotted to the violent, the passionate individual, who, unchaining the elemental principles of human impulse under favouring circumstances, points out to greed and self-indulgence the speedy pathways to their satisfaction. To the fear of violence from this quarter, as also to a modicum of knowledge thus acquired of basic human nature, we owe the *State*. In it the Need is expressed as the human Will's necessity of establishing some workable agreement among the myriad blindly-grasping individuals into which it is divided. It is a contract whereby the units seek to save themselves from mutual violence, through a little mutual practice of restraint. As in the Nature-religions a portion of the fruits of the field or spoils of the chase was brought as offering to the Gods, to make sure of a right to enjoy the remainder, so in the State the unit offered up just so much of his egoism as appeared necessary to ensure for himself the contentment of its major bulk.* Here the tendence of the unit naturally makes for obtaining the greatest possible security in barter for the smallest possible sacrifice: but to this tendence, also, he can only give effect through equal-righted fellowships ; and these diverse fellowships of individuals equally-entitled in their groups make up the parties in the State, the larger owners striving for a state of permanence, the less favoured for its alteration. But even the party of alteration desires nothing beyond the bringing about a state of matters in which it, too, would wish no further change ; and thus the State's main object is upheld from first to last by those whose profit lies in permanence.

Stability is therefore the intrinsic tendence of the State. And rightly ; for it constitutes withal the unconscious aim in every higher human effort to get beyond the primal need : namely to reach a freer evolution of spiritual attributes, which is always cramped so long as hindrances forestall the satisfaction of that first root-need. Everyone thus strives by nature for stability, for maintenance of quiet : ensured can it only be, however, when the maintenance of existing conditions is not the preponderant interest of *one* party only. Hence it is in the truest interest of all parties,

* Cf. Vol. II., 186-187.—TR.

and thus of the State itself, that the interest in its abiding-
ness should not be left to a single party. There must
consequently be given a possibility of constantly relieving
the suffering interests of less favoured parties : in this regard the more the nearest need is kept alone in eye, the
more intelligible will be itself, and the easier and more
tranquillising will be its satisfaction. General laws in provision of this possibility, whilst they allow of minor alterations, thus aim alike at maintenance of stability ; and that
law which, reckoned for the possibility of constant remedy
of pressing needs, contains withal the strongest warrant
of stability, must therefore be the most perfect law of
State.

The embodied voucher for this fundamental law is the
Monarch. In no State is there a weightier law than that
which centres its stability in the supreme hereditary power
of one particular family, unconnected and un-commingling
with any other lineage in that State. Never yet has there
been a Constitution in which, after the downfall of such
families and abrogation of the Kingly power, some substi-
tution or periphrasis has not necessarily, and for the most
part necessitously, reconstructed a power of similar kind.
It therefore is established as the most essential principle of
the State ; and as in it resides the warrant of stability,
so in the person of the King the State attains its true
ideal.

For, as the King on one hand gives assurance of the
State's solidity, on the other his loftiest interest soars high
beyond the State. Personally he has naught in common
with the interests of parties, but his sole concern is that
the conflict of these interests should be adjusted, precisely
for the safety of the whole. His sphere is therefore equity,
and where this is unattainable, the exercise of grace
(*Gnade*). Thus, as against the party interests, he is the
representative of purely-human interests, and in the eyes
of the party-seeking citizen he therefore occupies in truth a
position wellnigh superhuman. To him is consequently
accorded a reverence such as the highest citizen would

never dream of distantly demanding for himself; and here, at this summit of the State where we see its ideal reached, we therefore meet that side of human apperception (*Anschauungsweise*) which, in distinction from the faculty of recognising the nearest need, we will call the power of *Wahn*.* All those, to wit, whose simple powers of cognisance do not extend beyond what bears upon their nearest need—and they form by far the largest portion of mankind—would be unable to recognise the importance of a Royal Prerogative whose exercise has no directly cognisable relation with their nearest need, to say nothing of the necessity of bestirring themselves for its upholding, nay, even of bringing the King their highest offerings, the sacrifice of goods and life, if there intervened no form of apperception entirely opposed to ordinary cognisance.

This form is *Wahn*.

Before we seek to gain intelligence of the nature of *Wahn* from its most wondrous phases, let us take for guide the uncommonly suggestive light thrown by an exceptionally deep-thinking and keen-sighted philosopher of the immediate past † upon the phenomena, so puzzling in themselves, of animal instinct.—The astounding aimful-

---

* "Wahn-Vermögen." As the word "Wahn" is frequently used in these pages, and is absolutely untranslatable, I shall mostly retain it as it stands. It does not so much mean an "illusion" or "delusion," in general, as a "semi-conscious *feigning*" (such as the 'legal fiction'), a "dream," or a "symbolical aspiration"—its etymological kinship being quite as near to "fain" as to "feign"; but the context will leave the reader in no doubt as to its particular application in any sentence. It will be remembered that "Wahn" plays an important part in Hans Sachs' monologue in *Die Meistersinger*, act iii; the poem of that drama, containing the Wahn-monologue in a somewhat more extended form than its ultimate version, had already been published in 1862.—TR.

† Arthur Schopenhauer, in "*Die Welt als Wille und Vorstellung*," vol. ii, cap. 27. The philosopher there compares the operations of this "animal instinct" with a case of what we now should call hypnotism, and says that "insects are, in a certain sense, natural somnambulists . . . They have the feeling that they *must* perform a certain action, without exactly knowing why." He also compares this "instinct" to the "daimonion" of Socrates, but does not absolutely employ the expression "Wahn" in this connection. Neither does the "spirit of the race" (or "species"), mentioned by Wagner

ness (*Zweckmässigkeit*) in the procedures (*Verrichtungen*) of insects, among whom the bees and ants lie handiest for general observation, is admittedly inexplicable on the grounds that account for the aimfulness of kindred joint procedures in human life ; that is to say, we cannot possibly suppose that these arrangements are directed by an actual knowledge of their aimfulness indwelling in the individuals, nay, even of their aim. In explanation of the extraordinary, ay, the self-sacrificing zeal, as also the ingenious manner, in which such animals provide for their eggs, for instance, of whose aim and future mission they cannot possibly be conscious from experience and observation, our philosopher infers the existence of a *Wahn* that feigns to the individual insect's so scanty intellectual powers an end which it holds for the satisfaction of its private need, whereas that end in truth has nothing to do with the individual, but with the species. The individual's egoism is here assumed, and rightly, to be so invincible that arrangements beneficial merely to the species, to coming generations, and hence the preservation of the species at cost of the transient individual, would never be consummated by that individual with labour and self-sacrifice, were it not guided by the fancy (*Wahn*) that it is thereby serving an end of its own ; nay, this fancied end of its own must seem weightier to the individual, the satisfaction reapable from its attainment more potent and complete, than the purely-individual aim of everyday, of satisfying hunger and so forth, since, as we see, the latter is sacrificed with greatest keenness to the former. The author and incitor of this Wahn our philosopher deems to be the spirit of the race itself, the almighty Will-of-life (*Lebenswille*) supplanting the individual's limited perceptive-faculty, seeing that without its intervention the

---

a few sentences farther on, occur in so many words with Schopenhauer. Nowadays for " the spirit of the race " some of us might be inclined to read "the principle of the survival of the fittest " ; but the explanation of its *mode* of action, through a " Wahn," would hold as good to-day as thirty years ago.—Tr.

individual, in narrow egoistic care for self, would gladly sacrifice the species on the altar of its personal continuance.

Should we succeed in bringing the nature of this Wahn to our inner consciousness by any means, we should therewith win the key to that else so enigmatic relation of the individual to the species. Perhaps this may be made easier to us on the path that leads us out above the State. Meanwhile, however, the application of the results of our inquiry into animal instinct to the products of certain constant factors of the highest efficacy in the human State —factors unbidden by any extraneous power, but arising ever of their own accord — will furnish us with an immediate possibility of defining Wahn in terms of general experience.

In political life this Wahn displays itself as *patriotism*. As such it prompts the citizen to offer up his private welfare, for whose amplest possible ensurement he erst was solely concerned in all his personal and party efforts, nay, to offer up his life itself, for ensuring the State's continuance. The Wahn that any violent transmutation of the State must affect him altogether personally, must crush him to a degree which he believes he never could survive, here governs him in such a manner that his exertions to turn aside the danger threatening the State, as 'twere a danger to be suffered in his individual person, are quite as strenuous, and indeed more eager than in the actual latter case ; whereas the traitor, as also the churlish realist, finds it easy enough to prove that, even after entry of the evil which the patriot fears, his personal prosperity can remain as flourishing as ever.

The positive renunciation of egoism accomplished in the patriotic action, however, is certainly so violent a strain, that it cannot possibly hold out for long together ; moreover the Wahn that prompts it is still so strongly tinctured with a really egoistic notion, that the relapse into the sober, purely egoistic mood of everyday occurs in general with marked rapidity, and this latter mood goes on to fill the actual breadth of life. Hence the Patriotic Wahn requires a lasting symbol, whereto it may attach itself amid the dominant mood of everyday—thence, should exigence again arise, to promptly gain once more its quickening force; something like the colours that led us formerly to battle, and now wave peacefully above the city from the tower, a sheltering token of the meeting-place for all, should danger newly enter. This symbol is the King; in him the burgher honours unawares the visible representative, nay, the live embodiment of that same Wahn which, already bearing him beyond and above his common notions of the nature of things, inspirits and ennobles him to the point of shewing himself a patriot.

Now, what lies above and beyond Patriotism—that form of Wahn sufficient for the preservation of the State—will not be cognisable to the state-burgher as such, but, strictly speaking, can bring itself to the knowledge of none save the King or those who are able to make his personal interest their own. Only from the Kinghood's height can be seen the rents in the garment wherewithal Wahn clothes itself to reach its nearest goal, the preservation of the species, under the form of a State-fellowship. Though Patriotism may sharpen the burgher's eyes to interests of State, yet it leaves him blind to the interest of mankind in general; nay, its most effectual force is spent in passionately intensifying this blindness, which often finds a ray of daylight in the common intercourse of man and man. The patriot subordinates himself to his State in order to raise it above all other States, and thus, as it were, to find his personal sacrifice repaid with ample interest through the might and greatness of his fatherland. Injustice and violence toward other States and peoples have therefore been the true dynamic law of Patriotism throughout all time. Self-preservation is still the real prime motor here, since the quiet, and thus the power, of one's own State appears securable in no other way than through the powerlessness of other States, according to Machiavelli's telling maxim: "What you don't wish put on yourself, go put

upon your neighbour!" But this fact that one's own
quiet can be ensured by nothing but violence and injustice
to the world without, must naturally make one's quiet
seem always problematic in itself: thereby leaving a door
forever open to violence and injustice within one's own
State too. The measures and acts which shew us violently-
disposed towards the outer world, can never stay without a
violent reaction on ourselves. When modern state-polit-
ical optimists speak of a state of International Law,* in
which the [European] States stand nowadays toward one
another, one need only point to the necessity of maintaining
and constantly increasing our enormous standing armies,
to convince them, on the contrary, of the actual lawlessness
of that state (*Rechtslosigkeit dieses Zustandes*). Since it
does not occur to me to attempt to shew how matters
could be otherwise, I merely record the fact that we are
living in a perpetual state of war, with intervals of
armistice, and that the inner condition of the State itself
is not so utterly unlike this state of things as to pass
muster for its diametric opposite. If the prime concern
of all State systems is the ensurance of stability, and if
this ensurance hinges on the condition that no party shall
feel an irresistible need of radical change; if, to obviate
such an event, it is indispensable that the moment's
pressing need shall always be relieved in due season; and
if the practical common-sense of the burgher may be held
sufficient, nay alone competent, to recognise this need: on
the other hand we have seen that the highest associate
tendence of the State could only be kept in active vigour
through a form of Wahn; and as we were obliged to
recognise that this particular Wahn, namely that of
Patriotism, neither was truly pure, nor wholly answered
to the objects of the human race as such,—we now have
to take this Wahn in eye, withal, under the guise of a
constant menace to public peace and equity.

* "Von einem allgemeinen Rechtszustande,"—literally, "of a general (or
universal) state of right (or law);" the expression seems to refer to the so-
called "Balance of power," and may also be paraphrased by the more modern
European concert."—TR.

The very Wahn that prompts the egoistic burgher to the most self-sacrificing actions, can equally mislead him into the most deplorable embroglios, into acts the most injurious to Quiet.

The reason lies in the scarcely exaggerable weakness of the average human intellect, as also in the infinitely diverse shades and grades of perceptive-faculty in the units who, taken all together, create the so-called *public opinion.* Genuine respect for this "public opinion" is founded on the sure and certain observation that no one is more accurately aware of the community's true immediate life-needs, nor can better devise the means for their satisfaction, than the community itself: it would be strange indeed, were man more faultily organised in this respect than the dumb animal. Nevertheless we often are driven to the opposite view, if we remark how even for this, for the correct perception of its nearest, commonest needs, the ordinary human understanding does not suffice—not, at least, to the extent of jointly satisfying them 'n the spirit of true fellowship : the presence of beggars in our midst, and even at times of starving fellow-creatures, shews how weak the commonest human sense must be at bottom. So here already we have evidence of the great difficulty it must cost to bring true reason (*wirkliche Vernunft*) into the joint determinings of Man : though the cause may well reside in the boundless egoism of each single unit, which, outstripping far his intellect, prescribes his portion of the joint resolve at the very junctures where right knowledge can be attained through nothing but repression of egoism and sharpening of the understanding, — yet precisely here we may plainly detect the influence of a baneful Wahn. This Wahn has always found its only nurture in insatiable egoism; it is dangled before the latter from without, however, to wit by ambitious individuals, just as egoistic, but gifted with a higher, though in itself by no means high degree of intellect. This intentional employment and conscious or unconscious perversion of the Wahn can avail itself of none but the form alone accessible to the burgher, that of Patriotism, albeit in some disfigurement or other; it thus will always give itself out as an effort for the common good, and never yet has a demagogue or intriguer led a Folk astray without in some way making it believe itself inspired by patriotic ardour. Thus in Patriotism itself there lies the holdfast for misguidance; and the possibility of keeping always handy the means of this misguidance, resides in the artfully inflated value which certain people pretend to attach to "public opinion."

What manner of thing this "public opinion" is, should be best known to those who have its name forever in their mouths and erect the regard for it into a positive article of religion. Its self-styled organ in our times is the "Press": were she candid, she would call herself its generatrix, but she prefers to hide her moral and intellectual foibles—manifest enough to every thinking and earnest observer,—her utter want of independence and truthful judgment, behind the lofty mission of her subservience to this sole representative of human dignity, this Public Opinion, which marvellously bids her stoop to every indignity, to every contradiction, to to-day's betrayal of what she dubbed right sacred yesterday. Since, as we else may see, every sacred thing seems to come into the world merely to be employed for ends profane, the open profanation of Public Opinion might perhaps not warrant us in arguing to its badness in and for itself: only, its actual existence is difficult, or well-nigh impossible to prove, for *ex hypothesi* it cannot manifest as such in the single individual, as is done by every other noble Wahn; such as we must certainly account true Patriotism, which has its strongest and its plainest manifestation precisely in the individual unit. The pretended vicegerent of "public opinion," on the other hand, always gives herself out as its will-less slave; and thus one never can get at this wondrous power, save—

by making it for oneself. This, in effect, is what is done by the "press," and that with all the keenness ot the trade the world best understands, industrial business. Whereas each writer for the papers represents nothing, as a rule, but a literary failure or a bankrupt mercantile career, *many* newspaper-writers, or all of them together, form the awe-commanding power of the "*press*," the sublimation of public spirit, of practical human intellect, the indubitable guarantee of manhood's constant progress. Each man uses her according to his need, and she herself expounds the nature of Public Opinion through her practical behaviour—to the intent that it is at all times havable for gold or profit.

It certainly is not as paradoxical as it might appear, to aver that with the invention of the art of printing, and quite certainly with the rise of journalism, mankind has gradually lost much of its capacity for healthy judgment: demonstrably the plastic memory,* the widespread aptitude for poetical conception and reproduction, has considerably and progressively diminished since even written characters first gained the upper hand. No doubt a compensatory profit to the general evolution of human faculties, taken in the very widest survey, must be likewise capable of proof; but in any case it does not accrue to us immediately, for whole generations—including most emphatically our own, as any close observer must recognise —have been so degraded through the abuses practised on the healthy human power of judgment by the manipulators of the modern daily Press in particular, and consequently through the lethargy into which that power of judgment has fallen, in keeping with man's habitual bent to easygoingness, that, in flat contradiction of the lies they let themselves be told, men shew themselves more incapable each day of sympathy with truly great ideas.

The most injurious to the common welfare is the harm thus done to the simple sense of equity : there exists no form

* "Das plastische Gedächtniss"—evidently the mental record of things in their visual, concrete form, as opposed to their abstract labels.—TR.

of injustice, of onesidedness and narrowness of heart, that does not find expression in the pronouncements of "public opinion," and—what adds to the hatefulness of the thing —forever with a passionateness that masquerades as the warmth of genuine patriotism, but has its true and constant origin in the most self-seeking of all human motives. Whoso would learn this accurately, has but to run counter to "public opinion," or indeed to defy it : he will find himself brought face to face with the most implacable tyrant; and no one is more driven to suffer from its despotism, than the Monarch, for very reason that he is the representant of that selfsame Patriotism whose noxious counterfeit steps up to him, as "public opinion," with the boast of being identical in kind.

Matters strictly pertaining to the interest of the King, which in truth can only be that of purest patriotism, are cut and dried by his unworthy substitute, this Public Opinion, in the interest of the vulgar egoism of the mass; and the necessitation to yield to its requirements, notwithstanding, becomes the earliest source of that higher form of suffering which the King alone can personally experience as his own. If we add hereto the personal sacrifice of private freedom which the monarch has to bring to "reasons of State," and if we reflect how he alone is in a position to make purely-human considerations lying far above mere patriotism—as, for instance, in his intercourse with the heads of other States—his personal concern, and yet is forced to immolate them upon the altar of his State: then we shall understand why the legends and the poetry of every age have brought the tragedy of human life the plainest and the oftenest to show in just the destiny of Kings. In the fortunes and the fate of Kings the tragic import of the world can first be brought completely to our knowledge. Up to the King a clearance of every obstacle to the human Will is thinkable, so far as that Will takes on the mould of State, since the endeavour of the citizen does not outstep the satisfaction of certain needs allayable within the confines of the State. The General and States-

man, too, remains a practical realist ; in his enterprises
he may be unlucky and succumb, but chance might also
favour him to reach the thing not in and for itself impossible : for he ever serves a definite, practical aim. But
the King desires the Ideal, he wishes justice and humanity;
nay, wished he them not, wished he naught but what the
simple burgher or party-leader wants,—the very claims
made on him by his office, claims that allow him nothing
but an ideal interest, by making him a traitor to the idea
he represents, would plunge him into those sufferings which
have inspired tragic poets from all time to paint their pictures of the vanity of human life and strife.*   True justice
and humanity are ideals irrealisable : to be bound to strive
for them, nay, to recognise an unsilenceable summons to
their carrying out, is to be condemned to misery.   What
the throughly noble, truly kingly individual directly feels
of this, in time is given also to the individual unqualified for
knowledge of his tragic task, and solely placed by Nature's
dispensation on the throne, to learn in some uncommon
fashion reserved for kings alone : upon the height allotted
to it by an unavoidable destiny, the vulgar head, the
ignoble heart that in a humbler sphere might very well
subsist in fullest civic honour, in thorough harmony with
itself and its surroundings, here falls into a dire contempt,
far-reaching and long-lasting, often in itself unreasoning,
and therefore to be accounted wellnigh tragic.   The very
fact that the individual called to the throne has no personal
choice, may allow no sanction to his purely human leanings, and needs must fill a great position for which nothing
but great natural parts can qualify, foreordains him to a
superhuman lot that needs must crush the weakling into
personal nullity.   The highly fit, however, is summoned to
drink the full, deep cup of life's true tragedy in his exalted
station.   Should his construction of the Patriotic ideal
be passionate and ambitious, he becomes a warrior-chief
and conqueror, and thereby courts the portion of the
violent, the faithlessness of Fortune ; but should his nature

* Cf. Amfortas ; at this epoch our author was drafting his *Parsifal.*—TR.

be noble-minded, full of human pity, more deeply and more bitterly than every other is he called to see the futility of all endeavours for true, for perfect justice.

To him more deeply and more inwardly than is possible to the State-citizen, as such, is it therefore given to feel that in Man there dwells an infinitely deeper, more capacious need than the State and its ideal can ever satisfy. Wherefore as it was Patriotism that raised the burgher to the highest height by him attainable, it is *Religion* alone that can bear the King to the stricter dignity of manhood (*zur eigentlichen Menschenwürde*).

Religion, of its very essence, is radically divergent from the State. The religions that have come into the world have been high and pure in direct ratio as they seceded from the State, and in themselves entirely upheaved it. We find State and Religion in complete alliance only where each still stands upon its lowest step of evolution and significance. The primitive Nature-religion subserves no ends but those which Patriotism provides for in the adult State : hence with the full development of patriotic spirit the ancient Nature-religion has always lost its meaning for the State. So long as it flourishes, however, so long do men subsume by their gods their highest practical interest of State ; the tribal god is the representant of the tribesmen's solidarity ; the remaining Nature-gods become Penates, protectors of the home, the town, the fields and flocks. Only in the wholly adult State, where these religions have paled before the full-fledged patriotic duty, and are sinking into inessential forms and ceremonies ; only where "Fate" has shewn itself to be Political Necessity *—could true Religion step into the world. Its basis is a feeling of the unblessedness of human being, of the State's profound inadequacy to still the purely-human need. Its inmost kernel is denial of the world—

* Cf. Vol. II., 178, 179. Upon coupling the present parallelism with that noted on page 11 *antea*, it would appear highly probable that King Ludwig had been studying Part II. of *Oper und Drama,* and had directed Wagner's attention to this section—surrounding the Œdipus-Antigone myth—in particular.—TR.

i.e. recognition of the world as a fleeting and dreamlike state [of mind] reposing merely on illusion (*auf einer Täuschung*)—and struggle for Redemption from it, prepared-for by renunciation, attained by Faith.

In true Religion a complete reversal thus occurs of all the aspirations to which the State had owed its founding and its organising : what is seen to be unattainable here, the human mind desists from striving-for upon this path, to ensure its reaching by a path completely opposite. To the religious eye (*der religiösen Vorstellung*) the truth grows plain that there must be another world than this, because the inextinguishable bent-to-happiness cannot be stilled within this world, and hence requires another world for its redemption. What, now, is that other world ? So far as the conceptual faculties of human Understanding reach, and in their practical application as intellectual Reason, it is quite impossible to gain a notion that shall not clearly shew itself as founded on this selfsame world of need and change : wherefore, since this world is the source of our unhappiness, that other world, of redemption from it, must be precisely as different from this present world as the mode of cognisance whereby we are to perceive that other world must be different from the mode which shews us nothing but this present world of suffering and illusion.*

In Patriotism we have already seen that a Wahn usurps the single individual prompted merely by personal interests, a Wahn that makes the peril of the State appear to him an infinitely intensified personal peril, to ward off which he then will sacrifice himself with equally intensified ardour. But where, as now, it is a question of letting the personal

---

* "So weit die intellektualen Vorstellungfähigkeiten des menschlichen Verstandes reichen, und in ihrer praktischen Anwendung als Vernunft sich geltend machen, ist durchaus keine Vorstellung zu gewinnen, welche nicht genau immer nur wieder diese selbe Welt des Bedürfnisses und des Wechsels erkennen liesse : da diese der Quell unserer Unseligkeit ist, muss daher jene andere Welt der Erlösung von dieser Welt genau so verschieden sein, als diejenige Erkenntnissart, durch welche wir sie erkennen sollen, verschieden von derjenigen sein muss, welcher einzig diese täuschende leidenvolle Welt sich darstellt."

egoism, at bottom the only decisor, perceive the nullity of all the world, of the whole assemblage of relations in which alone contentment had hitherto seemed possible to the individual ; of directing his zeal toward free-willed suffering and renunciation, to detach him from dependence on this world : this wonder-working intuition—which, in contradistinction from the ordinary practical mode of ideation, we can only apprehend as Wahn *—must have a source so sublime, so utterly incomparable with every other, that the only notion possible to be granted us of that source itself, in truth, must consist in our necessary inference of its existence from this its supernatural effect.—

Whosoever thinks he has said the last word on the essence of the Christian faith when he styles it an attempted satisfaction of the most unbounded egoism, a kind of contract wherein the beneficiary is to obtain eternal, never-ending bliss on condition of abstinence [or " renunciation "—*Entsagung*] and free-willed suffering in this relatively brief and fleeting life, he certainly has defined therewith the sort of notion alone accessible to unshaken human egoism, but nothing even distantly resembling the Wahn-transfigured concept proper to the actual practiser of free-willed suffering and renunciation. Through voluntary suffering and renunciation, on the contrary, man's egoism is already practically upheaved, and he who chooses them, let his object be whate'er you please, is thereby raised already above all notions bound by Time and Space; for no longer can he seek a happiness that lies in Time and Space, e'en were they figured as eternal and immeasurable. That which gives to him the superhuman strength to suffer voluntarily, must itself be felt by him

---

* " Diese wunderwirkende Vorstellung, die wir, der gemeinen praktischen Vorstellungsweise gegenüber, nur als Wahn auffassen können " etc. I here have translated the first " Vorstellung " as " intuition," though " idea " is the word generally employed for rendering the Schopenhauerian term ; literally it signifies an image " *set before* the mind," and hence any " mental concept,' but with a less *abstract* shade of meaning than " Begriff "—the bare " idea " ; a difficulty arises at times, in the translation of this term, from its connoting not only the " mental picture " itself, but also the act of forming it.—TR.

already as a profoundly inward happiness, incognisable by any other, a happiness quite incommunicable to the world except through outer suffering: it must be the measure-lessly lofty joy of world-overcoming, compared wherewith the empty pleasure of the world-conqueror seems downright null and childish.*

From this result, sublime above all others, we have to infer the nature of the Divine Wahn itself; and, to gain any sort of notion thereof, we have therefore to pay close heed to how it displays itself to the religious world-Over-comer, simply endeavouring to reproduce and set before ourselves this conception of his in all its purity, but in nowise attempting to reduce the Wahn itself, forsooth, to terms of *our* conceptual method, so radically distinct from that of the Religious.—

As Religion's highest force proclaims itself in *Faith*, its most essential import lies within its *Dogma*.† Not through its practical importance for the State, i.e. its moral law, is Religion of such weight ; for the root principles of all mor-ality are to be found in every, even in the most imperfect, religion : but through its measureless value to the Indi-vidual, does the Christian religion prove its lofty mission, and that through its Dogma. The wondrous, quite incomparable attribute of religious Dogma is this : it presents in positive form that which on the path of reflection (*des Nachdenkens*), and through the strictest philosophic methods, can be seized in none but negative form. That is to say, whereas the philosopher arrives at demonstrating the erroneousness and incompetence of that natural mode of ideation in power whereof we take the world, as it commonly presents itself, for an undoubt-able reality : religious Dogma shews the other world itself, as yet unrecognised ; and with such unfailing sureness and distinctness, that the Religious, on whom that world has dawned, is straightway possessed with the most unshatter-

* Cf. "Doch wenn der mich im Himmel hält, dann liegt zu Füssen mir die Welt." *Die Meistersinger*, act ii.—Tr.

† " Wie die höchste Kraft der Religion sich im *Glauben* kundgiebt, liegt ihre wesentlichste Bedeutung in ihrem *Dogma*."

able, most deeply-blessing peace. We must assume that this conception, so indicibly beatifying in its effect, this idea which we can only rank under the category of Wahn, or better, this immediate vision seen by the Religious, to the ordinary human apprehension remains entirely foreign and unconveyable, in respect of both its substance and its form. What, on the other hand, is imparted thereof and thereon to the layman (*den Profanen*), to the people, can be nothing more than a kind of allegory; to wit, a rendering of the unspeakable, impalpable, and never understandable through [their] immediate intuition, into the speech of common life and of its only feasible form of knowledge, erroneous *per se*. In this sacred allegory an attempt is made to transmit to wordly minds (*der weltlichen Vorstellung*) the mystery of the divine revelation : but the only relation it can bear to what the Religious had immediately beheld, is the relation of the day-told dream to the actual dream of night. As to the part the most essential of the thing to be transmitted, this narration will be itself so strongly tinctured with the impressions of ordinary daily life, and through them so distorted, that it neither can truly satisfy the teller—since he feels that just the weightiest part had really been quite otherwise—nor fill the hearer with the certainty afforded by the hearing of something wholly comprehensible and intelligible in itself. If, then, the record left upon our own mind by a deeply moving dream is strictly nothing but an allegorical paraphrase, whose intrinsic disagreement with the original remains a trouble to our waking consciousness; and therefore if the knowledge reaped by the hearer can at bottom be nothing but an essentially distorted image of that original : yet this [allegorical] message, in the case both of the dream and of the actually received divine revelation, remains the only possible way of proclaiming the thing received to the layman. Upon these lines is formed the Dogma; and this is the revelation's only portion cognisable by the world, which it therefore has to take on authority, so as to become a partner, at least through Faith, in what its eye has never seen. Hence is Faith so strenuously commended to the Folk: the Religious, become a sharer in salvation through his own eye's beholding (*durch eigene Anschauung*), feels and knows that the layman, to whom the vision (*die Anschauung*) itself remains a stranger, has no path to knowledge of the Divine except the path of Faith; and this Faith, to be effectual, must be sincere, undoubting and unconditional, in measure as the Dogma embraces all the incomprehensible, and to common knowledge contradictory-seeming, conditioned by the incomparable difficulty of its wording.*

The intrinsic distortion of Religion's fundamental essence, beheld through divine revelation, that is to say of the true root-essence incommunicable *per se* to ordinary knowledge, is hence undoubtedly engendered in the first instance by the aforesaid difficulty in the wording of its Dogma; but this distortion first becomes actual and perceptible, from the moment when the Dogma's nature is dragged before the tribune of common causal apprehension. The resulting vitiation of Religion itself, whose holy of holies is just the indubitable Dogma that blesses through an inward Faith, is brought about by the ineluctable requirement to defend that Dogma against the assaults of common human apprehension, to explain and make it seizable to the latter. This requirement grows more pressing in degree as Religion, which had its primal fount within the deepest chasms of the world-fleeing heart, comes once again into a relation with the State. The disputations traversing the centuries of the Christian religion's development into a Church and its complete metamorphosis into a State-establishment, the perpetually recurring strifes in countless forms anent the rightness and the rationality of religious Dogma and its points, present us with the sad and pain-

---

* "Und dieser [Glaube] muss, soll er erfolgreich sein, in dem Maasse innig, unbedingt und zweifellos sein, als das Dogma in sich all' das Unbegreifliche, und der gemeinen Erkenntniss widerspruchvoll Dünkende enthält, welches durch die unvergleichliche Schwierigkeit seiner Abfassung bedingt war." The obscurity of this sentence—*credo quia impossibile*—will be cleared up in the next paragraph.—TR.

fully instructive history of an attack of madness. Two absolutely incongruous modes of view and knowledge, at variance in their entire nature, cross one another in this strife, without so much as letting men detect their radical divergence: not but that one must allow to the truly religious champions of Dogma that they started with a thorough consciousness of the total difference between their mode of knowledge and that belonging to the world; whereas the terrible wrong, to which they were driven at last, consisted in their letting themselves be hurried into zealotism and the most inhuman use of violence when they found that nothing was to be done with human reason (*Vernunft*), thus practically degenerating into the utmost opposite of religiousness. On the other hand the hopelessly materialistic, industrially commonplace, entirely un-Goded aspect of the modern world is debitable to the counter eagerness of the common practical understanding to construe religious Dogma by laws of cause-and-effect deduced from the phenomena of natural and social life, and to fling aside whatever rebelled against that mode of explanation as a reasonless chimera. After the Church, in her zeal, had clutched at the weapons of State-jurisdiction (*staatsrechtlichen Exekution*), thus transforming herself into a political power, the contradiction into which she thereby fell with herself—since religious Dogma assuredly conveyed no lawful title to such a power—was bound to become a truly lawful weapon in the hands of her opponents; and, whatever other semblance may still be toilsomely upheld, to-day we see her lowered to an institution of the State, employed for objects of the State-machinery; wherewith she may prove her use, indeed, but no more her divinity.

But does this mean that Religion itself has ceased?—

No, no! It lives, but only at its primal source and sole true dwelling-place, within the deepest, holiest inner chamber of the Individual; there whither never yet has surged a conflict of the rationalist and supranaturalist, the Clergy and the State. For *this* is the essence of true

Religion: that, away from the cheating show of the day-tide world, it shines in the night of man's inmost heart, with a light quite other than the world-sun's light, and visible nowhence save from out that depth.*—

'Tis thus indeed! Profoundest knowledge teaches us that only in the inner chamber of our heart, in nowise from the world presented to us without, can true assuagement come to us. Our organs of perception of the outer world are merely destined for discovering the means wherewith to satisfy the individual unit's need, that unit which feels so single and so needy in face of just this world; with the selfsame organs we cannot possibly perceive the basic Oneness of all being; it is allowed us solely by the new cognitive faculty that is suddenly awoken in us, as if through Grace, so soon as ever the vanity of the world comes home to our inner consciousness on any kind of path. Wherefore the truly religious knows also that he cannot really impart to the world on a theoretic path, forsooth through argument and controversy, his inner beatific vision, and thus persuade it of that vision's truth: he can do this only on a practical path, through *example*,† through the deed of renunciation, of sacrifice, through gentleness unshakable, through the sublime serenity of earnestness (*Heiterkeit des Ernstes*) that spreads itself o'er all his actions. The saint, the martyr, is therefore the true mediator of salvation; through his example the Folk is shewn, in the only manner to it comprehensible, of what purport must that vision be, wherein itself can share through Faith alone, but not yet through immediate knowledge. Hence there lies a deep and pregnant meaning behind the Folk's addressing itself to God through the medium of its heart-loved saints; and it says little for the vaunted enlightenment of our era, that every English shopkeeper for instance, so soon as he has donned his sunday-coat and taken the right book with him, opines

* "Da erdämmerte mild erhab'ner Macht im Busen mir die Nacht; mein Tag war da vollbracht." *Tristan und Isolde*, act ii.—TR.

† "Nicht darf sie Zweifels Last beschweren; sie sahen meine gute That." *Lohengrin*, act ii.—TR.

that he is entering into immediate personal intercourse with God. No: a proper understanding of that Wahn wherein a higher world imparts itself to common human ideation, and which proves its virtue through man's heart-felt resignation (*Unterworfenheit*) to this present world, alone is able to lead to knowledge of man's most deep concerns; and it must be borne in mind, withal, that we can be prompted to that resignation only through the said example of true saintliness, but never urged into it by an overbearing clergy's vain appeal to Dogma pure and simple.—

This attribute of true religiousness, which, for the deep reason given above, does not proclaim itself through dis-putation, but solely through the active example — this attribute, should it be indwelling in the King, becomes the only revelation, of profit to both State and Religion, that can bring the two into relationship. As I have already shewn, no one is more compelled than he, through his exalted, well-nigh superhuman station, to grasp the profoundest earnestness of Life; and—if he gain this only insight worthy of his calling—no one stands in more need, than he, of that sublime and strengthening solace which Religion alone can give. What no cunning of the politician can ever compass, to him, thus armoured and equipped, will then alone be possible: gazing out of that world into this, the mournful seriousness wherewith the sight of mundane passions fills him, will arm him for the exercise of strictest equity; the inner knowledge that all these passions spring only from the one great suffering of unredeemed mankind, will move him pitying to the exercise of grace. *Unflinching justice, ever ready mercy— here is the mystery of the King's ideal!* But though it faces toward the State with surety of its healing, this ideal's possibility of attainment arises not from any tendence of the State, but purely from Religion. Here, then, would be the happy trysting-place where State and Religion, as erst in their prophetic days of old, met once again.

We here have ascribed to the King a mission so uncommon, and repeatedly denoted as almost superhuman,
that the question draws near: how is its constant fulfilment
to be compassed by the human individual, even though he
own the natural capacity for which alone its possibility is
reckoned, without his sinking under it? In truth there
rules so great a doubt as to the possibility of attaining the
Kingly ideal, that the contrary case is provided for in
advance in the framing of State-constitutions. Neither
could we ourselves imagine a monarch qualified to fulfil
his highest task, saving under conditions similar to those
we are moved to advance when seeking to account for the
working and endurance of everything uncommon and un-
ordinary in this ordinary world. For, when we regard it
with closer sympathy, each truly great mind—which the
human generative-force, for all its teeming productivity,
brings forth so vastly seldom—sets us a-wondering how
twas possible for it to hold out for any length of time
within this world, to wit for long enough to acquit itself
of its tale of work.

Now, the great, the truly noble spirit is distinguished
from the common organisation of everyday by this : to *it*
every, often the seemingly most trivial, incident of life and
world-intercourse is capable of swiftly displaying its widest
correlation with the essential root-phenomena of all
existence, thus of shewing Life and the World themselves in their true, their terribly earnest meaning. The
naïve, ordinary man—accustomed merely to seize the out-
most side of such events, the side of practical service for
the moment's need—when once this awful earnestness
suddenly reveals itself to him through an unaccustomed
juncture, falls into such consternation that self-murder is
very frequently the consequence. The great, the exceptional man finds himself each day, in a certain measure, in
the situation where the ordinary man forthwith despairs
of life. Certainly the great, the truly religious man I
mean, is saved from this consequence by the lofty earnest
of that inner ure-knowledge (*Ur-erkenntniss*) of the essence

of the world which has become the standard of all his
beholdings ; at each instant he is prepared for the terrible
phenomenon : also, he is armoured with a gentleness and
patience which never let him fall a-storming against any
manifestation of evil that may haply take him unawares.

Yet an irrecusable yearning to turn his back completely
on this world must necessarily surge up within his breast,
were there not for him—as for the common man who lives
away a life of constant care—a certain distraction, a
periodical turning-aside from that world's-earnestness
which else is ever present to his thoughts. What for the
common man is entertainment and amusement, must be
forthcoming for him as well, but in the noble form befitting
him ; and that which renders possible this turning aside,
this noble illusion, must again be a work of that man-
redeeming Wahn which spreads its wonders wherever the
individual's normal mode of view can help itself no farther.
But in this instance the Wahn must be entirely candid ; it
must confess itself in advance for an illusion, if it is to
be willingly embraced by the man who really longs for
distraction and illusion in the high and earnest sense I
mean. The fancy-picture brought before him must never
afford a loophole for re-summoning the earnestness of Life
through any possible dispute about its actuality and
provable foundation upon fact, as religious Dogma does :
no, it must exercise its specific virtue through its very
setting of the conscious Wahn in place of the reality.
This office is fulfilled by *Art* ; and in conclusion I therefore point my highly-loved young friend to Art, as the
kindly Life-saviour who does not really and wholly lead
us out beyond this life, but, within it, lifts us up above it
and shews it as itself a game of play ; a game that, take it
ne'er so terrible and earnest an appearance, yet here again
is shewn us as a mere Wahn-picture, as which it comforts us
and wafts us from the common truth of our distress (*Noth*).
The work of noblest Art will be given a glad admittance
by my friend, the work that, treading on the footprints of
Life's earnestness, shall soothingly dissolve reality into

that Wahn wherein itself in turn, this serious reality, at last seems nothing else to us but Wahn : and in his most rapt beholding of this wondrous Wahn-play (*Wahnspiel*) there will return to him the indicible dream-picture of the holiest revelation, of meaning ure-akin (*urverwandt sinnvoll*), with clearness unmistakable,—that same divine dream-picture which the disputes of sects and churches had made ever more incognisable to him, and which, as wellnigh unintelligible Dogma, could only end in his dismay.   The nothingness of the world, here is it harmless, frank, avowed as though in smiling : for our willing purpose to deceive ourselves has led us on to recognise the world's real state without a shadow of illusion.—

Thus has it been possible for me, even from this earnest sally into the weightiest regions of Life's earnestness, and without losing myself or feigning, to come back to my beloved Art.   Will my friend in sympathy understand me, when I confess that first upon this path have I regained full consciousness of Art's serenity ?

GERMAN ART AND GERMAN POLICY.

Deutsche Kunst und Deutsche Politik.

Deutsche Kunst und Deutsche Politik *appeared originally in the feuilleton of the* Süddeutsche Presse *in the autumn of* 1867 *; this will account for the division into chapters, and into chapters of so very few pages each. Early in* 1868 *the essay was reprinted, and issued separately, by J. J. Weber of Leipzig.*

I.

N his admirable "Inquiry into the European Balance of Power"* Constantin Frantz closes with the following paragraph his exposition of the influence, outspoken in the Napoleonic propaganda, of French politics upon the European system of States :—

"But it is on nothing else than the power of French civilisation that this propaganda rests; without that, itself would be quite powerless. To extricate ourselves from the tyranny of that materialistic civilisation, is therefore the only effectual dam against this propaganda. And this is precisely the mission of Germany; because Germany, of all Continental countries, alone possesses the needful qualities and forces of mind and spirit to bring about a nobler culture, against which French civilisation will have no power any more. Here would you have the rightful German propaganda, and a very essential contribution to the re-establishment of European equipoise."

We place this saying of one of the most comprehensive and original political thinkers and writers—of whom the German nation might well be proud, had it only learnt to listen to him—at the head of a series of inquiries to which we are incited by the certainly not uninteresting problem of the relation of Art to Politics in general, of German art-endeavours to the struggle of the Germans for a higher political standing in particular. The first glance reveals this particular relation as of so peculiar a kind, that it seems worth while to proceed from *it* to a comparative examination of that more general relation,

---

* "*Untersuchungen über das europäische Gleichgewicht*": published in Berlin, 1859. In Volume II. of the present series will be found Richard Wagner's dedication (1868) of the second edition of *Oper und Drama* to this same author.—TR.

—worth while for rousing the Germans to a noble sense
of self-reliance, since the universal import of even this
particular relation, while it meets the efforts of other
nations in a conciliatory temper, at like time very evidently assigns to the qualities and development of just
the German spirit the pre-eminent calling to that work
of reconciliation.

That Art and Science pursue their own path of evolution, of efflorescence and decay, completely aside from
the political life of a nation, must have been the conclusion of those who have paid their chief attention to
Art's Renaissance amid the political relations of the
expiring Middle Ages, and have deemed impossible to
accord to the downfall of the Roman Church, to the
prevalence of dynastic intrigues in the Italian States, as
also to the tyranny of the ecclesiastical Inquisition in
Spain, any furthersome connexion with the unparalleled
artistic flourishing of Italy and Spain at the same epoch.
That present-day France is standing at the head of
European civilisation, and yet betrays the deepest bankruptcy of truly spiritual * productivity, is a fresh apparent
contradiction : here, where splendour, power, and acknowledged supremacy over almost every other land and nation
in every conceivable form of public life are undeniable
facts, the best spirits among this people, that accounts
itself so eminently spirituel, despair of ever mounting
from the mazes of the most degrading materialism to
any sort of outlook on the beautiful. If one is to grant
the justice of the never-ceasing French laments about
the restriction of the nation's political freedom (and
people flatter themselves with assigning this as the only
ground for the ruin of the public art-taste), these laments
might still be met, and not without good reason, by a
reference to those flowering periods of Italian and Spanish

* The word "*geistig*" (derived from "*Geist*," i.e. "mind" or "spirit")
having no comprehensive equivalent in the English language, one must render
it by "intellectual," "mental," or "spiritual"; as a rule I propose to employ
the last-named, but must claim a certain amount of elasticity in the interpretation.—TR.

Art when outward lustre and decisive influence upon the
civilisation of Europe went hand in hand with so-called
political thraldom, pretty much as now is the case in
France. But, that at no epoch of their lustre have the
French been able to produce an Art even distantly approaching the Italian, or a poetic Literature of equal
standing with the Spanish, must have a special reason of
its own. Perhaps it may be explained through a comparison of Germany with France at a time of the latter's
greatest splendour and the former's deepest downfall.
There Louis XIV, here a German philosopher [Leibnitz]
who .believed he must recognise in France's brilliant
despot the chosen ruler of the world : indisputably an
expression of the German nation's deepest woe! At that
time Louis XIV and his courtiers set up their laws for
even what should rank as beautiful, beyond which, at the
real heart of the matter, the French under Napoleon III
have not as yet exceeded ; from that time dates the
forgetting of their native history, the uprooting of their
saplings of a national art of poetry, the havoc played with
the art and poesy imported from Italy and Spain, the
transformation of beauty into elegance, of grace into
decorum (*der Anmuth in den Anstand*). Impossible is
it for us to discover what the true qualities of the French
people might have engendered of themselves ; it has so
completely divested itself of these qualities, at least in so
far as concerns its " Civilisation," that we can no longer
argue as to how it would have borne itself without that
transformation. And all this happened to this people
when it was at a high stage of its splendour and its power,
when, forgetting itself, it took its likeness from its Princes ;
with such determinant energy did it happen, this civilised
Form of its impressed itself so indelibly upon every
European nation, that even to-day one can picture nothing
else but Chaos, in an emancipation from that yoke, and
the Frenchman would rightly think he had lapsed into
utter barbarism if he swung himself from out the orbit of
his Civilisation.

If we consider the positive murder of freedom involved in this influence, which so completely dominated
the most original German ruler-genius of latter times,
Frederick the Great, that he looked down upon everything
German with downright passionate contempt, we must
admit that a redemption from the manifest bankruptcy
of European manhood might be deemed of moment not
unlike the deed of shattering the Roman world-dominion
and its levelling, at last quite deadening civilisation.   As
there a total regeneration was needed of the European
Folk-blood, so here a rebirth of the Folk-spirit might be
required.   And indeed it seems reserved for the selfsame
nation from whom that regeneration once proceeded, to
accomplish this rebirth as well ; for demonstrably, as
scarce another fact in history, the resurrection of the
German Folk itself has emanated from the German Spirit,
in fullest contrast to the " Renaissance " of the remaining
culture-folks of newer Europe—of whom in the French
nation's case at least, instead of any resurrection, an un-
exampledly capricious transformation on mere mechanical
lines, dictated from above, is equally demonstrable.

At the very time when the most gifted German ruler
could not look beyond the horizon of that French civilisation without a shudder, this rebirth of the German Folk
from its own spirit, a phenomenon unparalleled in history,
was already taking place.   Of it Schiller sings :

> No Augustan age's flower,
> No Medici's bounteous power,
>   Smiled upon our German Art ;
> She was never nursed in lustre,
> Opened wide her blossoms' cluster
>   Ne'er for royal Princes' mart.

To these eloquent rhymes of the great poet we will add
in humdrum prose that, when we talk of the rebirth of
German Art, we are speaking of a time at which, on the
other hand, the German Folk was scarcely recognisable
outside its royal families ; that, after the unheard ruin of
all civic culture in Germany through the Thirty Years'

War, all right, nay, all capacity to move in any walk or sphere of life lay in the Prince's hands alone; that these princely courts, in which alone the might and even the existence of the German nation found expression, behaved themselves with almost scrupulous conscientiousness as threadbare imitations of the French King's court: and we shall have a commentary, at any rate challenging earnest meditation, to Schiller's strophe. If we arise from that meditation with a feeling of pride in the German spirit's indomitable force; and if, encouraged by this feeling, we may dare assume that even now, despite the wellnigh unbroken influence of French civilisation upon the public spirit of European peoples, this German spirit stands facing it as a rival equally-endowed at bottom then, to mark the situation's political significance withal, we might frame the following brief antithesis :—*French Civilisation arose without the people, German Art without the princes; the first could arrive at no depth of spirit because it merely laid a garment on the nation, but never thrust into its heart; the second has fallen short of power and patrician finish because it could not reach as yet the courts of princes, not open yet the hearts of rulers to the German Spirit.* The continued sovereignty of French civilisation would therefore mean the continuance of a veritable estrangement between the spirit of the German Folk and the spirit of its Princes; it thus would be the triumph of French policy, aiming since Richelieu at European hegemony, to keep this estrangement on foot, and make it total : just as that statesman made use of the religious strifes and political antagonisms between Princes and Empire [or "Realm"—*Reich*] for founding French supremacy, so, under the changed conditions of the age, it would be bound to be the persistent care of gifted French dictators to employ the seductive influence of French civilisation, if not to subjugate the remaining European peoples, at least to openly control the spirit of German courts. Complete success attended this means of subjugation in the past century, where with a blush

we see German Princes snared and alienated from the
German Folk by presents of French ballet-dancers and
Italian singers, just as savage Negro-princes are beguiled
to-day with strings of beads and tinkling bells. How to
deal with a Folk from whom its indifferent Princes have
at last been actually kidnapped, we may see by a letter
of the great Napoleon to his brother, whom he had
appointed King of Holland : he reproached him with
having given way too much to the national spirit of his
subjects, whereas, had he better Frenchified the country,
the Emperor would have added to his kingdom a slice
of Northern Germany, "*puisque c'eût été un noyau de peuple,
qui eût dépaysé davantage l'esprit allemand, ce qui est
le premier but de ma politique,*" as the sentence runs in
the letter in question.—Here stand naked, face to face,
this "*esprit allemand*" and French civilisation : between
the two the German Princes, of whom that noble strophe
of Schiller's sings.—

Clearly, then, it is worth while to inspect the closer
relations of this German Spirit with the Princes of the
German people : it well might give us serious pause.
For we are bound some day to reach a point, in the
contest between French civilisation and the German spirit,
where it will become a question of the continuance of the
German Princes. If the German Princes are not the
faithful guardians of the German spirit ; if, consciously
or unconsciously, they help French civilisation to triumph
over that German spirit, so woefully misprised and disregarded by them : then their days are numbered, let
the fiat come from here or there. Thus we are fronted
with an earnest question, of world-historical moment :
its more minute examination will plainly teach us whether
we err when, from our standpoint, that of German Art,
we assign to it so great and grave a meaning.

II.

It is good and most encouraging for us, to find that the German Spirit, when with the second half of last century it raised itself from its deepest decay, did not require a new birth, but merely a resurrection: across two desert centuries it could stretch its hands to the selfsame spirit, which then strewed wide its lusty seeds through all the Holy Roman Empire of the German Nation,* and whose effect upon even the plastic shape of Europe's civilisation we can never deem of small account if we remember that the beautiful, the manifoldly individual, the imaginative German costume of those days was adopted by every European nation. Look at two portraits: here Dürer, there Leibnitz; what a horror at the unhappy period of our downfall is awoken in us by the contrast! Hail to the glorious spirits who first felt deep this horror, and cast their gaze across the centuries to recognise themselves once more! Then was found, that it had not been drowsiness that plunged the German Folk into its misery; it had fought its war of thirty years for its spiritual freedom; that was won, and though the body was faint with wounds and loss of blood, the mind stayed free, even beneath French full-bottomed wigs. Hail Winckelmann and Lessing, ye who, beyond the centuries of native German majesty, found the German's ure-kinsmen in the divine Hellenes, and laid bare the pure ideal of human beauty to the powder-bleared eyes of French-civilised mankind! Hail to thee, Goethe, thou who hadst power to wed Helena to our Faust, the Greek ideal to the German spirit! Hail to thee, Schiller, thou who gavest to the reborn spirit the stature of the " German stripling " (*des "deutschen Jünglings*"), who stands disdainful of the pride of Britain, the sensuous wiles of Paris! Who was this "deutsche Jüngling"? Has anyone heard of a French,

* Cf. Hans Sachs' closing speech in *Die Meistersinger*, particularly its last words : " Und gebt ihr ihrem Wirken Gunst, zerging' in Dunst das heil'ge röm'sche Reich, uns bliebe gleich die heil'ge deutsche Kunst."—TR.

an English "Jüngling"? And *yet* how plain and clear beyond mistake, we understand this " German Jüngling "! This stripling, who in Mozart's virginal melodies beshamed the Italian capons ; in Beethoven's Symphony grew up to courage of the man, for dauntless, world-redeeming deeds ! And this stripling it was, who threw himself at last upon the battle-field when his princes had lost everything, Empire, country, honour ; to reconquer for the Folk its freedom, for the Princes e'en their forfeit thrones. And how was this " Jüngling " repaid ? In all history there is no blacker ingratitude, than the German princes' treachery to the spirit of their people ; and many a good, a noble and self-sacrificing deed of theirs, will it need to atone for that betrayal. We hope for those deeds, and therefore let the sin be told right loudly !

How was it possible that the Princes should have passed in total silence the incomparably glorious resurrection of the German Spirit, not even have thence derived the smallest change in their opinion of their people's character ? How explain this incredible blindness, which absolutely knew not so much as how to use that infinitely stirring spirit for the furthering of their dynastic policy ? —The reason of the German heart's perversity in these highest regions of the German nation, of all places, lies certainly both deep and far away ; in part, perchance, in just the universal scope of German nature. The German *Reich* was no narrow national State, and far as heaven from what hovers nowadays before the longing fancy of the weaker, downtrod and dissevered races of the nation. The sons of German Kaisers had to learn no less than four distinct European languages, to fit them for due converse with the members of the *Reich*. The fortunes of all Europe were assembled in the political forecast of the German Kaiser's court; and never, even at the Empire's lowest ebb, did this dispensation wholly change. Only, the Imperial court at Vienna, through its weakness over against the *Reich*, at last was rather led by Spanish and Romish interests than exercised its influence over them; so that at its most fateful era the *Reich* was like an inn in which the host no longer, but the guests make out the reckoning. Whilst the Viennese court had thus completely fallen into the Romo-Spanish rut, at its only substantial rival, the court of Berlin, the mastering tendence was that of French civilisation; which had already fully drawn into its groove the courts of lesser princes, the Saxon at their head. By the fostering of Art these courts, at bottom, meant nothing more than the procuring a French ballet or an Italian opera; and, taken strictly, they have not advanced one step beyond the notion till this day. God knows what would have become of Goethe and Schiller if the first, born well-to-do, had not won the personal friendship of a minor German prince, the Weimar wonder, and eventually been enabled in that position to provide to some extent for Schiller! Presumably they would not have been spared the lot of Lessing, Mozart, and so many another noble spirit. But the "deutsche Jüngling" was not the man to need the "smile of Princes," in the sense of a Racine or a Lully: he was called to throw aside the "curb of rules," and as there, so here in the people's life, to step forth a liberator from oppression. This calling was recognised by an intelligent statesman at the time of utmost want; and, when all the red-tape armies of our monarchs had been utterly routed by the holder of French power—invading no longer as a curled and frizzled Civiliser, but as a ravenous lord of War; when the German princes were no longer servants to mere French civilisation, but vassals to French political despotism: then was it the German "Jüngling" whose aid was invoked, to prove with weapons in his hand the mettle of this German Spirit reborn within him. He shewed the world its patent of nobility. To the sound of lyre and sword* he fought its battles. Amazed, the Gallic Cæsar asked why

---

* An allusion to Körner's patriotic songs, as set to music by Weber in September 1814. These songs were the means of arousing the utmost patriotic enthusiasm among the youths and younger men of Germany.—TR.

he no longer could beat·the Cossacks and Croats, the Imperial and Royal Guards? Perhaps his nephew is the only man, on all the thrones of Europe, who really knows the answer to that question: he knows and *fears* the German "Jüngling." Learn ye to know him too, for ye should *love* him!

But in what consisted the huge ingratitude wherewith the German princes recompensed the saving deeds of this German spirit? They were rid of the French oppressors; but French civilisation they enthroned again, to hug its leading-strings as ever. Merely the great-grandsons of that Louis XIV were to be installed in power once more; and indeed it looks as if their only care besides, was to enjoy their Ballet and their Opera in peace again. To these regained delights they merely added one thing: fear of the German Spirit. The "Jüngling" who had rescued them, must pay for having shewn his undreamt power. A more lamentable misunderstanding, than that which now prevailed throughout a whole half-century in Germany twixt Folk and Princes, history would find it hard to point to; and yet that misunderstanding is the only decent shadow of an excuse for the ingratitude exhibited. If the German spirit had erewhile stayed unnoticed merely out of lethargy and corrupted taste, now, when its strength had proved itself upon the battle-field, the rulers confounded it with the spirit of the French Revolution—for everything had really to be looked at through French spectacles. The German stripling who had doffed his soldier's uniform and, in lieu of the French tail-coat (*Frack*), had reached back to the old-German gown (*Rock*), was soon considered a Jacobin who devoted his time at German universities to nothing less than universal schemes of regicide. Or is this taking the kernel of the misunderstanding a shade too literally? So much the worse, if we are to suppose that the spirit of German Rebirth indeed was grasped correctly, and hostile measures taken against it of set purpose. With deep sorrow must we confess that ignorance and knowledge here appear to stand not all too

wide apart; for that would mean that the deplorable
consequences of a purposely-fostered misunderstanding
could be explained on none but the lowest grounds of lax
and vulgar love of pleasure. For how did the " deutsche
Jüngling" bear himself, returning home from war?
Assuredly he strove to bring the German spirit into active
efficacy in Life itself; but no meddling with actual
Politics was his object; no, nothing but the renewing and
strengthening of personal and social morality. Plainly
is this spoken in the founding of the " Burschenschaft." *
It well became the young fighters of the nation's battles,
to take strong arms against the savage brawls and
hectorings of German student-life, to put down debauchery
and drunkenness; on the other hand, to institute a
strenuous and systematic training of the body, to do

* According to Brockhaus' *Conversations-Lexikon*, the first "Burschenschaft" (from " Bursch," a " fellow, youngster"—one might say, a "scrub")
was founded at Jena University, on June 12, 1815, partly by students who
had fought in the War of Liberation, partly by members of the old university-
"Landsmannschaften." Its motto was : " Honour, Freedom, Fatherland."
Its objects were those stated above, and its example was soon followed by
almost every university in Germany proper. In two or three years' time a
general conclave, with annual sittings, was formed from among these
Burschenschaften, under the name of " Burschentag." At this sort of minor
parliament the chief business from 1827 to 1831 was a dispute between the
so-called *Germanen*, a more practically political party, and the *Arminen*
(henceforth in a minority) who made chiefly for an *ideal* unity of the Fatherland and its attainment by means of the original objects of the Burschenschaft.
Already after Kotzebue's murder by a German student in March, 1819, the
Burschenschaft had been denounced, and some of its members ' examined ' for
" demagogism"; but after the " Frankfort Attempt " of 1833 (a rising in
which certain students had taken part) the legal prosecutions became
numerous ; sentences of death, etc. were passed, though nothing more severe
than personal imprisonment—which had a trick of being quite severe enough
—was really put into execution. In later years milder counsels appear to
have prevailed again, on both sides.

The "Landsmannschaften" date almost as far back as the universities
themselves. In these the members were enrolled according to what one may
call sub-national districts—at least the divisions were given territorial names—
with all the evil consequences of inflaming local, or at least sectional,
animosity. At the time when Wagner was at the Leipzig University both
species of groups seem to have co-existed, an interesting account whereof will
be found in a note on the " Corps Saxonia " in Glasenapp's Appendix to the
third edition of his *Leben Richard Wagner's*.—TR.

away with cursing and swearing, and to crown true piety
of heart with the vow of noble chastity.*   French civilisation had found the degenerate mercenaries of the Thirty
Years' War besotted with the vices here attacked : to
polish down and tinker up that rawness, with its aid, to
the Princes seemed sufficient for all time.   But now the
German Youth itself designed to earn the praise erewhile
bestowed by Tacitus upon the "deutsche Jüngling."   What
other people has a similar event to shew in all the history
of its culture?

Truly a quite unparalleled phenomenon.   Here was
nothing of that gloomy, tyrannous asceticism which at
times has passed across Romanic peoples and left no trace
behind : for this Youth was—wonderful to say!—devout
(*fromm*) without being churchly.   It is as though the
spirit of Schiller, the tenderest and noblest of his ideal
creations, here meant to take on flesh and blood upon a
soil of ancient home.   The social and political development to which it could not but have led, if the Princes had
only understood this youthful spirit of their Folk, is surely
past our rating high enough, our imagining its beauty.
The aberrations of the un-advised were soon made use of
for its ruin.   Taunts and persecution tarried not to nip its
flower in the bud.   The old *Landsmannschaften* system,
with all its vicious and deranging influence on youth, was
given another lease of life, to oppose and ridicule the
Burschenschaft; till at last, when the certainly not unintentionally aggravated blunders had begun to take a
sinister and passionate character, the time had come for
instructing the criminal courts to put a violent end to this
German "league of demagogues."—The only thing left
over from the time of Germany's revival, was the military
organisation retained by Prussia : with this last remnant of
the German spirit, uprooted everywhere else, the Prussian
crown won the battle of Königgrätz,† to all the world's

* Cf. "The German's Fate in Paris," in *The Meister*, No. XIX, p. 86.—Tr.
† Commonly, but erroneously, known in England and France as the Battle
of Sadowa, in which Prussia inflicted a crushing defeat upon Austria, July 3,
1866.—Tr.

amazement, after the lapse of half a century. So great was the terror at this host in every European Ministry of War, that an anxious longing needs must seize the French commander-in-chief himself [Marshal Niel], regarded as the mightiest of them all, to introduce a something like this " Landwehr " into his so rightly famous army. We have seen, not long ago, how the whole French people kicked against the thought. So that French Civilisation has not accomplished what the downtrod German Spirit so quickly and so lastingly succeeded in : the formation of a true Folk-army. As makeweight, it is busying itself with the invention of new weapons [chassepots], breech-loaders and infantry-cannon. How will Prussia reply to that ? Likewise by perfecting her armour, or—by putting to good use the knowledge of its true means of power, at present not to be learnt from it by any European people ? —Since that memorable battle, on whose eve the fiftieth anniversary of the founding of the German Burschenschaft was celebrated, a great turning-point has arrived, and an immeasurably weighty resolution stands at halt : almost it looks as if the Emperor of the French more profoundly judges this importance, than the governments of German princes seem to do. One word from the victor of Königgrätz, and a new power stands erect in history, whereagainst French civilisation will pale its fires for ever.

Let us look closer at the consequences of what we have called that treachery to the German spirit, and see what since, in the course of a full half-century, has become of the seeds of its then so entrancingly hopeful bloom ; in what manner German Art and Learning, which once had summoned forth the fairest phases of the people's life, have worked upon the evolution of this people's noble qualities since they were accounted and treated as foes to the quiet, or at all events the ease, of German thrones. Perhaps this survey may lead us to a plainer knowledge of the sins committed ; and we then shall try to mildly think of them as failings, as to which we should merely have to stipulate

for betterment, and not for expiation, when we finally
admonish to a genuinely redeeming, inner union of the
German Princes with their Folks, their imbuement with
the veritable German Spirit.

<hr />

III.

If one takes for granted that it needs times of great
political upsoaring, to force the mental qualities of a
people to high florescence, one is faced with the question :
how comes it, on the contrary, that the German War of
Liberation was plainly followed by a terribly rapid falling-
off from the previous steady rise ? Two issues are included
in the answer, one shewing us the dependence, the other
the independence, of a nation's artistic genius on the actual
stage of its political life. No doubt, the birth of even a
great art-genius must stand in some connexion with the
spirit of his time and nation ; but if we don't propose
to seek at random for the secret bonds of that connexion,
we certainly shall not do wrongly to leave to Nature her
own mystery, and confess that great geniuses are born by
laws we cannot fathom. That no genius, such as those the
middle of last century brought forth in rich variety, was
born in the beginning of the present century, has certainly
nothing strictly to do with the political life of the nation ;
on the other hand, that the high stage of mental receptivity
whereto the artistic genius of the German Rebirth had
lifted us, so quickly settled down again, that the Folk
allowed its ample heritage to be reft from it wellnigh
untasted—this, at any rate, may be explained by the
spirit of reaction from the fervour of the war of freedom. That the womb of German mothers at that time
conceived for us no greater poets than Houwald, Müllner
and their compeers, may belong to the inscrutable secret
of Nature ; but, that these minor talents should have
abandoned the free highways of their great German
fathers, to wander with quite childish insipidity in a

mournful imitation of misunderstood Romanic models, and that these wanderings should have met with actual consideration, allows us to argue with much certainty to a mournful spirit, a mood of great depression, in the nation's life. Nevertheless in this mutual mood of mourning there lingered still a trace of spiritual freedom: one might say, the exhausted German spirit was helping itself as best it could. The true misery begins when it was to be helped along in another fashion.

Indisputably the most decisive effect of the spirit of German Rebirth upon the nation itself had finally been exerted from the Theatre, through dramatic poetry. Whoever pretends (as impotent literati are so fond of doing nowadays) to deny to the Theatre a most preponderant share in the art-spirit's influence upon the ethical spirit of a nation, or even to belittle it, simply proves that he himself stands quite outside this genuine interaction, and deserves notice neither in literature nor in art. For the Theatre, had Lessing begun the war against French tyranny, and for the Theatre great Schiller brought that war to fairest victory. The whole aim of our [two] great poets was to give their poems their first, their true, convincing life through the Theatre; and all their intervening literature, in its truest sense, was merely an expression of that aim. Without finding in the existing Theatre a technical development even somewhat preparatory for the high tendence of German Rebirth, our great poets were driven regardless onward in advance of such development, and their legacy was bequeathed to us on express condition that we first made it truly ours. If, then, no genius such as Goethe and Schiller was born to us any more, it now was the very task of the reborn German spirit to rightly tend their works and thus make ready for a long florescence, which Nature necessarily would have followed with the bringing forth of new creative geniuses: Italy and Spain once lived to see this reciprocity. Nothing more would have been needed, than to set the Theatre in train to duly celebrate

the deeds of Lessing's fight and Schiller's victory.—But
as the youthful idealism of the Burschenschaft was parried
by the vicious tendence of the old Landsmannschaften, so,
with an instinct only owned by those whose subjects are
profoundly helpless, the rulers took possession of this
Theatre, to withdraw the wondrous platform of the
German spirit's noblest deeds of freedom from just the
influence of that spirit's self.   How does a skilful general
prepare the enemy's defeat ?   By cutting off its communi-
cations, its commissariat.   Napoleon the Great "*dépaysait*"
the German spirit.   From the heirs of Goethe and
Schiller one took the Theatre.   Here Opera, there
Ballet : Rossini, Spontini, the Dioscuri of Vienna and
Berlin, who behind them dragged the Pleiades of German
Restoration.   Yet here, too, the German spirit was to try
to break itself a path ; if verse was dumb, yet tune rang
out.   The fresh, sweet breath of the youthful German
breast, still heaving with noble aspiration, breathed out
of glorious Weber's melodies ; a new life of wonders was
won for German feeling (*Gemüth*) ; with cheers the German
Folk received its Freischütz, and now seemed minded to
throng anew the French-restored magnificence of the
Intendant-ruled court-theatres — there, too, to conquer
and to vivify.   We know the long-drawn torments which
the nobly popular German master suffered for his crime
of the Lützow-chasseurs' melody,* and whereof at last he
pined away and died.

   The most calculating wickedness could not have gone to
work more cleverly, than here was done, to demoralise and
slay the German art-spirit ; but no less horrible is the supposition that perchance sheer stupidness and trivial love
of pleasure, on the potentates' part, achieved this havoc.
After the lapse of half a century the result is palpable
enough, in the general state of spiritual life among the

   * In August 1820, Weber was serenaded by the Göttingen students with
his song " *Lützow's wilder Jagd,*" the words by Körner.   Lützow had been
allowed in 1813 to form a " free corps," which soon won celebrity for its
dash and spirit in the War of Liberation ; it was joined by Körner, Jahn,
Friesen, etc., etc.—TR.

German people : 'twere a lengthy task, to follow it through all its strangely complex phases. We propose to offer later our contribution to that task, from several points of view. For our present purpose let it suffice to indicate the fresh-won power, over the German spirit, of a civilisation which since has taken so fearfully demoralising a turn in its own country that noble minds beyond the Rhine are casting glances, longing for redemption, across to us. From what they then behold, to their amazement, we best may gather how matters really stand with ourselves.

The Frenchman disgusted with his own civilisation has read the book of Mdme. Stael on Germany, let us say, or B. Constant's report on the German Theatre; he studies Goethe and Schiller, hears Beethoven's music, and believes he cannot possibly be mistaken if he seeks in close and accurate acquaintance with German life both consolation and a hope for his own people's future also. " The Germans are a nation of high-souled dreamers and deep-brained thinkers." Madame de Stael found stamped on Schiller's genius, upon the whole evolution of German science, the influence of Kant's philosophy: what is there for the Frenchman of to-day to find with us ? He will merely discover the remarkable consequences of a philosophic system once nursed in Berlin,* and now brought into thorough world-renown under cover of the famous name of German Philosophy; a system which has succeeded in so incapacitating German heads for even grasping the problem of Philosophy, that it since has ranked as the correct philosophy to have no philosophy at all. Through such an influence he will find the spirit of all the sciences so altered that, in regions where the German's earnestness had made itself proverbial, superficiality, running after effect, and positive dishonesty—no longer in the discussion of any problems, but in personal bickerings

---

* That of Hegel; whereof Feuerbach's was an offshoot. Cf. Vol. I., 25, concerning Feuerbach's " bidding farewell to Philosophy," to which the end of the present sentence appears to refer.—TR.

mixed with calumnies and intrigues of every species—
almost alone supply the food-stuff for our book-mart,
which itself has become a simple monetary speculation of
the booksellers. Luckily he will find, however, that the real
German public, just like the French, reads no more books
at all, but gains its information almost solely from the
journals. In these latter he will find with sorrow that,
even in an evil sense, the process is no longer German—as
at least is the case with the wranglings of the university-
professors ; for he will here observe the final consummation
of a jargon that has more and more departed from resemblance to the German language. In all these manifestations
of publicity he will also note the obvious trend toward for-
saking any connexion with the nation's history, so highly
honourable to the German, and " operating " (" *anbahnen* ")
a certain European dead-level of the vulgarest interests of
everyday, whereon the ignorance and fatuity of the journalist may frankly make its comfortable confession, so
fondly flattering to the Folk, of the uselessness of thorough
culture.—To the Frenchman, amid such circumstances, the
remains of the German people's love for reading and writing won't rank of special value ; rather will he deem the
people's mother-wit and native common-sense thereby en-
dangered. For if he has been revolted in France by the
nation's practical materialism, he will scarcely comprehend
why this evil should be theoretically instilled into the
German Folk through a journalistic propaganda based
on the most unspiritual conclusions of an arrogantly shallow Nature-science ; seeing that, upon this path, even the
presumable results of naïve practice are made unfruitful.

Our guest next turns to German Art, remarking in the
first place that the German knows nothing by that name
but Painting and Sculpture, with Architecture perhaps
thrown in. From those days of the German rebirth he
recalls the fair, the noble beginnings of a development of
the German art-spirit on this side too : yet he perceives
that what was meant in grand and genuine earnest by the
noble P. Cornelius, for instance, has now become a flippant

pretext which flings its heels for mere Effect, just the same
as Science and Philosophy; but as far as Effect is concerned, our Frenchman knows that none can beat his
friends at home.—Onward to poetic Literature. He believes he is reading the journals again. Yet no! Are
these not books, and books of nine internally consecutive
volumes?* Here must be the German spirit; even if
most of these books are mere translations, yet here at last
must come to light what the German really is, apart from
A. Dumas and E. Sue? He undoubtedly is something
else, to boot: a trader on the name and fame of German
greatness (*Herrlichkeit*)! Everything bristles with patriotic
assurances, and "German," "German," so tolls the bell
above the cosmopolitan synagogue of the "now-time." †
'Tis so easy, this "German"! It comes quite of itself, and
no wicked Academy looks us up and down; nor is one
exposed to the constant chicane of the French author, who,
for one solitary linguistic solecism, is dismissed forthwith
by all his colleagues with the cry that he can't write French.
—But now to the Theatre! There, in the daily, direct
communion of the public with the intellectual leaders of
its nation, must assuredly come out the spirit of the thoughtful German people, so self-conscious in the practice of its
morals; the people of whom a certain B. Constant had
assured the Frenchman that it did not need French rules,
since the Seemly was a thing inherent in the inwardness
and pureness of its nature. It is to be hoped our visitor
won't make his first acquaintance with our Schiller and
Goethe at the theatre, as in that case he could never comprehend why we had lately been erecting statues to the
former in the squares of all our cities; or he would be led
to suppose that it was in order to have done with the
excellent, worthy man and his undeniable services, in some
right handsome way, for good and all. In particular, in
his encounter with our great poets on the stage, he would

---

* See note to Vol. II., 148—Gutzkow's "*Ritter vom Geiste.*"—TR.

† "Der 'Jetztzeit'", in place of "Gegenwart"; our slang expression, "up
to date", would be a fair equivalent.—TR.

be astounded at the extraordinarily dragging tempo in the recitation of their verses, for which he would feel bound to seek a stylistic ground until he became aware that this drawling arises merely from the actor's difficulty in following the prompter ; for this mimetic artist has plainly not the time to commit his verses properly to memory. And the reason soon grows obvious enough ; for one and the same actor, in course of the year, has to offer nearly all the products of the theatric literature of every age and every people, of every genre and every style—about the most remarkable collection one can anywhere find—to the subscribing public of the German theatre.   With this unheard extension of the duties of the German mime, it naturally is never taken into consideration *how* he shall fulfil his task : both critics and public have got far beyond that.   The actor is therefore compelled to found his popularity upon another quarter of his doings : the " now-time " is always bringing him something to set him in his congenial, his " self-intelligible " element ; and here again, as in the case of Literature, is found the help of the peculiar modern traffic of the newest German spirit with French civilisation. As A. Dumas was Germaned there, so here the Parisian stage-caricature is " localised " ; and in measure as its new " locale " compares with Paris, does this main support of the German Theatre's repertory cut a presentable figure on our stage.   A surprising awkwardness of the German's adds its quota to all this, producing complications which must awake in our French visitor the thought that the German far outstrips the Parisian in frivolity : what goes-on in Paris really quite beyond the pale of good society, in the smaller hole-and-corner theatres, he will see reproduced in our most stylish of Court-theatres, with vulgar loutishness to boot, and set before the exclusive circles of society without a scruple, naked and unashamed, as the newest piece of drollery ; and this is found quite as it should be.   Recently we lived to see Mdlle. Rigolboche—a person only explicable by means of Paris, and advertised in monster type as the Parisian " Cancan-dancer "—summoned to perform at

a Berlin theatre the dances which she there had executed,
by special agreement with the well-known ballet-caterers,
for enlivening the most disreputable rendezvous of the
travelling world;* moreover a gentleman of high position
in the Prussian aristocracy, and in the habit of patronising
the world of Art, paid her the honour of fetching her away
in his carriage. This time we had our knuckles rapped for
it in the Parisian press: for the French felt rightly shocked
to see how French civilisation looked without the French
decorum. Indeed, we may conclude that it is a simple
feeling of decency on the part of those peoples who were
erewhile influenced by the German spirit, that now has
turned them quite away from us and thrown them wholly
into the arms of French civilisation: the Swedes, Danes,
Dutch, our blood-related neighbours, who once had stood
in innermost spiritual communion with us, now draw their
requirements in the way of art and intellect direct from
Paris, as they very properly prefer at least the genuine
articles to the counterfeits.

But what will our French visitor feel, when he has
feasted upon this spectacle of German civilisation? To
be sure, a desperate home-sickness for at least the French
decorum; and in that feeling, pondered well, there is won
a new and most effectual engine of French supremacy,
against which we may find it very hard to shield ourselves.
If nevertheless we mean to make the attempt, let us
proceed to test with care, and without a shred of idle
overweening, the resources haply still remaining to us.

IV.

To the intelligent Frenchman, whom we have just seen
reviewing the present physiognomy of intellectual life in
Germany, we yet might speak a final word of comfort—
namely, that his eye had merely skimmed the outer
atmosphere of true German spiritual life. That was the

* 1867 was the year of the French International Exhibition.—TR.

sphere wherein one let the German spirit struggle for a semblance of power and public agency: once it quite desisted from that struggle, corruption might naturally also lose all power over it.   It will be both saddening and of profit, to seek that spirit out within its home, where once, beneath the stiff perruque of a Sebastian Bach, the powdered locks of a Lessing, it planned the wonder-temple of its greatness.   It says nothing against the German spirit's capacity, but merely against the intelli-gence of German Policy, if there, in the depths of German individuality with its so universal aptitudes, a fund of gold lies buried without the power of bearing interest to the public life.   Repeatedly in the last few decads have we reaped the strange experience, that German publicity has been first directed to minds of foremost rank in the German nation by the discoveries of foreigners.   This is a beautiful feature, of deep significance, however shaming to German Policy: if we weigh it well, we shall find therein an earnest admonition to German Policy to do its duty and thus ensure for the whole family of European nations that healing which none of them is able to originate from its own spirit.   Ever since the regeneration of Euro-pean Folk-blood, considered strictly, the German has been the creator and inventor, the Romanic the modeller and exploiter : the true fountain of continual renovation has remained the German nature.   In this sense, the dissolu-tion of the " Holy Roman Empire of the German Nation " gave voice to nothing but a temporary preponderance of the practically-realistic tendence in European culture ; if this latter now has reached the abysm of sordidest mate-rialism, by a most natural instinct the nations turn back to the fount of their renewing ; and, strange to say, they there find the German *Reich* itself in an almost inexplicable state of suspended animation, yet not a victim to advanced decay (*aber nicht in seinem vollen Untergange*), but engaged in a very obvious inner struggle towards its noblest resurrection.

Let us leave it to men of practical judgment to deduce

from the efforts last-indicated the outlines of a truly
German policy, and here content ourselves, in keeping
with our theme, with addressing our attention — aloof
from that department of the German's public spiritual
life which has been devastated by official misunderstanding
—to the persistence of the German spirit in pursuing its
peculiar line of evolution albeit abandoned to the anarchy
of its own initiative; for thus we may haply light upon
the point where both directions of Public Life might fitly
meet in a concord full of promise for the eventual raising
of that hidden treasure.

More easily to reach that point, let us therefore seek
the manifestations of the German spirit where they still
perceptibly impinge upon publicity; and here, too, we
shall meet with unexceptionable evidence of the German
spirit's pertinacity, its reluctance to give up again a thing
once grasped. The strictly federative spirit of the German
has never thoroughly denied itself: even in the days of its
deepest political downfall it has proved for all time, through
the dogged maintenance of its princely dynasties against
the centralising tendence of the Hapsburg Kaiser-dom, the
impossibility of absolute (*eigentlichen*) Monarchy in Germany. Ever since the uprousing of the Folk-spirit in the
War of Liberation, this ancient federative bent has entered
life again in every sort of form; where it shewed itself
the best equipped for life, in the associations of perfervid
German Youth, it was looked upon at first as hostile to
monarchic ease, and violently repressed; yet no one could
prevent its forthwith transferring itself to every sphere of
spiritual and practical social interests. But here again we
are called to melancholy reflection, when we find ourselves
compelled to admit that the wonderful vitality of the
German spirit of Association has never yet succeeded in
gaining an actual influence upon the fashioning of public
spirit. In truth on every field of science, of art, of common
social interests, we see the essence of German organisation
still hampered with much the kind of impotence that
cleaves, for instance, to our Turnvereins [gymnastic unions]

and their aimings at a general arming of the people, as against the standing Troops, or to our Chambers of Deputies, copied from French and English models, as against the Governments. With sorrow the German spirit therefore recognises that even in these self-flattering manifestations it does not in truth express itself, but merely plays a piteous game of make-believe. And finally what must make this in itself so encouraging appearance of German unionism quite odious, is that the self-same spirit of gain and outer Effect which we before discovered as reigning in all our official art-publicity, has been allowed to get the mastery of the German nature's manifestations on this side too : where everyone is so glad to dupe himself about his powerlessness for sake of at least doing something, and willingly acclaims the barrenest function as splendid productivity if one only is gathered together in good round numbers, there we may next expect to see a company in shares brought out to keep the thing afloat ; and the true heir and administrator of European civilisation will soon put in an appearance here, as everywhere else, with a Bourse-speculation on " *Deutschthum* " and " German solidness." *

That no associations of ever so sensible heads can bring into the world a genius or a genuine work of art, is patent enough : but, that in the present state of public intellectual life in Germany they are not even equal to bringing· knowably before the nation the works of genius, which naturally are begotten quite outside their sphere, they demonstrate by the mere fact of the art-abodes, in which the works of the great masters of the German Rebirth might be represented for the people's culture, being altogether withdrawn from their influence and turned into a nursery-ground for the ruin of German art-taste. Here on the side of Art, as there on the side of Politics, is irrefutable proof how little the German spirit has to await from all this mass of Unions, radically German as may be their underlying principle.

* Cf. " *Judaism in Music*," in Vol. III.—TR.

Yet precisely in their case may we shew the plainest, how, with one right step from the region of power, the most fruitful relation might be established for the good of all. For this we will refer once more to the Turnvereins, merely coupling with them the no less numerously supported Schützenvereins [rifle-unions]. Sprung from a desire to exalt the Folk-spirit, their present agency—viewed from the ideal side—serves rather to narcotise that spirit, seeing that it is given a pretty toy to play with, and, especially when the fire of eloquence rules high at the yearly banquet of the founders' festival, is flattered into the belief that in this guise it really *is* of some account, that the welfare of the Fatherland hangs out-and-out on *it*; whereas, from the practical side, these unions serve the advocates of our standing troops for just as irrefragable a proof that it would be impossible to institute a reliable army upon the basis of Folk-arming.* Now, the example of Prussia has already shewn how the above contradictions may be almost completely adjusted : on the practical side, that of compassing a whole people's preparedness for war, the problem may be considered completely solved by the Prussian military organisation ; nothing lacks but on the ideal side, as well, to give the weaponed Folk the ennobling sense of the true value of its arming and its readiness for action. It certainly is characteristic, that the last great victory of the Prussian host was ascribed by its commanders to other, to newer counsels, in the sense of returning to the principle of a standing army pure and simple, whereas all Europe took in eye the Landwehr's constitution, as the origin of that success and an object for most serious meditation. In that a very accurate knowledge of an army's needs, in the way of organisation, is assuredly at bottom of the Prussian monarch's estimate—in itself a perhaps not quite unbiased one—it would not be difficult

* It may be of interest to recall the fact that August Roeckel (part-editor of the *Süddeutsche Presse*, in which these articles appeared) had published a pamphlet in the troublous times of 1848-49, at Dresden, upon the subject of " *Volksbewaffnung*," i.e. a " general arming of the people."—TR.

to discover in what relation the whole system of Folk-unions should stand to organisations proceeding from the Governments in order to help forward a state of matters expedient from every point of view and, in our opinion, conducive to true and general salvation. For, that a host, to be at all times fit for service, needs a specially practised nucleus such as only the newer army-discipline can per-fect, is just as undeniable as it would be preposterous to want to train a country's whole able-bodied population for absolutely professional soldiers — an idea whereat the French, as known, were lately so horror-struck. On the other hand the Government has only to present to German unionism, in every branch of public life therein involved, just what has been brought to meet Folk-arming in the constitution of the Prussian army—namely the effective earnestness of Organisation, and the example of the real professional soldier's valour and endurance—to extend to the dilettantism of a male population merely playing with firearms the strengthening hand of universal welfare.

Now, we ask what an unheard, what an incommensur-able wealth of quickening organisations might not the German State include within it, if *all* the various leanings toward true culture and civilisation, as exhibited in German unionism, were drawn, in due analogy with the example of Prussian military organisation, into the only sphere of power to further them, into that sphere in which the Governments at present hold themselves close-hedged by their bureaucratism ?

As we here proposed to deal with Politics merely inso-far as, in our opinion, they bear upon the German art-spirit, we leave it to other inquiries to yield us more precise conclusions as to the political development of the German spirit, when brought into that leavening union with the spirit of the German princes which we desire. If we reserve to ourselves, however, a further discussion of the German spirit's artistic aptitudes, both social and indi-vidual, upon the lines of the root-idea last-broached—we beg, for all our later researches on that domain, to carry

over the result of this preliminary disquisition in something like the following sentence.

Universal as the mission of the German Folk is seen to
have been, since its entrance into history, equally universal
are the German spirit's aptitudes for Art ; the Rebirth of
the German spirit, which happened in the second half of
the preceding century, has shewn us an example of the
activation of this universality in the weightiest domains of
art : the example of that Rebirth's evaluation to the end
of ennobling the public spiritual life of the German Folk,
as also to the end of founding a new and truly German
civilisation, extending its blessings e'en beyond our
frontiers, must be set by those in whose hands repose the
political fortunes of the German people : for this it needs
nothing but that the German Princes should themselves be
given that right example from their own midst.

V.

It is encouraging, to be able to draw our invoked
example of a German Prince's understanding and futher-
ance of the German Art-spirit from the midst of the
Bavarian land.   Here was this high example already first,
nay only, set ; and as we have not accustomed ourselves
to building mere speculations in the air, we will confess
at once that the idea of that invocation itself would
probably never have come to us, had the lesson of just this
already-given example and its effect not lain before us.
Do we need to name King Ludwig I. of Bavaria, to afford
a clue to our meaning ? Is it first necessary for us to
designate the uncommon energy of initiative wherewith
this prince, aflame with the true fire of German zeal,
despite the prejudices of inertia and stupidity, proved far
and wide to German princes through his own example,
and through the example incited by him, that there was
in very truth a German art, that it was a beauteous and a
worthy thing to cherish it ? He proved that this art was

first cousin to the noblest archetype of Art, the Grecian :
Goethe's marriage of Helena to Faust he had celebrated
for him in works of plastic art, and thus disclosed the
loftiest calling of the German spirit, distinct to sight and
seizable to touch. Nor did the virtue of example stay
wanting in effect : thenceforward other German princes,
as if ashamed, took thought for the adornment of their
capitals with noble German works ; from Munich they
summoned the masters, and gave them tasks that erst had
not been dreamt at all, or merely in the sense of a corrupting luxury, to be indulged through nothing but the
appropriately frivolous media of abroad.

What here could be done from one sole point and in one
direction, was brought to pass ; and the example, as the
deeds, of Ludwig I. may be accounted thoroughly, entirely
fulfilled. Nevertheless the question which necessarily
obtrudes itself, why the German plastic art, after so incomparably energetic a stimulus, merely made a start at
blossoming but never fully flowered, in a higher sense,—
nay, why this start itself at last so dwindled down in force,
that to-day the time of flowering stands farther off than at
the commencement of the royal renascence, and we no
longer can shut our eyes against the witness of a manifest
decay,—this question would be but poorly answered, did
we not begin with an attempt at answering it in accordance with the broader purpose of our present inquiries.

Our answer will be much facilitated, if we set in its
proper light the uncommonly suggestive action of the
exalted son of the rewakener of German plastic art, the
dearly loved and unforgettably lamented Maximilian
II.* A thorough German in his meditative nature, his
country's deep need of political uprising seems to have
filled him with consuming care, since it could only be
achieved in union with the political re-shaping of the
whole great German Fatherland, and for this he could
not find the leverage within his special power. To look

* Succeeded his father, Ludwig I., in 1848; died 1864; and was
succeeded by his son, Ludwig II. —TR.

for any success, he must account his only possible task the raising of the intellectual standard of his personal sphere of power, the furtherance of the German spirit in every region thitherto neglected by the policy of German princes. Here, then, he began by seeking to supplement the action of his illustrious father. In the matter of the plastic arts he addressed his chief regard to Architecture, but already in the practical sense of preparing adequate houseroom for his people's spiritual culture. His notable aim in this direction is shewn by his greatest undertaking, alas left unachieved, the building and destination of the Maximilianeum. In this magnificently situated edifice, commanding all the city, an institute of quite new and individual kind was to be established: everything worth knowing in art and science was here to be collected and arranged in such an aimful fashion, and so intelligent and many-sided a professional instruction was to be provided, that the pupils of this unique school should be given the opportunity of acquiring a comprehensive culture, such as the judgment of this enlightened prince deemed needful, in particular, for all the higher servants of his State. In the idea of this foundation there lies a sublimely sorrowful confession, that conscious Want (*Noth*) had for the first time truly entered a monarch's breast. King Ludwig I. could satisfy his eagerness for visible and tangible deeds of Art with all success, so soon as ever he found the fitting artists; for the unhindered prosecution of their tasks he needed but the material which, as king and lord, he very well could come by. But, to make a people's mind receptive toward Art's beauteous deeds, it needed an education such as could not be attained by storm, and still less after so long a period of desolation in this quarter, but only through a careful nursing; which, again, must be presided over by officials who above all needed culture for themselves—and comprehensive human culture, not mere professional specialism. King Maximilian II might say to himself with a sigh: what boots us these fair works of art, if they seem wellnigh hostile to the people's spirit, if they cannot be called to

E

life with the will of it, but rather against its will ?—Was he
to turn his face about, or march straight onward ?—To be
sure, his whole State-paid-officialdom advised him candidly
to do the first. He held his tongue : but sagely set his
hand to work to fashion for himself right truly-cultured
officers. Do we correctly understand the Maximilianeum?

Wellnigh he meant nothing but a making good, a filling
up the chasms left necessarily by the gallant art-deeds of
his ardent father, the almost terrifying gulf betwixt his art-
creations and the spirit of his Folk, when the good King
Maximilian II bestirred himself with tireless strain for
German Literature and Learning. But, beyond the
veritable inner bent towards these branches of spiritual
life, which alone could give him his unexampled energy
in that direction, the exalted prince was haply guided by
a feeling of the intrinsic unsuccess, each day more obvious,
of the artistic labours of his illustrious father : no more
than any man of mind, could it escape him that the wellnigh opened flower of German plastic art had never really
come to full unfolding, and was already falling into premature decay ; he could not but recognise that the cause
was to be sought, as in the isolation of a whole art-tendency
that touched not yet the people's life, so, too, in the one-
sidedness of a nurture theretofore bestowed upon no branch
but that of plastic art.

Now, if the works of plastic art had left the Folk un-
moved and coldly passive, it is extremely apposite to the
issue of our inquiries to remark that, despite his earnest
forethought for his people's welfare, King Maximilian II
approached in doubt, perchance mistrust, the one art-branch
capable of embracing all the others, and the branch
which comes in contact with the people's life as ne'er
another, the art of *drama*. Benevolently wistful for each
and every, he sought indeed to give to Culture a voice
in the administration of the Theatre : but for him this
merely took the light of literary culture ; and, as his was
simply a benevolent regard for dramatic art, but no desire
to raise from out the Theatre's unknown mine the incom-

parable riches of a truly national art, so the fostering of literary culture pure and simple remained the chief endeavour of a prince who yet was bent on elevating the Folk-spirit as none before him. How impotent are Literature and Learning, when not already borne upon a genuinely art-productive spirit in the Folk itself, when they want instead to summon that Folk-spirit into life —this was manifested here; and the admirable prince, true father of his Folk, whose aim was no indulgence of a personal taste for literature and science, but, as the founding of the Maximilianeum shews us, the elevation of his people's spirit, must assuredly have felt the lesson's sharpest sting.

Insofar as the many and ample institutes wherewith he endowed the sciences, as no other monarch and in the noblest national sense, must conduce to their great and undeniable furtherance — in so far his fostering of his people's spiritual welfare is certainly not to be made light of; for if the gain herefrom is like that of a capital whose interest must be sunk for the eventual use of later days, it still remains a fund whose amassing proves that its founder's thoughts were not confined to a mere hand-to-mouth existence. Nevertheless we cannot put aside the fear that, if this immediate existence continues turning more and more away from an evolution of the *beauties* of the spirit, those heaped-up treasures may some-day sink to valueless and useless chattels. Nor has the special fostering of Science — which, the higher its conception, the less can it directly operate upon the Folk-spirit — any culture-historical meaning unless it crowns a Folk-culture already at its prime of beauty; and Art is the only cultivatrix of the Folk. Accordingly, with obvious wish to build this necessary bridge, the highly-cultured King Maximilian endeavoured withal to further the cause of belles lettres and literary poetry; and it was here that the failure of his great-hearted efforts came to plainest show. His noble example, the example longed for, was given just too late; the vibrant earnestness that still had illumined the national mind at the beginning of the century, had lately flickered out.   Even the chain of gifted epigones who, from Kleist to Platen, still manfully made known the exhaustless dowry of the German spirit, had come to end : it was only the other day, that collections were made at home for the erection of a worthy monument above the Syra-cusan grave of the last of German poets, long since de-parted.   Another era had dawned : the " now-time," large as life.   From Paris, the homeland of his choice, the vanquisher of Platen was sending us his witty couplets in German-versified prose ; and Heine's spirit now became the father of a literature whose intrinsic character consisted in its mocking at every kind of earnest literature.   Just as Dantan's caricatures at like time cheered the heart of the Parisian grocer by shewing him, right plain for any eye to see, that all greatness and earnestness was really sent into the world for nothing but a laughing-stock : so Heine's witticisms relieved the feelings of the German public, which now might console itself for the falling-off of German spiritual beauty with the thought, made almost visible, that after all 'twas no great loss.   This joyful consolation, received with special welcome by our poetic literati, has become the keynote of all the newest poetical literature.   One strikes the pose of beginning all over again, lets oneself be misled by no appeal to our great masters, and claims the true poetic right to " harmless " shuffle on as best one can.*   Heine having provided the wit, bold grasps into the epic realm are expedited by a heed to Byron's poems ; what Britons, French and Russians have already copied, is copied once again in valiant German ; and if the publisher is clever enough to push matters to the semblance of a twelfth edition, there stands a new celebrity in the German poet's-grove of some *all-gemeine Zeitung*, and behold ! the thing is done.

* An allusion to W. H. Riehl, the apostle of "harmlessness" (i.e. mild, unsophisticated innocence), to whom Wagner devotes a critique in the later pages of this volume.—TR.

Unhappy noble Prince, who here believed he could, he must, protect and further something! What could his generous will lay bare, but just the final palsy-stroke of German poetical literature?—

As we now have seen two examples set by German Princes, and have been forced to recognise them as each at bottom unsuccessful, what may justify us in nevertheless awaiting succour from the renewed example of a German Prince?

VI.

Certainly the high-souled patron of German intellectual efforts, whose noble example we last adduced, looked also with kindly expectation on the attempts at last addressed to the Theatre by literary poets of his favour: himself he prompted those attempts, by offering prizes. Here, too, an example; but with what a deterrent result!—In course of our inquiries we hope to shew the reason why, not merely mediocre, but even talented literati can never rightly prosper in their dealings with the stage until, through an entire new-shaping of the German Theatre, they reach a proper insight into the nature of this artistic organism that stands beyond comparison with any other. The true pity of the present failure, however, consisted in the effort's having been engaged-in as a last attempt to help this incomprehensible Theatre. But the theatre itself remains just what it was before, does much what always has been done by like establishments elsewhere; the same old order reigns, and it occurs to no one that in this quite derelict institute *there lies the spiritual seed and kernel of all national-poetic and national-ethical culture, that no other art-branch can ever truly flourish, or ever aid in cultivating the Folk, until the Theatre's all-powerful assistance has been completely recognised and guaranteed.*

If we enter a theatre with any power of insight, we look straight into a dæmonic abyss of possibilities, the lowest as the loftiest.—In the Theatre the Roman solemnised his gladiator-games, the Greek his tragedies; the Spaniard, here his bull-fights, there his autos; the Englishman the coarse buffooneries of his clowns, as the searching dramas of his Shakespeare; the Frenchman his cancan-dance, and eke his prudish alexandrine buskin; the Italian his operatic arias,—the German? What might the German solemnise within his theatre?—This we will try to make clear to ourselves. At present he celebrates the whole symposium— naturally in his own fashion!—but, for sake of either completeness or effect, he adds to it Schiller and Goethe, and lately Offenbach. And all this goes on amid circumstances of communion and publicity such as are repeated nowhere else in life: in Folk-assemblies questions passionately-debated may kindle rancour, in Church the higher self collect its thoughts to rapt devotion, but here in the Theatre the whole man, with his lowest and his highest passions, is placed in terrifying nakedness before himself, and by himself is driven to quivering joy, to surging sorrow, to hell and heaven. What lies beyond all possibility of the ordinary man's experiencing in his own life, he lives it here; and lives it in himself, in his sympathy deep-harrowed by the wondrous duping. One may weaken this effect through the senseless abuse of a daily repetition (which, again, draws after it a great perversion of the receptive powers), but never suppress the possibility of its fullest outburst; and finally, that outburst may be played on, according to the ruling interest of the day, for any manner of corruptive end. In awe and shuddering, have the greatest poets of all nations and all times approached this terrible abyss; 'twas they devised the aimful laws, the sacred conjurations, to bann the demon lurking there, by aid of the good genius; and Æschylus with priestly rites led e'en the chained Erinnyes, as divine and reverend Eumenides, to the seat of their redemption from a baneful curse. 'Twas this abyss great Calderon arched over with the heavenly rainbow, conducting to the country of the saints; from out its depths stupendous Shakespeare conjured up the demon's self, to set it plainly, fettered by his giant force, before the astonished world as its own essence, alike to be subdued; upon its wisely measured, calmly trodden verge, did Goethe build the temple of his *Iphigenia*, did Schiller plant the passion-flower * of his *Jungfrau von Orleans*. To this abyss have fared the wizards of the art of Tone, and shed the balm of heaven's melody into the gaping wounds of man; here Mozart shaped his master-works, and hither yearned Beethoven's dreams of proving finally his utmost strength. But, once the great, the hallowed sorcerers yield place, the Furies of vulgarity, of lowest ribaldry, of vilest passions, the sottish Gnomes of most dishonouring delights, lead high their revels round its brink. Banish hence the kindly spirits—(and little trouble will it cost you : ye merely need to not invoke them trust-fully !)—and ye leave the field, where Gods had wandered, to the filthiest spawn of Hell; and these will come uncalled, for there have they ever had a home whence naught could scare them but the advent of the Gods.

And this prodigy, this pandæmonium, this awesome Theatre, ye thoughtless leave its traffic to mechanical routine, to the censorship of ruined students, to the bidd-ing of amusement-hunting panders, to the management of used-up bureaucrats ?—This Theatre, which the Protest-ant clerics of last century denounced, with much discern-ment, as a gin of the Devil; from which to-day ye turn your right hand in disdain, while with your left ye load its walls with pomp and glitter, and—when any grand occasion comes—can think of nothing better than a " performance at the theatre," to shew yourselves in all your finery ?—

And ye wonder that plastic art, poetic literature, and all that makes for beauty and significance in a nation's spiritual life, will not march forward; that retrogression follows on the heels of each advance ? How can ye so

---

* "Den Gotteswunderbaum " — literally " God's wonder-tree." The " wonder-" or " miracle-tree " is the *palma Christi*; but, as no translation could possibly convey the beauty of the compound word invented by our author, I have preferred a mere *suggestion* of its meaning.—TR.

much as dream of true artistic influence on the Folk, when
ye pass this Theatre by with shrugging shoulders, or—
worse still—sit therein with leering eyes ?—

A truce to questions ! The goal of our inquiries must
now be clear to every reader. While proposing to prove
the unparalleled importance of the Theatre, through a demonstration of its illimitably ruinous, as of its illimitably
helpful influence ; while, for the insurance of its loftiest,
most beneficial agency, we invoke a royal example like to
those already set so finely and so hopefully, in plastic art
and science, by two enlightened princes of Bavaria : we
own that it is not without a shudder, that we approach a
field of public discussion from which all truly-cultured
Germans have long congratulated themselves on being
able to keep aloof ! It says enough to stamp the downfall
of the German Theatre, when no one can dispute the fact
that the last remnant of truly German-cultured men in
each profession have abandoned every hope thereof, and
scarcely treat it as still existing. This verdict, moreover,
is endorsed in silence by all the literature-poets who of
late have wooed the theatre again ; for the surprising
feebleness of their dramatic concoctions, as compared with
their doings in other walks—whereas great poets have
erewhile done their greatest in the Drama—is only explicable on the hypothesis that they have held so low an
opinion of the Theatre, as to believe they could place
themselves on a footing with its present demands by
nothing but sinking their own productive powers to much
the level which Goethe deemed compulsory when writing
operatic texts. Hence such forces alone are left in
energetic action, for the Theatre, with whom a mere contact on the part of any earnest-minded man must forthwith lead to the grossest, most ridiculous misunderstandings. Yet, despite this danger, let us venture the attempt ;
for without it we can never acquaint ourselves with those
who nowadays, outside the hubbub of publicity, nurse
quietly a grief and memory as mournful as our own. To
these mostly unknown, yet, as we may conclude from

many a cheering experience, forthcoming friends of a nobler fashion of our public art-life—to them we turn. For if, to supplement and bring to fruit the unique and generous efforts once begun in Munich for German Art and Learning, to crown the work through raising the German Theatre to the importance once assigned it by our great spirits, we now invoke the stirring example of the august heir of those two great benefactors of the German Spirit,—we plant a banner from whose shade the Vulgar has to hide its head in awe.

VII.

For the more searching inquiries which we now propose to address to the *German Theatre* we shall still retain the general heading of these articles : " German Art and German Policy." Our reason might well coincide with the very cause of many people's presumable surprise that this parasite of an irrational state of culture—as which the theatre appears—should be held to have aught to do with Politics, since it is hard enough to imagine what the theatre may have in common with Art itself. To such persons, whom the evil character of the German Theatre has plunged into the most total confusion as to the Theatre's significance in general, it is our desire to shew that precisely Plastic-art—which alone means " Art " for them, as one may read in all our books and journals— has been so strongly influenced by the Theatre that her present increasingly hideous mannerism, as also, wherever she has withdrawn from its influence with painful purpose, her dullest unproductiveness, are only explicable through this ill condition of the Theatre itself.

Two main and characteristic stages present themselves in European Art : its birth among the Greeks, its re-birth among the modern nations. The re-birth will never wholly round itself to an ideal, before it reaches once again the birth's departure-point. The Renaissance lived upon the re-discovered, studied, imitated works of Grecian art, and this could only be the plastic art; to the true creative strength of antique art it can only come by pressing forward to the fountain whence that art derived this strength. Exactly as the symbolical conventions of the temple-ceremony compare with the performance of an Æschyleian drama, compares the older plastic art of the Greeks * with the products of its prime : this prime so closely followed the perfecting of the Theatre, that Phidias was merely the younger contemporary of Æschylus. The plastic artist never overcame the tethers of symbolical convention, till Æschylus had shaped the priestly choral-dance into the living Drama. If it be possible that for modern Life, re-shaped through Art's renascence, there shall arise a Theatre in equal answer to the inmost motive of its culture as the Grecian Theatre answered to the Greek Religion, then plastic art, and every other art, will at last have reached once more the quickening fountain whence it fed among the Greeks ; if this be not possible, then reborn art itself has had its day.—The Italians, with whom this reborn art both took its rise and ripened to its highest modern bloom, found not the drama of the Christian Church ; they did invent the Christian Music. This art, new as the Æschyleian Drama to the Greeks, bore the same relation to Italian plastic art (thus pre-eminently painting) as the Theatre to Greek plastic art (pre-eminently sculpture). The attempt to arrive through Music at a reconstruction of the antique Drama, led to Opera : an abortive attempt, drawing after it the downfall of both Italian music and Italian plastic art. From the genuine Folk-spirit, on the contrary, was Drama newly born. The same relation borne by Thespis and his car to the rites of Grecian temples, that relation bore the modern bands of merry-Andrews to the sublimely mournful ritual of the Holy Passion : had the Catholic clergy already clutched at a popular enlivenment of this earnest

* One is forcibly reminded, by this passage, of the Æginetan marbles in the Munich Glyptothek—the marbles which were among the first King Ludwig's earliest acquisitions.—TR.

Passion by aid of those performers; had the great Spaniards actually built the Modern Drama on the soil thereby prepared, and the wondrous Briton filled it with the contents of every form of human life : so in our great German poets there awoke the consciousness of this new creation's meaning, and across two - thousand years they stretched to Æschylus and Sophocles the hand of understanding. Thus arrived again at the fecund wellspring of all true, Folk-cultivating art, we ask : would ye foul this source anew, would ye let it turn into a ditch for breeding vermin ? That it urged onward to this Theatre of our great poets, was the sole true progress in the evolutionary march of reborn art ; what held back, nay, altogether stemmed that progress with the Italians, the invention of Modern Music, has—thanks again to great German masters equally unique—become the last enabling element for the birth of a dramatic art of whose expression and effect the Greek could not have dreamed. Every possibility of attaining to the highest has now been won : there stands a platform in front whereof, throughout all Europe, the Folk each evening throngs as driven by an unconscious longing to learn, where it is merely lured to idle pastime, the answer to the riddle of existence,—and ye still can doubt that here indeed is the one thing wanting, the thing ye toil in vain to reach by every aimless byway ?—

If, then, we wish to find a prosperous channel for this Theatre, as to whose mission both intelligent and unintelligent persons nurse the utmost doubts, we first must take a closer glance at the special idiosyncrasy of histrionic art, and its relation to those art-varieties which now are held alone for Art.

What is revealed so plainly by a practical survey of the Theatre's historical bearings on the evolution of the arts in general, is explained convincingly and surely, from the theoretic side, by a consideration of the precise nature of those artistic faculties of man which enter here into play. —Clearly, each artistic impulse springs in the first instance from the bent-to-*imitation*, from which there then evolves

the bent-to-*interpretation*.* By an ever more complex use
of media, the plastic artist, and finally the literature-poet,
'interprets' what the mime directly copies in his own
person and with the most deceptive likeness. Through
many an intermediation the literature-poet arrives at his
material, of abstractions (*der Begriffe*), out of which he
constructs his imitation of life, the plastic artist at his
material of æsthetic forms : here the intended illusion,
without which no kind of effect is compassed in any of
these arts, can therefore only prosper through means of
an agreement based upon the laws of technique, on the
artist's side, on the public's upon a certain grade of acquired artistic culture, enabling it to willingly accept those
laws of technique. Now it is to be noted that in the con-
veyance of the idea (*Vorstellung*) presented by the plastic
artist, as also by the literary poet, the weightiest link is not
the direct incident of life, but, in the former's case the
incident as brought before his own æsthetic judgment
through a lifelike imitation, in the latter's case the incident as brought him through report : thus, in neither case
the natural, immediate act or incident of life. But what
the model is to the plastic artist, the reported incident to
the literary poet, to the Folk are the Mime and the theatric
Action : from these it receives directly what those could
only offer through the laws of technique to the more abstract art-intelligence. To the plastic artist the question
of prime moment will therefore be, the quality of his
model ; to the poet the bringing of the incident of life,
that hovers before his mental vision, to direct portrayal
through this model : but to us, for the object of our present
inquiry, it is of moment to prove from the nature of the
Mime himself what *he* requires, for all his uncommonly

* " *Nachahmungs*trieb " and " *Nachbildungs*trieb." The first of these terms
is easy enough to render, but we have no satisfactory English equivalent for
the second ; its meaning is "to form, or model, *after*," i.e. to follow the
essential lines of Nature, without a slavish adherence to her so-called accidentals. In this sense I propose, in general, to employ the word ' interpret ' ;
to mark its specific use, I shall place it between single inverted commas.
—T<small>R</small>.

potent artistic aptitudes, to first become in truth—a man and not a monkey.

What ranks the art of the Mime so low in the eyes of other artists, is the very thing that makes his doings and effects so universal. Everyone has a feeling of kinship with the actor : each person is liable to some 'trick' or other, in which he unwittingly copies the mien, the gestures, the bearing and language of others : the art simply consists in doing this without 'trick,' and of set purpose. In this sense dissimulation serves the ordinary man in lying ; only, to imitate another human being deliberately, without 'trick,' and so illusively as to make us believe that other being stands before us—the sight of *this* sets the crowd in an astonishment all the more agreeable, as each man detects the germs of such an art-dexterity within himself, and merely finds them here developed to a pitch of high effectiveness. It is for this reason, also, that everyone holds himself qualified to judge the doings of an actor.—Now let us figure to ourselves the painter's and sculptor's model passing into continuous movement and action, representing at each moment the very model of the situation, and at last possessing itself [or "himself"] of the words and accents of the real incident—that life-incident which the poet labours to relate and, through a process of crystallising his abstractions, to bring home to his reader's Phantasy* ; further, let us figure this model as finally turning itself into a corporation of such, and reproducing its local surroundings with as realistic an illusion as its gestures and its speech,—and we may easily conclude that this will suffice in itself to carry away the mass, no

* "Welchen der Dichter zu erzählen und durch Fixirung seines Begriffsvermögens der Phantasie seines Lesers vorzuführen sich bemüht." Literally, this would be : "which the poet labours to relate and, through a fixing of his powers of ideation (or abstract thought), to lead before his reader's phantasy ;" but, like all terms imported into Germany from France, there is some ambiguity about the word "*Fixirung,*" as the French themselves employ "*fixer*" in two or three different shades of meaning ; and as our author has never used the word before, we can only interpret it by the general light of the context. —TR.

matter what the subject chosen : the mere charm of the
machinery for duping, with its imitation of some living
incident, sets everybody in that agreeable amazement
which takes the forefront of our pleasure at the theatre.
Viewed from this natural base, one might liken the Theatre
to the result of a successful mutiny of slaves, a reversal of
the relations between master and servant.   And in fact the
theatre of nowadays shews a very similar result : it needs
neither the poet nor the potter* ; or rather, it presses both
poet and potter into its service.   They do exactly as it bids
them ; the critic signs its warrant, which in slave-States
may be bought by niggers, and in power whereof a black
may call himself a white ; the no less easily appeased
authorities lend their sanction to the trick; Majesty throws
its mantle over it, a shelter and a pomp—and lo ! you have
the " Court-theatre " of our German days.

Before it stand, again, the painter, sculptor and literature-
poet, and can't think what they have to do with it.   Do
they suspect, perhaps, that they now must thresh their
brains without a model, and work by sheer abstraction
from older, once vital styles of art ; or, should they still
require a model, that they must take it from this curious
university-school of the revolted slaves, where it has become another being, and learnt to bear itself quite otherwise, than can prove of any service to their art?   What is
left for them, but, precisely through their own continued
makings, to visibly expose the enormous influence of the
Theatre ?   For, either their talent will run dry, without its
genuine source of renovation ; or, if artistic effect be made
for, it will take the shape of that mannered aiming at
Effect which nowadays, and in an evil sense, is rightly
called " theatrical."   And what do we signify, in every
sphere, in the bearing of the private person, in the unlovely
cut of clothes, in the talk, nay, the behaviour of the student
alike with the statesman, and finally in art and literature,
when we brand it as " theatrical " ?   We signify a weaken-

* "Bildner"—literally the "former, modeller, or moulder," i.e. the so-called
"plastic artist"; but perhaps I may here be allowed the figurative term.—TR.

ing, a perversion and derangement of general taste, proceeding from the present Theatre; but, seeing that the Theatre's unbounded popularity gives it also an irresistible influence upon manners, through its influence on taste, we signify withal a profound decline of public morality, to rescue whence appears an earnest and a noble task. But only through taking the Theatre itself most earnestly in eye, can success be promised to such a toil.

So much, at present, for the Theatre's power. How to get at that power, we cannot learn before we have rightly grasped its mainspring; and this we shall only do when, without unmerited disdain, we acknowledge it to be Mimetic-art itself.

VIII.

When we described the relation of the merely imitative Mime to the truly poetic 'interpretative' artist as resembling that of the monkey to the man, nothing was farther from our mind than an actual belittlement of his qualities. However easily comparisons of this kind may lend themselves to such a construction, especially in the heat of argument, we here were moved by quite another motive —namely to draw from one of Nature's methods, falling well within the popular comprehension, the most striking analogy for the relation we were about to discuss. Were the poetising artist ashamed to recognise himself as an originally merely-imitative mime developed into an 'interpreter' of Nature, then Man himself must be no less ashamed at finding himself again in Nature as a reasoning ape : but it would be very foolish of him, and simply prove that he had not got very far with the thing which distinguishes him from an un-reasoning ape.—The analogy adduced, however, will prove most luminous if, granting our descent from monkeys, we ask why Nature did not take her last step from Animal to Man from the elephant

or dog, with whom we meet decidedly more-developed
intellectual faculties than with the monkey? For, very
profitably to our object, this question can be answered by
another : why from a pedant no poet, from a physiologist
no sculptor or painter, ay—to borrow the well-known
answer given by the lips of beauty to a Czar—why from a
Russian privy-councillor can one create no ballerina?—In
Nature's election of the ape, for her last and weightiest
step, there lies a secret which calls us to deep pondering :
whoso should fully fathom it, perchance could tell us why
the wisest-constituted States fall through, ay, the sublimest
Religions outlive themselves and yield to superstition or
unbelief, whilst Art eternally shoots up, renewed and young,
from out the ruins of existence.

In view of the significance thus assigned by us to the
theme, we may hope to expose ourselves to no more mis-
constructions if we commence our further inquiry by tack-
ing it in all earnest to the analogy of man and monkey.
For we believe that in this analogy, when taken as representing the relation of man's merely imitative to his ' interpretative ' faculties, we have won a very helpful light
wherewith to lighten the relations of *realism* and *idealism*
in Art, about which there's such a vast amount of slipshod
talk.

What scares the plastic and poetic artists from contact
with the mime, and fills them with a repugnance not
entirely unakin to that of the man for the monkey, is not
the thing wherein they differ from him, but that wherein
they resemble him.   Moreover what the one imitates, and
the other ' interprets,' is one thing and the same : Nature ;
the distinction lies in the How, and in the means employed.   The plastic artist, who cannot reproduce his
model, the poet who cannot reproduce the reported incident in full reality, forgoes the exhibition of so many of
his object's attributes as he deems needful to sacrifice in
order to display one principal attribute in so enhanced a
fashion that it shall make known forthwith the character of
the whole, and thus one glance at this one side shall reveal

what a demonstration of the object's every side can make intelligible to none but the physiological, or, in questions of Art, the æsthetic judgment : i.e. to the judgment of just the plastic or poetic artist. Through this restriction the plastic artist and poet arrive at that intensifying of their object and its re-presentment which answers to the conception of the Ideal, and through a wholly successful idealisation, that is to say, a realisation of the Ideal, they obtain an effect completely indemnifying us for the impossible inspection of every facet of the object's manifestation in Time and Space ; and to such an extent, that this mode of representment is acknowledged to be the only resultful, nay, the only possible method of dealing with real objects, their aspects being inexhaustible.

To this ideal, this only veritable art, however, the mime steps up with all the matter-of-fact-ness of an object moving in Time and Space, and gives the man who compares him with the picture * somewhat the terrifying impression as though a mirror-image were descending from its glass and walking up and down the room before our eyes. To the æsthetic eye this phenomenon must needs have something positively ghostly ; and if one makes the acquaintance of mimetic art through performances such as have been the daily work of great comedians,—if, sitting as guest to a Garrick, we see at one moment a despairing father with his dead child in his arms, at another a money-grubbing miser, or again a drunken sailor cudgelling his wife, then, possessed with the ideality of pure plastic and poetic art, our breath may easily forsake us, and with it all desire to meet the fearsome man a-joking cheerfully at Art's expense—a thing he is always very fond of doing.—Is this Mime an incomparably higher being, or a being small beyond compare ? Nay, neither one thing nor the other : merely he is a being quite other. He presents himself as Nature's intermediate link, through which that absolutely realistic Mother of all Being incites the ideal within you. Like as

* " Dem vom Bilde auf ihn Blickenden "—lit. " the man looking at him from the picture," or " from the image."— TR.

F

no human Reason (*Vernunft*) can discharge the commonest
diurnal act of Nature, and yet she never tires of forcing herself in constant newness on Reason's apprehension : so the
mime reveals to the poet or potter ever new, untold and
countless possibilities of human being, to be fathomed by
him who could invent not one of these possibilities,* by
him to be redeemed into a higher being.—This is Realism
in its relation to Idealism.   Both belong to Art's domain,
and their difference lies in that between the *imitation* and
the *interpretation* (Nachbildung) of Nature.

How far this realism can become an art, without the
slightest brush with idealism, we may see by French
theatric art ; which has raised itself, and altogether of itself,
to such a pitch of virtuosity, that the whole of modern
Europe pays obedience to its laws.   Very helpful for the
further pursuance of our physiological analogy, appears to
us a saying of Voltaire's, when he described his countrymen
as a cross between tiger and ape.   It is surprising, in fact,
how speedily this nation has made itself known to other
European nations mainly under two distinctive types :
natty to the point of finnicking, particularly in its capers
and its chatter ; cruel to bloodthirstiness, springing furious to
attack.   History shews us such a springing, and yet capering tiger, in the real founder of modern French civilisation :
Richelieu (no less than his great precursor, Sully) was
passionately fond of dancing Ballet, and—we are told—
made himself so ridiculous through a scandalous dance
before the Queen of France herself, that he avenged his
mortification with all the tiger's fury.†   This was the man
'fore whom no noble head in France sat firmly on its trunk,
the man who founded withal the almighty Academy,
whereby he coerced the spirit of France into adopting that
Convention, entirely foreign to it thitherto, whose laws
still govern it to-day.   These laws permitted anything but

---

* Cf. Vol. III., 305—concerning Frau Schröder-Devrient.—TR.

† The vengeance was taken on the so-called " Day of Dupes," November
11, 1630, when the Queen-mother, Maria de Medici, the Duke of Orleans
et al, were outwitted by Richelieu and had to escape to Brussels.—TR.

the cropping-up of ideality; on the contrary, a refinement
of realism, a supernal prettifying of actual life, attainable
only by guiding the monkey-nature, which Voltaire twitted
in his countrymen, to a successful imitation of the courtier's
etiquette. Under this influence the whole life of everyday
assumed a theatrical shape; and the only difference
between real life and the Theatre proper, was that public
and players changed places at times, as if for mutual recreation.—It perhaps is hard to say whether it was a general
talent for the Theatre, that brought about this conformation
of French life, or whether it was the conventionalising of
life that turned all the French into talented actors. The
actual result is, that every Frenchman is a good comedian;
and for this reason, again, the French Theatre with all its
customs, idioms and requirements, is simply imitated
throughout all Europe. Now, this would not be of positive
harm to Europe, if theatric art in France itself had only
been able to approach the Theatre's true aim, in a higher
sense, through adopting the plastic artist's and poet's Ideal.
But not one piece of an ideal scope or import has ever been
written for the French stage; no, their Theatre has always
been kept to a direct copy of real life—so remarkably easy
for it, too, since life itself was nothing but a theatrical convention. Even in the portrayal of socially-exalted or
historically-distant spheres of life, where the ideal trend has
come quite of itself to every poetic nation, it has been
turned from that direction by the spectre of Convention,
and here most utterly of all. To keep forever to a copy of
reality, the Versailles court—which, again, was planned
with a single eye to theatrical effect—was held up as
unique type of the sublime and noble; if one meant to set
Greek and Roman heroes in their worthiest light, it would
have seemed absurd, and in the worst possible taste, to let
them speak loftier language, strike nobler attitudes, or in
any way think and deal otherwise than the Great King and
his court, the flower of France and the *grand siècle*. Nay,
God himself must at last submit to being addressed with
the courtier's " *Vous.*"

Thus, however high the French spirit might try to lift itself above the common life, the loftiest spheres of its imagination were everywhere delimited by tangibly and visibly realistic life-forms, which could only be copied, but not 'interpreted': for Nature alone supplies a model for æsthetic moulding (*Nachbildung*), whereas Culture * can become an object of nothing but mechanical imitation. A wretched state of things indeed, in which none but a monkey-nature could really feel at ease. Against it no rebellion of the *man* was possible ; for only through a glance at the Ideal, does he consciously outstep the circle drawn by Nature. But the "tiger" could rebel. After his tigress had—danced once more, around the guillotine (for nothing will pass off well in France without a dance !), and he himself had grown tipsy with the blood of his Culture's lawgivers (we know the loving-cup of the September Feast!), this wild beast was tamable by nothing but letting it loose upon the neighbouring nations. Marat—the tiger ; Napoleon—the tiger-tamer : that is the symbol of new France.— Without the Theatre, however, the tiger was not to be broken in : the monkey must help in the taming. Known for centuries as the worst of soldiers, and jeered at by the Germans in particular, since the Revolution the French army has ranked as the best. We are aware that this result has been effected on the one side by a discipline which crushes out all sense of self, but it has been maintained, on the other, by a happy blending of the interests peculiar to the tiger's and the monkey's natures : the new phantasm, that has replaced the old court-nimbus of Versailles, is the sufficiently notorious, specifically Gallic "*gloire*," which we here need mention merely in so far as it has become the new expression for that same theatrical Convention which has taken the place of Nature for good and all with the Frenchman, and beyond whose pale, as we have put it once before, he would believe himself plunged into Chaos.

* "*Die Kultur*"—our author invariably uses the foreign term to signify "artificial culture" ; for "culture" in its best sense, he employs "*Bildung*." —Tr.

What notable alterations the baptism of the French Revolution has effected in the character of this great people, this people destined for such important fortunes, we should be glad to see explained in detail by some qualified Culture-historian, from a similar standpoint to our own. The blends and shadings of this Folk-character—which in so episodic a notice we naturally have been able to consider merely according to its general type, as from a bird's-eye view—these nuances, when reviewed from quite close, will surely shew no less a natural disposition to culture of the Purely-human, than is to be found among the other members of the European family. Nevertheless the open-minded Frenchman, of all persons, will regard with despair the possibility of his nation's character undergoing a total new-birth. In view of the state of things to-day, he must confess to feeling uneasy at any thought of dissipating the phantom "gloire," since he knows not whether, once this glittering canvas drawn aside, the tiger might not spring forth again. Perhaps one might set his mind at rest by telling him that behind this stage-coulisse, merely painted on its outer face, there lurks the capering monkey, already well-acquainted with its realistic back. Would it comfort him to find that perchance the vanity and light-mindedness of his nation, which stand even its military bravado in such good stead, have helped no less than the Imperial discipline to tame the tiger; and—as pleasure is so much the Frenchman's summum bonum, that he classes Art itself under the rubric of Amusement—to find that these qualities may after all be competent to resume unaided their ancient duties of police?

But enough! We possibly may find some other source of comfort. Let us therefore turn from the French, with whom we had nothing to note but Theatre and theatrical virtuosity, and come back to Germany; paying our first attention to how this Theatre and its virtuosity stand out upon our native soil.

IX.

"German, strive for Roman strength, for
Grecian beauty! Both have sped thee; but
never yet the Gallic spring!"

Thus Schiller invokes the German genius.

But how if the bear must dance like the monkey, to earn
his daily bread?—A revolting sight, ridiculous at once and
mournful!—

The German tempo is the walk (*der Gang*), the
"Andante"; which therefore also has been so richly and
expressively developed in German music, that music-
friends have rightly called it the typical German style, and
have declared its maintenance and studious cultivation to
be a question of vital moment in German æsthetics. With
this deliberate walk the German reaches everywhere in
time, and manfully can make the farthest-lying thing his
own. Germans have learnt and taught the plastic arts in
Italy; in German poets the great Spaniards lived on, when
driven from their country's stage by power of French
influence; and while Englishmen had turned the performances of their Shakespeare into circus-evolutions, the
German spelled for himself the mysteries of human nature
from this their miracle. With this walk Goethe, setting
out from Götz, reached Egmont, that type of German
nobility and true distinction by whose side the overreach-
ing Spanish don seems an automaton oiled with venom:
for this transformation of the rugged, rough-hewn Götz
into the graceful, freely-moving Netherlander, it needed
but a stripping of the bear-hide, thrown round us for protection from the rawness of the age and climate, to let the
supple, sinewy body—whose natural tendency to beauty
even Winckelmann, so enthusiastically engrossed in all
things Southern, acknowledged with delight—attest its
inner warmth. The calm patrician gait, wherewith this
Egmont trod the scaffold, led the favoured poet through
the wonder-land of myrtle and laurel, from hearts a-droop
with tenderest soul-griefs in marble palaces, to knowledge

and proclamation of the sublime mystery of the Ever-womanly, of the likeness that passeth not away; and should Religion ever vanish from the earth, 'tis this would keep the sense of its divinest beauty sempiternally alive, so long as Goethe's "Faust" itself had not been lost.

How strange that, whenever German literary-æsthetes begin to talk of idealism and realism, Goethe is straight-way called a representant of the latter, and Schiller an idealist! Though sayings of Goethe's own have given rise to this, yet the whole character of his productivity, and especially his conduct toward the Theatre, shews how little such a designation hits the mark. Plainly, in regard of his truly great creations, his bearing toward the Theatre was far more that of an idealist than Schiller's : for scarcely had the ground of an agreement with this Theatre been trodden, than Goethe ruthlessly transgressed the bounds mapped-out by the scanty predevelopment of German histrionic art for the poet's commerce with it. Nor was it the "Gallic spring" that tempted him ; but the swing of German genius drove him far, far hence, and left the German actor staring after him with much the indifference of Mephistopheles when Helena's magic-mantle floats away in clouds. For Goethe lived longer than Schiller, and came to despair of German history : Schiller lived merely long enough to cherish a doubt—which doubt he took such noble pains to conquer. Never has a friend of man done for a neglected people what Schiller did for the German Theatre. If the whole ideal life of the German spirit is illustrated in the course of his poetic evolution, so in the sequence of his dramas we may read the history of the German Theatre, and of its attempted raising to a popularly-ideal art. It might indeed be hard to draw a parallel between the "Robbers" and "Fiesco," instinct already with full poetic greatness, and the raw spirit of the German Theatre's beginnings in so-called English-comedi-anism : in every comparison of the creations of our great masters with what faced them from the wasted Folk-life, however, we shall always stumble on this sad, this indomitable disproportion. Better will the harmony appear, from the point where we find in Schiller himself the result of his observation of the character and capabilities of the Theatre. This is past mistaking in "*Kabale und Liebe*": perhaps that piece is the strongest proof, supplied as yet, of what could be done in Germany by a full accord between Theatre and Poet.—The excellent, the veritably German-breathing players of the happy epoch of the German Theatre's rebirth, as well, had brought matters as far as a naturalistic imitation of the surrounding burgher-world: for this they shewed no less a talent than any other nation, and did no little honour to that German nature for which Lessing had fought his energetic battles. Though the ideal of all Art remained unknown to them, yet they copied with realistic truth a sterling, unaffected nature, from whose simplicity, whose goodness of heart and warmth of feeling, one well might await in course of time an out-look on the beautiful. What first discredited and made the German burgher-play repulsive,—what Goethe and Schiller lamented in despair, was not that honest beginning, but its caricature, the Sensational-piece inflicted on us by the reaction against the ideal trend of our great poets.

For the present let us follow Schiller in his strong-winged progress from that burgher sphere to the realms of the Idea. "Don Carlos" was to decide whether the poet should finally turn his back upon the theatre, like Goethe, or draw it by his loving hand into those higher regions with him. What the German spirit here achieved, will ever be astounding. In what language of the world, among Spaniards, Italians or French, shall we find beings from the highest spheres of life, monarchs and Spanish grandees, queens and princes, expressing themselves in the most passionate and the tenderest emotions with such dis-tinguished, such humanly - noble naturalness, at once so polished, so witty and full of deeper meaning, so unforcedly highbred, and withal so visibly sublime, so drasticly uncommon? How conventional and stilted must even Calderon's royal figures, how utterly laughable the courtly-

theatrical marionnettes of a Racine, appear beside them!
Shakespeare himself, who yet could give his kings and yokels
equally appropriate truths to speak, was here no all-sufficient
pattern ; for that sphere of the Sublime which the poet of
" Don Carlos " trod, had not opened out before the gaze of
the great Briton. And it is intentionally that we here confine ourselves to the speech, the gestures of the characters
in "Don Carlos," because we have to ask ourselves at once:
how was it possible for German players, who had previously
no other model but the human nature of everyday, to adopt
this speech, these gestures ? What did not forthwith and
wholly prosper, at least succeeded to a hopeful pitch : for
here was shewn, as in poet so iñ players, the German's aptitude for the ideal. His starting-point was a naturalistic
imitation of his own familiar burgher-life, itself in correspondence with the natural German manner—the " Andante " :
what remained to win, was the loftier swing, the tenderer
passion of the more sublime " Allegro " ; and attainable
they were, for Schiller's figures wore no made, conventional, unnatural gentility, but the true, the nature-noble,
the purely-human eminence of heart. These actors were
so conscientious in their self-appraisement, that they feared
to fall into un-nature and affectation through an unaccustomed recitation of the un-burgherlike iambics ; to keep
faith with themselves on the new path, they elected to
have these iambics written out in prose for their preliminary study, and thus to not attempt the rhythmic
pathos until the natural accent of the words had been
ensured—much as it would be sensible in Opera, however
trivial the text, to teach the singers to first pronounce it
properly, before they begin to practise singing it. The
only danger in this phase of evolution, by no means un-
lovable in itself, was lest the German actor's fundamental
sense of naturalness should degenerate into grotesque over-
emphasis and downright ranting, in the more emotional
parts.* Goethe and Schiller, intelligently taking stand by

* " Die an sich wahrlich nicht unliebenswürdige Gefahr lag bei dem Fort-
schreiten in dieser Entwickelungsphase der deutschen Schauspieler nur darin,
dass der gründliche Natürlichkeitssinn beim Affekt nicht in groteske Heftigkeit
und allzu wahre Sinnfälligkeit ausarte."—

Goethe's side, adopted the selfsame expedient for checking this natural impetuosity, as the lawgivers of the French Theatre had long employed to banish Nature out-and-out. In this regard it is very instructive to note how Benj. Constant expresses himself in his " *Réflexions sur le théâtre Allemand*": the naturalism of the German Theatre he highly admires, seeing that it is applied with so much chasteness, loyalty, and tender conscience; but he believes that it should stay forbidden to the French, since on the one hand they have aimed at nothing but the opportune, i.e. theatrical Effect, whilst on the other hand the true-to-Nature affords so strong an engine of effect that, were it once conceded to them, they would deal in none but such effects, and their exaggerations would soon destroy all truth, good taste, nay, even any possibility of the truly natural.   And in the further evolution of the French Theatre the consequence of giving up its rules has fully borne out this foreboding : to our deep disgrace we presently shall have to see how hence again, under sway of the reaction against the German spirit, the final ruin of the German Theatre, nay, of German Art in general, was brought about.   With wise precaution our great poets let the players practise a few orthodox French pieces, to learn to feel the artistic benefits of Culture too, and thus, like stout Ulysses shunning Scylla as Charybdis, to steer the ship of the German Theatre, freighted with the last and highest glory of the long-suffering nation, into the haven of its new, its ideal home.

Henceforth the glorious couple worked and wrought together in newly-kindled hope : for very joy at Schiller's work, Goethe forgot his own poetic gifts, and helped the dear one all the better.   Thus, in direct formative interaction with the Theatre, arose those splendid dramas; each of them, from " Wallenstein " to " Tell," the landmark of a conquest on the unknown realm of the Ideal, and standing now as pillars of the German spirit's only veritable hall-of-Fame.   And this was compassed *with* the Theatre.   Without seeing any startling geniuses appear within its ranks the whole body of actors was inspired with the breath of the Ideal : with result that a potent sympathy seized every cultured person of that age, seized youth, the Folk itself, for the Theatre ; for upon these had dawned the spirit of their great poets, wellnigh clad in flesh, and made them through this Theatre the partners in their poets' great ideas for man's ennobling.—

But the worm was already gnawing at this blossom : to have come to actual fruit-bearing, the tree must have been able to strike strong roots into the depth and breadth of the people's life, moulding and fashioning its every particle of soil. We have seen how the people opened wide its breast to take the boon : we have viewed its deeds—but we have also learnt what was its wage.—It is highly significant, and peculiar to the unexampled character of German history, that the worm which gnawed at the blossom of German Art was the selfsame fiend that wrought the ruin of the German nation's political revival, — a fact not recognisable until viewed from a distance, the distance of our days.

If the Czar had not succeeded in making a ballet-dancer from a Russian privy-councillor, yet he found it possible to create a Russian privy-councillor from a German zany. At the hearth and home of their gigantic labours, the tranquil, tiny Weimar, *August von Kotzebue* was preparing for Schiller and Goethe their first annoyances and troubles of disturbance and confusion. A strange, a certainly not ungifted, a flippant, vain and evil-hearted mortal, whom the glory of the Gods annoyed. All their doings were so new and dauntless : could not one derange them ? He made stagepieces of every style that seemed at all likely to suit ; chivalry-pieces, farces, and finally—to strike the nail right home—sensational-pieces. Whatever ill leanings, whatever bad habits and evil passions existed among the public or the players, he stirred them up and set them going. Benj. Constant's prophecy was beginning to be fulfilled in Paris : the monster of Melodrama was born ; to Germany must it be brought with all one's might, were it only,

through the " Dog of Aubry," to make Goethe lay down
the reins of Weimar management.   But one meant to introduce the actual sovereignty of the Abject (*des Nieder-
trächtigen*).   A particularly novel blend was just the thing
for that.   The blunt had been the first foundation of
German naturalness, at the theatre too : no cleanly soul
had taken umbrage at " Götz," the " Robbers,"—at Shakespeare, ay, at Calderon, who could play his hand of blunt-
ness with the rest ; only to the French had it been pro-
hibited, and for the same good reason as the true-to-Nature,
because with them the blunt is but another name for the
obscene.   Nature, suppressed, avenged herself : what was
not suffered as obscenity, assumed the garment of frivolity.
Kotzebue adapted the " suggestive " [*das " Schlüpfrige "*—
lit. the " slippery "], i.e. the absolutely fatuous, which betrays its nothingness so signally that one seeks beneath its
every fold for Something, until at last awakened curiosity
is shewn the well-disguised obscene—but so gingerly that
the police can have nothing to say against it.   Behold !
the archetype was won, for a new theatrical development
in Germany.   Kotzebue wrote his privy-councillor reports
to Petersburg, upon the charming turn of things in Germany,
and was in the best of spirits.   Then on March 23rd, 1819,
a stripling in the old-german gown found entrance to his
chamber, and stabbed the privy-councillor to death.   An
unheard, a deed of fateful presage.   It all was instinct :
the Russian Czar had dealt from instinct, when he got his
privy-councillor to write him those really nothing worse
than flippant reports ; and so did *Sand*, who could make no
other answer to the plain proofs of Kotzebue's political harmlessness, than—that this man was the corrupter of German
Youth, the betrayer of the German Folk.   The judges
racked their brains : there *must* be some terrible conspiracy
afoot ; the murder of the privy-councillor was surely nothing
but a prelude ; the masters of the State, the State itself,
would follow next for certain.   Nothing was to be ex-
torted from the youthful murderer, but that he hugged his
deed, would gladly do it over again, thanked God who had en-

lightened him and now was leading him towards a righteous death of expiation in peace and surety of salvation. And he abode by this without a moment's blenching, through fourteen-months' imprisonment, devoured by festering wounds, racked on the sordid plank of suffering.—It was a clever Jew, Börne by name, who first made merry at this deed ; nor did Heine, if our memory serves us, allow it to escape his wit. What the nation felt, is not quite clear; the only certainty is, that the German Theatre belonged to Kotzebue's spiritual heirs. At this theatre we still will look a little closer, and that in earnest.

X.

The line now struck by the German Theatre, in force of the reaction already described by us, could hardly be kept to its full corruptive tendence without a direct and definite influence from the sphere of political power. The new, seductive social station, now allotted to the Theatre, became the weightiest engine of that influence. Entirely alienated from the spirit of their people, the Princes hitherto had entertained their courts with nothing but Italian and French opera-, ballet-, and comedian-companies : the German play and *Singspiel* had been set before the genuine public in wretched show-booths, by ill-nourished, mostly strolling players, conducted and hawked around on strictly industrial principles. They alone comprised the real stage-handicraft, in its good and evil sense. But now that everything was taking a nobler, more human form of energy through the rebirth of the German art-spirit, the municipal and royal authorities, led by men of good will and artistic feeling (among whom the German nobles, then mindful of their rank and freedom, shewed out to marked advantage), bethought them of extending to these strolling troops, which they were surprised to find displaying certain sterling talents, a social patronage conducive to the weal of Art itself. A shining

example (great Princes' weightiest means of influence) had
been set by the fervid Kaiser Joseph II. of Austria: in
Vienna had arisen the first Court- and National-theatre;
in its two divisions,* together with Opera and Ballet at
least, the German Play was cultivated by well-tended
companies, now taken into the Imperial pay.   For a considerable time, in fact until it likewise fell beneath the
universally ruinous influence of the Abject—a curious art-
tendence which we soon shall have to characterise a little
more precisely—Germany owed to this earliest institute its
best school of acting and the longest preservation of the
style peculiar to the German, the so-called "true-to-
Nature": a tendence not itself directed to the Ideal, but
at all events the basis whence the German may arrive at
the Ideal.   This admirable example was swiftly copied
almost everywhere.   The courts, inspired by nothing but
a feeling of philanthropy (for one left them in undisturbed
possession of their Italian Opera and Ballet, and even of
French Comedy where needful) committed the technical
conduct of the Theatre to men well-versed in Art, and
mostly by profession: the Duke of Weimar handed it to
his friend Goethe; in Berlin it was directed by a great
comedian, Iffland.   That was the time of promise; then
things went Germanly and honestly.   Had they continued
in this happy vein, the shortcomings of every standing
theatric enterprise on German soil would soon have come
to observation; the proper remedy, the way to organise
the German Theatre in the sense of all truly healthy
German institutions — which have to answer needs and
usages quite other than those, for instance, of the Parisian
public—and the way to make it nobly productive, must
soon have been discovered, and discovered it would have
been.—

    But now the whole thing took another aspect: Kotzebue
had been murdered; a student in the old-German gown
had stabbed him.   What did it mean?   Plainly something
most insidious lurked behind.   In any case it seemed pru-

* Cf. Vol. III., page 365.—TR.

dent to effect a clearance of the old-German gowns, and make Kotzebue's cause one's own. "Out upon the German lumber! The Theatre has become a *point d'honneur* of the Court. Out, ye men who know your business, or to your rightful place as humble hodmen! The regular court-cavalier alone understands the new tendence." We have been told of a twenty-two-year-old hunting-page, who, simply because he knew nothing whatever about it, was made Intendant of a theatre; he directed the art-establishment, entrusted to him, for considerably over a quarter of a century* ; once we heard him candidly declare that now-adays, at any rate, Schiller would never have dared to write a thing like "Tell." Here everything worked by instinct, with no real hint from lucid consciousness, as indeed at most turnings in the world's career; that consciousness began to glimmer only when one had to say straight out what one would *not* have. What one *would* have—it followed so easily and palpably from the foolishest arrangements: why shame oneself by confessing it aloud?

Naturally the ideal point of contact of the mime with the poet must first be blotted out. That was an easy matter. One fed the mime with sugarplums, and let the poet starve. Now were the actor and, especially, the actress clad in brave array: but when the prima donna, or the mighty ballerina came along, the stately Intendant himself sank on his bended knees. Why shouldn't the poor comedian take it in good part? The whole class was lacquered with a certain glistening varnish, giving it the appearance, from a distance, of something between a peer and a demigod. What had formerly been reserved for famed Italian cantatrici and French ballet-danseuses, now spread like a vapour over the whole poor German player-class: to the most admired and oftenest applauded, it smelt as perfume; to the unregarded stopgap, at least as fragrance of baked meats. All the heartlessness and bad

* Baron von Lüttichau, Intendant of the Dresden Court-theatre in Wagner's time.—TR.

propensities that lurked in the histrion's nature, were assiduously coaxed forth and solely fostered—again, by the all-directing Instinct: the most repulsive vanity and the most harlot-like complaisance.   The monkey, in its most atrocious shape, had been carefully shelled from its Goethe-Schiller chrysalis, and the only remaining question was: what to give it now to imitate?—'Twas easy, and not so easy.   As for clothes, so for the Theatre, one held by Paris fashions.   Botched and copied: oh! it was soon got ready, and it answered too.   But not at every season.   In Paris, where each new piece can be played off the reel for over a hundred nights to an immense and constantly changing public, at many theatres at least, one doesn't bring out so much in a whole year as the theatre of a little German provincial city, with its diminutive public, devours in a month. From one entirely disregarded root-offence of our modern German theatric system, the mistake of being obliged to cut an entertaining figure before one and the selfsame public, night in, night out—from this evil, which was bound to result in the utter ridicule of its performances, there have evolved alike the Nemesis upon the whole criminal attempt and the last possibility of rescue from a death by drowning.

What one intended with the Theatre, when one brought it under the immediate management of parade-struck courts, was at any rate assisted by the demoralising influence that could not but extend itself to the more or less industrial establishments still subsisting in the towns. The directors of these minor theatres, mostly non-subventioned and a prey to simple speculation, were forced to try and turn an honest penny out of the superabundance of theatre-evenings by clutching at every drifting straw that offered a distraction.   In this wise the German repertory became packed with a monstrous mass of specially-adapted pieces, the property of every age and nation.   Seeing that at divers times and in divers tongues a fair amount, nay, much of excellent work has been written for the stage, it also took its bounden turn of penal exercise.

The great Court-theatres fell at last into an altogether similar plight. The gruesome ghost, Finance, which Frederick the Great foresaw would threaten the Papacy itself some day, and most unpleasantly, appeared before the Court-theatre Intendants. The very institution of the new Court-theatre was nothing but a compromise between the Court and Public of a capital: the Court merely furnished the pompous show and the mismanagement; the Public must stand bail for the loss (*Noth*). Thus a second power evolved itself, the revenue-voting Lower House, one of the most remarkable of phenomena — the German theatre-subscriber. The subterranean war in sieges can scarcely shew more interesting tactics, than the wondrous battle-of-the-mines between the Subscriber and the Intendant. They can never come to terms without reciprocal concessions; for the Intendant himself—particularly if his monarch is out of temper at the extravagances for singers, dancers, etc.—has to accommodate his ways to the subscribers; in the long run he has to fly to the expedient of the profit-needing Town-theatre Director, and slip into his sack of bad a grain of good for once in a way. And as the Subscriber takes an occasional trip, if not exactly to Paris, yet to somewhere in the nearer or remoter German neighbourhood where exceptional circumstances have helped something really worth regarding into a provincially timid light of day, he brings back with him and publishes, the news that all that glitters is not gold: whereupon the ruling tendence toward the Abject is somewhat shaken from its orbit, now and then; which, vexatiously enough, leads on to fresh concessions, nay, finally to the utmost confusion. Then should it chance that a foreign ambassador expresses the longing to taste a little of the Romantic stage-literature of Germany, discussed from time to time abroad (much as the Emperor of Russia wished the Grand-Duke of Weimar to shew him the famous Jena students); or if it happens that a junior prince or, for a rarity, the Monarch himself avows a weakness on any classical side or other,—then Chaos comes to stay.

G

Reviewers are begged for their literary advice, the learned are dragged on as poets, architects as decorators: everyone shakes hands, exhibits mutual reverence, and the Court-theatre becomes the Pantheon of modern art.   And all this groups itself around the happy Mime, who now feels perfectly warranted in babbling of art and the classics. To be sure, an aside, a sly wink of the Intendant's teaches him that things are really not so parlous: "What the gentry are really driving at, good God! these art-twaddlers don't seem to have a notion of.   You know!"—"But the subscribers—the ghost?"—"Ah well! Isn't there a way of bringing them to reason?"— One has nothing against Schiller and Goethe; on the contrary, one is only too happy to throw in all the classic poets, right back to Sophocles: only, you musn't expect the actor to duly learn the stuff by heart, when one can give it after all so very seldom, alas! like everything else; but with this distinction, that everything else is much easier to get by heart, and can very well be "played to the prompter."

For beautiful times had come for the mime, when he felt himself in clover, could take a nap for once, and lounge about.   From the tedious, tiresome rehearsal, often without waiting it out, to the coffee-house; before the performance billiards or skittles, after the performance beer-house. There you have his faithful round.   Admittance behind the wings was still reserved for the aristocrats; in compensation to the town-populace proper, the wings, with all that passes behind them, were brought into the restaurant or tavern.   The interest in what one heard there, soon swallowed every other interest that formerly might occupy a city's population.   An actor's marriage, a new amour, a quarrel about rôles; whether one would be "called out," increases of salary, star-engagements, how much was to be paid for them,—these were henceforth the grand topics on which the attention of society, the passionate sympathy of the whole public and domestic life, was concentrated in every city where a standing theatre, especially under Court protection, had taken thorough root.   Then came the favourites, their rivals, their personal war, and the warfare of their parties. Now the actor's 'shop,' the comedian's slang became the soul of wit, the jargon of the wings the speech of public and of press; and the most utterly non-sensical words, such as "self-intelligible" ("*selbstverständlich*"), which had plainly been invented for a knockabout parody, were rolled on the tongue with such lasting delight that the grammarian felt bound at last to explain, the foreigner to translate them, had both not been impossible. —Goethe bewailed the improvement of the universities insomuch as it sensibly reduced the number of ruined students, who, having come into some manner of contact with higher intellectual culture, had formerly supplied the Theatre with at least a serviceable material; whereas it now was besieged by the discharged counterjumper, whose only qualification for the stage consisted in a smooth face and a certain shop-agility. Had Goethe been able to foresee into whose hands German trade itself would one day fall, and from what exclusive nationality our Theatre would consequently have to recruit its ranks, he would never have let his "Faust" be so much as printed in book form; for any, were it even the remotest resemblance to a theatre-piece, would certainly have scared him back from publishing his wonder-work. And it was just upon this "Faust" that the full vengeance of theatrical Abjectness was wreaked.

To two summits did the genius of Germany mount up, in its two great poets. The idealistic Schiller reached his in the staunch and solid core of German Folk-nature; to the point whence Goethe had set out, did Schiller return; after he had paced the glorious round of ideality to the transfiguration of Catholic Dogma in "Maria Stuart," with majestic valediction he turned back to "Tell," journeying from the sunset to the sunrise full of hope for nobly German manhood. From the bottomless depths of sensuous-suprasensual yearning, our Goethe soared to the hallowed mystic mountain-top, from whence he gazed into the glory of the world's redemption: with this gaze, which no ecstatic could ever have cast more raptly or more reverently upon that land beyond approach, the poet parted from us, and left us in his " Faust " his testament.

Two points denote the phases of the German Theatre's descent into the Abject : their names are " Tell " and " Faust."

At the beginning of the 'thirties of the present century, about the middle of the " now-time," the German spirit seemed inclined to shake itself up a little (the Paris July-revolution had given it a nudge) : also, one was making a few concessions here and there. The Theatre wanted its share of them : old Goethe was still living. Well-meaning literarians hit upon the thought of bringing his " Faust " to the theatre. It happened. What in itself, and with the best-regulated Theatre, was a fool's attempt, was bound just then to still more cryingly expose the Theatre's already far-advanced decline : but Gretchen proved a " grateful rôle." The noble poem dragged its maimed and mutilated carcase mournfully across the boards : but it seemed to flatter the young people, in especial, to get the public chance of cheering many a remembered word of wit and wisdom.—The theatres had better luck with " Tell," at much about the same time : people in Paris had made it into an opera-text, and no less a man than Rossini himself had set it to music. It was a question, indeed, whether one durst offer the German his " Tell " as a French translated opera ? Whoso would fathom once for all the unbridgeable gulf that separates the German spirit from the French, had only to compare this operatic text with Schiller's drama, which had reached the height of popularity in Germany. This was felt by every German, down from the professor to the lowest gymnasiast, even by the comedians themselves, and shame covered them at seeing that hideous travesty of their own best nature ; but,—hm !—an opera,—one doesn't take that sort of thing so strictly ! The overture, with its noisy ballet-music at the close, had already been received with thunders of applause at classical concert-establishments, close beside the Beethovenian symphony. People shut

one eye. And after all, this opera's goings-on were really
very patriotic, in fact more patriotic than in Schiller's
" Tell " : " *esclavage* " and " *liberté* " made an enormous effect
in music. Rossini had taken great pains to compose as
solidly as possible : indeed, when listening to many of the
ravishingly effective numbers, one could clean forget about
" Tell." It went, and is going still ; and, looked at in the
light of to-day, this " Tell " was quite a classical event
in our operatic calendar.—And things went on, and sank,
and drowned. After some years, Germany had a Revolution of its own: the colours of the old Burschenschaft *
floated above the palace of the Frankfort Bund. Goethe's
hundredth anniversary was dragged on as a sedative.
What should one give ? " Faust " was no longer of any
use. A Parisian composer once more comes to the rescue†:
without any other ambition, he gets the Goethian poem
translated into the effect-ive jargon needful for his boule-
vard-public ; a repellent, sugary-vulgar patchwork, with
all the airs and graces of a lorette, wedded to the music
of a second-rate talent that fain would bring itself to
something and stretches out an anguished hand to everything. People who had attended a performance in Paris,
declared that with *this* opera it would surely be impossible
to repeat in Germany what had been gone through, in its
day, with Rossini's " Tell." Even the composer, who had
simply wished to score a success with his own particular
public, there in the Boulevard du Temple, was far from
the pretension of venturing to exhibit himself in Germany
with this work. But matters turned out otherwise. Like
an evangel of bliss, this " Faust " at last swelled full the
heart of the German theatre-public, and from every point
of view both fools and sages found it really not at all
amiss. If to-day one still gives the " Faust " of Goethe as
a curiosity, it is merely to shew what a decided progress
the Theatre has made since the olden times.

* The red, yellow and black, adopted by the students (see page 47) as a
symbol of German unity.—Tr.

† Strictly speaking, not for ten or eleven years ; for Gounod's *Faust* was
1st produced at the Théâtre Lyrique, on March 19th, 1859.—Tr.

And certainly the progress is immeasurable. Should the noble example of a sovereign devotee of Art succeed in bringing the Theatre to such a point of efficiency as to open our eyes to its present downfall, that success, were it even to reach the highest thinkable, would be of no more than equal dimensions with our recent progress to the apogee of naked Abjectness.

XI.

We have endeavoured to throw a beam of light upon the characteristic physiognomy of affairs whose accurate delineation might occupy the lifetime of some gifted writer. The French have found such a genius, to delineate the ethical condition of their society—yet a genius who, by reason of his choice of subject, the hitherto-unknown realism and tireless perseverance of his drawing of that subject's details, and above all through the utter hopelessness in which he leaves us, appears more like a demon. Balzac, whom the French cannot but marvel at, but would prefer to leave unnoticed, gives striking evidence that only by duping himself can the Frenchman preserve an illusion as to the awful contents of his Culture and his Civilisation: viewed and apprehended with the same eagerness as guides the German in his thorough examination of a Nature-truth, this Culture was bound to reveal to the poet a chaos of ghastly details, strictly connected withal, and mutually explanatory; to have undertaken whose unravelling and reproduction, and to have carried it out with the incredible patience of a poet genuinely in love with his subject, makes of this remarkable writer a phenomenon quite unparalleled in the domain of literature.—'Twere a more than mournful, a pitiable task, to become a Balzac of those evils which have fastened upon the whole public life of the German people through the desolation of its Theatre. To see this public life, not temptingly embellished with the Theatrical as in France, to conceal that hateful substance of French civilisation which Balzac has exposed, but weighed down by the Theatrical, as has been the case with the Germans, in such wise that a valiant, truthful native substance (which B. Constant so admired in us) has been transformed into a ridiculous grotesque, for every passer-by to scoff at,—this scarcely could inspire the most malicious demon to write a second *Comédie humaine*: at the very least its title would have to be concocted from one of the newer German jargons now in vogue.*

For ourselves, we know but one way of bringing the problem, inherent in the deeply humiliating state of things above-denoted, to anything like a conscious understanding : namely, by adopting a negative expedient—somewhat curious in itself, but here the only one available—and proving that no sort of consciousness of this problem can be existent, for the simple reason that everyone is person-ally involved and implicated in that state. We will there-fore address a circular interrogatory to all the classes and members of German society, as constituted by the only public life that comes within the purview of the Culture-researcher, asking each in turn for their opinion of the agency of the modern German Theatre: whether they ascribe to it any influence at all ; of what kind they deem that influence ; and whether, if they recognise that influence as harmful, they know of any remedy ?

As standing nearest to the Theatre, our first witnesses shall be the representatives of the ideal tendency in art, the literature-poets and plastic artists. Their temper and attitude towards the Theatre we have already characterised, and therefore, seeking now alike for counsel, we need tarry but a little with them.—When the reaction against the German spirit set in, the literary poet saw himself excluded from the theatre: he cast himself upon the literature drama, either not reckoned, or else unfitted, for theatrical performance. A first fall : for it was through his aimful observance of stage-requirements, that Schiller became our

---

* Perhaps one might suggest : "*Selbstverstand des jetztzeitlich aufgebesserten und bereiften deutschen Kunstvertriebs.*"—R. WAGNER.

greatest dramatic poet. When the literature-dramatist turned once more to the theatre, it had become a stranger to him, and already something quite distinct from what it was in Schiller's time : the newer French Effect-piece was now the ruling fashion. To copy this as faithfully as possible, and chiefly to clothe themselves about with the skilful mannerism of Parisian Scribe, became the plumb-line for these poets' dealings with the theatre. Moreover, from the leading-article they brought into the theatre the journalist's harangue upon political interests of the day and "time-tendences" so-called ; from the beloved actor's mouth there spouted the catchword of the parliamentary orator, an unfailing fillip to the audience's applause. Thus: an aping of the foreign, and a falsification of the Drama, reacting upon Literature itself : theatrical - journalistic mongreldom. We shall have to ask the politician and the statesman for the further results on the spirit of the journal-nourished Folk, but will take the present oppor-tunity of renewing our question to the plastic artist : what incentive could he reap from a model which offered itself to him in this manner of stage-trappings, or from a public life under influence of this stage ? The literature-poet, how-ever, reduced by this Theatre to a bad, at best a clumsy writer of Effect-pieces,—how can we expect him to tell us that the Theatre has corrupted him, to advise us how to purge away theatrical corruption, when all the time, con-ceitedly enough, he sets such store by his literary existence as to believe he may view his dealings with the stage in the light of a condescension ? What is his only grievance against the Theatre? That he cannot do good business there, because he is throttled by French competition : he wants patriotism at the theatre, wants protective duties to clear those unquestionably better-manufactured French Effect-pieces from the path of his bad imitations. Nothing but this does he think of, when there's talk of theatric reform. Is it of any use turning to him for help? Will he so much as be able to understand us ?

Must it be an even harder undertaking, to bring to the

plastic artist's consciousness the Theatre's ruinous influence upon his art in particular, since he fancies he stands quite beyond its reach, we will pass him by for now, and address ourselves somewhat more definitely to the *musician.*—What is the complaint of the German musician? Firstly, that he can make no headway outside the concert-room,— whereby he confesses that his relation to the Theatre is exactly the same as the literature-poet's: namely, since ever he gave up composing un-theatric operas, and tried to copy the Parisian Opera, the maladroitness of his imitation has left him handicapped by the original; and he, too, must therefore wish for patriotic measures at the theatre, when everything would go quite otherwise and he would be able at last to bring off something. But our good friend the German musician has another, and a very different ground for startled outcry; a ground he would have to explain by the desolation of the German Theatre, were he only able to explain a thing like that at all. Whence this imbecile uncertainty and unreliableness in the musical taste of just the German public, which in other respects is really the most musical of publics, and has seen the German Folk give birth to the greatest musicians of the world? That even in the closest-guarded concert-establishments one is compelled, beside the nurture of the noblest, purest art, to make the most dishonouring concessions to vulgarest virtuoso-triviality; and moreover has to admit that the very audience which here assembles for Bach and Beethoven, falls into still greater ecstasies when a famous Italian bravura-singeress drives away all memory of music,—this rolls around in the gentlemen's heads, no doubt; but when they have digested it so long, that they fancy they may as well print it, on whom do they pin the blame? Look you! upon the poor public itself, for being what it is.*

The sordid tendence that has prevented the Theatre from raising itself to an equally noble height with German

* See Ferd. Hiller's "*Aus dem Tonleben der Gegenwart. Gelegentliches.*" Second Volume: "*Die Musik und das Publikum.*"—R. WAGNER.

Instrumental-music, and the overwhelming influence of the
Theatre in general, which not even the best propensities of
the public are able to withstand—it never occurs to the
gentlemen to think of this.   They opine, indeed, that the
Theatre is harmful to the musical good-sense of the public:
but that what thus harms the latter is still more harmful to
the former, and that this is not the Theatre itself, but the
evil tendency imposed upon it, they never dream of; no,
they assume that by no possibility can the Theatre be
anything else, than just what it has become.   If one looked
to the German musician for help, in what a ridiculous
dilemma it would place him !   For this is what he thinks,
at bottom : what on earth has the Theatre to do with
Music ?   That without the pursuit of a tendence funda-
mentally different from that of the present Theatre, the
German sense of music, nay, the spirit of German Music
itself must sink into a desolation exactly like that now
arrived-at by the Theatre,—how is it possible to make this
intelligible to these gentry, notwithstanding that they hear
their condemnation bellowed out from every alley, and the
very Frenchman already knows better how to render their
best music than they themselves ?—

Let us now turn from the artistic classes that only
indirectly work upon the spirit of the nation, to those
representatives of public intellectual culture into whose
immediate tutelage the nation is given over.—

How stands the *School* towards the Theatre ?—

In the past century, when the School was labouring
under the full incubus of pedantry and what we now
call "*Zopf*" ("pigtail"), there evolved from it a Winckelmann, a Lessing, Wieland, and a Goethe.   When Lessing
cast himself upon the Theatre, he was excommunicated by
the School : yet Lessing, of all men, is quite unthinkable
without the education he received in just that School.
Rightly enough : for that School still clove to the classic
principle of Humanism, whence had issued the great figures
and great movements of the era of Rebirth and Reformation.   Greek and Roman classics formed the groundwork

of these schools, in which the purely utilitarian was as
good as unknown, or not yet advocated. Despite the
character of utter dryness and sterility that necessarily
stamped itself upon classical studies in the days of the
German spirit's deepest decline, through their lack of any
living fecundation from just that spirit, the Schools at least
maintained alive the source of all fair humanising culture
of more recent times; in a similar, though converse, fashion
as the Mastersingers of Nuremburg, at the prime of classic
Humanism, preserved for the eye of genius the old-German
mode of poetry. It was a time of fairest hope, when
Goethe, nursed in that school of Classic pedantry, sang
his stalwart praises of the scoffed-at and forgotten Hans
Sachs; when he triumphantly expounded Erwin's Strassburg
minster to the world,—when the spirit of old Classicism
took fresh life unto itself from the poet-warmth of our
great masters, and from the stage the " Bride of Messina "
re-illumed in age and youth the study of the mighty
Greeks. Then 'twas no shame for the School, to go
hand in hand with the Theatre : the teacher knew that
what his pupils could not learn from him, they there would
learn, and with him—noble, vibrant warmth in the judgment of those great problems of life to which the pupil
was then brought up.

Here came to consciousness and received its plain expression, what *German* is : to wit, the thing one does for
its own sake, for very joy of doing it ; whereas Utilitarianism, namely the principle whereby a thing is done for sake
of some personal end, ulterior to the thing itself, was
shewn to be un-German. The German virtue herein expressed thus coincided with the highest principle of
æsthetics, through it perceived, according to which the
' objectless ' (*das Zwecklose*) alone is beautiful, because,
being an end (*Zweck*) in itself, in revealing its nature as
lifted high above all vulgar ends it reveals at like time
that to reach whose sight and knowledge alone makes ends
of life worth following ; whereas everything that serves an
end is hideous, because neither its fashioner nor its on-

looker can have aught before him save a disquieting conglomerate of fragmentary material, which is first to gain
its meaning and elucidation from its employment for some
vulgar need.—None but a great nation, confiding with
tranquil stateliness in its unshakable might, could ripen
such a principle within itself, and bring it into application
for the happiness of all the world : for it assuredly presupposes a solid ordering of every nearer, every relation
that serves life's necessary ends ; and it was the duty of
the political powers to found that order in this lofty, world-
redeeming sense,—that is to say : *Germany's Princes should
have been as German, as were its own great masters.* If this
foundation fell away, then the German must come to the
ground for very reason of his merit : and that's what he
has done to-day, where German he has stayed.

But, let us have no care ! People knew of a means of
rescue. The " Now-time " had arrived. Let us see how
things go with the School, in it !—

XII.

About the School, especially in Catholic Germany, the
Church and State to-day are striving : manifestly because
each has its own end in view. The Church upbraids the
State with aiming at nothing in the School but a materialistic, a utilitarian education of the people, and claims it
as her duty to see that man's highest spiritual interests,
which undeniably are his religious interests, shall not
suffer harm from this training for sheer utilitarian ends.
Plainly the Church here appears in the most advantageous
of lights. Only, the State replies with the proof, or at
least the apprehension, that the Church is merely endeavouring through the School to found for herself a
political power, an imperium in imperio ; that religion is
simply her means, whereas her end is Hierarchy, which
would give rise to great confusion in the State and finally
would burden it with an uneducated populace, unfitted for

the ends of life, unable to help itself, and cast upon the State for a shelter and a sustenance at last impossible.

Indeed it might be hard, wellnigh impossible, to say which is the greater evil menacing a Folk : the ill foreboded by the Church, or that foretokened by the State !

Certain it is, that dating from the reaction, so often mentioned by us, of the German governments against the German spirit, the new tendence of the State itself has strongly influenced the School : an ever greater aversion to ' objectless ' æsthetic culture supervened ; classical studies were more and more exclusively reserved for philologists by profession ; of Philosophy one took possession for objects of the State—and easily enough, for whoso declined to trim his philosophy to suit these ends, simply got appointed to no post * and was hurled into the opposition, where he might see for himself how well he fared between philosophy and the police.   In this the State was everywhere backed by the Church, both Protestant and Catholic.   The Polytechnic schools arose, those highschools of industrial Mechanics : to prepare the sons of the Folk for admission to these schools, became more and more the State-subserving object of the better class of lower Folk-schools ; the Universities, on the other hand, where not intended to directly qualify for service of the State, became more and more a luxury for the rich, who " didn't need " to learn anything save what they had a fancy for. Classical education proper, i.e. the foundation of all humanising culture upon a knowledge of the Greek and Roman tongues and literature, is already openly decried — by persons, too, who as artists make a claim to culture—and dubbed both useless and easy of replacement : it is looked on as a waste of time, disturbing, and good for nothing but being forgotten.   Altogether of this opinion is the Catholic Church of nowadays, though upon different grounds from our artists'.   Herein she rather shares the secret reasons of the un-German newer State : all phenomena upon the field of intellectual life which have fallen

* Arthur Schopenhauer. —Tr.

out of favour with them both, they deem the result of those humanistic classical studies. This change originated in their terror of the French Revolution, their amazement at the fire of German revival in the War of Liberation. Down to that time the Jesuit Fathers had rendered the greatest services to classical education, and thus to the cause of spiritual rewakening in Catholic countries, fast decaying beneath the most unspiritual political oppression. Then the Church (as influenced by the Jesuits, at least) and State were really and intrinsically antagonists. How we are to construe their antagonism of to-day, is more difficult to comprehend : after the mournful turning taken by the Church's spiritual life under dread of political re-volution, it would rather seem as if the State had stepped into the position toward the Church which the Jesuits ere-while occupied so honourably towards the State. Yet how the State could venture, with a good conscience and any prospect of success, to take into its hands again the intellectual elevation of the Folk-life, after, in common with the Church, it had left, or even led the public in-tellectual life of the nation itself to a desolation such as our present inquiries have forced upon our knowledge,— that certainly is easier said than thought. With justice might the Church, like ourselves, be amazed at seeing the State now want to drag on Art as substitute for the spiritual fount of life once issuing from Religion : on the other hand, though the State had no valid answer to the scoffs it thus invited, it would surely be no less justified in hesitating to ascribe any such quickening efficacy to the Church, in her present so very mundane form, for only too visibly there likewise clings to her the stain of that theatrical element which we have shewn to be the character-istic mark of all our social and artistic life that faces toward publicity.

Since the School has necessarily brought us into im-mediate contact with the *Church* and *State*, we hold it our duty to at once give plainer expression to the idea we cherish of the supremely salutary effect of a genuine

German Art-revival even upon these weightiest of all the world's affairs; a course to which we are chiefly prompted by the hope of bringing about at least a glimmer of agreement where it hitherto has seemed to be the farthest off.

It has become an easy thing to-day, to taunt the Church: on the political tribune, in diplomatic intercourse, and by newspaper-authors in the service of them both, she commonly, and according as the particular interest dictates, is treated with not much more respect than an establishment of the *crédit mobilier*. If, then, we undertake to prove to the representatives of ecclesiastical interests that this want of reverence has an actual correlation with the dishonour put on public art in modern days, it is quite obvious that the barest self-regard would oblige us to adopt a more becoming tone. Again, as we do not feel that our thesis calls us in the slightest to touch upon the intrinsic substance of the Church, her religious Dogma, but simply on the outer shape wherein she steps before the burgher's public life and strikes his senses,—and even though that outer shape, whereby she fain would point the layman's phantasy to the depths of her unutterable content, must ineluctably submit itself to the laws of the æsthetically beautiful: yet we are so remote from the almost universal spirit of irreverence, that we ourselves should account it unhandsome to wish to make these laws apply to her exactingly, or without reserve. Merely we would rouse the representatives of Churchly interests to meditate on this; and for that purpose we, too, will have recourse to parable, in a certain sense, to wit an illustration from historically patent facts.

It was a beauteous time for the Roman Church, when Michael Angelo adorned the walls of the Sistine Chapel with the sublimest of all works of painting; but what is the import of a time in which these works, upon occasions of great ceremony, are swathed with theatrical draperies and tinsel gewgaws?—It was a beauteous time, when a Pope was determined by Palestrina's lofty music to retain for God's service the adornment of the art of Tone, against whose rank corruption he had meant to take

strong measures by banishing it forever from the Church;
what now shall we say of a time in which the latest
favourite operatic aria and ballet-tune sound out for the
credo and *agnus* ?—It was a fairer time, when the Spanish
auto brought the sublimest mysteries of Christian Dogma
upon the stage, and set them in dramatic parables before
the Folk, than when the capital of the Church's temporal
protector sent forth to all the world an opera in which
murderers and incendiaries (as in the "Huguenots"), in
the most sacred garment of the Church, attune their hideous
priestly jargon to the strains of their by all means effect-
full trios.   Nor has it an import less deserving of reflection
by the representatives of Catholic interests, when the
recently canonised dogma of the Immaculate Conception
called forth full many a frivolous quip in the French and
the Italian press, whereas the greatest German poet closed
his grandest poem with the beatific invocation of the *Mater
gloriosa*, as the loftiest ideal of spotless purity.   Might they
not be of opinion, that the last Act of Schiller's "Maria
Stuart" affords an other, and a more commendable explanation of the purport of the Catholic Church, than
Mons. L. Veuillot can ever reach to-day in Paris through
his bickerings and his sorry wit ?

In his "Wanderjahre" Goethe draws the imaginary
picture of an educational establishment according to his
own ideas: the father, committing his son to its care, is
conducted round the building wisely furnished for instruction in Religion; after the Life of the Saviour down to the
Last Supper has been also shewn him, in beautiful paint-
ings on the wall, he asks the overseer in amazement
whether the Passion and Death of the Redeemer are
kept a secret from the pupils.   The Elder answers: "Of
this we make no secret; but we draw a veil over those
sufferings, even because we reverence them so highly.
We hold it a damnable effrontery to expose that instrument of torture, and the Holy One who hangs thereon,
to the light of that same sun which hid its face when a
flagitious world forced such a sight upon it; to take these

deepest mysteries, in which the godlike depths of Holiness lie hid, and play with them, dandle them, trick them out, and rest not till the most sublime seems vulgar and insipid. I invite you to return when a year has elapsed, to attend our General Festival, and see for yourself how far your son has progressed ; then shall you, as well, be inducted to the sanctuary of Sorrow." *—

This lesson well might teach us how the School must finally be governed in its dealings with Religion, if the same tendence which has brought the Church to the degradation suggested in the instances adduced above is to remain the only one in force for her further evolution, and thus if her "*non possumus*" is no longer to express a will, but a sheer incapability.—The words cited from Goethe, however, are not attributable to the Protestant, but to the *German*. And indeed it might not seem amiss, to counsel the representatives of ecclesiastical interests to ponder earnestly what we understand, and with full authority, by this " German ": its æsthetic principle, as previously defined, might be imagined in no unhelpful harmony with the highest religious principle of the Church. Perchance the leaders of the Roman Church of old committed the same mistake, in their judgment and treatment of the German spirit, as we have shewn attaching to the German Princes in more recent history: what was quickening for their rescue, may easily have been misprised and rejected by them both, as ruinous alike to every party. But, if the latest incidents in history make it seem more doubtful every-day whether the spirit of the Romanic nations is destined to prove a lasting buttress to the Roman Church, one might recommend the deeper-thinking advocates of Catholic interests to take more keenly and affectionately in view the hopes and endeavours, as sincere as beautiful, which the never-to-be-forgotten King Maximilian II. of Bavaria addressed to a re-uniting of the severed Christian

---

* With exception of a few minor changes, I have taken the above translation from Carlyle's English version of " *Wilhelm Meister*," Vol. III., chapter xi. —TR.

H

creeds in Germany,—to take this project more affectionately into their consideration than the policy, said to be
more than tolerated by them, of a final partition of
Germany into a Catholic and a Protestant half, to be
effected by a main-divisor leaving nothing politically over,
save Austria and Prussia.

In any case may the immediate object of these hints
have been so far attained, that the representatives of
Churchly interests, even should they not deem good to
second with friendly earnestness our efforts toward ennobling the spirit of public art in Germany, at least will
not allow them to be cried down with hostile jests—as,
alas! has become so common in the public organs that
serve their party.* With this pious wish, and surely no
extravagant one, we believe we must for this time turn
away from School and Church; not, however, as though
we feared our further plan would ever lead us to a region
where we should find ourselves compelled to leave out of
count, not to say wantonly sacrifice, the highest and
weightiest interests of these most saving powers for culture
of the human mind and heart.

XIII.

To want to bring the *State* directly into play for Art, as
has already occurred to many a well-meaning mind, reposes
on an error which takes the faults in organisation of the
modern State for its truest and intrinsic essence. The
State is the representative of absolute expedience †; it

---

* For the Ultramontane newspapers of Munich were as hostile to Wagner
and his friends, as was the Jewish press; he stood between the two opposing
fires.—TR.

† "Zweckmässigkeit"; this word—derived from "Zweck," an "end, aim,
or object"—is not fully covered by "expedience," but implies the principle
upon which a thing is done for some purely temporal or mechanical end,
something akin to "utilitarianism"; the latter term, however, being likewise
employed by our author—either actually or in the more strictly German form
of "Nützlichkeit"—I have found it necessary to observe a distinction between
the two.—TR.

knows nothing but expedience; and therefore, with the utmost propriety, it flatly declines to concern itself with anything that cannot plead a directly useful end. The blunder, against which indeed the whole newer development of the State is labouring either consciously or unconsciously, consists in the organisation of the Expedient having issued from above, thereby completely reversing the poles of the State. Frederick the Great was the conscious founder of this State, and the Prussian State is his handiwork, down to our own day of misunderstandings. After the dissolution of the Estates of the Realm * nothing was left but the Patriarchal State, established on the basis of territorial possession : to administer the country in such a fashion that it should yield the utmost revenue as a mere inhabited territory, was the task of his Government. The more exactingly high that end was pitched, the more carefully must the doctrine of expedience be instilled into the administration. We certainly should underrate this Frederick's importance, if we took the definition of his policy solely from a chance remark of his, that he wanted nothing from the State but money and soldiers ; yet it is quite certain that we cannot attribute any very lofty grandeur of aim to the exclusively French-cultured prince, with his rooted contempt for the German spirit, without falling into gross contradictions in our estimate of his actions. The consequences of his conception of the State, and the success of his State-organisations, come out the sharpest in the modern French Imperial State. In German, and particularly in South-German States, on the contrary, the Prussian State-idea has refused to work out either profitably or purely : sufficient remnants of the older *Reichsstand*-constitution had survived, though only just sufficient, to hinder any pure development of the Prussian State-idea, and thus to help its intrinsic impurity quite plainly into light of day.

* " Reichsstände "—the *immediate* members of the old Reich, who had the right of sitting in the Reichstag ; they comprised the Reichs-towns, Free-towns, and various spiritual and temporal powers, down even to a few Freiherrs, or Barons.—TR.

The most terrible result of an organisation founded on expedience, must undeniably be its proving inexpedient; for then the State, and all that lives and moves therein, must be involved in an eternally *bootless* struggle for the satisfaction of vulgar life-needs, can never even reach the glimmer of a knowledge of the essential aim of all Expedience, and thus must sink into a state unworthy of the human being.   Moreover in the State the most purely constructed on the principle of expedience, and just because its organisation proceeded from above, and from above to below one prided oneself on nothing but the Expedient, it was inevitable that the officials entrusted with the execution of its measures of expedience should be regarded both by Throne and Folk as the State itself, the only State with which one had to do.   In the mechanism of this officialdom the State was bound to grow so rigid, that its only object seemed comprised in these official establishments and the posts they offered ; so that the right to such appointments—and hence to sustenance by the State—became in turn the only aim of efforts from below, the preferment thereto the only end-of-State considered from above.

It warrants great hopes for the future, that in wellnigh every German land alike, from below as from above, the need has recently been felt of ennobling the tendence of the State, and weighty changes in this sense have already been commenced.   For our present object it is sufficient to say that we prefer to interpret the different social edicts, in their various stages of maturity, as attempts to raise the State's expediency-tendence, starting from satisfaction of the commonest need, to a knowledge and assuagement of the most universal, the highest need ; and thus through an ascending series of the most expedient, i.e. the most natural organisations, to reach at last its veritable goal. For Bavaria itself the wisest step towards this goal we hold to be the completion of the Maximilianeum, that school for higher State-officials where an education directed purely to the ends of usefulness would reach its hand already to the only truly humanistic, i.e. the ideal education, an end unto itself. And the State which builds itself from below upwards, in this project, will also shew us finally the ideal meaning of the *Kingship;* an office as to whose expediency so strong a doubt has been engendered in the minds of many political theorists by the ill-success of the expediency-tendence when conducted from above, that the constitution of the American United States has already been discussed and recommended, with much the same regardless volubility as bandies questions of the Church, for adoption by the German States.—At the hand of our guiding principle, derived in turn from our full conviction of the sterling value of the German spirit, we venture to briefly state our thoughts anent the destination of the German Kingship, that Kingship which must set the ideal crown upon the new true Folk-State now in course of building.

The true meaning of Kinghood is expressed in the prerogative of *pardon* (Begnadigung). The exercise of grace (*Gnade*) is the only act of positive freedom conceivable within the State, whereas in every other State-relation freedom can take effect in none but its original negative sense : for the etymologic meaning of the word is a "being freed from," a " being rid of"; which, again, is only thinkable as the negation of a constraint or pressure, either antecedent or presupposed. To free oneself as much as thinkable from the constraint and pressure of natural Want, as also of Want arising from the conflict of individual and social interests—this is the principle of Expediency that lies at bottom of every organisation of the State : in the happy event of all these organisations working together in peace and harmony, we reach the point where each unit has the least to sacrifice in order to reap the utmost profit from the whole ; but there always remains the relation of sacrifice and gain ; and absolute freedom, i.e. emancipation from all constraint, is quite beyond our thinking : its name were Death.—Only from quite another sphere of being, a sphere which the throughly realistic State must deem exclusively pertaining to an ideal order of the world, can a law of truly ideal expedience come into effect, as the exercise of positive, i.e. of active freedom, determined by no ordinary constraint, a freedom truly free ; and thus, at the very point we have termed impassable, it decks the work of the State with the crown which is that law itself. This crowning of its edifice the State-organisation attains through the King's being loosed, from first to last, from the principle of expedience that binds the entire State, and thus completely freed from every Want (*Noth*) engendered by that general principle. He consequently represents the attained ideal of negative freedom, the sole ideal within the knowledge and purview of the State and all its tendencies ; but this freedom, ensured to him by every available means, has the further object for the State, of raining down the ideal law of purest freedom, both blessing and ennobling it.

As said above, this ideal law shews out the plainest, and comes within the range of every man's perception, in the exercise of Grace. Here Kingly freedom steps into immediate contact with the weightiest basis of all Civil organisation : with Justice. In this latter is embodied the general law-of-expedience of the whole State, which strives through it for equity. Were Justice altogether sure that, while complying with the most cogent of Expedience's laws, she had perfectly fulfilled withal the idea of purely-human equity, then she would not feel obliged to lay her verdict first before the King : but even in pure democracies it has been thought necessary to establish a surrogate, however scanty and inadequate, for the King's prerogative of pardon ; and where this was not the case, as at the height of Athenian democracy, but the Demos exercised its power of ostracism according to the common reading of expediency—as in the best event it could not but do—there the State itself was already half-way toward the reign of pure Caprice. Now, to the verdict of Justice the King in any case accords a full validity *per se*, as answering to the expedience of the State's control in matters of right ; but of pure freedom he resolves on pardon, where it seems good to him to let

Grace prevail before Right; and in that he has to give a reason to no one, he testifies to that state of freedom, attainable by none besides, in which he is supported by the will of all. As no human resolves, not even the seemingly freest, are formed without a motive, so the King must here be guided by some aimful reason (*Zweckmässigkeitsgrund*) : but this reason itself resides in that quite other sphere, averted from the organisation of the State, that sphere which, in distinction from the latter's tendences, we can only term the ideal; it remains unspoken, because unutterable, and only lets itself be seen within its work, the act of Grace,—just as the motives of the idealistic artist spring no less from a law-of-aim, yet from a law which likewise cannot be expressed, but only gathered from the fully fashioned artwork.*—It is obvious, be it said in passing, that this lofty freedom can dwell in none but a legitimate Prince: whereas the prince to whom there hangs a shade of usurpation, has fallen beneath the law of vulgar expedience, and in each resolve he must ever keep a watch upon his personal hard-fought interests; wherefore he resembles an artist who fain would pass for something other than he is, and thus must see himself compelled to employ the Expedient for all his fashionings — a means which neither can produce an artwork, nor a work of Grace.

The right of Grace, as characterised above, is the type of every normal function of the King within the State, and he is every inch a King only when in all his acts he shews himself controlled by that unwritten law of Grace; wherefore his each decision, too, is rightly announced as flowing from his "most gracious motion" ("*allergnädigster Bewegung*"), and even the term "his pleasure"† very aptly designates the frame in which the King resolves : a tyrant

* That our professors of æsthetics fain would undertake this, notwithstanding, merely proves how far they stand from even the bare perception of the problem; a sufficient explanation of the muddle in which they jog along from book to book.—R. WAGNER.

† "*Geruhung*," derived from "*Ruhe*," "rest," or "tranquillity"; it is in this sense that Wagner says the term cannot apply to the "tyrant," who must always be "uneasy."—TR.

cannot "please."—Just as Grace is the highest expression of benignity, here carried even to compassion for the evil-doer, so it preserves this character in face of all the decisions of the civil power, which can never deal with anything beyond the publicly-useful; where these latter own themselves entirely impotent, the King goes on before them with his example of compassionateness, to draw the moral movement of the burgher-world directly into his sphere of Grace. In like manner he draws into his sphere the public merits of the burgher, so soon as ever they amount to purely-human virtue, either transcending the immediate object of the State, or no longer to be re-quisitioned for its service. The bestowal of an *order* does not mean the rewarding of an official's normal merit, but the recognition, and the bringing to the recognition of others, of services that exceed the imperative claims of the mere law of utility. The order conferred on military men sets a mark upon the virtue of valour, with its accompany-ing higher grade of discretion and personal sacrifice: the soldier who has thoroughly fulfilled his duty, in and for itself, merely attracts the attention of the military authori-ties, and they take note of the fact for his further em-ployment, in accordance with their only guiding pre-cept of expedience. The ideal import of this bestowal of an order may be very plainly perceived in the frequent in-stance of whole regiments having earned the highest meed of valour by their joint and free-willed sacrifice, when one must accord to every individual an equal claim to highest recognition: in this case the entire regiment has been en-nobled by the simple expedient of decorating one member with the order, a member whom the regiment itself has singled in accordance with the unspeakable law of Grace.

Analogously, the favour of the King exalts from every sphere of civic and social organisations those persons whose achievements or capacities surpass the common standard of requirements erected for mere utilitarian ends, those persons who thereby enter of themselves the sphere of Grace, i.e. of active freedom, and makes them in a true

and noble sense his peers.—But the idea, at any rate
originally inherent in the institution of Orders, would
never come to operative life in all its purity until these
orders ceased to mean a mere symbolic decoration, but
consisted in truly active fellowships, as at their first inception. The idea indeed is still extant, and is expressed
herein :—as the King is the foremost bearer of the highest
grade of orders, so is he considered the Grand Master of an
actual lodge (*Ordenskörper*).   In the case of certain higher
and exclusive orders, in fact, all the usages and functions
of a closer fellowship are still preserved : but no one who
reflects will have much difficulty in doubting that any true
and active vital spirit is here expressed, either in the relations of the members to one another, or in their relations
to the order's Master or the remaining organisations of the
State.   In any case, the plurality and the graduated rank
of orders bear witness to the mistake into which the whole
ordinal system has fallen, owing undoubtedly to the confusion of history itself.   To her Revolution, which swept
away all orders, France has to thank the establishment of
one single, all-embracing order, the "*légion d'honneur*" :
with the State's progressive evolution, every country will
be obliged at last to follow the very proper example of
France, in this point of the consolidation of its orders.*
For if a Prince chose even now to found an order with the
significance of a league conferring active rights in return for
active duties, must not all the special orders—sprung from
times and tendences quite other, and merely lingering on
as lifeless, often senseless baubles—so lose in meaning, ay,
in estimation, as soon to dwindle clean away ?—As Grand
Master of the order we suppose, already existing *in potentiâ*
and needing only to be woken to a life of actual fellowship,
—an order whereto, exactly as in the earliest of such com-
munities, even the greatest services should entitle to admission upon nothing but a vow of continued devotion to

* The example of France could scarcely be appealed to nowadays, with its
shower of " legions of honour " upon successful tradesmen, after the Exhibition
of 1889, and its still more recent " decoration-scandals."—TR.

higher and the highest ends,—the King would be the living link between his ideal tendence and the realistic tendence of the State, and have won the atmosphere essential for his motion, a body of like - minded men, emeriti (*eximirten*), i.e. set free by their self-sacrifice from the common law of expedience, banded to serve him sans reserve, pledged fulfillers of his gracious will.

For our time and the times to come, this Order would take the meaning once possessed by the *German peerage* at the flower of its prime and toward another age's claims. One might inquire, indeed, whether the surviving German nobility—which has been obliged to abandon most of its privileges as a civic class already, but still retains a standing involuntarily acknowledged by the burgher-world as socially exempt (*eximirte*)—would not form the very fittest basis of the Order imagined by us, and thus, while furnishing the monarch with the willing initiative for that creation, rejuvenate itself for its own honour and the common weal?

As it would lead us too far afield, to devote a more minute inquiry to the point itself, we should merely wish to have given some qualified person a sufficient incitation to pursue it; and from this sketch of the general character of a fellowship exempted from the common law of utility by the pledge of joint self-sacrifice—a body whose members, supported by material wealth, may even now be found sporadically strewn in every station—we will now proceed to draw our conclusion as to the share which such a fellowship might take in raising the desolated spirit of German public art.

XIV.

It was impossible for us to indicate the degeneration into which German theatric art has fallen, in particular, without exposing the pernicious tendences and promptings whose influence had brought about that ill result : to clear the Theatre from the assumption of an absolutely vicious tendence indwelling in itself, it was indispensable to prove

that mischievous result to be a consequence of the suppres-
sion, or at least the neglect, of the good qualities inherent in
it [the Theatre]. Even for the exercise of this injurious influence we have assigned no wilfully evil motive, but simply
a misunderstanding of the German Spirit, in the very sphere
which should have been the most active to protect it. In
all our censure of the sad result we have never laid the
blame on human wickedness, but purely on human error:
to tell the truth, this error's one effect has been to keep in-
flamed the evil side of the human passions here coming
into play, albeit we have not suggested any lucid consciousness thereof, but rather superficiality and slothful love of
pleasure. We have also found it possible to discuss a relation so important, involving every section of society and
undeniably developed by our history itself, without in any
way employing the showy catchwords of a party, or the
ideas that lie beneath them : we have appealed to neither
aristocratic nor democratic, to neither liberal nor conservative, neither monarchical nor republican, to neither catholic
nor protestant interests ; but in each demand of ours we
have relied on nothing but the character of the *German
Spirit*, which we have already had occasion to define.
Though this may have remained unrecognised or been
misunderstood by those who have completely alienated
themselves from that spirit, yet in the eyes of every well-
intentioned person we hold ourselves assured of the advantage of being able to proceed in like fashion now that we
undertake, in conclusion, to shew the possibility of a
thorough reform of the evil relation investigated ; when,
as that side has stirred up the hurtful qualities, so we
attempt to rouse the good and beneficial qualities of the
social elements concerned. Moreover we shall profit by
the advantage of supposing every extant element to retain
its natural attributes, albeit capable of evolution and reform ; and this will allow us, as touching the social basis
of the State, to take that absolutely-conservative standpoint which we will call the idealistic, in opposition to the
formally realistic—which latter is no less a senseless error,

than formally-realistic Radicalism itself. Yet again, we shall enjoy the noblest and most charitable of all advantages, that of henceforth being able to keep entirely out of sight the evil aspects of existing social elements ; for we now shall most expediently assail them by drawing forth their good sides only, and trying to set them in a state of action which needs must make their evil harmless.—

The ancient German nobleman by birth, in spite of all the reduction in his political privileges, as already noted, still retains a social standing undisputed by the Feeling of the burgher ; a remark confirmed by the obvious fact that the bestowal of a patent of nobility, little as it can transform the recipient into a compeer of the old nobility by birth, is yet a cherished goal of the burgher's ambition, especially when he has made his money. The rich financier who no longer needs to carry on his business, but makes for sheer enjoyment of the leisure bought him by his wealth, seeks in the patent of nobility, so to say, a binding authorisation. One takes for granted that a lord will ply no trade. And even though the partial impoverishment of the real hereditary peerage has given things an opposite appearance, yet here again we may mark a special token of the noble : the nobleman who decides to pursue a business reckoned for sheer profit, entirely lays aside his title ; or if he enters the public service, it is with the distinct and honourable assumption that he has chosen this career because it leads to heights where attainments directed to mere utilitarian ends will be of less advantage to the State, than an independent personal character. However much these lines may cross and blend with one another, in any case the tendence of the preservation of the old nobility is plain enough : it ensures the continuance of a whole class of persons who account themselves raised by nature above the need of making for the merely useful. Now, the right-minded nobleman can find employment for his energy, in keeping with his natural bent, only when he directs it to ends so lofty as to lie far beyond the tendence of the burgher, or even of the State-official. Through this tend-

ence, ingrained as if by a Nature-necessity, he enters of
himself the sphere we have termed the virtual sphere of
royal Grace. Hence the Nobility surviving to the German
Folk, together with its Princes, would only have of its own
free-will to raise this tendence to a law incumbent on its
station, and to give that law the outspoken force of binding rules, such as pledged the oldest orders of Knights,—
when Germany would have won from a class now deemed
superfluous, nay, wellnigh harmful, a boundlessly beneficent
and active spiritual league of character. Then its already-
forced abandonment of civic privileges must be held by this
class for the sacrifice attaching to every vow of ordination ;
but a sacrifice whereby it would have secured the right of
exemption from the common law of utility, to devote its
energies to none but higher ends, ungoverned by that law.
The constant renovation of this order through the accession
of fresh members raised by royal Grace, in accordance with
the principle defined above, would set it in a beneficial
relation, at once a human link and balance, with the social
and official organisations non-exempt by nature ; and its
example would serve to spur the exempt in virtue of
mere riches, encouraging him to give to his enjoyment of
freedom from common utilitarian interests, simply based
upon material possessions, a higher meaning and a nobler
trend.

Let one imagine the general utilitarian objects of the
State never so perfectly attained, on the path of a progressive development of its organisation, yet an ample field
will always remain open to the energy of these Emeriti
[or " exempt "—*Eximirten*], for never will there lack occasion for special sacrifice. Let us suppose, however, that
the efforts of the best-organised State-forces, strained and
stimulated by a proper burgher-pride, must at last succeed
in removing all occasion for self-sacrifice to general and
purely-human ends in even matters of the moral order
of the world : to the Emeriti there would still remain a
field whereon they must feel the more committed to medi-
ative, to sacrificial energy, as it is a field on which they

have been accorded an advantage that in itself first
stamped their station as a sphere of Grace; for this
advantage consists in an 'object'-less interest, possible
to them alone, the pure enjoyment of Art and Science
in themselves. For those who rightly know its pleasures,
this advantage is so unique and blessed, that its maintenance must seem worth any sacrifice. In the past century
it was pre-eminently members of the peerage, who knew
to prize it actively. The history of the German land may
plume itself on instances. 'Twas a Saxon Count Bünau,
under whose protection our great Winckelmann enjoyed
his earliest freedom from the common cares of life, and
leisure to push his free researches in the region of artistic
learning. But only in a grand, wide-reaching sense, could
this noblest and most enviable advantage be turned to
account for the ennoblement and blessing of the Folk and
Burgher world. We will explain our meaning, with a perhaps audacious tack to our immediate object, by adducing
a warning example from history. Assuredly the world is
indebted to the free leisure of the Roman nobles, after the
extinction of the Republic had cut them off from all strictly
political activity, for the origin and nurture of a valuable
and instructive literature, notwithstanding that it cannot
compare with the creative works of the Greek spirit—without whose incitation it is not so much as thinkable, and to
which, in a measure, it bears the mere relation of a commentary: those works had issued from a living communion
of great spirits with the spirit of the Folk, particularly in
the case of the Lyric and the Tragedy. This communion
the finely-cultured Roman nobles did not seek, presumably
since they despaired of finding it: indifferent, they left the
scene of popular pleasures to gladiators, to battlers with
wild beasts; the attempt to concern themselves with
jesters they proudly left to their emancipated slaves.
History knows the foundering of these nobles, of this
people, in growing demoralisation and materialistic mud.
—At the time of the great revival of the German nation,
heralded and stimulated by the undreamt successes of the

German spirit on the realm of Drama and Music, it was all the more incumbent upon the German nobles to holdfast these successes for the ennobling of the Folk-spirit, as the contemporary development of German Constitutional-government was progressively depriving them of their former political privileges.   To-day, when this political power is even more pronouncedly crippled than then, it might perhaps be not too late for them to make a stren-uous effort to regain lost opportunities.   It would secure them a field of action of boundless benefit; for that same German Spirit which alone can yield a beauteous import to their being, is in so great straits by now—we have seen it—that we cannot but wellnigh despair of getting our lament so much as understood.

Without any beating of the bush, we will name the point where the cultured art-taste of the Emeriti, imagined and described above, would encounter that need which drives the Folk and Burgher-world to seek a transitory pleasure, a distracting entertainment: it is the Theatre.   The daily tax upon his mental forces, for the direct utilitarian ends of life, allows the burgher no purposeless preoccupation with Literature and Art: all the more need has he of recreation through a diverting entertainment, distracting in a good sense, which must cost him little or no personal preparation.   This is the need.   To answer it, the Mime at once steps in ; the public's need supplies him with a means of livelihood, as hunger helps the baker.   He knocks up his platform : behold ! the Theatre.   The whole concern is naïve and honest : the mime proffers his art, the public pays him for its entertainment.   Everything in this relation is direct : the spectator holds by what he sees and hears ; the story, or the history, here becomes for him an agreeably exciting fact : he laughs with the merry, weeps with the sad, and, suddenly aware of the deception put upon him, he claps his hands in pleased approval of the clever trick. Upon this relation, and its using for the highest ideal ends, are based the sublimest artworks of the greatest poets of all time.--It has a defect, which escapes attention in its

earliest, naïve state : its subjection to the utilitarian law of
burgher traffic prevents this relation from expressing itself
purely ; the public pays and demands, demands without
judgment or knowledge ; the mime takes his pay, and, observing with swift and accurate instinct the public's lack of
judgment, for profit's sake he gives it—not what is wholesome for it, but, like the pampered child, what tempts its
palate. Hence that confusion which, given an evil tendence, may lead the Theatre to the ruin of the Folk's best
moral qualities, of the best artistic qualities of Art itself.
We see that ruin almost reached. But upheave this root-
defect, or at least reduce it to the smallest possible power
of harm, and that relation—in whose naïvest form the
æsthetic instinct of the Folk-spirit speaks out as a genuine
social need—will offer the unique, the incomparable starting - point, replaceable by none besides, for the highest
conjoint operation of the spiritual and moral forces of a
people's soul and of its leading minds.—After all the
evidence from our prior inquiries into the ethical, as the
æsthetic import of this relation, we may now conclude by
taking in eye the possibility of a remedy for that root-
defect, which we have just exposed, in the organisation
of the modern Theatre itself.

XV.

The principle of our imagined reform of the German
Theatre, in the sense of the German spirit, we will found
upon one and the same relation, repeating itself in divers
spheres : it is that which we have discussed at length in
the relation of poet to mime, which proves itself identical
in that of the cultured Emeritus to the public proper, and
in its grandest aspect as that of the King to his Folk.
Here the realistic force of Need, there the ideal power
of supplying that which is unreachable by the highest
demands of Need. The greatest relation, that of King
to Folk, embraces all the relations like it ; wherefore, when

it is a question of bringing all these forces into conjoint action, the stimulus must issue from the King. Just as he gives the finishing touch to the utilitarian law of every social and State organisation, by securing it through his 'mere motion' the attainment of what it could not reach *in proprio motu* (*in seiner reinen Konsequenz*), so his authority must intervene wherever the law of usefulness has arrived at this point; and it therefore is presupposed, once and for all, that this point shall be reached through fittest organisation of the unhindered burgher forces of the State. Yet we are not to figure this relation as a chronologic one, but as a synchronistic, an architectonic equipoise. The view that the Useful must *first* be established, and it will *then* be time to think about the Beautiful, leads with much certainty to the second tendence never setting in at all; for it is to be anticipated that the first will by then have usurped the whole architecture of the State, as we have styled it, and consequently will have absorbed the store of force reserved for the second. No: both tendences have to work side by side, though always so that the first shall be the motive force, which propounds the problem, the second the conclusive force, which solves it. An example will make this clear. A city requires an aqueduct: this is a need whose satisfaction implies a useful end, concerning the whole city; should the burgher commune be hindered from completing the building of its conduit through failing funds, for instance, that would mean a defect in the commune's Expedience-organisation, and in the interest of its most vital principle, that of common usefulness to the town, the defect would have to be remedied by the commune's own exertions; to appeal directly to the King would be a humiliating confession of inefficient organisation, on the part of the town-commune. Whereas this one particular city, if its financial means are exhausted at the moment, should seek its natural helpers in the other cities of the land; together with these to enter an organised alliance of communes, in which all municipal utilitarian-interests should become a question of joint concern, and in power whereof all local and partial detriments should be remedied in accordance with the law of reciprocal aid and guarantee—as, for instance, in the case of fire- and life-insurance companies,—this would be the way beseeming every good organisation within the State itself. To the King there is only one appeal to make : to see to it that the aqueduct shall be *beautiful* of plan, and, just as it is useful, shall also be an ornament to the town. On the other hand, if the King wanted to erect in this selfsame town a sumptuous building designed for purely æsthetic ends, and to throw its cost on the town-community, the latter would be perfectly justified in accounting that a tyrannical proposal, a mockery of the utilitarian object of its whole organisation : nevertheless, as the King had pro-vided for the beauty of its conduit, it would not place any mere utilitarian hindrances in his path, on the score, forsooth, of this building's serving no directly useful end.

Now the Theatre, as we have seen, owes its origin to a need experienced by citizen Society, that of recreation and distraction after the strain of business toil. The actual utilitarian ground for retaining the Theatre would be adduced by all the town with great alacrity, were one to want to close its theatre for good, or even to diminish the number of performances. In this matter, as in everything else, we start from an existing practical relation. It is possible that Radical utilitarians may wish to see this relation entirely done away with, as harmful *per se* to the commonwealth—against which, to be candid, we should have nothing to advance if the Theatre were bound to keep unchanged its present tendence, and even to develop a still greater power of harm. However, as we have not placed ourselves on the utilitarian-radical, but the ideal-conserva-tive standpoint, let us hold fast to this one proved fact, that the Theatre, as a place of entertainment for the burgher population of a city, owes its origin and maintenance to a genuine need. It being a question, then, of meeting this need with services of that high character which the Theatre is proved pre-eminently capable of, but which cannot be

compassed in the sheer utilitarian traffic between Public
and Mime, no reasonable doubt can arise as to the right,
nay, the necessity of intervention on the part of the highest
power in the State, aiming as it should at the Ideal. In
fact this right and this necessity are fully recognised already,
in the standing compacts between State and Crown : only,
by neither side could the object of placing a Court-theatre
upon the royal Civil List be plainly spoken out, because
this particular State-endowment sprang from quite another
principle than the rest. When the newer Constitutions
were framed, and the finances of the State were regulated
by fixing the formerly voluntary contributions of the Crown
at their previous average figure, as the definite quantum
of a royal Civil List, one also took the sum set down at
that particular date in the accounts of the Royal Household for the maintenance of a Court-theatre and fixed it
as a permanent allowance to be made for the same purpose
in the future. Here there was no ulterior thought of the
meaning and true requirements of dramatic art, but merely
an existing factor in the royal establishment was acknowledged, and retained, as befitting the dignity of the Crown.
Through application of this sum to the superior equipment
of a theatre in the chief city of the land, the King enters
into a distinct relation with the public of that city ; but,
after as before, the public pays for admission to this theatre,
and remains at bottom in a primitive, naïve attitude towards
it, that of seeking entertainment in return for entrance-
money. We will abide by this given relation too—again
in an ideally conservative sense—though it has merely
sprung from circumstances without reflection ; and we now
will ask how it is to be made the best of, in promotion of
German dramatic art, since we have seen that its pursuance
hitherto has led to the positive ruin of that art.

Let us put the question thus : in what manner can one
effect such an ennoblement of the general taste for theatric
representations as needs must be the meaning of the royal
Grace bestowed upon the Theatre ?

Plainly, through nothing but an improvement in the

character of the representations themselves. The public is willing to fall in with everything that offers satisfaction of its natural root-needs ; excellent performances of admirable works it always receives with heightened mood and glad acknowledgment. But, with much justice, it rebels against the presumptuous attempt to teach it in an abstract, didactic fashion. An imitation of the American game of culture, which sends the servants to scientific and æsthetic lectures while the masters spend their dollars on the windfalls of the European stage, has not as yet found favour with the German public. As touching this public, the only doubt is whether it will be possible to accustom it, by the excellence of what is offered, to a more abstemious, a rarer enjoyment thereof. For only by a moderation of the quantity of theatrical performances, on the other hand, could one hope to influence the standard of their quality ; for simple reason of the leisure needful to mature and give effect to technical laws and their requirements, to say nothing of the present difficulty in imagining a worthy repertoire of adequate variety. Now as, in spite of the ideal goal we have set before us, we hold by our motto of not letting ourselves be carried into the suggestion of any sort of formally Radical tactics, to meet the aforesaid evil we should merely wish to see an adoption of palliative measures such as would recommend themselves to everyone as being in the true, and even the commercial interest of a number of theàtres subsisting in one city side by side; and these measures must necessarily result in a reduction of the sum-total of theatric representations.

Upon this path, however, were progress never so willingly helped onward in all quarters, it yet might lead to merely feeble possibilities of raising the general spirit of theatric doings : a decisive transformation could be compassed only through the force of a sufficiently-repeated *example* of the effect of doings excellent in every respect. This is impossible of attainment in the daily intercourse of Theatre and Public, particularly upon a basis of commercial interests—at least, impossible with the existing relations of

German theatres in general. That example can be given only upon a soil exempt from all the needs and necessitations of a daily traffic, upon a soil which nowhere can be found but in the sphere of what we have termed, in a broader sense, the royal Grace. Its primary condition is, that each and everything shall be *out of the ordinary* ; and, in the first instance, that can be ensured by nothing but a greater rarity. We do not propose to stop and characterise this out-of-the-ordinary-ness through a criticism of the unsuccessful efforts already made in that direction, as this is not at all the place to specify the technical requirements for the realisation of our idea: we will merely mention that all previous so-called " model performances " (" *Mustervorstellungen* ") have never really quit the soil of daily traffic of the stage, have simply distinguished themselves by a heaping-up and setting-together of ordinary theatric virtuosities, and as such have been accepted. On the contrary, the truly regal performances we mean, to be given at rarer intervals, would bear the following characteristic marks. Once for all, only such dramatic works would there be represented as really make it possible to evolve and perfect a hitherto entirely-lacking *German style*, on the field of living Drama : by this Style we understand *the attainment of thorough harmony between the stage-representation and the truly German poet-works performed, and the raising of that harmony to a fundamental law*. Through a most careful employment of existing histrionic talents, to be assembled expressly for this purpose, and starting with the representation of existing truly German works, one would advance to the instigation of new works adapted for a like standardising of Style. The commercial tendence in the intercourse of Theatre and Public would here be wholly done away with : the spectator, led no longer by the need of distraction after the day's exertions, but by that of collection (*Sammlung*) after the distractions of an infrequent holiday, would enter the special art-building—remote from his wonted nightly haven of entertainment, and opened only for the purpose

of these un-ordinary, these 'exempt' performances—he
would enter it to forget, in a nobler sense, the toil of life,
for sake of life's supernal ends.

We have hinted enough, to permit the kindly reader to
judge for himself the influence and ultimate effect of our
invoked Example, upon theatric art, upon the spirit of our
poets, on the spirit of Art in general, and thereby on the
fashioning of a Life which shall truly bring the German
soul to show.

As cap to our now-ended inquiries, we beg to be allowed
a brief, but broader survey.

When Prussia was setting about the overthrow of the
Bund, she spoke of her *German calling*.   Now that Bavaria
is bracing herself to turn her new position to honourable
account, her statesmen make no less appeal to the in-
cumbence of a German calling.   What may that calling
be?   Surely it is the meaning of her Ministers, to form
of her a model German State; whereto she is alike compelled by the cotemporaneous pressure of her inner social
needs, and qualified by her position on the map, hemmed
in, but central and secure.   And what spirit alone can
serve to mould this German model State, to make of it a
pattern for the others?—When the Prussian Crown drove
three old princely houses from their ancient homes, it
advanced the utilitarian plea*: with the utmost, wellnigh
appalling energy, it laid bare thereby the inmost spirit of
the Prussian system, that creation of Frederick the Great's
which we characterised before.   To what goal would it
lead Bavaria, if in the progressive organising of her State
she dogged the footsteps of the Prussian State?   Necessarily, to a point where both would meet some day, and

---

* Schleswig-Holstein, Hanover, and Hesse-Nassau; the annexation had
been ratified by the Prussian Landtag about a year before these articles were
first published, i.e. late in 1866.--Tr.

clash with one another : the stronger utilitarian plea would
then prevail once more ; and on which side must the
verdict fall ?   Were it not therefore an end utilitarian
above all others, that the Bavarian State in all its organisations should keep steadfastly in eye that beyond all ends
of utility there lies a high Ideal ; and that only in so far
as Bavaria approaches that Ideal, can she still fulfil a
German calling by the side of Prussia ?   If the Prussian
Crown has to keep sharp watch from above, lest anywhere
or anywhen it should lose sight of the utilitarian law ; and
if it must even trim its Grace to fit the mandates of that
law : would not Bavaria have to pursue its utilitarian
object from below, and carry it to such a lofty pitch, that
the fulfilled utilitarian law should permanently ensure the
Crown the freest exercise of Grace ?   Even Prussia must,
and will, perceive that it was the German Spirit, in its
rebound against French despotism, that gave her once the
power she now directs by nothing but utilitarianism : here,
then, will be the right point at which—for the weal of all—
a happy guidance of the Bavarian State may bring the two
together.   But, this point alone : there is no other prospering.   And this is the *German Spirit* : about which it is
easy to talk and boast in nothing-saying phrases ; but
which is visible to our sight, and sensible to our feeling,
only in the ideal uprise of the great authors of German
Rebirth in the past century.   And to give this Spirit a
fitting habitation in the system of the German State, so
that in free self-knowledge it may manifest itself to all the
world, is tantamount to establishing the best and only
lasting Constitution.

APPENDIX TO "GERMAN ART AND GERMAN POLICY."

As certain foolish people have lately made it a charge against Richard Wagner, that he did not include in the Collected Works his now celebrated Vaterlandsverein (Fatherland Club) Speech, delivered on June 14th, 1848, I deem the present a fitting opportunity for translating it. Whether our author knew not where to procure a copy, at the time of issuing the Ges. Schr., whether he considered it an insufficiently digested product, and so forth, I cannot presume to say—but it is astonishing to find how similar are his views, as expressed in 1848, to those of 1867 : in no substantial principle do they differ ; merely maturity has brought a riper mildness.

The Speech was published as supplement to a short-lived news-paper, the Dresdener Anzeiger, *of June 16th 1848 ; the original being inaccessible, at least in London, I have followed Wilhelm Tappert's German reprint of 1883 ; the italics are as given by Herr Tappert, and obviously existed in the original.*

To the Speech itself I have thought it well to couple a letter written four days later by Wagner to von Lüttichau, Intendant of the Dresden Court-theatre, as it sets forth not only the external circumstances, but also the internal motives of the Speech.

· ————

WHAT RELATION BEAR REPUBLICAN ENDEAVOURS TO THE KINGSHIP?

Let us become quite clear upon this question, and therefore settle in the first place : what is the gist of Republican efforts.

Do ye seriously believe that, if we mean to push onward from our present standpoint, we must promptly arrive at a bare King-less Republic? Do ye believe this, or merely wish to foist untruth upon the nervous? Are ye ignorant, or are ye evil-willed?

I will tell you the aim of our by all means "Republican"

efforts : our efforts *for the good of all* make for treating the so-called attainments of the immediate past, not as a *goal* in themselves, but as a *beginning*.

The goal taken firmly in eye, then, we wish first to see *the extinction of the last glimmer of aristocratism*; as our gentlemen of the nobility no longer are feudal lords with power to enslave and clout us as they please, so, to wipe out all offence, they should give up the last remnant of a distinction which some sultry day might easily become a shirt of Nessus, burning them to the very bone, had they not cast it far away from them betimes. Should ye recall your ancestors and hold it impious to discard the privileges inherited from them, reflect that we, as well, have memories of our forefathers, whose deeds—and good deeds too !—have not been written down by us in family-archives, but whose sufferings, bondage, oppression and thraldom of every kind, stand inscribed with ink of blood upon the great unerring *records of the History of the last millennium.* If ye forget your fathers, if ye cast off every title, every smallest token of distinction, then we promise to be generous and strike the recollection of *our* fathers completely from our memory, that henceforth we may all be children of *one* father, brethren of *one* family ! Hear ye the admonition, fulfil it gladly and of your own accord ; for it is past dismissing, and Christ says : " If a limb offend thee, cut it off and cast it from thee : for it is profitable for thee that one of thy members should perish, and not that thy whole body should be cast into hell."

And once again ! Renounce for good and all the exclusive honour of standing nighest to our prince ; beseech him to release you from the whole useless tangle of court-offices, the rights and privileges that make a Court to-day the object of impatient glances ; be no more Lords and Pages of the Chamber, who call our King "*their* King" ; take from him those heyducs and those motley lackeys, the frivolous outcrop of an evil time, the time when every prince throughout the world believed he must copy the French Louis XIV. Stand free of this Court, the court of idle sustenance for nobles, that it may become a court of the whole blithe happy Folk, where every member of that people through its joyous deputies may smile upon its prince (*Fürst*), may tell him he is First of a free Folk !

Therefore we further wish : *no longer a First Chamber* ! The Folk is but *one*, and accordingly there can and should be but *one* sole House of the people's Deputies ; and that house should be but one noble, simple building, a lofty dome on strong and shapely pillars : how ye would mutilate this building, did ye drive a trivial party-wall straight through it, that in lieu of one great chamber ye might have two dwarfed ones !

Further, we want assigned to every adult *human being,** born in the land, the unconditional right of vote and franchise ; the poorer, the needier he is, the more natural is his claim to share in framing the laws that henceforth are to shield him against poverty and neediness.

And further, in our " Republican " endeavours, we want *one great and general Volkswehr* (Folk-levy), not a standing Army and a recumbent Communal Guard : what ye prepare, should neither be a lessening of the one, nor a mere enlarging of the other ; but a new creation, which, stepping little by little into life, shall let both Communal Guard and Army dissolve into the one efficient *Volkswehr*, abolishing each class-distinction.

When all the classes hitherto at enmity, and parcelled off by envy, have been united in the one great class of the free Folk, embracing all that on the dear German soil has received its human breath from God,—think ye we then shall have reached our goal ? No, then shall we first begin in earnest ! For then must be taken firmly and deedfully in eye *the question of the root of all the misery in our present social state,*—then must be decided whether Man, that crown of the Creation, whether his lofty spiritual, his artistically stirring bodily powers and forces, were meant by God to serve in menial bondage to the stubbornest, the most lifeless product in all Nature, to sallow *metal*?

It will have to be settled whether this minted matter is to be accorded the right of making the king of Nature, the express image of God, its servitor and tributary,—whether Money is to be left the power of stunting the fair free Will of Man to the most repulsive passion, to avarice, to usury and the sharper's itch ? This will be the great War of Liberation for deep-dishonoured, suffering mankind : not one drop of blood, not a single tear, nay, not one deprivation will it cost : merely one conviction shall we have to gain, and that will thrust itself upon us past withstanding : the conviction *that it must bring about the highest happiness, the perfect*

* " *Menschen* "—italicised : apparently to include both man and *woman*.— TR.

wellbeing of all, if as many vigorous human beings as ever the soil of Earth can nourish, combine in well-ordered unions, through exchange of the products of their various and manifold abilities, to mutually enrich and benefit each other.* We shall recognise it as the most sinful state for a human Society to be in, when the energy of individuals is pronouncedly hampered, when available forces can neither move in freedom nor thoroughly expend themselves; providing always—and this is the only reservation—the earthly soil is broad enough to yield them nurture. We shall perceive that Human Society is maintained by the *activity of its members*, and not through any fancied agency of *money*: in clear conviction shall we found the *principle*—God will give us light to find the rightful *law* to put it into practice; and like a hideous nightmare will this demoniac idea of Money vanish from us, with all its loathsome retinue of open and secret usury, paper-juggling, percentage and bankers' speculations. That will be the *full emancipation of the human race*; that will be the *fulfilment of Christ's pure teaching*, which enviously they hide from us behind parading dogmas, invented erst to bind the simple world of raw barbarians, to prepare them for a development towards whose higher consummation we now must march in lucid consciousness. Or does this smack to you of *Communism*? Are ye foolish or ill-disposed enough to declare the necessary redemption of the human race from the flattest, most demoralising servitude to vulgarest matter, synonymous with carrying out the most preposterous and senseless doctrine, that of Communism? Can ye not see that this doctrine of a mathematically-equal division of property and earnings is simply an unreasoning attempt to solve that problem, at any rate dimly apprehended, and an attempt whose sheer impossibility itself proclaims it stillborn? But would

---

* "Die Ueberzeugung, *dass es das höchste Glück, das vollendetste Wohlergehen Aller herbeiführen muss, wenn so viele thätige Menschen, als nur irgend der Erdboden ernähren kann, auf ihm sich vereinigen, um in wohlvergliederten Vereinen durch ihre verschiedenen mannigfaltigsten Fähigkeiten, im Austausch ihrer Thätigkeit sich gegenseitig zu bereichern und zu beglücken.*" The last half of this clause is somewhat difficult to render into English, chiefly owing to the expression " *im Austausch ihrer Thätigkeit,*" which I have translated " through exchange of the products of their " &c., whereas it strictly means "in exchange of their activity," or " of their energy"; the idea, of course, is that of a ' distribution of labour.'—The next sentence is obviously allied to the first Napoleon's famous maxim : " *la carrière ouverte aux talents.*"—TR.

ye denounce therewith the task itself for reprehensible and insane, as that doctrine of a surety is? *Have a care!* The outcome of three-and-thirty years of unruffled peace shews you Human Society in such a state of dislocation and impoverishment, that, at end of all those years, ye have on every hand the awful spectacle of pallid Hunger! Look to it, or e'er it be too late! Give no *alms*, but acknowledge a *right*, the God-given *right of Man*, lest ye live to see the day when outraged Nature will gird herself for a battle of brute force, whose savage shout of victory were *of a truth that Communism*; and though the radical impossibility of its continuance should yield it but the briefest spell of reign, that short-lived reign would yet have sufficed to root up every trace, perchance for many an age to come, of the achievements of two thousand years of civilisation. Think ye, I *threaten*? Nay, I *warn*!—

When our Republican endeavours shall have brought us as far as an answer to these weightiest of all questions, to the happiness and wellbeing of the social State (*der staatlichen Gesellschaft*); when we have entered fully on the rights of man's free dignity: shall we then have reached our journey's end? No! Then first will come the true beginning! When arrived at the complete rebirth of man's Society, through a legislative answer to the last Emancipation question; when thence there springs a free new race, brought up to fullest exercise of all its energies: then first shall we have won the strength to march towards the highest tasks of Civilisation—its *activation and its spread*. Then will we take ship across the sea, plant here and there a fresh young Germany, befruit it with the outcome of our toils and struggles, beget and bring up noblest children, children like unto the gods. Better will we manage than the *Spaniards*, to whom the new world became a papal slaughterhouse, otherwise than the English, who have made thereof a peddler's tray. We will do things *Germanly* and grandly; from its rising to its setting the sun shall look upon a beautiful free Germany, and on the borders of the daughter-lands, as on the frontiers of their mother, no downtrod, unfree folk shall dwell; the rays of *German freedom* and *German gentleness* (Milde) shall light and warm the French and Cossacks, the Bushman and Chinese.

Look ye! our Republican ardour has here no goal nor end; unresting it forges on, from century to century, for blessing of the whole wide race of Man! Is this a dream, Utopia? It is, if we only bandy it to and fro, half-hearted and self-seeking balance and dispute its possibility: it is *not*, if only we act in buoyant courage, if every day beholds us do a new good *deed* of progress.

But ye ask: wouldst reach this all, and *with* the Kingship?— Not an instant have I had to leave its preservation out of sight,— but held *ye* it for impossible, 't would be yourselves had uttered its death-warrant! Should ye, however, be bound to recognise its possibility, as I perceive its more than possibility, then our Republic were indeed the right one, and merely we durst ask *the King to be the first and sterlingest Republican of all.* And who is more called to be the *truest, faithfulest* Republican, than just the *Prince*? RESPUBLICA means: the affairs of the nation. What individual can be more destined than the Prince, to belong with all his feelings, all his thoughts and actions, *entirely to the Folk's affairs*? Once persuaded of his glorious calling, what could move him to belittle himself, to cast in his lot with one exclusive *smaller* section of his Folk? However warmly each of us may respond to feelings for the good of all, so pure a Republican as the Prince can he never be, for *his* cares are undivided: their eye is single to the One, the Whole; whilst each of us must needs divide and parcel out his cares, to meet the wants of everyday.

And in what would consist the Prince's sacrifice, in answer to his recognised, his unspeakably beautiful calling? Could he account it a sacrifice, to see no longer in the State's free citizens his "*subjects*"? Through the fact of our laws, that notion is already done away with; and *he*, who ratified those laws, fulfils their spirit with such lealty, that the *announcement* of subjection's surcease would seem no more to him a sacrifice. Must it rank in his eyes as a sacrifice, to put away those relics of an idle Court-parade, its superannuated honours, its outlived titles and orders? How poorly should we judge the simplest, truest prince in all our age, did we reckon as his sacrifice the accomplishment of such a wish; when we may safely assume that even an actual sacrifice would willingly be brought by him, if he saw in it the removal of a hindrance to free outflow of his people's love?

What authorises us to grasp so deep into the soul of this rare prince, to express convictions about him, such as we might scarce deem prudent in regard of many a burgher on an equal footing with ourselves?—'Tis the spirit of our age, 'tis the unprecedented hap of things, as brought by the Present into light of day, and gifting even the homeliest man with prophet's range of vision. Decision's urgence stands before us: two camps are pitched among the civilised nations of Europe: here rings the cry *Republic*! there *Monarchy*! Can ye deny that this question is pressing for determinate answer, that it holds within it whatsoever convulses human society to its deepest roots? Would ye misprise the spirit of this God-appointed time, aver that this all had taken place before, and, once the fit of madness over, that things would put on their old shape again? Then to all eternity would God have smitten you with blindness!

No! we recognise not only the hour, but the necessity, for *decision*: the thing that is a lie, can not endure; and Monarchy, i.e. the *Rule of One* (die Alleinherrschaft), is a lie, become such through our Constitutionalism. Now, when he who quite despairs of reconcilement is boldly and defiantly throwing himself into the arms of the red Republic, the man who still hopes directs a last inquiring glance to the peaks of the Existing. He sees that, if war is declared against Monarchy, only in special cases will it be waged against the *person of the Prince*, but in every case against the *party* that selfishly uplifts the Prince upon its shield; beneath whose shadow it fights for its own privilege, of profit or of vanity. This *party*, then, is what has to be vanquished: is the fight to be a bloody one? It must be, it must strike at like time at Party and Prince, if there be left no means of reconcilement. But we conceive that means to be the Prince himself: is he the genuine free Father of his Folk, then with a single high-hearted resolve he can plant peace where war seems unavoidable. Now, if we seek upon the thrones of Europe the prince whom God has chosen to fulfil the fair and lofty work,—what do we behold? What a purblind, deep-degenerated race, unfit for any higher calling! What spectacle is offered us by Spain, Portugal, Naples? What sorrow fills us when we look upon the German countries, Hanover, Hesse, Bavaria*—ah! let us close the vista! God has passed his sen-

---

* King Ludwig I. of Bavaria had abdicated on March 20th, 1848, partly owing to the scandal about Lola Montez, the Spanish dancer, but chiefly in disgust at Ultramontane opposition. At Munich, where the first Ludwig's memory was still cherished by the people, Wagner learnt to form a different estimate of his character: see page 63.—TR.

tence on the weak and wicked: their weakness waxeth from generation to generation.*

We turn our eyes away from distance, we raise them in our home again, and *there we see a prince whom his people loves*, not in the mere sense of old-traditional allegiance to his family, no! *of pure love for himself, for his ownest I.* We love him because he is what he is, we love his pure virtue, his high sense of honour, his probity, his clemency. So from a full heart I cry aloud in joy:—

That is the man of Providence.

If Prussia wills to maintain a monarchy, 'tis for sake of the idea (*Begriff*) of Prussiandom: a vain idea, that soon will be exploded! If Austria wills to retain its prince, in his dynasty it perceives the only means of holding an unnatural conglomerate of lands together: an impossible union, that soon will fall to pieces!—But if the Saxon wills the Kingship, he is prompted before all else by *pure affection for his prince*, by the happy knowledge that he may call this Best his own: here is no cold and calculating State-*idea*,—'tis the full warm *confidence of Love*. And this Love, it shall decide; not for now alone, can it decide, *for henceforth and forever*! Filled with this thought, of weight past telling, I cry with all the courage of conviction: *We are Republicans*, through the accomplished facts of our age we are on the verge of a republic; but delusions and offences of all kinds still hang around that name,—let them be banished by *one* word of our dear prince! Not we, will proclaim the republic, no! *this prince, the noblest, worthiest King, let him speak out:*—

"**I declare Saxony a Free State.**"

And let the earliest law of this Free State, the edict giving it the fairest surety of endurance, be:—

"*The highest executive power rests in the* **Royal House of Wettin**, *and descends therein from generation to generation, by right of primogeniture.*"

The oath which we swear to this State and this edict, will never be broken: not *because* we have sworn it (how many an oath is sworn in the unthinking joy of taking office!) but because we have sworn it in full *assurance* that *through that proclamation, through that law, a new era of undying happiness has dawned, of*

* "Gott sprach sein Urtheil über die Schlechten und Schwachen: ihre Schwäche wuchs von Glied zu Glied."

utmost benefit, of most determinant presage, not alone for Saxony, no ! for Germany, for Europe. He who thus boldly has expressed his enthusiasm, believes with all his heart that never was he *more loyal* to the oath he, too, has sworn his King, than when he penned these lines to-day.

Now, would this have brought about the downfall of the *Monarchy* ? Ay ! But it would have published the *emancipation of the Kinghood.* Dupe not yourselves, ye who want a " Constitutional Monarchy upon the broadest democratic basis." As regards the latter (the basis), ye either are dishonest, or, if in earnest, ye are slowly torturing your artificial Monarchy (*die künstlich von Euch gepflegte Monarchie*) to death. Each step forward, upon that democratic basis, is a fresh encroachment on the power of the Mon-arch, i.e. the *sole*-ruler ; the principle itself is the completest mockery of Monarchy, which is conceivable only as actual *alone*-ruling : each advance of Constitutionalism is a humiliation to the ruler, for it is a vote of want-of-confidence in the monarch. How shall love and confidence prevail, amid this constant, this often so unworthily manœuvred contest twixt two opposing principles ? The very existence of the monarch, as such, is embittered by shame and mortification. Let us therefore redeem him from this miserable half-life ; let us have done altogether with Monarchism, since Sole-rule is made impossible by just the principle of Folk's-rule (Democracy) : but let us, on the contrary, emancipate the *Kinghood* in its fullest, its own peculiar meaning ! At head of the Free State (the republic) the hereditary King will be exactly what he should be, in the noblest meaning of his title [*Fürst*] : *the First of the Folk, the Freest of the Free* ! Would not this be alike the fairest commentary upon Christ's saying : " And whosoever of you will be the chiefest, shall be servant of all " ? Inasmuch as he serves the freedom of all, in his person he raises the concept of Freedom itself to the loftiest, to a God-implanted consciousness.

The farther back we search among Germanic nations for the Kinghood's meaning, the more intimately will it fit this new-won meaning, and prove it strictly naught but re-established ; the historic cycle of the Kinghood's evolution will have reached at last its goal, have rounded back upon itself, and we shall have to look on *Monarchism*, that foreign and un-German notion, as the farthest aberration from that goal.

For this outspoken, heartfelt wish, ought we to gather signatures in form of a Petition? Certain am I that hundreds of thousands would sign it, for its purport offers reconciliation to all conflicting parties, at least to those among them who mean honestly. But one sign-manual alone can be the right and crucial, here : *that of our beloved Prince,* to whom with fervour of conviction we wish a fairer lot, a happier station, than that assigned him now.

Dresden, June 14th, 1848.

A MEMBER OF THE VATERLANDSVEREIN.

As said above, this Speech was succeeded on June 18th, 1848, by the following letter, from Wagner to von Lüttichau.

YOUR EXCELLENCY,

Obediently I crave the favour of a leave of absence, perchance for fourteen days, in order to undergo the necessary treatment for a gastric trouble which appears to be threatening me.*

At like time I consider it my personal duty to justify myself in regard of a step, which had absolutely no relation to my artistic office, but with respect to which I should wish not to be misunderstood, above all by yourself.

At a time when the right is accorded even to the most uneducated person, to utter his opinions on the drift of current events, the educated feel all the more bound to exercise such right. The party friction of the past fortnight has forced the opposing views of dwellers in our city to such a climax, that no onlooker could escape a painful tension. For my part, I joined that Club (*Verein*) in which the party of Progress is the most decided in its utterances : firstly, because I recognise that the party of Progress is the party of the Future ; but secondly, from the consideration that it is this party that needs the most to be restrained by temperate thought from raw excesses. I have seldom attended these gatherings, and never mixed in their debates, but merely looked on ; and thus in the last few days I came to the con-

* The *Letters to Uhlig* shew how frequently Wagner suffered from this trouble and its cognate maladies ; his water-cures, &c., supply the matter for many a page.—TR.

K

clusion that, precisely through the violent attacks of the so-called
Monarchists, a defiant spirit had there begun to manifest itself in
a more and more hazardous fashion. In the declaration that a
Republic is the best form of State, there is, according to present
ideas, no crime *per se;* but the corollary of the idea of a Republic,
in the minds of the generality, is the belief in the necessity of
doing away with the Kingship. I had nowhere seen any speaker
or political writer grasp the notion that the Kinghood could
remain the hallowed centre round which each popular institution
might be erected; but, with the idea of a Republic there was
always closely knit the assumption of a ceasing of the Kingship.
It therefore was this assumption alone, that held back the masses
and their leaders from at once deciding for the introduction of
that form of State; but folk coupled it with all manner of conditions, in which there certainly was nothing criminal uttered, though
they might, and must, lead to every conceivable misconstruction.
Hence it lay at my heart to shew these people clearly, once for
all, that whatever attainable thing we strove for, yet the Kingship
itself was not immediately opposed to such endeavours: that with
the Kingship, in fact, all might be very well attained, and would
only prove more lasting.

To the People's party the existing aspect of the Court, with all
its survivals from an earlier age, is a vexation of spirit. In this
regard I have heard expressions used, and by persons who in
nowise belong exclusively to the most unpolished classes, which
have given me a deep glimpse into the spirit of the Folk. Their
upshot is somewhat this: Were the King away, we were rid of
this Court! I now ask myself: Should the Kingship itself be
imperilled for sake of such externals? No! They well might
vanish, and with them a source of the discontent that at last is
becoming fastened on the King himself. Under these circumstances, and following this line of thought, I weighed the whole
real matter of attack, and arrived at the conclusion that, were *this*
abolished, then all the ill-humour against the Kingship would
vanish too. Hence it was natural that the wish should rise in me,
to convince both parties, alike Monarchists and Republicans, of
the truth of the opinion to which I had come, and, if I succeeded
in that, to incline both parties to one common goal: the maintenance of the Kingship, and therewith of the land's internal
peace. At like time it must be my object to make clear the noble

meaning of the word "Republic," so little understood by its own party, and then to shew that in it the Kingship first would find its fairest setting. This wish alone impelled me to the writing of that essay; and if, to reach my desired conclusion, I was forced to strike at the existing, here and there, yet the fear of making enemies ought not to prevent me from speaking out a deeply-felt conviction, whose aim was not discord, but peace and unity. The warmth of that conviction must bear the blame that I went so far as to champion it in my own person. Upon entering the Club the other day, I heard once more those phrases that perpetually connect the idea of a Republic, which of late has undeniably become the chief topic of a large section of the people, directly with the abolition of the Kingship. In full assurance that now, of all times, I should be speaking a good and beneficial thought to this assembly, I swiftly resolved to at once read out my essay; and even supposing that step had been bare of any good intention, yet *one* it undeniably fulfilled: for never in that Club was there uttered so enthusiastic a eulogy of our King, nor ever received with such acclamation, as greeted the passage of my speech wherein I praised his lofty virtues.

Now, it is precisely this applause, as also its ground, that has woken me jealous enemies. I will not here give further vent to my opinion of many of these popular leaders,—it fills me with the gloomiest apprehensions, since especially my enthusiasm for the Kingship has displeased them. What I hear from this side might well be indifferent to me personally; but the case is otherwise, if I must fear that I have been completely misunderstood by the other side, if even the King, how unpractical soever he might deem the formal aspect of my plan, should see some sinister purpose in my endeavour to hold before a most prosaically-guided throng a poetic image of how I pictured to myself the Kingship. I admit that I now am heartily perturbed to see from various tokens that, as a matter of fact, I have been misunderstood: therein I recognise the danger, in these times, of speaking out an independent thought, and such as does not fully bear the hallmark of one party or the other; and it did not need the entreaties of my wife, to win my promise never again to take a personal part in questions of the day. To my great distress, I see that it no longer is the season for fighting with the weapons of the spirit; a gloomy, a terrible foreboding invades my mind, that the war will

soon be waged by the raw element of the Masses only.   We have
Prague not far from us ; in Austria horrible things are under way,
things which easily may take a regicidal turn.   Into the mass of
Dresden's population I have also cast a glance : nothing criminal
lurks therein to-day ; but who shall answer for the storm of
madness, when once it spreads from outside to our home ?

In this anxiety, this deep concern, I believed the aforesaid step
would ease my mind : in my sincere conviction it seemed to me
the fittest path of reconcilement.   Now, if my black forebodings
were ungrounded,—O, much the better ! If, on the other hand, my
step has stirred but bitterness, then has it not fulfilled its aim.
Has it not *reconciled*, but *only* wounded—at least it sprang from
an illusion, for which I heartily crave forgiveness from everyone I
may have wounded.

Yours, in greatest esteem,

RICHARD WAGNER.

WHAT IS GERMAN?

Was ist deutsch?

For a similar reason as in the case of the Vaterlandsverein Speech, I have chosen "Was ist deutsch?" *to follow after* "German Art and German Policy." *The author's introductory note explains the intimate connexion of the two articles.*

"Was ist deutsch?" *was evidently written, either entirely or in part, towards the* end *of* 1865; *for the review of C. H. Bitter's* "Johann Sebastian Bach," *quoted on page* 163, *appeared in the Augsburg* Allgemeine Zeitung *of September* 22nd 1865.

The article itself was first printed in the second Number of the Bayreuther Blätter, *namely for February* 1878. *It was reprinted in the last, i.e. the tenth, volume of Richard Wagner's* Gesammelte Schriften, 1883, *the contents whereof were collected by Baron Hans von Wolzogen soon after the author's death.*

Translator's Note.

HEN lately searching through my papers, I found in disconnected paragraphs a manuscript of the year 1865 ; to-day, at wish of my younger friend and colleague in the publication of the " Bayreuther Blätter," I have decided to hand over the greater portion for issue to our more distant friends of the Patronatverein.

If the question " What is German ? " was in itself so hard for me to answer, that I did not presume to include the all-unfinished article in the Collected Edition of my writings, my recent difficulty has been the matter of selection ; for several of the points discussed in these paragraphs had already been treated by me at greater length in other essays, particularly in that on " German Art and German Policy." May this be my apology for the present article's shortcomings. In any case I have still to close the train of thought I then sketched out ; and that close—to which, after thirteen years of fresh experience, I have certainly to give a colour of its own—will this time be my final word upon the sadly earnest theme.—

It has often weighed upon my mind, to gain a clear idea of what is really to be understood by the expression " *deutsch* " [" German "].

It is a commonplace of the Patriot's, to introduce his nation's name with unconditional homage ; the mightier a nation is, however, the less store it seems to set on repeating its own name with all this show of reverence. It happens seldomer in the public life of England and France, that people speak of " English " and " French virtues " ; whereas the Germans are always appealing to " German depth," " German earnestness," " German fidelity " (*Treue*) and the like. Unfortunately it has become patent, in very

151

many cases, that this appeal was not entirely founded; yet we haply should do wrong to suppose that the qualities themselves are mere figments of the imagination, even though their name be taken in vain. It will be best to seek upon the path of History the meaning of this idiosyncrasy of the Germans.

The word "deutsch," according to the latest and most profound researches, is not a definite Folk's name; in history there has been no people that could claim the original title "Deutsche." Jacob Grimm, on the contrary, has proved that "diutisk" or "deutsch" means nothing more than what is homelike to ourselves, "ourselves" being those who parley in a language mutually intelligible. It was early set in contrast with the "wälsch," whereby the Germanic races signify the "proper to the Gaels and Kelts." The word "deutsch" reappears in the verb "deuten" [to "point, indicate, or explain"]: thus "deutsch" is what is plain (*deutlich*) to us, the familiar, the wonted, inherited from our fathers, racy of our soil. Now it is a striking fact, that the peoples remaining on this side of the Rhine and Alps began to call themselves by the name of "*Deutsche*" only after the Goths, Vandals, Franks and Lombards had established their dominion in the rest of Europe. Whilst the "Franks" spread their name over the whole great conquered land of Gaul, but the races left on the hither side of the Rhine consolidated themselves into Saxons, Bavarians, Swabians and East-Franks, it is at the division of the empire of Karl the Great [Charlemagne] that the name "Deutschland" makes its first appearance; and that as collective-name for all the races who had stayed this side the Rhine. Consequently it denotes those peoples who, remaining in their ancestral seat, continued to speak their ure-mother-tongue, whereas the races ruling in Romanic lands gave up that mother-tongue. It is to the speech and the ure-homeland, then, that the idea of "*deutsch*" is knit; and there came a time when these "Deutschen" could reap the advantage of fidelity to their homeland and their speech, for from the bosom of that home there sprang for centuries the ceaseless renovation and freshening of the soon decaying outland races. Moribund and weakened dynasties were recruited from the primal stock of home. To the enfeebled Merovingians succeeded the East-Frankish Carlovingians; from the degenerate Carlovingians, in their turn, Saxons and Swabians took the sceptre of the German lands; and when the whole might of Romanised Frankdom passed into the power of the purely-German stock, arose the strange, but pregnant appellation "the Roman Empire of the German Nation." * Finally, upon this glorious memory we could feed the pride that bade us look into the Past for consolation, amid the ruins of the Present. No great culture-Folk has fallen into the plight of building for itself a fanciful renown, as the Germans. What profit the obligation to build such a fantastic edifice from relics of the Past might haply bring us, will perchance grow clear if first we try to realise its drawbacks, free from prejudice.

These drawbacks, past dispute, are found above all in the realm of Politics. Curiously enough, the memory of the German name's historic glory (*Herrlichkeit*) attaches precisely to that period which was so fatal to the German essence, the period of the German's authority over non-German peoples. The King of the Germans had to fetch the confirmation of this authority from Rome; the Romish Kaiser belonged not strictly to the Germans: The cavalcades to Rome were hateful to the Germans, who could be made at most take kindly to them as predatory marches, during which, however, their chief desire was a speedy return to home. Peevishly they followed the Romish Kaiser into Italy, most cheerfully their German Princes back to home. This relation is responsible for the constant powerlessness of so-called German Glory. The idea of this Glory was an un-German one. What distinguishes the "Deutschen" proper from the Franks, Goths, Lom-

---

* "Und als die ganze Macht des romanisirten Frankenreiches in die Gewalt der reindeutschen Stämme überging, kam die seltsame, aber bedeutungsvolle Bezeichnung 'römisches Reich deutscher Nation' auf."

bards &c., is that the latter found pleasure in the foreign land, settled there, and commingled with its people to the point of forgetting their own speech and customs. The German proper, on the contrary, weighed always as a stranger on the foreign people, because he did not feel himself at home abroad ; and strikingly enough, we see the Germans hated to our day (1865) in Italy and in Slavonic lands, as foreigners and oppressors, whereas we cannot veil the shaming truth that German nationalities quite willingly abide beneath a foreign sceptre, if only they be not dealt with violently in regard of speech and customs, as we have before us in the case of Elsass [Alsace].—

With the fall of outer political might, i.e. with the lost significance of the Romish Kaiserdom, which we bemoan to-day as the foundering of German glory, there begins on the contrary the real development of genuine German essence (*Wesen*). Albeit in undeniable conjunction with the development of all other European nations, the German homeland assimilates their influences, especially those of Italy, in so individual a manner that in the last century of the Middle Ages the German costume actually becomes a pattern for the rest of Europe, whereas at the time of so-called German glory even the magnates of the German Reich were clad in Romo-Byzantine garb. In the German Netherlands German art and industry were powerful rivals of Italy's most splendid bloom. After the complete downfall of the German nature, after the wellnigh total extinction of the German nation in consequence of the indescribable devastations of the Thirty Years' War, it was this inmost world of Home from whence the German spirit was reborn. German poetry, German music, German philosophy, are nowadays esteemed and honoured by every nation in the world : but in his yearning after " German glory " the German, as a rule, can dream of nothing but a sort of resurrection of the Romish Kaiser-Reich, and the thought inspires the most good-tempered German with an unmistakable lust of mastery, a longing for the upper hand over other nations. He forgets how detrimental to the

welfare of the German peoples that notion of the Romish
State had been already.

To gain a clear idea of the only policy to help this
welfare, to be worthy the name of German, we must before
all ascertain the true meaning and peculiarity of that
German essence which we have found to be the only prominent power in history itself. Therefore, still to keep an
historical footing, let us somewhat more closely consider
one of the weightiest epochs in the German people's evolution, that extraordinarily agitated crisis which it had to
pass through at time of the so-called Reformation.

The Christian religion belongs to no specific national
stock: the Christian dogma addresses purely - human
nature. Only in so far as it has seized in all its purity
this content common to all men, can a people call itself
Christian in truth. However, a people can make nothing
fully its own but what becomes possible for it to grasp
with its inborn feeling, and to grasp in such a fashion that
in the New it finds its own familiar self again. Upon the
realm of Æsthetics and philosophic Criticism it may be
demonstrated, almost palpably, that it was predestined for
the German spirit to seize and assimilate the Foreign, the
primarily remote from it, in utmost purity and objectivity
of intuition (*in höchster objektiver Reinheit der Anschauung*).
One may aver, without exaggeration, that the Antique
would have stayed unknown, in its now universal world-
significance, had the German spirit not recognised and
expounded it. The Italian made as much of the Antique
his own, as he could copy and remodel; the Frenchman
borrowed from this remodelling, in his turn, whatever
caressed his national sense for elegance of Form: the
German was the first to apprehend its purely-human originality, to seize therein a meaning quite aloof from usefulness,
but therefore of the only use for rendering the Purely-
human. Through its inmost understanding of the Antique,
the German spirit arrived at the capability of restoring the
Purely-human itself to its pristine freedom; not employing

the antique form to display a certain given 'stuff,' but moulding the necessary new form itself through an employment of the antique conception of the world.* To recognise this plainly, let anyone compare Goethe's *Iphigenia* with that of Euripides. One may say that the true idea of the Antique has existed only since the middle of the eighteenth century, since Winckelmann and Lessing.

Now, that the German would have apprehended the Christian dogma in equally preeminent clearness and purity, and would have raised it to the only valid Confession-of-faith, just as he had raised the Antique to a dogma in Æsthetics,—this can not be demonstrated. Perhaps on evolutionary paths unknown to us, and by us unimaginable, he might have arrived hereat; and certain attributes would make it appear that, of all others, the German spirit was called thereto. In any case 'tis easier for us to see what hindered its solution of the problem, since we recognise what enabled it to solve a like one in the region of Æsthetics. For here there was nothing to hinder it: Æsthetics were neither interfered with by the State, nor converted to its ends. With Religion things were otherwise: it had become an interest of the State, and this State-interest obtained its meaning and its guidance, not from the German, but quite definitely from the un-German, the Romanic spirit. It was the incalculable misfortune of Germany that, about the time when the German spirit was ripening for its task upon that high domain, the legitimate State-interests of all German peoples were entrusted to the counsels of a prince to whom the German spirit was a total stranger, to the most thorough-paced representative of the un-German, Romanic State-idea: Charles the Fifth, King of Spain and Naples, hereditary Archduke of Austria, elected Romish Kaiser and Sovereign of the German Reich, devoured by ambition for

* "Durch das innigste Verständniss der Antike ist der deutsche Geist zu der Fähigkeit gelangt, das Reinmenschliche selbst wiederum in ursprünglicher Freiheit nachzubilden, nämlich, nicht durch die Anwendung der antiken Form einen bestimmten Stoff darzustellen, sondern durch eine Anwendung der antiken Auffassung der Welt die nothwendige neue Form selbst zu bilden."

world-supremacy, which would actually have fallen to him if he had been able to master France,—this sovereign felt no other interest in Germany, than to weld it with his empire, an iron-bound monarchy like Spain.

With him arrived the grave fatality that later doomed wellnigh each German prince to misunderstanding of the German spirit; yet he was opposed by the majority of the Reichs-princes of that time, whose interests then coincided, as good fortune would have it, with those of the German Folk-spirit. One can never conjecture the mode in which the actual religious question, too, would have been answered to the honour of the German spirit if Germany then had had a sterling patriotic overchief for Kaiser, such as the Luxemburgian Heinrich VII. At any rate the original Reformatory movement in Germany made not for separation from the Catholic Church; on the contrary, it was an attempt to strengthen and reknit the Church's general union, by putting an end to the hideous abuses of the Roman Curia, so wounding to German religious feeling. What good and world-significant thing might here have come to life, we can scarce approximately measure; but we have before us the results of the disastrous conflict of the German spirit with the un-German spirit of the German Reich's supreme controller. Since that time—cleavage of religion: a dire misfortune! None but a universal religion is Religion in truth: divers confessions, politically established and ranged beside or over one another by contract with the State, simply confess that Religion is in act of dissolution. In that conflict the German Folk was brought near its total foundering, nay, wellnigh it altogether reached it through the outcome of the Thirty Years' War. If therefore the German Princes had mostly worked in common with the German spirit, I have already shewn how since that time, alas! our Princes themselves almost quite unlearnt an understanding of this spirit. The sequel we may see in our public State-life of to-day: the sterling German nature (*das eigentlich deutsche Wesen*) is withdrawing ever farther from it; in part the German is following his native bent to phlegma, in part that to fantasticism : and since the lordling and even the lawyer is becoming quite old-fashioned, the royal rights of Prussia and Austria have gradually to accustom themselves to being upheld before their peoples by—Israelites.*

In this singular phenomenon, this invasion of the German nature by an utterly alien element, there is more than meets the eye.   Here, however, we will only notice that other nature in so far as its conjunction with us obliges us to become quite clear as to what we have to understand by the "German" nature which it exploits.—It everywhere appears to be the duty of the Jew, to shew the nations of modern Europe where haply there may be a profit they have overlooked, or not made use of.   The Poles and Hungarians did not understand the value, to themselves, of a national development of trade and commerce : the Jew displayed it, by appropriating that neglected profit.   None of the European nations had recognised the boundless advantages, for the nation's general œconomy, of an order- ing of the relations of Labour and Capital in accordance with the modern spirit of burgher-enterprise : the Jews laid hand on those advantages, and upon the hindered and dwindling prosperity of the nation the Jewish banker feeds his enormous wealth.   Adorable and beautiful is that foible of the German's which forbade his coining into per- sonal profit the inwardness and purity of his feelings and beholdings, particularly in his public and political life : that a profit here, as well, was left unused, could be cog- nisable to none but a mind which misunderstood the very essence of the German nature.   The German Princes sup- plied the misunderstanding, the Jews exploited it.   Since the new-birth of German poetry and music, it only needed the Princes to follow the example of Frederick the Great, to make a fad of ignoring those arts, or wrongly and unjustly measuring them with French square and com-

* In the original there occurs a Stabreim, unfortunately irreproducible, of "Junker, Jurist and Juden."—TR.

passes, and consequently allowing no influence to the spirit which they manifested,—it only needed this, to throw open to the spirit of alien speculation a field whereon it saw much profit to be reaped. 'Tis as though the Jew had been astounded to find such a store of mind and genius yielding no returns but poverty and unsuccess. He could not conceive, when the Frenchman worked for "*gloire*," the Italian for the *denaro*, why the German did it simply "*pour le roi de Prusse*." The Jew set right this bungling of the German's, by taking German intellectual labour into his own hands; and thus we see an odious travesty of the German spirit upheld to-day before the German Folk, as its imputed likeness. It is to be feared, ere long the nation may really take this simulacrum for its mirrored image: then one of the finest natural dispositions in all the human race were done to death, perchance for ever.

We have to inquire how to save it from such a shameful doom, and therefore first of all will try to signalise the characteristics of genuine "German" nature.—

Once more let us briefly, but plainly recite the outer, historical documents of German nature. "Deutsche" is the title given to those Germanic races which, upon their natal soil, retained their speech and customs. Even from lovely Italy the German yearns back to his homeland. Hence he quits the Romish Kaiser, and cleaves the closer and the trustier to his native Prince. In rugged woods, throughout the lengthy winter, by the warm hearth-fire of his turret-chamber soaring high into the clouds, for generations he keeps green the deeds of his forefathers; the myths of native gods he weaves into an endless web of sagas.* He wards not off the influences incoming from abroad; he loves to journey and to look; but, full of the strange impressions, he longs to reproduce them; he therefore turns his steps toward home, for he knows that here alone will he be *understood*: here, by his homely hearth, he

---

* Cf. *Die Meistersinger* : " Am stillen Heerd in Winterszeit, wenn Burg und Hof mir eingeschnei't . . . ein altes Buch, vom Ahn' vermacht, gab das mir oft zu lesen."—Tr.

tells what he has seen and gone through there outside. Romanic, Gaelic (*wälische*), French books and legends he transposes for himself, and whilst the Latins, Gaels and French know nothing of him, he keenly studies all their ways. But his is no mere idle gaping at the Foreign, as such, as purely foreign ; he wills to understand it " Germanly." He renders the foreign poem into German, to gain an inner knowledge of its content. Herewith he strips the Foreign of its accidentals, its externals, of all that to him is unintelligible, and makes good the loss by adding just so much of his own externals and accidentals as it needs to set the foreign object plain and undefaced before him. In these his natural endeavours he makes the foreign exploit yield to him a picture of its purely-human motives. Thus " Parzival " and " Tristan " were shaped anew by Germans : and whilst the originals have become mere curiosities, of no importance save to the history of literature, in their German counterparts we recognise poetic works of worth imperishable.—

In the same spirit the German borrows for his home the civic measures of abroad. Beneath the castle's shelter, expands the burghers' town ; but the flourishing town does not pull down the Burg : the " Free Town " renders homage to the Prince ; the industrial burgher decks the castle of his ancient lord. The German is conservative : his treasure bears the stamp of all the ages ; he hoards the Old, and well knows how to use it. Fonder is he of keeping, than of winning : the gathered New has value for him only when it serves to deck the Old. He craves for nothing from without ; but he wills no hindrances within. He attacks not, neither will he brook attack.—Religion he takes in earnest : the ethical corruption of the Roman Curia, with its demoralising influence on the clergy, irks him to the quick. By Religious Liberty he means nothing other than the right to deal honestly and in earnest with the Holiest. Here he waxes warm, and disputes with all the hazy passionateness of the goaded friend of peace and quiet. Politics get mixed therein : shall Germany become a Spanish monarchy, the free Reich be trodden under foot, his Princes made mere eminent courtiers? No people has taken arms against invasions of its inner freedom, its own true essence, as the Germans: there is no comparison for the doggedness with which the German chose his total ruin, rather than accommodate himself to claims quite foreign to his nature. This is weighty. The outcome of the Thirty Years' War destroyed the German nation; yet, that a German Folk could rise again, is due to nothing but that outcome. The nation was annihilated, but the German spirit had passed through. It is the essence of that spirit which we call "genius" in the case of highly-gifted individuals, not to trim its sails to worldly profit.* What with other nations led at last to compromise, to a practical ensurance of that profit through accommodation, could not control the Germans: at a time when Richelieu forced the French to accept the laws of political advantage, the German nation was completing its shipwreck; but that which never could bend before the laws of this advantage, lived on and bore its Folk afresh: the German Spirit.

A Folk reduced to a tenth of its former numbers, its significance could nowhere survive but in the memory of units. Even that memory had first to be revived and toil-somely fed, to begin with, by the most prescient of minds. It is a wonderful trait of the German spirit's, that whereas in its earlier period of evolution it had most intimately assimilated the influences coming from without, now, when it quite had lost the vantage-ground of outward political power, it bore itself anew from out its own most inward store.—Recollection (*Erinnerung*) now became for it in truth a self-collection (*Er-Innerung*); for upon its deepest inner self it drew, to ward itself from the now immoderate outer influences. 'Twas no question of its external exist-ence, for that had been ensured by the continuance of

---

* "Es ist das Wesen des Geistes, den man in einzelnen hochbegabten Menschen 'Genie' nennt, sich auf den weltlichen Vortheil nicht zu verstehen." The colloquialism "not to be up to" is really the best translation for what I have rendered "not to trim its sails to."—Tr.

the German Princes; ay! survived there not the title of
"Romo-German Kaiser"? But its truest essence, now
ignored by most of these its Princes,—that was the German
spirit's object to preserve and quicken to new force. In
the French livery and uniform, with periwig and pigtail
(*Zopf*), and laughably set out with imitations of French
ga'' ntry, the scanty remnant of its people fronted it;
while its language even the burgher, with his garnish of
French flourishes, was about to abandon merely to the
peasant.—Yet when its native countenance, its very speech
was lost, there remained to the German spirit one last, one
undreamt sanctuary wherein to plainly tell itself the story
of its heart of hearts. From the Italians the German had
adopted Music, also, for his own. Whoso would seize the
wondrous individuality, the strength and meaning of the
German spirit in one incomparably speaking image, let
him cast a searching glance upon the else so puzzling,
wellnigh unaccountable figure of Music's wonder-man
SEBASTIAN BACH. He is the history of the German
spirit's inmost life throughout the gruesome century of
the German Folk's complete extinction. See there that
head, insanely muffled in the French full-bottomed wig;
behold that master, a wretched organist and cantor, slink-
ing from one Thuringian parish to another, puny places
scarcely known to us by name; see him so unheeded, that
it required a whole century to drag his works from oblivion;
finding even Music pinioned in an art-form the very effigy
of his age, dry, stiff, pedantic, like wig and pigtail set to
notes: then see what a world the unfathomably great
Sebastian built from out these elements! I merely point
to that Creation; for it is impossible to denote its wealth,
its sublimity, its all-embracing import, through any manner
of comparison. If, however, we wish to account for the
amazing rebirth of the German spirit on the field of poetic
and philosophic Literature too, we can do so only by
learning from Bach what the German spirit is in truth,
where it dwelt, and how it restless shaped itself anew,
when it seemed to have altogether vanished from the

world. A biography of this man has recently appeared, and the Allgemeine Zeitung has reviewed it. I cannot resist quoting the following passages from that review: "With labour and rare force of will he struggles up from poverty and want to the topmost height of art, strews with full hands an almost incommensurable plenty of most glorious masterworks, strews it on an age which can neither comprehend nor prize him, and dies beneath a burden of downweighing cares, lonely and forgotten, leaving his family in poverty and privation. . . . The grave of the Song-dispenser closes over the weary home-gone man without a song or sound, because the household penury cannot afford the grave-chant fee. . . . Might the reason, why our composers so seldom find biographers, lie partly in the circumstance that their end is usually so mournful, so harrowing?"— —And while this was happening with great Bach, sole harbourer and new-bearer of the German spirit, the large and little Courts of German princes were swarming with Italian opera-composers and virtuosi, bought with untold outlay, too, to shower on slighted Germany the leavings of an art that nowadays cannot be accorded the least consideration.

Yet Bach's spirit, the German spirit, stepped forth from the sanctuary of divinest Music, the place of its new-birth. When Goethe's "Götz" appeared, its joyous cry went up: "That's German!" And, beholding his likeness, the German also knew to shew himself, to shew the world, what Shakespeare is, whom his own people did not understand. These deeds the German spirit brought forth of itself, from its inmost longing to grow conscious of itself. And this consciousness told it—what it was the first to publish to the world—*that the Beautiful and Noble came not into the world for sake of profit, nay, not for sake of even fame and recognition.* And everything done in the sense of this teaching is " *deutsch* "; and *therefore* is the German great; and *only what is done in that sense, can lead Germany to greatness.*

To the nurture of the German Spirit, the greatness of

the German Folk, nothing can lead, then, save its veritable understanding by the rulers. The German Folk arrived at its rebirth, at unfolding of its highest faculties, through its conservative temper, its inward cleaving to itself, to its own idiosyncrasy: once it shed its life's blood for the preservation of its Princes. 'Tis now for them to shew the German Folk that they belong to it ; and where the German spirit achieved its [deed of rebearing the Folk, *there* is the realm whereon the Princes, too, have first to found their new alliance with the Folk. It is highest time the Princes turned to this re-baptism : the danger that menaces the whole of German public life, I have already pointed out. Woe to us and the world, if the nation itself were this time saved, but the German spirit vanished from the world ! *—

How are we to conceive a state of things in which the German *Folk* remained, but the German *Spirit* had taken flight ? The hardly-thinkable is closer to us than we fancy. When I defined the essence and functions of the German spirit, I kept in view a happy development of the German people's most significant attributes. But the birthplace of the German spirit is alike the basis of the German people's failings. The capacity of diving deep within, and thence observing lucidly and thoughtfully the world without, always presupposes a bent to meditation ; which, in the less gifted individual, quite easily becomes a love of doing nothing, a positive phlegma. What in its happiest manifestation places us nearest the supremely gifted folk of ancient Indus, may give the mass the character of common Oriental sloth (*Trägheit*) ; nay, even that neighbouring development to utmost power can become a curse for us, by betraying us into fantastic self-complacency. That Goethe and Schiller, Mozart and Beethoven have issued from the German people's womb,

---

* Cf. *Die Meistersinger*, act iii: "Habt Acht ! Uns drohen üble Streich' :— zerfällt erst deutsches Volk und Reich, in falscher wälscher Majestät kein Fürst bald mehr sein Volk versteht ; und wälschen Dunst mit wälschem Tand sie pflanzen uns in's deutsche Land,"—TR.

far too easily tempts the bulk of middling talents to consider these great minds their own by right of birth, to
persuade the mass with demagogic flatulence that they
themselves are Goethes and Schillers, Mozarts and
Beethovens. Nothing flatters more the bent to sloth and
easygoingness, than a high opinion of oneself, an opinion
that quite of oneself one is something great and needs take
no sort of pains to first become it. This leaning is root-
German, and hence no people more requires to be flicked
up and compelled to help itself, to act for itself, than the
German. But German Princes and Governments have
done the very opposite. It was reserved for Börne the
Jew, to sound the first challenge to the German's sloth ;
and, albeit in this sense unintentionally, he thereby raised
the Germans' great misunderstanding of themselves to the
pitch of direfulest confusion. The misunderstanding that
prompted the Austrian Chancellor, Prince Metternich, in
the day of his leadership of German Cabinet-policy, to
deem the aspirations of the German " Burschenschaft "
identical with those of the bygone Paris club of Jacobins,
and to take hostile measures accordingly,—that misunderstanding was most advantageous to the [Jewish] speculator
who stood outside, seeking nothing but his personal profit.
This time, if he played his game well, that speculator had
only to swing himself into the midst of the German Folk
and State, to exploit and, in the end, not merely govern it,
but downright make it his own property.

After all that had gone before, it now had really become
a difficult matter, to rule in Germany. Had the Governments made it a maxim to judge their German peoples
by the measure of French events, there also soon arose
adventurers to teach the downtrod German Folk-spirit to
apply French maxims to its estimate of the Governments.
The *Demagogue* had now arrived indeed : but what a
doleful after-birth ! Every new Parisian revolution was
promptly ' mounted ' in Germany : of course, for every new
spectacular Paris opera had been mounted forthwith at
the Court-theatres of Berlin and Vienna, a pattern for all

Germany. I have no hesitation about styling the subsequent revolutions in Germany entirely un-German.* "Democracy" in Germany is purely a translated thing. It
exists merely in the "Press"; and what this German Press
is, one must find out for oneself. But untowardly enough,
this translated Franco-Judaico-German Democracy could
really borrow a handle, a pretext and deceptive cloak, from
the misprised and maltreated spirit of the German Folk.
To secure a following among the people, "Democracy"
aped a German mien; and "*Deutschthum*," "German
spirit," "German honesty," "German freedom," "German
morals," became catchwords disgusting no one more than
him who had true German culture, who had to stand in
sorrow and watch the singular comedy of agitators from a
non-German people pleading for him without letting their
client so much as get a word in edgewise. The astounding
unsuccessfulness of the so loud-mouthed movement of 1848
is easily explained by the curious circumstance that the
genuine German found himself, and found his name, so
suddenly represented by a race of men quite alien to him.
Whilst Goethe and Schiller had shed the German spirit on
the world, without so much as talking of the "German"
spirit, these Democratic speculators fill every book- and
print-shop, every so-called "Volks-," i.e. joint-stock theatre,
with vulgar, utterly vapid dummies, forever plastered with
the puff of "deutsch," and "deutsch" again, to decoy the
easygoing crowd. And really we have got so far, that we
presently shall see the German Folk quite turned to gabies
by it : the national propensity to sloth and phlegma is being
lured into fantastic satisfaction with itself; already the
German people is taking a large part, itself, in the playing
of the shameful comedy; and not without a shudder can
the thoughtful German spirit look upon those foolish festive
gatherings, with their theatrical processions, their silly
speeches, and the cheerless empty songs wherewith one tries

* " Ich stehe nicht an, die seitdem vorgekommenen Revolutionen in Deutsch
land als ganz undeutsch zu bezeichnen."

to make the German Folk imagine it is something special and does not need to first endeavour to become it.—

So far the earlier article, from the year 1865. My project was to get a political journal founded for the purpose of advocating the tendences expressed therein: Herr Julius Fröbel declared his readiness to undertake that advocacy: the "Süddeutsche Presse" came to daylight. Unfortunately I soon discovered that Herr Fröbel's view of the problem in question was different from my own, and one fine day we parted; for the thought that Art should serve no end of usefulness, but only its own honour (*Werth*), so sorely went against his grain that he fell into a fit of tears and sobbing.

However, I certainly had other grounds for leaving my task unfinished.—"What is German?"—The question puzzled me more and more. What simply aggravated my bewilderment, were the impressions of the eventful years which followed the time when that article was begun. What German could have lived through the year 1870 without amazement at the forces manifested here, as also at the courage and determination with which the man who palpably knew something that we others did not know, brought those forces into action?—Many an objectionable feature one might overlook at the time. We who, with the spirit of our great masters at heart, witnessed the physiognomic bearing of our death-defiant landsmen in the soldier's coat, we cordially rejoiced when listening to the " Kutschkelied," * and deeply were we affected by the " feste Burg " before the war and " nun danket Alle Gott " when it was over. To be sure, it was precisely we who

* A song very popular with the German troops in the Franco-German War, originally attributed to a fusilier by name of Kutschke, but later ascertained to have been written by Field-chaplain Herm. Alex. Pistorius (1811-1877).—The "determined man " of two sentences back is, of course, Prince Bismarck.— TR.

found it hard to comprehend how the deadly courage of our patriots could whet itself on nothing better than the "Wacht am Rhein"; a somewhat mawkish Liedertafel product, which the Frenchmen held for one of those Rhine-wine songs at which they earlier had made so merry. But no matter, they might scoff as they pleased, even their "*allons enfants de la patrie*" could not this time put down "lieb Vaterland, kannst ruhig sein," or stop their being soundly beaten.—When our victorious troops were journeying home I made private inquiries in Berlin as to whether, supposing one contemplated a grand solemnity for the slain in battle, I should be permitted to compose a piece of music for performance thereat, and to be dedicated to the sublime event. The answer was: upon so joyful a return, one wished to make no special arrangements for painful impressions. Still beneath the rose, I suggested another music-piece to accompany the entry of the troops, at the close of which, mayhap at the march past the victorious Monarch, the singing-corps so well supported in the Prussian army should join-in with a national song. No: that would have necessitated serious alterations in arrangements settled long before, and I was counselled not to make the proposal. My Kaisermarsch I arranged for the concert-room : there may it fit as best it can !—In any case, I ought not to have expected the "German spirit," new-risen on the field of battle, to trouble itself with the musical fancies of a presumably conceited opera-composer. However, divers other experiences made me gradually feel odd in this new "Reich ;" so that when I came to editing the last volume of my Collected Writings, as already mentioned, I could find no right incitement to complete my article on "What is German?"

When once I spoke my mind about the character of the Berlin performances of my "Lohengrin," * I was reprimanded by the editor of the "Norddeutsche Allgemeine Zeitung," to the effect that I must not consider myself sole lessee of the "German spirit." I took the hint, and

---

* Cf. Vol. III. p. 270—written in the year 1871.—TR.

surrendered the lease. On the other hand, I was glad to find a coinage minted for the whole new German Reich, particularly when I heard that it had turned out so original-German that it would fit the currency of no other of the Great Powers, but remained subject to a "rate of exchange" with "franc" and "shilling": people told me this was tricky for the common trader, no doubt, but most advantageous to the banker. My German heart leaped high, too, when Liberally we voted for "Free-trade": there was, and still prevails, much want throughout the land; the workman hungers, and industry has fallen sick: but "business" flourishes. For "business" in the very grandest sense, indeed, the Reichs-"broker" has recently been patented; and, to grace and dignify the wedding-feasts of Highnesses, with oriental etiquette the newest Minister leads off the torch-dance.

This all may be good, and well beseem the novel Deutsches Reich; but no longer can I plumb its meaning, and therefore I must hold myself unqualified for further answering the question: "was ist Deutsch?" Could not Herr Constantin Frantz, for instance, afford us splendid aid? Herr Paul de Lagarde, too? May they consider themselves most friendlily invited to take up the answer to that fateful question, for instruction of our poor Bayreuther Patronatverein. If they haply then should reach the realm whereon we had to take Sebastian Bach in view, in course of the preceding article, I might perchance be able to relieve my hoped-for colleagues of their task again. How capital, if I should gain these writers' ear for my appeal!

A MUSIC-SCHOOL

FOR

MUNICH.

Bericht

an

Seine Majestät den König Ludwig II.

von Bayern

über eine in München zu errichtende

deutsche Musikschule.

The translation of the full title of this essay is: "Report to His Majesty King Ludwig II. of Bavaria upon a German Music-School to be founded in Munich." *According-ing to Glasenapp* (Richard Wagner's Leben und Wirken), *the architect Gottfried Semper, one of Wagner's oldest and staunchest friends, had been given an audience by the King in February 1865 (i.e. about a month before the date of this Report) for the purpose of discussing the plans of a model-theatre for the* Ring des Nibelungen, *whereupon the Munich press had broken out into a positive tempest of wrath and revilings of Richard Wagner and all his ways. After presenting the following Report to the King, Wagner desired the appointment of a Commission to decide upon the feasibility of his scheme; it was constituted, accordingly, of Intendant von Perfall, as president, Franz Lachner, W. H. Riehl, Hans von Bülow and Wagner himself, and held its first sitting on April 24th. The scheme was then rejected as too "expensive"! But two years later (1867), a modification of the proposed institute was established in Munich, with von Bülow at its head; after another two years, however, the interminable machinations of the anti-Wagner party succeeded in driving von Bülow to resign the post and quit the town.*

TRANSLATOR'S NOTE.

Allerdurchlauchtigster grossmächtigster König!

OUR Majesty has expressed the wish that I should state my views as to what may reasonably be expected for Music from the action of a Conservatorium; what requirements should be founded on that expectation; and how those requirements might be met, by suitable arrangements at the Royal Conservatorium of Music in this city.

To the wide-reaching eye of the illustrious friend of my art I believe I can offer a satisfactory insight into this matter by nothing but displaying it in intimate connexion with the present status of all the art-branches that impinge upon it.

In the very title "Conservatorium" there lies a definition of the character of the functions required from it. Such a school should maintain, "conserve," the classic style of a ripe stage in Art's development; and that by fostering and loyally handing down the proper mode-of-rendering (*Vortragsweise*) for those standard-works, in particular, which have formed and rounded off a period of artistic prime and made it classical. We find Conservatories for Music established first in Italy, at a time when Italian vocal music, especially in Opera, had evolved itself to so pronounced a style that even in its greatest degeneracy, of nowadays, its Form may yet be termed essentially unchanged. The labours of the renowned Conservatoire in Paris, too, could base themselves on the preservation of a classic mode-of-rendering, according to French canons of taste, for the works of great masters who had rounded off a characteristic era in the composite French style. The mode of rendering, as cherished and maintained in these Conservatories, thus originated at those great musical art-institutes for which the most considerable artists of the nation had directly worked and written. The Conservatories of Naples, Milan and Paris preserved and fostered what the direct achievements of the theatres of *San Carlo, della Scala* and the *Académie de musique*, with assistance from the nation's own peculiar trend of taste, had previously matured into a recognised Classical Form.

When we extend our field of vision to the numerous Conservatoria established in Germany, we simply have to explain their non-success and uselessness—admitted by almost every disinterested onlooker—by the fact that an art-institute of the importance of the above-named great theatres, in France and Italy, does not exist in Germany : in our German schools it is impossible to maintain and nurse a classic style, because it is either totally unknown, or else unadvocated, at our public art-institutes.

To take proper stock of this, we Germans first must recognise the feeble status of our public art ; and that comes all the harder, as a legitimate pride in the great masters who have issued from our midst makes us far too ready to shut our eyes to the miserable manner in which we have supplied them with the media needed for their art. We shall never clearly see what ails us, till we turn our eyes from our great masters, themselves, to the mode in which their works are set before us.

The merest glance at the history of music in Germany shews us that, in respect of institutions for the practice of this art, we are in an utterly un-selfreliant, unripe and wavering condition, that nowhere have we even taken the first step towards evolving a Style in harmony with the German spirit. Whereas, of their own unaided means, the Italians at the middle of the bygone century formed such a style ; whereas about the end of the past and commencement of the present century the individuality of French taste, assisted by the artistic forces of every nation, founded the style of that Parisian institute whence the taste of wellnigh every European nation has been governed to this day,—the Germans have not as yet advanced beyond a mere aping and imitating the stylistic idiosyncrasies of the French and Italians, especially as concerns the mode-of-rendering current at our theatres.

To perceive how prejudicial this is for us, we have only to compare the result of foreign influences upon the French with that exhibited by ourselves.

In Paris the Italian and German became naturalised at once, and the far less musically-gifted Frenchman so stamped the seal of his own taste upon the importations from abroad, that, far beyond his frontiers, this taste of his has become in turn the standard for the doings of abroad. In Germany, upon the contrary, the course has been as follows. Italian music is imported in an utterly barbaric fashion, singers and all, as a wholly foreign product. German musicians take it up, and become Italians ; whilst one tries to make French Opera one's own, through a mangling reproduction. The resultant evils I have repeatedly endeavoured to expose. Little as my demonstration of the great incorrectness of the performances at our opera-houses and their ruin of all good artistic taste has been regarded, yet I have been so fortunate as to win the attention and interest of Your Majesty for precisely these complaints of mine, among other things ; in the present Report I may therefore assume that I am addressing a judge who will not require me to first bring forward circumstantial proofs.

To put it briefly : in our opera-houses we badly copy and distort the Foreign. Though the French and Italians are stricken with artistic palsy, their works are still in harmony with their national peculiarities, and their performances correct of style ; but we—for our daily entertainment we take these selfsame works, we mutilate them, and perform them incorrectly.

In face of facts like these, I ask, what mode-of-rendering has a German " Conservatorium for Music " to " conserve " ?

Very probably I shall be answered that, in addition to

those foreign products, we also perform *Mozart* and *Gluck*, and that our conserving care must remain directed to the works of these masters. In that plea we may discern the true root-error of the Germans. The operas of Gluck and Mozart we are obliged to decypher by light of the same French and Italian peculiarities of style, as every other foreign work; and in precisely the same incorrect and de-facing fashion, as with the latter, have we made Mozart and Gluck our own. But had we ever been in a position to render them stylistic justice, we were bound at last to lose that faculty under influence of the more and more profoundly corrupting taste of abroad, itself corrupted. And so it is. The quite specific art of singing and delivery, still based in the days of Gluck and Mozart on the special achievements of the Italian schools, but no-where fostered in Germany itself, has since been lost at even the fountainhead of that style; and nothing can more plainly prove the failings of our operatic personnel to-day, than the utter lifelessness and lack of colour in its perform-ances of just Mozart and Gluck—giving the lie to all our hypocritic praises of them.

To give just *these* works wholly rightly, to-day would need an artistic culture and stylistic development such as could only crown a long-continued, and a most intelligent, training in the utmost art of delivery. That we Germans can presume to speak of such a thing, without having stirred a finger for the first foundation of a rendering even adequate to the products of our time, merely proves that these preliminary requirements have not yet come within our consciousness, however self-sufficiently we may ward ourselves against the charge.

The gravamen of this charge is lessened when we take into account the uncommon difficulty of the task proposed us. The bewildering influences of those foreign forms of Style—which have controlled the German public's taste in every way, and (because incorrectly reproduced) have led astray and ruined it—were nowhere confronted with a centre of German culture, such as Paris in the case of

France, where the original taste of the nation might enrich itself with the foreign factors, but always through re-fashioning them to meet its own true needs.

Even the most important German theatres have pre-served an attitude of dependence upon Paris, similar to that adopted by the French provincial stage; but with the great disadvantage that their Parisian prototype was remote and unintelligible to them, whilst the direct influence of Italian Opera, coupled with attempts to copy foreign styles from their own resources, has raised the difficulty of correctly rendering all this into a complete impossibility.

How the German is to conquer that difficulty, whether by simply restraining himself and abandoning a spurious universalism, or through a most careful and correct training in all the stylistic idiosyncrasies of every country and every age,—this question we may be able to answer, if we con-sider the foremost requirement for laying the foundation of a truly German style of rendering.

Indisputably the weightiest matter is to call into life, in some suitable centre of German life and German culture, a standard institution for the mode of performing works of German style. The extraordinary, the wellnigh incom-parable influence upon the taste and spirit of the nation which the Theatre has acquired, as almost the sole diurnal organ of artistic entertainment, can leave us not an instant's doubt that the institution we have in mind could only be one that aims at stage-performances. It is an established fact that whatever may be done by the Concert-room, to give the nation's musical taste a more earnest and a nobler trend, has always been crossed and set awry again by the preponderating influence of the Opera; it therefore is evi-dent that from the Theatre alone, can the intended nobler tendency be lastingly impressed upon a people's taste.

In my opinion and experience, it would be quite useless to begin with an attempt to impose this cultivating tend-ence on one of the larger standing theatres, as the sole criterion for its doings: the obligation to cater without break, year in, year out, for the daily entertainment of one

M

and the same town-public, has brought in its inevitable train the ignorance, the immaturity and incorrectness, exhibited by all these theatres' doings ; and, after each abnormal effort, they necessarily would fall back upon their former tendence, so long as the obligations of their daily business remained in force.

The way in which a weighty share in the fostering of good taste may be allotted and ensured to the standing theatres, as well, shall presently transpire ; but I first must denote that institution which is to be assigned the initiative. As I believe that everything hinges upon our arriving at the possibility of really correct and thoroughly symmetrical performances of works of a noble class and German originality, and as that aim can only be attained exceptionally and rarely,—it follows that the proposed institution must consist in the establishment of Model-performances, for which the best and best-trained artistic forces, procurable at the time, should be gathered from existing German theatres.

Experience teaches us that in desperate situations, such as that before us, succour can never be gained from abstract theory, but solely through the prompt adoption of practical measures.

Your Majesty's profoundly earnest mind has recognised the straits (*Noth*) in which I find myself as regards the performance of my later works, and more especially the projected larger cycle of dramas "*der Ring des Nibelungen.*" In my preface to the public issue of the latter poem I sketched the only arrangements which to me seemed competent to solve the problem of a satisfactory rendering of those dramas, and my illustrious patron has resolved to take the needful steps for that solution. These would consist, substantially, as follows.

Since the existing Court- and National-theatre is fully occupied at all times with the public's daily need, we had to put aside any thought of using its building for our Model-performances, which were to be prepared-for with the utmost care ; instead thereof, a special structure was to be provisionally erected.   In the comprehensive judgment of Your Majesty, this temporary erection should itself contribute to the solution of certain weighty problems of æsthetic fitness, bearing upon the scenic and acoustic principles to be observed in building a standard theatre. Your Majesty therefore committed to an architect of eminent experience in this department * the task of constructing, before all else, an interior in which the æsthetically disturbing visibility of the orchestra should be avoided on the one hand, while enhancing as much as possible the beauty of its tone-effect, and on the other hand—particularly through devising new modes of 'lighting' to give the scenic decorations an importance truly worthy of the landscape-painter—the art of Theatric Representation should itself be raised to a nobler and a purer height than any it has reached as yet.   Your Majesty has consented to the architect's proposal to erect this provisional structure in one of the wings of the great Exhibition in this city, provided that prove feasible, and has thus ensured the enterprise the double advantage of smaller costliness (as there would be no provisional need of building outer walls) and of economy of time in the erection. Moreover Your Majesty has commissioned me to direct my energies to seeking among the members of German opera-companies for specially-gifted and well-trained performers, such as might be summoned to Munich, at the proper time, for the express purpose of studying my work undisturbed by other influences, and of setting it before a specially-invited German audience in a series of standard performances.   Performances brought about in this exceptional manner would undoubtedly pass away, in point of time, but their excellence could not fail of a lasting effect; and, while it would be reserved for recurrent intervals to repeat their like, the mere obligation to perform my works thus, and not otherwise, would afford the starting-point for an institution whose agency must eventually prove of utmost benefit to German art.

* Gottfried Semper—see page 172.—TR.

However, before losing myself in a description of the benefits possible to accrue from this institution after it had been called to life on the path of immediate need, I must remember the chief object of my humble communication, and detail the mode in which I consider the Munich Conservatorium not only may share in those prospective benefits, but may even now lay down the road for them in its capacity of a preparatory Music-school.

It is obvious that this share must at first confine itself, in essence, to a preparatory aid in founding the suggested institution, since it is only through the doings of the latter that an actual standard for the rendering of works of pronouncedly German originality can be established. Therefore, while reserving a discussion of the *didactic* path on which the higher German style may be prepared-for and acquired—in thorough keeping with the native idiosyncrasy of our artistic taste and its development under so many diverse influences—for the present I will merely take in eye the *practical* necessity, that of preparing the artistic organs absolutely indispensable for the intended Model-performances, of qualifying them to fulfil a task such as has never yet been earnestly and singly set before them.

For this, it is of the first importance that singers gifted with dramatic talent should receive a proper training in voice-production.—In Germany no branch of musical education is more neglected, and worse practised, than that of Song, particularly Dramatic Song. Irrefutable proof is furnished by the extraordinary dearth of first-rate singers available for higher ends. Among all the singers of our numerous theatres, often engaged at enormous salaries, it is quite astonishing how limited must be the choice when it is a question of summoning the needful artists, even at great outlay, to take part in standard representations of a strictly German style, as is now Your Majesty's generous will. By far the largest number of the singers required for the performance of my Nibelungen-work are absolutely not to be found at German opera-houses; for the majority almost entirely lack the requisite preliminaries for mastering the task proposed by me, and are mostly much too pampered and spoilt already, by an anomalous renown, to offer any hopeful prospect of their reformation.   Seeing that one can count on but little support from this quarter, then, even our nearest practical goal imperatively demands the founding of an efficiently organised *singing-school.*

To the instigation of General-music-director *Franz Lachner* we owe it, that the needful funds for establishing such a singing-school were allocated many years ago by the munificence of Your Majesty's exalted grandfather, King Ludwig I.   It is to be regretted that, without any notable increase in its revenue, and without any practical knowledge of the higher task therein involved, this singing-school should have been expanded to a universal music-school with all the pretensions of a Conservatorium.   While deferring an indication of the way in which this necessary first foundation, that of a Singing-school, may in course of time be built into a universal Music-school, a true " Con-servatorium," I have only to point to the issue of the path struck hitherto—an acknowledged failure, condemning the very existence of the institute—to prove that that path was not the right one.   Hence I thoroughly concur with General-music-director Franz Lachner's prudent view, that, in the first instance, this failure can only be remedied by restoring the Conservatorium to its original basis, that of a practical school of singing ; and I vote for the employment of its present funds upon the re-establishment of an effi-ciently organised Singing-school.   As to the meaning I should wish given to that school, and the tendence to be stamped upon it, I beg to express my general view as follows.

With us Germans the maturing of an art of Song is peculiarly difficult, infinitely more difficult than with the Italians, much harder even than with the French.   The cause resides not merely in the influences of climate on the voice itself, but the most demonstrably in our Speech's idiosyncrasies.   Whereas the extremely ductile vowels of the Italian language have simply been moulded into more effective sound-bodies by the graceful energy of

its consonants, and even the Frenchman has kept his far
more limited vowel-force in flow through a shaping of his
consonants which often leads, indeed, to unintelligibleness,
but is prompted solely by the need of euphony : the German language, after its downfall at the close of the Middle
Ages, and despite the exertions of the great poets of the
German renaissance, has not yet recovered sufficiently to
enable it to challenge any sort of comparison with its
Romanic, or even its Slavonic neighbours, in respect of
pleasing sound.   A tongue with vowels mostly short and
mute, extensible only at cost of intelligibility ; hemmed-in
by consonants, most expressive indeed, but heaped regardless of all euphony : such a Speech must necessarily com-
port itself to Song quite otherwise than those aforesaid.
This right relation has first to be discovered ; the influence
of speech on song, and at last perhaps (for our language is
not fully formed as yet) of song on speech, has first to be
made sure of ; but in no event can that take place upon
the path pursued at present by our singing-masters.   The
Italian style of vocalism, our only present model for the
classic, is inapplicable to the German language ; here
speech is spoilt, and song disfigured : with consequence,
the fatuity of our modern German opera-singing.   A right
development of Song, upon a groundwork of German
Speech, is therefore the first task for us to put our shoulders
to—extraordinarily difficult, as I admit.   Upon the other
hand, that task can prosper by nothing but an unbroken
practice of vocal works in which the 'song' is thoroughly
conformed to German speech.   The character of this
'song,' in contradistinction from the Italian long-drawn
play of vowels, will prove to be an energetic speaking-
accent, and therefore quite admirably fitted for dramatic
delivery.   Taking an opposite standpoint heretofore, German singers have been more incapable of dramatic singing
than those of other nations, and just because their vocal
training was governed by a foreign type which hindered
all evaluation of the German tongue's intrinsic merits ;
whereby elocution itself has been so maimed and neglected

that any German master who counts to-day upon the intelligible aid of speech, in the rendering of his works, cannot find a single singer for the purpose. This one circumstance, of our singers' altogether careless and unclear pronunciation, is of the most appalling import for the question of establishing a truly German style in Opera. I therefore forego all cataloguing the countless evils attendant on this root-defect in German singing, when the character of both the nation and its language so clearly points to its only suitable method of Dramatic Song; and for the present I consent to be deemed onesided when I claim it as a *sine quâ non* for the Singing-school, now about to be constituted, that its first aim shall be directed to solving the problem of how to bring the art of Song into due relation with the idiosyncrasies of German Speech.

That any such method should never permit euphony to be tampered with, goes without saying. Yet that is just the special difficulty for the German. Whilst to the Italian everything is made easy by Nature herself, and no doubt he just as easily grows lax and self-complacent, Nature has put difficulties in the way of the German's use of his artistic organs; but she has equipped him, on the other hand, with strength and perseverance in the application of Reflection to his culture. It is the peculiar mark of the German cycle of culture (*Bildungsgang*) that it takes its form and motive mostly from without, consequently that it tries to digest a conglomerate culture whose elements lie primarily remote from it, not merely in space, but also in time. Whereas the Romanic nations abandon themselves to a dubious life of the moment, and, strictly speaking, have a sense of nothing but what the immediate Present offers them, the German builds his world of the Present out of motives from all zones and ages. His enjoyment of the beautiful is consequently more reflective than is the case, in particular, with his Romanic neighbours. His art-media too—and his art-organs, as I soon shall shew—he has to acquire through a careful process of assimilation and a deliberate judgment of Art and her whole organism, such as can be acquired on none but the historic path   In the case before us, the special quality required of German dramatic singers is only to be made full use of, for the general good of Art, by our refusing to rob their education of the euphony of the Italian school.   In the curriculum of the proposed Singing-school we must therefore include a 'reflective' study of Italian Song, with retention of the Italian words, as indeed is indispensable.   This brings us to the rendering, for purposes of practice, of modes not only foreign, but belonging also to divers earlier periods; a practice to be conducted with fullest knowledge of the peculiarities of these several styles, but which I chiefly regard as a means of education for the pupils.   What consequences I await from this cultural factor and its application, as regards the significance and future extension of the institute itself, I will in due course endeavour to set in a brighter light.   To give that future extension a still broader basis, however, I will next allow myself to direct attention to those auxiliaries, in a fit and thorough education of the singer, which must be called upon for even a prosperous working of the Singing-school as such.

It is indispensable that the singer be also a good musician.   How ill we stand in this respect, for all our boasted superiority over the foreigner in solidity and thoroughness, can not be loud enough bewailed.   The first rudiment of musical grammar, a simple reading of the notes, is so much a stranger to most of our singers that the study of a vocal part does not mean for them a mastery of its phrasing and delivery (*Vortrag und Gehalt*), but a simple learning to hit the notes ; when that is accomplished, the study itself is viewed as strictly over.   If one considers the ratio borne by this neglected education of the singer to the character of German music, of all others,— so pre-eminently distinguished by the wealth and intricacy of its harmonic texture,—one will easily comprehend why it has occurred to so few German masters to carry the rich development won upon the field of Instrumental-music into the field of Opera.—It will therefore be expedient to com-

mence a thorough general instruction in Music simultaneously with the specific instruction in singing: by this
I mean a theoretical tuition and practical exercises in
Harmony, advancing to that department of the science of
'composition' which closes with an accurate knowledge of
a tone-work's structure, the build of its periods, the purport
and relation of its themes, as also a correct perception of
its phraseology. From this stage, essential in the singer's
education, one would have to start whenever the Singing-
school was meant to be developed and expanded to a
universal Music-school.

Before contemplating such an expansion, however, we
must first have complied with all the requirements for fully
educating the singer; and to do justice to him, especially
if his destination be dramatic, we must necessarily provide
for his rhetorical and gymnastic training. Both these
departments should be attended-to at the very beginning
of his purely vocal instruction. In order to bring his tones
into proper agreement with the words, the singer must
learn to pronounce both finely and correctly; to gain full
power over the immediate vocal organ, the throat and
lungs, he must have his whole body completely under
control. Steps should therefore be taken to furnish the
best instruction in both these branches at the commencement of practice in voice-production proper. The
elocutionary tuition will advance from a purely physical
training of the speaking-organ to a precise instruction in
the structure of the verse, the properties of the rhyme,
and finally the rhetoric and poetic contents of the poem
whereon the song is built. The gymnastic tuition, again,
beginning with an instruction in the proper poise of body
for bringing out the tone, will extend to the development
of plastic and mimetic aptitudes, to meet the requirements
of each dramatic action. This extension of the singer's
curriculum is indispensable, unless its true goal is to be
lost sight of in a onesided policy.

It is the total lack of training in these branches, that
makes the generality of our modern opera-singers so in-

capable of higher artistic tasks. 'Tis incredible what
indifference one meets among them, as touching the "text"
of their arias; scarce intelligibly, often wholly unintel-
ligibly declaimed, the verse and its contents remain almost
totally unknown, not only to the audience (unless it helps
itself by following with the text-book), but even to the
singer himself; and the result of this one circumstance is
an obtuse, an often idiotic state of mind, which makes
one's dealings with him, under circumstances, a positively
sickening pain.   That a singer who does not really know
the contents of the poem, and of the situations to be portrayed, but substitutes the traditional harum-scarum of
operatic routine—that such a singer's plastic and mimetic
action can only copy senseless customs, is self-evident;
and the truly cultured section of the nation may explain
from this one fact why it must seem positively childish and
degraded, in its own eyes, when constituting part of an
opera-public; wherefore, too, it very properly accounts its
visit to the Opera a frivolous excess, for which it feels
justly punished with a deadly ennui when the thing is
over.—

Though I have hitherto confined myself to the practical
object of training singers to fit them for taking part in the
intended Model-performances, I have repeatedly arrived
already at the bounds of the stricter Singing-school, where
it comes in contact on the one hand with the wider realm
of Music, on the other, and through the requirement last
set up, with the educational subjects of a purely Theatric
school.   Not only is it indispensable, but part of the task
wherewith I am entrusted, to cross these frontiers in my
plan—even should they have to be regarded as infranchis-
able for the actual present, in view of reaching our immediate goal; for, by exhibiting the practical need, I have
both to make clearer the obligation to gradually enlarge
our sphere in future, and to point out in advance the
means thereto.

To no musician, let him devote his career to whatever
speciality he will, can singing-lessons taken at the beginn-

ing of his artistic education be other than of the utmost profit. The neglect of Song in Germany avenges itself not merely on the singers, but even on the instrumentists, and most of all on the composer. Whoso knows not how to sing, himself, can neither write for the voice with full assurance, nor imitate Song on an instrument. How far each musician should take his share of vocal training, ought to depend on nothing but the limits of his vocal organ. Everyone, particularly when gifted with a musical bent, possesses in his organ of Speech a material which he should cultivate to the utmost of his ability, and thus develop his sense of the true attributes of Song—at least so far that they shall not be strangers to him, but intimate acquaintances. The human voice is the practical basis of Music, and however far the latter may journey on her primal path, the boldest combinations of the tone-setter, the most daring execution of the instrumental-virtuoso, will always have to hark back to the purely Singable, to find the law for their achievements. Hence I hold that elementary instruction in singing must be made obligatory upon every musician; and in the successful organisation of a Singing-school, upon the lines above-denoted, I consequently should also see the foundation of the intended universal Music-school. It then would have to first extend that frontier we have seen it reach with the necessity of instructing the singer in the elements of Harmony and the rudimentary Analysis of musical compositions.

But here I must emphatically repeat that I abide by the expressed character of our establishment, as a purely practical school for cultivating the media of performance required by works of a classical and German style of music; to want to introduce musical Science with all its branches into a Music-school, must turn us completely aside from the weightiest object, that of helping works of music to their perfect execution, and must lame and complicate their power of effect. The knowledge needful for the executant musician and composer can likewise best be learnt on a practical path, before all things by his taking part in good performances, and finally by his hearing and being taught to judge the same ; what lies between, namely a learning of the theoretic laws of so-called Composition, is a matter for private study, and in no larger town of Germany, least of all at the seat of the intended practical music-school, will there be a lack of teachers competent for that.   But whereas the musical student is able to learn the rules of musical science better, more easily and more thoroughly in Germany than in France or Italy, he has always been at a pinch to acquire consciousness of the laws of beauty and correct expression, by which to apply what he has learnt.   Wherefore at the flowering-time of Italian music German princes and French academies sent their protégés to Rome and Naples, because this education by listening to classic modes-of-rendering was not to be acquired at home.   In just this way Italian princes and magnates provided for the education of young painters, by the simple device of giving the masters the means for creating important works of art, which thus directly served their pupils as pattern alike and lesson.   The atelier, the workshop of the master while creating, and while he speeds his works, is the true school for the chosen pupil.   To give that workshop to the musicians of our day, let this be the shining goal of the illustrious patron of my art !

While, then, I banish actual theoretic instruction in Composition, such as the Science of Harmony and Counterpoint, from the practical curriculum of our Music-school, and confine it to the private personal intercourse of the studious pupil with the easily-selected teacher, I all the keener take in eye the means of cultivating a taste for the beautiful and expressive ; and the only profitable path to this, in my experience, is that of guidance in the right and lovely mode-of-rendering.   In this relation we had before all else to care for Song, because that branch of training —in my opinion the foundation *in se* of all musical culture —not only is of special difficulty in Germany, but has also been the most neglected.

We stand infinitely better in the Instrumental department. From the poorly-fostered voice, the German has always fled with predilection to the musical instrument. Every large town in Germany has a comparatively good, nay, here and there a quite admirable orchestra, to shew us ; there is no lack of good, nay, even excellent string- and wind - players. For every instrument each considerable orchestra owns a master, with whom the pupil can learn the technique of his chosen instrument to a point of greatest finish. I see no reason for forming a special branch of tuition at a Music-school ; joint studying of instrumental technique has no sense, and can at most be plied in Russian barracks with success. When the Music-school is extended on this side, only from humanitarian motives, in a manner of speaking, could one pay regard to the learning of instrumental technique : to wit, from among the members of the Orchestra a suitable master should be assigned to those talented young musicians who may have decided on any particular instrument, and in case of need, when the pupil really shewed great talent, the master should be repaid for his tuition out of a subventional fund.—It is a different matter, and quite in harmony with our expressed object, when we come to the point where the pupil, having gained a technical mastery through private tuition, is to advance towards the cultivation of his æsthetic taste for the beauty of right rendering. Here is the crux, where even our best orchestras are not yet warranted in "conserving," but in truth themselves still need that education which shall bring their achievements to an equal height with the works of the great German masters themselves ; and here the intervention of a higher Music-school, to aid in cultivating a classic German music-style, becomes a question of grave moment.

Let me therefore first throw a needful ray of light on the German so-called Concert-world.—

By side of the German opera-houses—in which one rings the changes upon every form of operatic music by new and old Italian and French masters, the classic operas of German masters, such as Gluck and Mozart, and so on—

Concert-establishments have arisen, which likewise make it their business to entertain their subscribers with every form of purely instrumental music, as also of mixed choral music. The character of these musical entertainments is twofold, founded on the one side upon virtuosity, on the other, upon the decline of music in the churches. The virtuoso who wanted to be heard on his particular instrument, bade-in the public of the city he was travelling through ; to back his personal efforts, and to give them the relief of contrast, he summoned the aid of other virtuosi, preferably of favourite singers, as also of an orchestra to open and fill up the programme with an overture or symphony. These were called "concerts," for reason of the contests of the virtuosi who appeared therein. Beside them, especially in Protestant countries, church-music emigrated to the concert-room under the title of Oratorios, and found both imitation and diffusion—gaining prominent favour in England on account of the religious label. Through a compromise and blend of these two elements, essentially most wide apart, have arisen the great Musical Festivals to which the Germans treat themselves each summer, at various places ; and each winter these, again, are copied on a smaller scale at so-called Subscription-concerts, for the social entertainment of a section of the city-public. People think themselves justified in viewing the intrinsic musical culture of the German public as issuing from these concert-establishments ; with good reason insofar as the most earnest and most inspired works of our great German masters belong precisely to the realm of Instrumental-music, and, being suited for the purpose, can here the most often be brought to hearing. But never yet have we learnt a little caution in our rating of that influence, from the fact that, by side of these more solid art-delights, the public notwithstanding pays its eager visits to the worst stage-performances of the vilest genre of Opera ; also that, immediately before or after a symphony by Mozart or Beethoven, the most nonsensical behaviour of a virtuoso, the most trivial aria of a prima donna, could often win applause, nay, rouse enthusiasm,—not even this has been able to shew our concert-givers the plague-spot of their undertakings, despite the straits to which they are put in compiling a good programme under the circumstances. The habit of seeing the room filled to suffocation with the large family-circles who here, for a relatively insignificant subscription-price, find place and opportunity to satisfy the social need of an innocent conceit and a just as harmless entertainment, may have contributed its share to blinding them; the readiness wherewith this public lets itself be led and governed in its taste, its often enthusiastic-seeming submission to what is christened classical and excellent, its willingness to recognise the authority of leading minds,—all this might so far delude them, that they dreamt they had reached in Concert-institutes the acme of German musical life.

Undeception would very soon arrive if our subscribers left us, one fine day, and sought for satisfaction of their social needs in some other kind of form; if haply scientific lectures, chemical experiments and so forth, were to offer a still cheaper opportunity of entertainment. Let us admit the case is possible. But what would then be adduced, to explain the lamentable, the astounding falling-off of sympathy? A decline in public taste for music? But didn't you say you had its cultivation in the hollow of your hands? It remained with you, to stamp your pleasure on it; and, as that was dubbed a classical good-pleasure, wherefore did you not succeed?

The fault is this, *we possess classical works, but as yet no classic rendering for them.* The works of our great masters have influenced the larger public rather through Authority, than through a genuine impression on the Feeling, and it therefore has as yet no sterling taste for them. And in this, but in precisely this, consists the hypocrisy of our cult of Classicality, upon which so much opprobrium has been cast from quarters not worth noticing. Only see what care and trouble the Italians and French have devoted to rendering the works of their respective classical epochs;

look, even to-day, at the quite admirable diligence wherewith French musicians and orchestras have sought to digest
the hardest works of Beethoven and make them appeal
directly to the Feeling : and it will be astonishing how
easily we Germans persuade ourselves that everything
comes to us of itself, through a miraculous gift of Nature.
Let anyone name me the school in Germany where the
authentic rendering of Mozart's music has been established
and preserved ! Does this come to our orchestras and
their appointed chiefs so absolutely of itself ? But who
has ever taught it them ?—Take the very simplest instance,
the instrumental works of Mozart (by no means the master's
true chef-d'œuvres, for those belong to Opera), and you
shall here see two things : their great claims upon a singable rendering, and its scanty indications in the scores
bequeathed us. We know how hurriedly Mozart wrote
down the score of a Symphony, for mere purpose of one
particular performance at a concert he was just about to
give ; and on the other hand, how peremptory he was with
regard to the expression of its song-like motives, when
rehearsing it with the orchestra. Everything here, you
see, was reckoned for the direct communion of the master
with his orchestra.   In the 'parts' it therefore sufficed
to mark the principal tempo, with simple specifications of
forte and *piano* for whole periods, because the conducting
master could dictate aloud to his bandsmen the rendering
he wanted for his themes, actually singing them for the
most part.   Even to-day, albeit we have accustomed ourselves to a most minute notation of the nuances of phrasing,
the more talented conductor often finds himself obliged to
teach his bandsmen very weighty, but delicate shadings of
expression by *vivâ voce* explanation ; and these communi-
cations, as a rule, are better understood and heeded, than
the written signs.   How important they were for the rendering of Mozart's instrumental works, of all others, is
obvious.   As distinguished from the so-called working-out,
and particularly the 'bridge-work' of his symphonic movements—traced, on the whole, with a certain flightiness—

the main stress of his invention is laid upon the tuneful-
ness of the themes. Compared with Haydn's, Mozart's
symphonies are of significance almost solely through this
extraordinarily feeling, *singing* nature of their instrumental
themes ; in it lies expressed the thing that makes Mozart
both great and inventive in this branch of music too.
Now, had there existed in Germany an institute of like
authority with the Paris Conservatoire, in the case of
France, and had Mozart performed his works there, or been
able to supervise the spirit of their performance, we may
take for granted that an authentic tradition would have
been preserved to us ; in much the same way as the Paris
Conservatoire, for all the degeneracy that has crept in even
there, has still maintained an often surprisingly conspicuous
tradition for the performance *e.g.* of Gluck's music. This
was not the case, however : once, at a concert given by
him with an orchestra engaged for the occasion, at Vienna,
Prague or Leipzig, he performed this one particular
symphony, and the tradition has vanished without a trace.
All that remained, was the scantily notated score ; and this
classical relic of a production once vibrant with life is
stored as only standard for the rendering, is made with ill-
judged piety the only reason of the reproduction. Now let
us imagine one of the feeling themes of that master who
was saturated with the classic nobleness of the Italian vocal
art of earlier times down to the inmost throbs and pulsings
of its accent, the very soul of his expression, and that
master who laboured to inspire the orchestral instrument
with this expression as none before him ; let us imagine
this theme enounced without inflection, without the smallest light and shade of accent, without one of those modifications of time and rhythm so needful to the singer, played
smooth and neat with the same expression as one might
give to a musical sum : let us compute the difference
between the impression originally intended by the master
and that now actually received, and we shall be able to
judge the kind of piety observed toward Mozart's music
by our music-conservators. To put it still more clearly,

N

through a definite example, let us compare the first
eight bars of the second movement of Mozart's famous
"Symphony in E-flat major" merely played in the sleek
fashion, apparently demanded by its marks of expression,
with the rendering instinctively imagined for this wondrous
theme by any musician of feeling; how much of the real
Mozart do we get, when set before us thus bare of life and
colour?   A soulless pen-music ; nothing more.—

I have dwelt at some length upon this simpler, plainer
illustration, to enable me to sketch with fewer strokes the
incalculable injury to which a like procedure must needs
expose the abundant riches of Beethoven's instrumental
music, for whose rendering and execution we have hardly
one reliable tradition.   It is an established fact, that Beethoven himself could never obtain an entirely adequate performance of his difficult instrumental works.   As he had to
bring one of his hardest symphonies to light of day in two
brief rehearsals, and himself in a state of deafness too, we
may imagine with what a desperate indifference he regarded
the experiment ; particularly if we remember with what
unparalleled care and minute exactitude he was wont to
formulate his claims upon Expression when an artistic
union, such as the eminent Schuppanzig Quartet, stood at
his beck with needful blind devotion.   In the scores bequeathed to us by Beethoven we certainly find by far more
definite indications for the rendering, than with Mozart ;
but the task itself not only is higher and higher-pitched—
it is just so much the more difficult, as Beethoven's thematism is more complex than Mozart's.   Quite new demands
on rendering arrive with Beethoven's works, through their
uncommonly expressive use of Rhythm ; and to find the
right tempo for a movement of a Beethovian symphony,
above all to discover that tempo's perpetual, intensely
delicate, and speaking modifications—without which the
import of the extraordinarily eloquent musical phrase often
stays completely unintelligible—is a task which every
appointed orchestra-leader of nowadays has no scruple in
embarking on, but only because he has not the faintest

notion of what it means. Add to this the nature of Beethoven's treatment of the orchestra, which often offers obstacles to clearness in the music's rendering : its *idea*, indeed, was far in advance of the technical combinations of the orchestra of his day, but, through his adhesion to the only instrumental usage handed down by his forerunners, the tone-poet's thought not seldom failed of reaching due and palpable distinctness in its utterance.* Moreover in the weightiest periods of his life and work he was hindered from making this orchestra a speaking likeness of his thoughts, by the deafness which withdrew him from immediate converse with its world of timbres. In many most important cases the master's thought is only to be brought to really cognisable utterance through a most intelligent, refined and dexterous combination and modification of its orchestral expression ; and this must be done with at least the care bestowed by the orchestra of the Paris Conservatoire, when it devoted three full years to the study of Beethoven's Ninth Symphony.

But, not content with leaving these nearest problems entirely unsolved as yet, the conservators of our concert-establishments have hunted up the works of far remoter masters, and finally of every age and style ; to find in an aggravation of the difficulties of their task, as it would seem, an apology for really solving none of them. Since

---

* " Halten wir hierzu noch die, der Deutlichkeit des musikalischen Vortrages nicht selten hinderliche, Beschaffenheit der Beethoven'schen Behandlung des Orchesters, für welche er in der Idee weit den technischen Kombinationen des ihm zeitgenössischen Orchesters vorausgeeilt war, so ergiebt es sich, dass oft der Gedanke des Tondichters durch die Verwendung der Instrumente, wie sie ihm von seinen Vorgängern als einziger Gebrauch überliefert war, nicht zu entsprechender sinnfälliger Deutlichkeit gelangte."—For clearness' sake I have been obliged to somewhat alter the structure of this sentence, preserving as far as possible, however, the literal sense of each several clause. The "instrumental usage handed down by his forerunners " (quite literally, " the employment of the instruments as handed down to him, as only usage, by his forerunners ") evidently refers to the traditional 'register' or compass observed by Beethoven's predecessors, and retained by himself, for the violin, flute, &c.—as specified by our author in his essay on "Conducting," where he shews that Beethoven, finding a phrase exceed the traditional compass, for instance, would continue it an octave lower.—TR.

one surely can make nothing further out of Beethoven, one lately takes Sebastian Bach for choice ; as though it must needs be easier, to find an answer to that most stupendous riddle of all time !   To comprehend Bach's music, requires so special, so profoundly reflective a musical culture, that the folly of foisting it upon the public, in the modern flippant manner of performance too, can only be explained by the offenders' utter ignorance of what they are doing. Passing over the intrinsic character of this music, we have simply to remark that its mode-of-rendering has become one of the very hardest problems for us, since here the tradition itself, supposing it even provable, could never help us to success ; for, as far as we can ascertain how Bach himself performed his works, he was quite peculiarly a victim to the misfortune incident on every other German master, that of not having at his disposal the fitting *means* for a perfectly correct performance.   We know with what utterly threadbare means, and under what uncommonly disheartening circumstances, was Bach empowered to bring his excessively difficult music-works to even a hearing ; and from this one fact we may judge how resigned, how in-different at last, the master became to their rendering, and how for him it left their contents wellnigh nothing but a thought-play of the inmost soul.—It therefore will be an outcome of the highest and most complete artistic culture, to discover and establish for the works of this most won-drous master, too, that mode-of-rendering which shall make them entirely understandable to Feeling, shall set them open for all future ages.   What an exertion it first will need, however, we now will try to make clear.

To indicate the path hereto, I must commence by re-ferring once more to the essential tendence of the proposed Music-school, which can be of profit only when it rigidly confines its work to fostering the art of Rendering.   Just as with the pupil's purely scientific education in the theory of composition, the school should merely prescribe the main lines for his purely technical learning of the tools of tone, and direct him to the fittest media of instruction ;

but its general course of study must prepare him for acquit ing the best method.* The invisible bond, uniting the various branches of tuition, will always have to be the tendence of the Rendering. For this Rendering, then, not only must one mature the tools of tone themselves, but above all the æsthetic taste, the self-reliant judgment of the Right and Beautiful.† From the standpoint of a teaching-establishment one can only operate upon the first, the execution through the tools of tone, by the most aimful development of the second, the æsthetic taste and judgment. In keeping with the whole tendence of our Music-school, this cannot be pursued upon an abstract scientific path, mayhap through academic lectures and the like ; but here, too, we must strike the purely practical path of direct artistic exercise, under higher guidance for the rendering. Music's need in this direction has led to the invention and elaboration of the rightful instrument, which enables the single musician, by dint of certain abstractions and reductions, to completely represent to himself the idea of complex polyphonic pieces. The *pianoforte* is of the greatest significance for the evolution of modern polyphonic music, inasmuch as it supplies to self-dependence a directly practical and quite unreplaceable means of mastering the content and expression of almost every kind of music, even the most complicated. At the pianoforte, not only can the educated musician directly set before his solitary self the form and contents of a polyphonic tone-piece ; he also can plainly and definitely impart to the somewhat more advanced pupil the art of Rendering. Upon no single instrument can the idea of modern music be more clearly expounded, than through the ingenious mechanism of the

---

* "Wie der rein wissenschaftlichen Ausbildung des Schülers im Kompositionsfache, soll sie auch der rein technischen Erlernung der Tonwerkzeuge nur durch Feststellung der Grundrichtung die geeignetsten Mittel nachweisen und, allgemein bildend, auf die beste Methode hierfür vorbereitend wirken."—

† "Für den Vortrag sind daher nicht nur die Tonwerkzeuge selbst, sondern namentlich der ästhetische Geschmack, das selbstständige Urtheil für das Schöne und Richtige auszubilden." *Here* the comprehensive term, "the tools of tone," evidently refers more particularly to the performers.—TR.

pianoforte; and it therefore has become for our music the virtual chief-instrument—were it only through our greatest masters having written a considerable portion of their finest, and their works the weightiest for Art, expressly for this instrument. Thus, when we wish to denote the acme of German music, we place immediately beside the Beethovenian Symphony the Beethoven Sonata; and from the standpoint of our school we cannot go to work more hopefully or more instructively, for the formation of a correct and fine taste in rendering, than by starting with an education in the rendering of the Sonata, to develop the faculty of correct judgment of the rendering for the Symphony.

A quite peculiar care will therefore have to be bestowed on proper pianoforte-tuition, when the Music-school is established; only, that tuition must be conducted on quite other lines than heretofore, to answer to the higher end we have kept alone in view. As with the orchestral instrument, we relegate the learning of the sheer technique of the pianoforte to private tuition, and only to the already finished technician would the school stand open for instruction in the higher art of rendering.

This higher instruction would operate in two distinct directions: whereas the maturing of virtuosity pure and simple, in the special case of pre-eminent talent, would again be a matter for [?—pecuniarily assisted] private tuition, our instruction in the correct and beautiful rendering of classical pianoforte-music would aim at the formation of good pianoforte-teachers, on the one side, of good orchestral and choral conductors on the other. As touching the first side, we must pay special attention to training good pianoforte-teachers for simple reason that this instrument, the widest-spread of modern times and to be found in every family, has become the virtual ambassador of Music to the public. Therefore if we mean to rightly influence the taste of the uncommonly numerous body of amateurs, we here already have a road that pierces straight into the entertainment of the home. Nothing can more bitterly avenge itself, than the disregarding of

this influence ; and a great part of the deep-seated failure
of all Classical efforts, especially at our concert-institutes,
explains itself when we find that here, in the home-circle
and for the self-amusement of the amateur, the vilest
music, or the worst style of rendering, is harboured commonly without a check.   It is not our amateurs themselves,
however, whom the Music-school is to instruct ; as said,
it has to train their future teachers in the right course of
beautiful rendering, so that their subsequent instruction of
the amateurs may become, in turn, a fountain of noble
taste for music within the public's midst.   But here, with
the doings of our pianoforte-players, the case is just the
same as with the doings of our orchestras.   The correct
rendering for the Beethoven Sonata has never yet been
formed and fixed into a classic style ; still less have the
right modes of rendering for pianoforte-works (*Klavier-
werke*) of earlier periods been once for all laid down and
cherished.

In what we have termed the second direction, the prospective musical conductor will therefore best prepare himself at the pianoforte, and by close acquaintance with the
so immensely important literature of our classical pianoforte-compositions, for his most weighty office.   It is not
requisite for him to know the instruments of the orchestra,
which he is one day to direct, as an executant musician
himself; for their compass, their idiosyncrasies and the
suitable mode of treating them, a listening to excellent
performances, coupled with a study of the score itself, will
give him the best of lessons ; so far as he ought to be more
intimately acquainted with delivery (*Vortrag*) through his
personal experience, he will learn enough by sharing in
the singing-lessons : the æsthetic means of mastering the
more complex rendering of larger tone-pieces he will best
acquire through the pianoforte.   Besides private tuition in
the theory of composition, the pupil intending to become a
conductor of musical performances would therefore advance
through his share (*Theilnahme*) in the higher practice of
the pianoforte to the power of correctly judging the form

and substance of the nobler works of our classical masters
—the closest acquaintance with which, and in correct performance too, alone can yield the fitting finish to his
education.

It would ill beseem our only tendence, that of a practical
introduction to the correct rendering of good music, if,
finally arrived at the climax of preparatory education, we
were to follow the example of purely scientific establishments and make the last attainment of our goal a course
of academic lectures on the Æsthetics of the art of Tone,
forsooth, or the History of Music. The true æsthetics and
the sole intelligible history of music, on the contrary, we
must teach in nowise save by beautiful and correct performances of works of classical music ; and, with the scheme for
such performances, we now have touched the quick of all
our efforts to plan a truly efficient curriculum for the
higher Music-school we have in mind.

What has hitherto been taken all unprepared and un-
led-up-to, without a reasoned choice or aimed conjunction,
and set before an audience of mere amateurs, at our concert-
establishments ; the rich, but scrambled, treasure of the
classical music-literature of every age and nation : this now
should be first taken for the culture and instruction of the
pupils of our school, in well-devised selection, in aimful
sequence and conjunction, and performed in such a fashion
that before all else the participants in these performances
themselves shall have the essence and value of the works
disclosed to them by practice in their truest rendering.

To frame a plan of selection and graduated sequence, to
be followed in bringing on the works aforesaid, will certainly demand the utmost thought ; and perhaps the complete and successful solution of this problem not merely
must depend on circumstances, but can only result from a
long series of intelligently conducted tests. Thus much
is certain : the present compilation of our best concert-
programmes has simply proved a snare and delusion to
any culture of sound taste. As we have already had occasion to denounce their evil consequences from the outside

point of view, we here must chiefly note the harmful influence of such wayward assortments of works of the most diverse style upon the executants themselves. To set Bach, Mozart, and finally a composer of the latest school, directly side by side, is every whit as injurious to the rendering of their works as it bewilders the audience— which in such a case, indeed, will give vent to its feelings in boisterous applause of Rossini's overture to "William Tell," for instance, at the selfsame concert where it has just heard Beethoven and Händel, as I myself once witnessed at one of the celebrated Leipzig Gewandhaus concerts. To be of any use in cultivating a healthy musical judgment among the public, too, the latter ought not to be admitted to hear the classical works of older periods until their execution has been arranged upon an aimful plan, which should above all aim at a first-class rendering. Since its tradition has been entirely lost to us, the right mode-of-rendering can be discovered only by a close consideration of the requirements of these works themselves, and settled only by directly practical tests of its effect. What has heretofore been attempted in the way of so-called Historical Concerts, arranged by æsthetes not really musicians themselves, sometimes with an honest aim, sometimes out of sheer speculation on the public's curiosity; and what, in the best event, could only produce on the audience an impression much akin to that made on the reader of a scientific treatise by algebraic illustrations printed in the text: this now should be undertaken with the primary object of establishing the most correct and suitable mode-of-rendering for those works, and at like time forming and fostering in the executants themselves the sense and judgment of true and beautiful delivery. A graduated progress from works of earlier to those of the latest epochs of music will not only be of profit to the exercise of artistic understanding, but suited also to the various grades of technical attainment among the executants themselves; and the joint rehearsals founded on this method would consequently make out the very pith of the plan of teaching at our Music-school.

While executants and conductors thus familiarise themselves with the rendering of masterworks of various schools
and epochs, for cultivation of their own taste and judgment,
they are accumulating a store of musical art to impart to
the lay public for cultivation, in turn, of the taste and
judgment of the amateur.   And should there remain any
doubt in the School itself as to the correct method for this
or that musical work of a remoter period, the lay public,
unbiased by scholastic study and solely guided by instinctive Feeling, would mostly give the right and final
verdict.*   Lastly, after we had made our ripest selection
and arrangement of the programme, and performed its
pieces in the faithfulest mode-of-rendering we could devise
for them, an audience thus unimplicated in the strict experiments of the school would also give us the best information as to whether we had failed in any detail, or
even whether the tone-works themselves, which we had
hunted up, really contained that genuine beauty and fairest
truth which appeal to purely-human Feeling throughout
all time.   These weighty meetings of our executants with
the public proper, formative and instructive to both parties
alike, in future would fill the place of the customary classical or mixed concert-entertainments, whose weakness we
have shewn above ; and our School would thus extend
itself on this side to culture of the Public's self, by directly
offering it the most perfect musical enjoyment.

Making first for measures to promote a true artistic taste
in the musical profession, I defer a discussion of their effects
upon the inventive productivity of the present day; but,
not to leave one-sided the proposed institution's conservative and formative influence upon Style, we have still to
consider its extension from the Concert-room to its nearest
of kin, the Theatre.   What would it profit us to cultivate
a nobler, sterling art-taste in our school, if we had ultimately
to abandon our pupils to exploitation by an establishment

* " Wollt ihr nun vor dem Volke zeigen, wie hoch die Kunst ihr ehrt . . .
so lasst das Volk auch Richter sein."   Hans Sachs, in *Die Meistersinger*, act i.
—TR.

which, nowise sharing in our culture and withdrawn from any responsibility for the spirit of its own doings, should pull down all that we had built up, through its senseless panderings to the so profoundly degraded operatic taste of our age? To find the proper starting-point for our School's indispensable influence upon the Theatre too, we have simply to bear in mind the latter's need of good and practised singers, whose paucity and costliness are so huge an obstacle to its subsistence. That the doings and productions of the Theatre are stricken with the same faults and imperfections as our Concert-establishments themselves, only in a greater measure, we scarcely need set forth at length; to claim for its doings the same tendence as claimed for the public performances of our School, however, we merely have to draw attention to the *universal* nature of the German repertoire, compiled as it is from works of every age and style, in quite the manner of our present concert-programmes.

As we have already come to terms about the Opera itself, I here will pass it completely over, and—to set my broader purpose in the clearest light at once—forthwith address myself to the requirements of the so-called Recited Play.

When Gluck and Mozart wrote their operas, the needful style of singing could be studied in Italy and Paris; but when Goethe and Schiller gave their noblest poems to the Play, there existed neither the merest semblance of a school nor any kind of prototype for the delivery of their verses, the rendering of their refined and purely-human pathos. In their natural evolution our actors had not yet passed beyond the so-called Burgher-drama, and shortly before had changed the verse of Shakespeare into prose; they were completely set aghast by the problems suddenly proposed them by our great poets. Brought up in the so-called school of Naturalism, they believed it impossible to master these rhythmic verses save by reducing them to prose once more: since the claims of rhythm still held the upper hand, however, less conscientious declaimers practised these verses to a kind of banal melody, which soon became an unreasoning mannerism, wholly destroying both sense and content. Whoso has devoted any attention to the natural and promising development of German acting at about the middle of the eighteenth century, knows that it since fell victim to a swift decay. This dates from the appearance of the higher Drama of Goethe and Schiller. Here we have striking confirmation of the mournful feature peculiar to the evolution of German art : whilst the nation's general state of art-culture offers nothing even remotely resembling those artistic requisites (*künstlerischen Hilfs-mittel*) which abroad are so well-organised that the French or Italian author scarce needs more than to keep himself abreast of his nation's culture to put forth the best he has within him, creative geniuses arise among the Germans of such a grandeur and significance that, towering high above the heroes of abroad, they outtop in requirements for the portrayal of their works even everything which *there* could be supplied. Though we are minded to derive from this singular fate a warrant for boldest hopes of the ultimate greatness and glory of German Art, yet, to give those hopes a practical basis, at present we must lay chief stress upon the cheerless evils that have arisen from this amazing discrepance between Will and Can. Incapable of appro-priating Goethe and Schiller in such wise that a valid, veritable Style should have been evolved from solution of the problems posed by them, the German Play was turned from its more restricted natural development, by these invincible demands of Idealism, and fell experimenting with the works of every age and nation exactly as we have shewn to be the case with our concert-givers ; and just as there one ranged beside the un-understood and non-eluci-dated Beethoven the masters of all ages, up to Bach, so here one dragged on Molière, Calderon, Shakespeare, ay, Sophocles and Æschylus at last, as if by a general shuffling of the cards to conceal their individual want of finish. To mark the lamentable consequences plain for anyone to see, I will simply draw attention to one circumstance, namely

that it would be difficult, wellnigh impossible, to recommend from among our actors of to-day even the teacher of
correct pronunciation and declamation in classic modes of
verse whom we need for our very first department, the
intended Singing-school. Strictly speaking then, this
purely practical question would itself afford us the starting-
point for a much-needed reform of the Play ; I therefore
content myself with the above brief survey, in support
of my opinion that the Play, as well, should be drawn
into the circle of our efforts to found a genuine Style of
Rendering.

Indispensable to ensure our reaching our nearest goal,
on the one side, upon the other it will be of the utmost
consequence to that institute itself, if the Theatre—specifically inclusive of the Play—can be submitted to the
leading principles of our art-educational establishment,
which then must necessarily be widened to embrace a
Stage-school. For this we should find due motive in the
tendence stamped on the German Theatre by its practical
need, the tendence to compile its repertory from the
classical works of every age and nation ; making it incumbent upon us, just as in the case of purely musical works
and for exactly the same reasons, to first of all search out
with care, to teach, and finally establish, their right mode of
representation. Everything said anent the former case
applies with equal force to this ; both there and here, it is
primarily a question of mastering the spirit and form of
reproduction for works remote from our immediate humour,
and works that have been kept green by no manner of
ascertainable tradition. If the whole work of establishing
a school for the cultivation of artistic taste is not to be
undermined forthwith, we must be deterred by neither the
difficulties of possessing ourselves of such an influence nor
those of exerting it. Above all, the *public* will be speedily
won over to us, without a doubt ; for the classical works of
every age are already set before it from sheer exigence of
the repertoire, whether it understands them or no, and it
will soon comprehend that the share we ask it to take in

our earnest studies is limited to receiving those works henceforward in correct and living representation, intelligible to simple human Feeling. What attitude the public, once a proper understanding of classical works has fitted it for true enjoyment of the doings of theatric art in general, will adopt toward those dramatic products which can never arrive at a fine and fascinating rendering for very reason of their nugatory nature, belonging to no style but that of mere routine and mannerism,—this will easily be proved at last by experience, and surely will bear out the clear idea already formed by those who know the questions dealt with. So soon as we make it our invariable rule, that everything given at the theatre shall be given well and rightly, we denote at once the side of our repertoire alone worthy of the trouble. But since the Theatre has been assigned the at any rate dubious tendence of a place of Entertainment, as needed by the populace of our great cities ; and since it even might alarm the police, were we to brusquely oppose that tendence with a too great reduction of the number of theatre-nights, for instance: we should have to consider how to keep the absolutely trivial tendence away from that theatric institute which, on the other side, is called to contribute so decisively to the promotion of a nobler art-taste. What road we ought to take, so as to exercise a humane indulgence and offer no offence to naïve habits, yet to attain our end with open eyes, we must learn from a comprehensive judgment of the value and tendence of the present pursuits of practical life. We will shortly approach the solution of that riddle on a purely empiric path ; but, having already been led so far afield by the theoretic construction of our proposed educational establishment, we first must discuss the practical possibilities of its actual, its living institution.

While I should like to see a Commission of conscientious experts entrusted with the task of surmounting the great difficulties which purely personal considerations will certainly import into the execution of the scheme, I now feel bound to lay before *Your Majesty* my own view of the procedure necessary to call into practical life the arrangements I aim at. The one great difficulty, that of setting aside the present admittedly unsuccessful arrangements at the Royal Conservatorium of this city, I believe it my duty to pass entirely over, since they involve administrative problems of a purely personal character, for whose solution I under no circumstances could feel myself qualified. To unfold my plan, then, I must start with the assumption that the special Royal Commission for the purpose will succeed in satisfactorily overcoming the difficulties of that needful removal, and thus make room for our initial requirement, the reduction of the Royal Conservatorium to its original basis, that of a simple Singing-school.

The manning of this Singing-school I regard as an especially difficult task. The experience that in no German conservatoire has vocal instruction been carried on with real success, is sufficient evidence of that difficulty. For certain, no branch of study requires so assiduous a personal attention, as that of singing. To obtain a really faultless production (*Entwickelung*) of the human voice, particularly in Germany and under influence of the German tongue, demands incessant supervision of the smallest details, most patient and painstaking exercises. Whereas the technical laws for learning every instrument have been thoroughly established, and can be taught the pupil by any skilled executant, the technique of singing is even yet a positive enigma, and must therefore first be finally unriddled by our school. Our foremost care will consequently be the formation of a firstrate body of assistant teachers, under a thoroughly competent Singing-Director. Just as with the instruments and musical theory, the vocal tuition proper can only be a private one, *i.e.* to be imparted singly, not collectively: but whilst our teachers for every instrument are procurable already in the more distinguished members of the Royal Court-Orchestra, for song they must really be first created. The singing-teachers, either resi-

dent here or to be summoned from elsewhere—and in
time they would best be obtained from among the finished
pupils themselves—would first have to come to a mature
agreement upon the lines to be followed in establishing
the most expedient vocal method.* It would be the duty
of the Singing-Director to superintend and rectify the
prosecution of this method, through a most minute inspection of its results with individual pupils.

Now, as I believe that the whole question of a larger
Music-school must be made dependent on the issue of these
studies, I hold it indispensable to wait in patience for the
success of our efforts to form and eventually establish an
efficient method of voice-cultivation, and to bestow all our
care and all our available means upon that alone, before
thinking of enlarging the institute. If only we arrive at
this one thing, if a Singing-school upon a sure and stable
foundation has been crowned with success beyond all
doubt, then the hardest problem has been solved, the
problem nowhere rightly broached as yet, and we have
laid the solid ground for every further development.

Just as Speech and Tone meet one another in the rudi-
ments of Song, so in its higher development and application Music and Poetry join hands. Even the moulding of
tone requires the aid of *speech*, though here in none but the
lesser, the physical meaning of the term ; so that for mere
elementary instruction in voice-producing the singing-
master must himself supply our linguistic requirements.
But should the result of our preliminary efforts have
proved successful, now that we have reached the higher
stage of vocal training we shall need the help of a teacher
of elocution and declamation. Called-in at first to teach

---

* " Den vorhandenen und sonst noch zu berufenden Gesangslehrern, welche
mit der Zeit aus den gebildeten Schülern selbst am besten sich werden gewinnen
lassen, würde zunächst eine reiflich zu erwägende Verständigung über Annahme
und Feststellung der zweckmässigsten Methode aufzugeben sein."—As a good
many of the sentences in this particular essay suffer from the circumlocution
apparently inseparable from official documents, just possibly the meaning here
is, that the " method " must first be devised by some external authority, and
then committed to the teachers for carrying out.—TR.

the singer only, his value and efficiency would of themselves suggest an extension of his duties to the education
of disciples of the unmixed art of Play.   This very obvious
extension, which necessarily must be of the weightiest
consequence, we ought to take most seriously in view when
choosing the said teacher ; and, should we succeed in
finding a man peculiarly adapted for the post,* to him
should be made over the direction of the Stage-school
proper : an arrangement which would be completed, in my
opinion, by our giving him an under-teacher for the purely
elocutionary and declamatory studies, together with a really
cultured ballet-master for the pupil's higher requirements
in the way of plastic and mimetic training.   A share in
the exercises of the purely histrionic school, again, would
be good for those pupils of the Singing-school whose
powers were sufficiently developed to allow of their adopting a dramatic career.   Thus, with the constitution of a
Stage-school, the second phase of building up our training
establishment—its first phase having been occupied by the
Singing-school—would have come to a conclusion.

But when the Singing-school proper had proved successful in a more than elementary training of the voice, it
would supply the motive for a third phase of development,
that of Musical Theory, as concerns the needful knowledge
of Harmony and the capacity to analyse the compositions
about to be performed.   As the only practical basis for
this extension on the side of pure Music, to be directly
adopted by the school itself, I have already spoken at
length of Pianoforte-playing, with its direction to the
understanding and critical judgment of higher musical
Rendering.   Referring to my detailed, exposition of that
branch of musical education, I consider the last requirements for the strictly practical curriculum of the extended
Music-school would be met by the appointment of an
adequate staff for teaching pianoforte-expression, since
one would not need to appoint special teachers for the
other instruments (the orchestral instruments proper) but

* Obviously Ludwig Schnorr, as will be seen in the next essay.—Tr.

O

simply to organise and systematise the teaching-forces already existing.

I must somewhat explain my ideas on this point.

There would be no sense in the subsistence of a private body of musical teachers, left purely to their own devices, beside an official Music-school. Our school can fulfil the tendence repeatedly assigned to it above, only when its quickening and cultivating influence governs the whole line of taste of at least the city where it works. Instead of forming in addition to a scattered class of private teachers a limited official body shut off by its own walls, our school should therefore draw all the music-teachers of the city into the circle of its functions, and simply make itself the guiding head of members hitherto dissevered ; merely organising musical tuition, so to speak, and stamping it with its own higher tendence. The appointed chief-teacher of each single branch would accordingly become the Director of his respective teaching-division, and his duty would consist in the organisation—to be constantly renewed to meet fresh circumstances—and continual supervision of the instruction given by the departmental teachers who had associated themselves with the institute.

The proposed organisation of the various departments may be easiest illustrated by the relation which the Music-school would enter toward the musicians of the Royal Court-Orchestra, since we here have all the needful teaching - material united in an existing corporation. Plainly, it would be folly to think of appointing special teachers for the various orchestral instruments, seeing that due care has already been taken to acquire the best masters when manning their respective desks in the Royal Court-Orchestra. The Director of any particular teaching-department would accordingly hand over the pupils, whose general musical education the school had undertaken, to be taught the instruments of their choice by the respective masters of the principal first-instruments in the Orchestra ; and the Director's share in this tuition would be limited to overhauling its results, and keeping them in harmony with the expressed higher tendence of the school through a proper cultivation of æsthetic taste for classical expression. This would be effected on the one hand by periodical examinations, to be attended by the teacher—for his method itself must be subject to a needful criticism, if he is to retain the confidence of the Music-school ; on the other hand, by joint practice in the rendering of orchestral pieces, under the immediate direction of the Music-school's own conductor.

In the same manner as with the masters of the various instruments of the Royal Court-Orchestra, the easily-ascertainable foremost private-teachers of Munich in singing, pianoforte-playing, the theory of composition etc., would have to be called to assist in the school's instruction, as need arose. The means of supervising their tuition, and stamping it with the higher tendence of the Music-school, would remain the same as for the orchestral school: namely, periodical examinations of the scholars in presence of their teachers—upon a sliding scale of frequency—and joint rehearsals, extending to performances in public.

The last phase in the enlargement of the Music-school would therefore be its expansion to a complete Orchestral institute,* embracing the whole resident body of musical teachers and executants more or less directly in the operations of the school, and excluding no substantial talent. The effective staff of the school, however, when broadly based on this alliance of all existing teaching-forces, might be fairly simplified. With a thorough organisation and efficient supervision of private instruction, one would scarcely need more than the Directors of the single branches ; and I believe that in future, besides the Director of Song, the Director of the Stage-school, the Director of Pianoforte-playing and finally the Director of the Orchestra (upon both of whom it would be incumbent to

* "Ihre Ausbildung zu einem vollständigen Orchesterinstitute."—Either our author has made a slip of the pen, and meant to say " vocal *and* orchestral," or he uses the word " orchestra," as in Vol. II., page 336 (" Opera and Drama "), in a sense akin to the old Greek signification of the term.—TR.

teach the theory of Composition and higher Rendering), we should require at most an official under-master as substitute for each; whereas all direct tuition proper should be made over to the private teachers associated with the school, their services being rewarded upon an agreed scale of remuneration for single lessons.

To sum up the main functions of the Music-school, they would consist in *a continual testing of instruction, coupled with efficiently-conducted practice in common.* Moreover the school would come into contact with the public through presentation of the results of its practice, in the shape of concerts and stage-performances. While here suggesting no kind of interference with the continuance of the Court Orchestra and Theatre as independent administrative bodies (for even the co-operation of the whole Orchestra in the purely-musical performances of the School would have to be specially remunerated from the revenue of the latter), I merely wish to see the principle expressed, that the influence of the School should be exerted upon the *spirit* of the doings of both these institutes; that is to say, what has hitherto been brought before the public by the Theatre and Orchestra in a state of disorganisation, disruption, unripeness and incorrectness, and has therefore had an undecided, nay, a false effect, should henceforth be offered to publicity in the only right condition, beautifully and universally-intelligibly performed.

And this is the meaning of the true conservative tendence: to cherish and preserve the classical works of the past by establishing and putting in practice their correct mode-of-rendering, in such a way that not only shall the artists themselves acquire the sense of true and beautiful expression, a fine artistic taste, but the general sense of Art [among the public] shall also reach its highest power and cultivation, upon the only groundwork proper to the German spirit. Arrived at this height, of a genuine "Conservatorium" for music, our Music-school would at last have won the basis whence to exert an influence on the further evolution of Art itself; and simply through its furnishing, beyond the stimulus of classical example, above all the fit artistic media for the bringing forth of new and noble artworks. In what this stimulus and help would then consist, we may readily perceive, if first we picture to ourselves the result of efforts as conducted hitherto.

Indisputably a great mission lies prefigured in the whole temper of the German, and a mission scarce within the cognisance of other nations. The exceptional difficulties with which the evolution of German Art has had to battle, and which to make right clear has been a part of my endeavour in the preceding pages, repose almost principally upon that temper: when felicitously cultivated, it must be assigned the character of Universalism. What is a hindrance to the ripeness and correctness of our achievements, makes out alike the great significance of our artistic tendence. That only incorrectly are we able to set Bach, Beethoven, Goethe and Schiller before us, simply shews how high the temper of the German spirit is pitched, above the limit of its relations in Time and Space. What the grudge of these relations forbids our reaching here and to-day, must surely be reserved for us to reach some day, for a deeply inward reason moved those great masters to frame the conditions for their understanding precisely thus, and not otherwise. Whereas the Italian and French artist is borne in triumph on the shoulders of his nation, the noble German master reminds us of Frederick the Great when at Kollin he dashed on to take a battery and, looking round, discovered that his grenadiers had stayed behind. That fight was lost; but in the very same year his little army won the splendid victories of Rossbach and Leuthen, to the wonder of the world.

No character, however lofty, stands quite detached from the soil of its human surroundings : in *something* every German is akin to his great masters ; and this something, by the German's very nature, is capable of great, and therefore needs a slow, development. The German's feeling for true poesy and music is no fable. When to-day a German maiden bursts into tears at the most

farcical parody that ever travestied a noble German poet's-
work, at a performance of Gounod's Paris Boulevard-opera
"Faust," the more cultured observer is seized with a qualm
like that of Goethe's Faust upon entering the dungeon : he
marvels how the feeling for the true and sterling can be so
wondrously abused, and led astray, that loathing does not
at once fall back in horror from the grimacing lie. Yet
those tears of the German maiden have their source in an
emotion which cannot be far distant from the fountain
whence the great poet drew, himself, the inspiration for his
Gretchen. Not only that Beethoven and Goethe have
issued from our loins, but also that their works, despite
our present inability to conceive and represent them quite
distinctly, are yet remotely grasped and loved by us,—
bears witness to our natural capabilities. When in days
gone-by I heard Beethoven's enigmatic Ninth Symphony
work the audience at the Paris Conservatoire into an
ecstasy, so incredibly perfect had been the technique displayed that I fell doubting whether, after all, it was not just
that consummate virtuosity in the orchestra's performance
that had called forth this effect. Certain it is, that, being
in the position to contrast our now most frequent, but
mostly very indistinct performances of this wondrous work
with that Paris achievement, our praises—at last become
a positive habit—have woken doubts in me as to whether
the public's understanding of it be not a mere pretence.
Here, as there, a doubt too much inclined to one side
might go too far. Be that as it may, one must admit the
German public's closer kinship to the master's spirit, even
should its present acclamations be nothing more than
obedience to amiable Authority. To have introduced this
Authority, assuredly reflects no little credit on the estimable masters to whom we owe that introduction. True
Religion, no doubt, can only thrust into the deepest
chamber of the heart, as unshatterable and blessing Faith,
through the sublime and personal example of saints and
martyrs ; but it wellnigh always presupposes that this
Faith shall first have been accepted by the people on

authority. We will not be wroth with that Bishop of Paris who baptised wholesale the heathen hordes of Norman invaders, and made them Christians by casting white smocks upon them : through this white smock the idol-server was visibly detached from his former company and made distinguishable by the preacher, who could now proceed to pour the mysteries of the new doctrine into his heart. What has been done to spread belief in our great classics among the public, may be numbered with the most meritorious acts of German masters * ; and nowhere does experience offer us a more conspicuous occasion for valuing such services than here in Munich, where the propagation of this faith is due to the activity of a man who, even if as yet he has merely thrown upon his public those white garments of the first conversion of the heathen, had surely to begin with that, so as to prepare the soil for genuine musical culture.

Hereby alone has the path been broken, undoubtedly, for an understanding of the propagated works. But the question as to the degree of truth in that understanding becomes more serious and momentous, when we examine its effects upon the spirit and style of the creative musicians who have followed after. Here it is obvious that the veritable, the whole true Beethoven has hitherto remained without any real and wholesome influence upon the music-style of later days. The strangely flaccid, shapeless, superficial mannerism of the orchestral works of the post-Beethovenian school, woven from the most opposing strands of style, betrays no trace of influence from Beethoven's astounding plastique. The more frequent occupation in the last decad or two with the works of the master's latest period, and in particular with his last quartets, we can in no wise deem engendered by a growing

* Cf. *Die Meistersinger*, act iii. : " Verachtet mir die Meister nicht, und ehrt mir ihre Kunst ! . . . Ihr seht, wie hoch sie blieb in Ehr' : was wollt ihr von den Meistern mehr ? "—The allusion in the next clause is, obviously, to Franz Lachner ; see the essay on " Conducting," at the close of the present volume.—TR.

understanding; of this we are convinced on the one hand
by the unimpressive mode of rendering those works, on
the other, by their total lack of influence upon the manner
of more recent composers. Since we must explain the
latter largely by the former, here again we should have
sufficient cause to denounce the great mischief of the
present musical system in Germany. Precisely those last
quartets of Beethoven, still complete enigmas at deepest
bottom to the generality of German musicians, in Paris
have long been executed in consummate style by a society
of French musicians : these artists owe that result to the
upright diligence they have devoted to their only task for
years, a diligence prompted by a very proper feeling, and
solely directed to attainment of the correct rendering for
the song-like melody (*die gesangsmelodische Substanz*) of
these seemingly so hardly understandable works. They
held no bar acquitted, no ever so insignificant-looking
phrase, till they had succeeded in mastering its last
particle of melodic essence through discovery of the
corresponding technical expression ; and the truly surprising result is, that these music-pieces, erewhile reckoned
crude and turgid, suddenly appear so melodious, so limpid
and so prepossessing, that the most naïve audience cannot
at all comprehend why they should have been accounted
less intelligible than other compositions. This is a triumph
we no longer should allow French musicians to bear away ;
for among ourselves the intimate understanding of just
these wondrous works must necessarily exert a weightier,
and a more enduring influence, namely upon the forming
and fashioning of a Style in composition too, reserved for
none but German Music to achieve. Through those last,
and to us still unknown works of our wondrous master, of
all others, the power of Musical Expression has taken a
direction from which the music of earlier periods was often
bound to hold deliberately aloof: I here will call that
direction the *tenderly and deeply passionate*, through whose
expression Music first has raised herself to an equal height
with the poetry and painting of the greatest periods of the

past. Whilst Dante, Shakespeare, Calderon, and Goethe, like the great masters of painting in Italy and the Netherlands, with this expression took fee of every portrayable object in the world and man ; and whilst it was this, that first enabled them to really paint the world and man : in Music there had ruled an axiom which openly degraded her as a branch of Art, an axiom borrowed from the purely physical pleasure, the purely sensuous entertainment to be found in her. To what a point this narrow view of Music's mission still wanders to this day, particularly under the terrifying impression of the un-understood last works of Beethoven, we may perceive from the flat assertions of modern æsthetes when setting up their theories of the Beautiful in Music.* Us it behoves, on the contrary, to first take true and full possession of the whole rich heritage bequeathed us by our great masters, and, through full knowledge of the powers developed by Music hitherto, to procure ourselves due light on what development is still before her.

Naturally these questions, so far as amenable to a purely theoretic treatment, require the most careful and minute investigation, to obtain a scientific answer in step with the practical efforts of our School. Here we find the utmost hindrance in the deplorable state of Criticism, whose musical department is plied by our newspapers in a manner no longer to be let proceed unpunished. It surely is needless for me to add to the already excessive length of this memorandum by a closer illustration of the monstrosity of modern journalistic criticism. The unexampled levity, the unpardonable indifference, wherewith even the most conscientious editors of our newspapers abandon the rubric of "Music and Theatre " to the veriest gabblers, if only they know how to amuse the public a little, is a secret to no dispassionate observer. Since, then, the lesson of good taste is to issue from the School, one must further provide that the interesting information thereanent shall likewise be conducted in its sense.

* The title of Dr E. Hanslick's pamphlet.—TR.

Wherefore a journal, to be founded by the Music-school and edited by its head-masters, as Organ of the Munich Music-school, might advantageously be taken in eye at once. The numbers of this journal should first be occupied by the actual diary of the School, giving account and report of its doings ; next would come articles upon the tasks and problems propounded for settling the methods of instruction to be observed—treated in didactic fashion, as much for agreement among the teachers as for education of the pupils ; and finally a critical and speculative discussion of the higher aspects of any attempted extensions of Style—to form a channel between the artists themselves and the interested public.

So far, the direct agency of the School : to a real share in forming the *style* of the music-works of the future. That the actual creation of that Style can rest on nothing but the spirit evinced in the productions of creative artists now existing, is manifest ; that nothing but individual inspiration can give the whole its final shape, needs no authentication. But in what mode the struggling Artist of the Present may be supplied by our School with the proper media for performance of his works, what share the School is to take in the practical labours of our young composers, will best be gauged by the subject (*Gehalt*) and tendence of those labours. To the concerts and stage-performances of the institutes under influence of our School we primarily assigned a conservative tendence, that of forming and maintaining the correct style-of-rendering for masterworks of the past. In addition to that tendence, then, there must be given a cordial welcome, and the opportunity of most correct performance, to works of the struggling creative artist of the present. Now, such works as conform with a style of rendering already practised, and thus require no special study in the more important sense, might very well be ranged with the performances of older works, perhaps even given in some special conjunction with their nearest of kin. As to their value and admissibility, the School itself would have to decide.

Postponing a consideration of the mode of performance we should wish ensured to those works which, new of their kind and aiming at an extension of the style hitherto adopted, at like time call for innovation and extension in the mode-of-rendering, we now will deal with the case of musical or dramatic works to which one could assign no definite position upon either the one side or the other: works of sheer routine or mannerism. Manifest ineptitude in works of this class would naturally have to be dismissed with a word of counsel; but for works which, though higher grounds prevented our attaching them directly to the list of works of classic style, yet plainly possessed some individuality of invention, certain drastic qualities of expression, haply even a mere effectiveness attributable to their subject, there should at any rate remain open a path to public hearing. We refer to purely ephemeral works, born from the passing 'tendence of the day,' appealing to the crowd's delight in a less select entertainment, simply reckoned, perchance, as setting for some favourite performer; works often written with brightness and natural skill, frequently displaying great talent and developable originality, and thus [? constituting] the real source [or fountain—*Quell*] of immediate Folk-life, as, with all its faults and merits, it shapes itself according to its own bent. Against productions of this class we have no barriers to erect, but neither should their furtherance be committed to our care: we simply have to let them alone, since the spirit of the times will always see that those who flatter it shall not perish by the wayside. Folk-concerts and Folk's-theatre are the watchword of the day. I am of opinion that no obstacles should be laid in the path of our urban populace's ardent love of entertainment: only, the more we find the people trying to help itself to satisfy this need, as well as others, the more careful must we be that a truly cultivating influence shall extend from higher artistic circles to the taste of this side too,—and that, if we don't mean to simply forbid, can be compassed only through the instructive pattern, the good example. Wherefore the more room we have to allow the great Folk's-theatre now being built in Munich, the more freedom for the deploying of its forces, so much the more assiduously have we to insist upon excellence and purity in the doings of our School, as also of the musical and theatrical establishments affiliated to it. Nay, once the people's theatre had succeeded in acquiring a truly popular tendence, representing purely and unsulliedly the spirit of the Folk, our School would have to pay the keenest attention to its doings, if haply it [the School] might draw refreshing hints for form and substance from that fountain of directness. But in the path of so favourable an expectation from the labours of such a place of entertainment there stands full many a fear, alas ! but too well grounded—in part upon our opening judgment as to the whole condition of theatric art in Germany, in part upon the speculative character of all joint-stock establishments, which necessarily stamps them with the fundamental evil of every seemingly public-spirited enterprise in our commercial era.

While we therefore leave such undertakings entirely to their own devices, and prefer them to relieve us of what could only be a hindrance to the pursuit of our higher tendence, I must conclude by alluding once more to that institution which, I venture at least to promise myself, not only will further the highest interests of Art itself, but will also found and tend a genuine national feeling for them.

In the introduction to my Report I spoke of the simple groundplan of this momentous, this national, original-German institution. The conception of that groundplan was dictated to me by Need: faced with the ruling evils of the German Theatre, I could see no other possible means to good and correct performances of my newer dramatic works than that of Model-performances, to be given by a specially-selected company of artists, trained expressly for the purpose of correctly representing those works ; more-over, in a building planned expressly for such performances, where one would avoid all the disturbances arising from immediate contact with theatrical establishments engaged in nightly functions. I have been moved to make these stipulations in nowise by an overweening opinion of the special value of my works, but solely by the nature of their style, and their consequent demands upon a mode-of-rendering which has nowhere yet been nursed into the sureness of a genuine Style. In what these demands consist, and through what educational means they may be met by the executant artists, I have described at length in course of this memorandum, both theoretically and practically. That their fulfilment must be of great benefit to musical and dramatic art for all time, is obvious: to keep alive the zeal herefor, and kindle it anew, will need the constant stimulus of novel tasks, of tasks arising from new works by the creative masters of the nation.* On the other hand, the possibility of setting novel tasks can be smoothed for those masters only through the artistic means to their performance being kept in well-drilled readiness; and only this reciprocity between School and Masters can therefore ensure the welfare and the flourishing of both.

For its own nurture, then, the School in future should offer a perpetually open prize for works that, while related to some important aspect of the classic art it cherishes, yet propound new problems of performance and portrayal: this quality will be found indwelling in every truly original work, from whatsoever school or style it may take its starting-point; and the prize would consist in the work being commended to the nation through a special model-performance of the kind denoted. Finally, the arrangements in provision of such performances would obtain a monumental basis, so to speak, through there being built expressly for them a Model-theatre—whose inner construction, as regards a more efficient adaptation to higher artistic needs, Your Majesty has already committed to the inventive powers of a specially expert and famous architect. Thus, should every arrangement to that end have proved successful, the crowning of this momentous

---

* Cf. *Die Götterdämmerung*: "Zu neuen Thaten, theurer Helde, wie liebt' ich dich—liess' ich dich nicht?"—TR.

institution, of Festival-performances of nobly German original-works, would be formed by the dedication of a Festival-theatre, to nobly front the whole civilised world, a pattern for its purpose, a monument of the German Art-spirit. In this theatre, at a stated season in each returning year, the best and noblest works of its masters would be set before the German nation, in standard fashion; thereafter, their method of performance once thoroughly established, they could be made over to the remaining theatres, and in particular to the standing Court-and-National-theatre of Munich, for more frequent repetition in accordance with that pattern. And with the dedication of this Model-theatre I believe I have found a fitting close for the theme to which the present pages have been devoted,—a close already planned, at least in outline, in the inspired eyes of Art's illustrious Patron.

———————

Allerdurchlauchtigster, grossmächtigster König!

By nature and by education I have been fated to per-ceive the amazing discrepance between public achievements in the region of that art-branch wherewith I have become familiar and the requirements of the German genius, as expressed in the works and tendences of our great masters; and that discrepance has been so plainly thrust upon my consciousness, that it has forced me to move unceasingly for the needful reforms—an inner compulsion under which I have had to suffer, hitherto, more than the world can divine. At a time when this heartfelt grief had stirred me to the deepest, I gave it general expression through a series of art-writings, whose disregardal, misunderstanding or deliberate perversion, involved me in fresh annoyances and persecutions. Moreover at the various places where I worked, or where I merely sojourned for a longer time, I have repeatedly laboured to point out the road of reform, with special reference, and even detailed entry into local conditions, shewing by practical suggestions how they might be developed for the good of Art. At Dresden I drafted, in this sense, a plan of reorganisation for the Theatre in the kingdom of Saxony*; for Zurich, where I found asylum for a lengthy period, I devised a scheme to prove that even the most modest means, when rightly employed for noble ends, might compass a considerable result, and there I published it under the title: "A Theatre at Zurich."† Instigated by a "Goethestiftung"‡ once mooted at Weimar, I took that subject up, to shew by it, again, what we Germans needed in the way of organisation. A short while since, the question of a new and sumptuous opera-house, then about to be built in Vienna, incited me to publish certain practical proposals§ for raising the local institute from a downfall manifest to all the world. All these endeavours have passed without a trace of heeding. The public issue of my dramatic poem "Der Ring des Nibelungen" I opened with a preface,‖ already cited in the present Report; there, starting from the requirements for performance of my own work, I sketched a plan the carry-ing-out whereof would at least prepare the way for the only thorough solution of the problems exercising my mind. For this I turned to some unknown German "Prince," and, inwardly despairing, I concluded with the question: "Will this Prince be found?"—

More beautifully than I had dared to dream or hope, my timid question has been answered. It seems that Fate has refused to any of my narrower plans both notice and result,

---

* *Ges. Schriften und Dichtungen*, Vol. ii.—R. Wagner. † Ibidem, Vol. v.—R. W. ‡ Ibidem, Vol. v.—R. W. § Ibid., Vol. vii.—R. W. ‖ Ibid., Vol. vi.—R. W.—The last four of these essays will be found in Vol. III. of the present English translation; the first will eventually appear in Vol. VII.—TR.

only to furnish the execution of my broadest and most thoroughgoing with the truly puissant might. To-day then, as this last exhaustive labour has been undertaken solely in obedience to the will of my exalted patron, so I venture to commit it into the hands of Your Majesty in the supremely comforting assurance that, so far as reach the strength and power of the only Present that stands open to us, my plans will find consideration and fulfilment.

To the judgment of those persons whom Your Majesty will call to examine these proposals, as also to set in gradual motion whatever may be found therein of value, I may with a good conscience leave the verdict whether attainment of the suggested goal would, or would not, contribute alike to the welfare of Art and to the fame of Bavaria and its noble King.

For my own part, since e'er my good star let me find the longed-for "Prince," I know of a surety all my aims and all my labours are held within one thought, to serve that Prince ; and in the most respectful loyalty I remain

YOUR MAJESTY'S
most humble servant,
RICHARD WAGNER.

Munich, March 31st, 1865.

MY RECOLLECTIONS

OF

LUDWIG SCHNORR OF CAROLSFELD.

Meine Erinnerungen

an

Ludwig Schnorr von Carolsfeld.

(† 1865.)

The subject of the following brief memoir died on July 21st, 1865, at the age of twenty-nine, and was buried in Dresden on the 23rd of the month.   The article itself originally appeared in the Neue Zeitschrift für Musik *of June 5th and 12th, 1868, and was dated, at the end, "Luzern, May 5, 1868."*

T<small>RANSLATOR'S</small> N<small>OTE</small>.

F the young singer Ludwig Schnorr of Carolsfeld I first heard through my old friend Tichatschek, who paid me a visit at Zurich in the summer of 1856, and directed my attention to the future of this highly-talented young artist. The latter had just commenced his stage-career at the Carlsruhe Court-theatre; by the Director of that theatre [E. Devrient], who likewise visited me in the summer of the following year, I was informed of Schnorr's especial predilection for my music, as also for the tasks I set before the dramatic singer. On that occasion we agreed that I should destine my "Tristan," with whose conception I then was busied, for a first performance at Carlsruhe; for this purpose it was hoped that the Grand Duke of Baden, who was very kindly disposed towards me, would be able to overcome the difficulties which still stood in the way of my unmolested return to the dominions of the German Bund. From young Schnorr himself, a little later, I received a beautiful letter, with wellnigh passionate assurance of his devotion to me.

For reasons which contained a considerable element of vagueness, the realisation of our preconcerted plan for the Carlsruhe performance of my "Tristan," completed by me in the summer of 1859, was ultimately declared impossible. As to Schnorr himself, I was informed at the same time that, despite his great devotion to me, he considered it impossible to master the difficulties of the principal rôle, particularly in the last Act. Moreover his bodily health was represented to me as being in a critical condition: he was said to be suffering from an obesity that deformed his youthful figure. In particular the picture woken in me by this last report was very dismal. When in the summer of 1861 I visited Carlsruhe at last, and the execution of the earlier scheme was broached anew by the Grand Duke,—

who throughout had retained his friendly feeling toward me,—I was almost rebellious against the management's offer to open negotiations for the part of Tristan with Schnorr, then engaged at the Dresden Court-theatre; I declared that I had no manner of wish to make the personal acquaintance of this singer, since I feared lest the grotesqueness of his figure, occasioned by his malady, might even blind me to his real artistic gifts.

Soon afterwards a performance of my new work was projected at Vienna, but, as it in turn had not been made possible, I spent the summer of 1862 at Biebrich on the Rhine; thence I visited Carlsruhe for a performance of "Lohengrin," in which Schnorr appeared as 'guest.' I went to it in secret, and had intended to let myself be seen by no one, for sake of concealing my presence from Schnorr; for, abiding by my renouncement of him, and in dread lest the terrifying accounts of his misshapenness should be more than realised by actual impression, I was anxious to avoid even making his personal acquaintance. That timorous mood of mine was swiftly altered. Though the sight of this Swan-knight landing from a tiny shallop offered me the certainly somewhat estranging first impression of a youthful Hercules, yet his earliest entry placed me under the quite specific spell of the God-sent legendary hero in whose regard one asks not: How he is, but tells oneself: Thus is he! And indeed this instantaneous effect, piercing the very soul, can be compared with nothing but magic; I remember to have experienced it in my earliest youth with the Schröder-Devrient, determining the cast of my whole life, and since then never so definitely and strongly as with Ludwig Schnorr at his entry in "Lohengrin." In further course of his rendering, I noticed certain tokens of unripeness of conception and execution; but even these afforded me the charm of unspoilt youthful purity, of a soil still virgin for the choicest flowers of artistic cultivation. The warmth and tender inspiration, shed from the wondrous love-filled eyes of this scarcely more than youth, forthwith assured me of the dæmonic fire with which they once would flame ; to me he rapidly became a being for whom, on account of his boundless talent, I fell into a tragical suspense. Directly after the First Act I sought out a friend, and commissioned him to beg of Schnorr an interview with me after the performance. And so it fell out : late in the evening the young giant came untired to my room at the hotel, and the bond was sealed ; we had little need to talk, save jokes. But a longer meeting at Biebrich was arranged for the near future.

There by the Rhine we met for two happy weeks, to go through my Nibelungen works and particularly the " Tristan " to our heart's content, accompanied at the pianoforte by von Bülow, who then was on a visit to me. Here everything was said and done, to bring about an intimate agreement as to each artistic interest that filled our minds. As regards his doubts of the executability of the Third Act of " Tristan," Schnorr told me they had less arisen from any fear of over-taxing and exhausting the voice, than from his inability to understand one single passage ; but a passage which seemed to him the weightiest of all, namely the curse on Love, and especially the musical expression of the words : " from sweetness and suffering, laughter and sorrow " (" *aus Lachen und Weinen, Wonnen und Wunden* ") and so on. I shewed him how I had meant it, and what manner of expression, at any rate prodigious, I wanted given to this phrase. He swiftly understood me, recognised his mistake in imagining too quick a tempo, and now perceived that the resulting ' rush ' (*Ueberhetzung*) had been to blame for his failure to hit the right expression, and thus for his missing the meaning of the passage itself. I admitted that with this slower tempo I was certainly making a quite unwonted, perhaps a monstrous demand on the singer's strength ; but *that* he made utterly light of, and at once proved to me that precisely through this ritenuto he was able to render the passage to complete satisfaction.—To me that one feature has remained as un-forgettable as instructive : the utmost physical exertion lost all its fatiguingness, owing to the singer's having grasped the right expression for the words ; the spiritual understanding gave forthwith the strength to overcome the material difficulty. And this tender scruple had weighed for years on the young artist's conscience; his doubt of being able to reproduce one solitary passage had made him fear to match his talent against the whole task ; to 'cut' that passage—the ready expedient of our most celebrated opera-heroes—naturally could never occur to him, for he perceived in it the apex of the pyramid to which the tragic tendence of this Tristan towers up.—Who can measure the hopes which took possession of me, now that this wondrous singer had passed into my life?— —We parted ; and only after years, were new and strange destinies to bring us together again for final solving of our problem.

Thenceforward my endeavours for a performance of "Tristan" went hand-in-hand with those for Schnorr's co-operation in it ; they prospered only when a new-arisen, illustrious friend of my art granted me the Munich Court-theatre for that purpose. At the beginning of March 1865 Schnorr arrived in Munich, upon a brief visit, for sake of discussing the needful preliminaries of our soon forth-coming project; his presence led to a performance of "Tannhäuser," for the rest not specially prepared, in which he undertook the title-rôle with a single stage-rehearsal. I thus was limited to private conversation with him, for arranging with him his execution of this hardest of all my tasks for the dramatic singer. In general, I told him of the dismal dissatisfaction I had experienced from the previous stage-success of my "Tannhäuser," owing to the principal part having never yet been properly rendered, nay, even comprehended. Its chief feature I defined to him as *utmost energy, of transport alike and despair*, with no half-way-house betweeen the moods, but abrupt and downright in, its change. To fix the type for his portrayal, I bade him note the importance of the first scene with Venus; if the intended shock of this first scene hung fire, the failure of the whole impersonation needs must follow; for no jubilance of voice in the first finale, no girding and fury at the papal ban in Act III., could then avail to bring about the right impression. My new working of this Venus-scene, prompted by my recognition of just that importance and its insufficient definition in the earlier draft, had not as yet been put in rehearsal at Munich; Schnorr must therefore do his best, for the present, with the older version : the torturing conflict in Tannhäuser's soul being here still left more exclusively to the *singer*, all the more necessary would it be for him to give it due expression by the energy of his interpretation ; and in my opinion he would accomplish this only if he took the whole scene as one long climax leading to the catastrophic cry : " My weal rests in *Maria !* " I told him, this " *Maria !* " must burst forth with such vehemence that the instantaneous disenchantment of the Venusberg, and the miraculous translation to his native valley, shall be understood at once as the necessary fulfilment of an imperative behest of feeling driven to the utmost resolution. With that cry he had taken the attitude of one transported into loftiest ecstasy, and thus he must remain, without a motion, his eyes rapt heavenward ; ay, even until addressed by the knights who enter later, he must not quit the spot. How to solve this task—already refused me by a very celebrated singer, a few years previously, as quite inexecutable—I would direct him at the stage-rehearsal, placing myself beside him on the boards. There accordingly I took my stand, close by his side, and, following the music and surrounding scenic incidents bar by bar, from the goatherd's song to the departure of the pilgrims, I whispered him the inner cycle of the entranced's emotions, from the sublimest ecstasy of complete unconsciousness to the gradual wakening of his senses to their present environment, his ear being first to return to life—while, as if to shield the wonder from disturbance, he forbids his eye, now unchained from the magic spell of Heaven's æther, to look as yet upon the homely world of Earth. The gaze fixed movelessly on

high, merely the physiognomic play of features, and finally
a gentle slackening of the body's rigid upright pose, betray
the stir of gained rebirth ; till every cramp dissolves beneath the whelming miracle, and he breaks down at last in
humbleness, with the cry: "Almighty, to Thy name be
praise ! Great are the wonders of Thy grace ! " Then,
with the hushed share he takes in the pilgrims' chant, the
look, the head, the whole posture of the kneeling man, sink
ever deeper ; till choked with sobs, and in a second, saving
swoon, he lies prone, unconscious, face to earth.—Continuing to prompt him in undertones, to a like effect, I remained
by Schnorr's side throughout the rehearsal. On his part
my hints and very brief directions were answered by a
fleeting glance, just as gentle, and of so heartfelt a sincerity
that, assuring me of the most marvellous concordance, it
opened for myself new insights into my own work ; so that
through one example, at any rate unparalleled, I became
aware how fruitful to both sides may be the affectionate
communion of artists differently endowed, if only their gifts
are mutually and fully complemental.

After that rehearsal, not another word did we say about
"Tannhäuser." Moreover, after the performance on the
following night scarce a word fell from our lips about it ;
especially from mine no word of praise or recognition.
Through my friend's quite indescribably wonderful impersonation, of that evening, I had gained a glimpse into
my own creation such as seldom, perhaps never, had been
vouchsafed to an artist. That fills one with a certain
hallowed awe, in whose presence it beseems one to observe
a reverent silence.

With this one, this never repeated impersonation of
Tannhäuser, Schnorr had thoroughly realised my innermost artistic aim ; the Dæmonic in joy and sorrow had
never for one moment been lost from sight. The crucial
passage in the second finale, so often begged by me in
vain : " *Zum Heil den Sündigen zu führen* " &c.—ob-
stinately omitted by every singer on plea of its great
difficulty, by every Kapellmeister in virtue of the custom-

ary "cut"—for the first and unique time was it delivered by Schnorr with that staggering and thereby harrowing expression which converts the hero, of a sudden, from an object of abhorrence into the typic claimant of our pity. Through his frenzy of humiliation during the rapid closing section of the Second Act, and through his anguished parting from Elisabeth, his appearance as a man demented in Act III. was properly prepared for: from this broken being the outburst of emotion was all the more affecting ; till at last his renewed access of madness summoned the magic re-apparition of Venus with wellnigh the same dæmonic cogence as the invocation of the Virgin, in Act I., had miraculously called back the Christian world of home and day.   Schnorr was truly terrible in this last frenzy of despair, and I cannot believe that Kean or Ludwig Devrient in "Lear" could ever have attained a grander pitch of power.

The impression made upon the audience was most instructive to myself.   Much, as the wellnigh speechless scene after the exorcising of the Venusberg, gripped it in the right sense, and provoked tumultuous demonstrations of general and undivided feeling.   On the whole, however, I noticed mere stupefaction and surprise ; in particular the quite new, such as that eternally-omitted passage in the second finale, almost alienated people through upsetting their wonted notions.   From one friend, not otherwise dull-witted, I positively had to hear that I had no right to get Tannhäuser represented my way, since the public as well as my friends had everywhere received this work with favour, and thereby had plainly pronounced the former reading—the tamer but pleasanter one, however it might dissatisfy myself—at bottom the more correct.   My objection to the absurdity of such an argument was dismissed with an indulgent shrug of the shoulders, as much as to say, it made no difference.—In face of this general effeminacy, nay, debauchment, not only of the public taste, but even of the judgment of some of those with whom we came into closer contact, there was nothing for us but to possess our souls in patience; so we went on in our simple concord as to what was true and proper, quietly doing and working, without other expostulation than that of the artistic deed.

And that deed was preparing, with the return of my artistic ally at commencement of the ensuing April, and the beginning of our joint rehearsals for "Tristan." Never has the most bungling singer or bandsman let me give him such minute instructions, as this hero who touched the highest mastership of song; with him the seemingly most paltry stubbornness in my directions found naught but gladdest welcome, for their sense he caught at once; so that I really should have deemed myself dishonest, if, haply not to seem too touchy, I had withheld the tiniest comment. The reason of it was, that the ideal meaning of my work had already opened to my friend quite of itself, and truthfully become his own; not one fibre of this soul-tissue, not the faintest hint of a hidden allusion had ever escaped him, had failed of being felt to its tenderest shade. Thus it was a mere question of accurately gauging the technical means of singer, musician and mime, to obtain a constant harmony of the personal aptitude, and its in-dividuality of expression, with the ideal object of por-trayal. Whoso was present at these rehearsals, must remember to have witnessed an artistic consentaneousness the like whereof he has never seen before or since.

Only as to the Third Act of "Tristan" did I never say a word to Schnorr, beyond my earlier explanation of the one passage which he had not at that time understood. Whereas throughout the rehearsals of Acts I. and II. I had kept both ear and eye intent upon my player, with the commencement of Act III. I instinctively quite turned from sight of the death-wounded hero lying stretched upon his bed of anguish, and sat motionless upon my chair with half-closed eyes, to plunge myself within. At the first stage-rehearsal the unwonted duration of my seeming utter listlessness would appear to have inwardly embarrassed Schnorr, for in course of the whole protracted scene, even at the singer's most impassioned accents, I never once faced towards him, nay, not so much as stirred; but when at last, after the curse on Love, I reeled across and, bending down to throw my arms around the prostrate figure on the couch, I softly told the wondrous friend that no words could express my estimate of the ideal now fulfilled by him, his deep-brown eye shot fire like the star of love; a scarcely audible sob—and never did we speak another serious word about this final Act. Just to intimate my feelings, I would simply allow myself some such jest as the following: a thing like this Act III. was easy enough to write, but to be compelled to hear Schnorr sing it, was hard indeed, and so I could not even bring myself to look.—

In truth even yet, when jotting down these recollections after three years' interval, it is impossible for me to adequately express myself about that achievement of Schnorr's as Tristan, which reached its summit in my drama's final Act; and impossible, perhaps, for reason that it quite eludes comparison. Entirely at loss to furnish so much as an approximate idea thereof, I believe the only way to transfix that terribly fleeting miracle of musico-mimetic art will be to ask the genuine friends of my self and works, both now and in times to come, before all to take into their hands the score of this Third Act. They first would have to pay close heed to the orchestra, from the Act's commencement down ᵗo Tristan's death, and follow carefully the ceaseless play of musical motives, emerging, unfolding, uniting, severing, blending anew, waxing, waning, battling each with each, at last embracing and wellnigh engulfing one another; then let them reflect that these motives have to express an emotional-life which ranges from the fiercest longing for bliss to the most resolute desire of death, and therefore required a harmonic development and an independent motion such as could never be planned with like variety (*Kombinationsfülle*) in any pure-symphonic piece, and thus, again, were to be realised only by means of instrumental combinations such as scarce a purely-instrumental composer had been compelled as yet to press into his service to a like extent. Now let them observe that, regarded in the light of Opera, this whole enormous orchestra bears to the monologues of the singer —outstretched upon a couch, too—the mere relation of the accompaniment to a so-called solo : and they may judge for themselves the magnitude of Schnorr's achievement, when I call on every candid hearer of those Munich performances to testify that, from the first bar to the last, all attention, all interest was centred in the actor, the singer, stayed riveted to him, and never for a moment, for one single text-word, did he lose his hold upon his audience, but the orchestra was wholly effaced by the singer, or—to put it more correctly—seemed part and parcel of his utterance. Surely, to anyone who has carefully studied the score, I have said enough to signalise the incomparable artistic grandeur of my friend's achievement, when I add that already at the full rehearsal unbiased hearers had credited this very Act with the most popular effect in all the work, and prophesied for it a general success.—

In myself, while witnessing the public representations of " Tristan," a reverent amaze at this my friend's titanic deed developed to a positive terror To me it seemed at last a crime, to demand a frequent repetition of this deed, to enlist it perchance in the operatic repertoire ; and, after Tristan's love-curse in the fourth performance, I felt driven to definitely declare to those around me that this must be the last performance of " Tristan," that I would not consent to its being given any more.

It may be difficult for me to make this feeling clearly understood. No anxiety about victimising the physical forces of my friend entered into it, for any such consideration had been wholly silenced by experience. Anton Mitterwurzer, who, as Schnorr's colleague at the Dresden Court-theatre and his comrade, Kurwenal, in the Munich Tristan-performances, evinced the most intelligent interest in the doings, and the deepest sorrow for the fate of our friend,—that well-tried singer expressed himself most aptly in this regard : when his Dresden colleagues raised the cry that Schnorr had murdered himself with "Tristan," he very shrewdly replied that a man like Schnorr, who had shewn himself master of his task in the fullest sense, could never overtax his physical powers, since a victorious disposal of the latter was necessarily included in the spiritual mastery of the whole affair. As a matter of fact, neither during, nor after the performances was there ever detected the smallest fatigue in his voice, or any other bodily exhaustion ; on the contrary, whilst solicitude for their success had kept him in constant agitation *before* the performances, after each fresh success he was restored to the gayest of moods and the most vigorous carriage. It was the fruit of these experiences, very correctly estimated by Mitterwurzer, that led us earnestly to ponder, on the other hand, how it might be gathered for the establishment of a new style of musico-dramatic Rendering, a style in answer to the true spirit of German art. And here my encounter with Schnorr, now thriven to such an intimate alliance, opened a prospect full of unhoped promise for the outcome of our joint labours in the future.

The inexhaustibility of a genuinely gifted nature had thus become right plain to us, from our experiences with the voice of Schnorr. For that mellow, full and brilliant organ, when employed as the immediate implement for achieving a task already mastered mentally, produced on us the said impression of absolute indefatigableness. What no singing-master in the world can teach, we found was only to be learnt from the example of important tasks thus triumphed over.—But what is the real nature of these tasks, for which our singers have not yet found the proper Style ? —Their first aspect is that of an unwonted demand upon the singer's physical endurance ; and if the singing-master is called in, he believes—and rightly, from his standpoint— that he must fly to mechanical devices for strengthening the organ, in the sense of absolutely denaturalising its functions. In the first stages of its cultivation, as probably is inevitable, the voice is treated as a mere animal organ ; but when, in further course of training, its musical

soul is to unfold itself at last, standing specimens can alone
supply the scheme of voice-employment; therefore the
whole remaining matter resolves itself into a question of
the tasks proposed in them.* Now, the singing-voice has
hitherto been trained on none but the Italian model; there
existed no other. Italian vocalism, however, was informed
with the whole spirit of Italian music; at its prime its most
thorough exponents were the castrati, since the spirit of
this music made for merely sensuous pleasure, without a
spark of nobler passion—whilst the voice of the adolescent
male, the tenor, was scarcely then employed at all, or, as
later, in a falsetto masking as the voice of the castrato.
Yet, under the undisputed leadership of German genius,
and particularly of Beethoven, more modern music has
soared to the height and dignity of sterling Art through
this one thing: that, beyond the sensuously pleasurable,
it has drawn the spiritually energetic and profoundly passionate into the orbit of its matchless Expression. How
then can the masculine voice, trained to the earlier musical
tendence, take up the tasks afforded by our German art of
nowadays? Cultivated for a mere material appeal to the
senses, it here sees nothing but fresh demands on material
strength and sheer endurance, and the modern singing-master
therefore makes it his principal aim to equip the voice to
meet them. How erroneous is this procedure, may be
easily imagined; for any male singing-organ merely trained
for physical force will succumb at once, and bootlessly,
when attempting to fulfil the tasks of newer German music,
such as are offered in my own dramatic works, if the singer
be not thoroughly alive to their *spiritual* significance. The
most convincing proof of this was supplied us by Schnorr
himself; and, in illustration of the profound and total
difference we here are dealing with, I will cite my experi-

* "Hierbei ist die Stimme, wie für die erste Grundlage ihrer Bildung auch
wohl gar nicht anders verfahren werden darf, nur als menschlich-thierisches
Organ aufgefasst; soll nun im Gange der weiteren Ausbildung endlich die
musikalische Seele dieses Organes entwickelt werden, so können hierfür immer
nur die gegebenen Beispiele der Stimmanwendung zur Norm dienen, und auf
die hierin gestellten Aufgaben kommt es demnach für alles Weitere an."

ence of that Adagio passage in the second finale of
" Tannhäuser " (" *zum Heil den Sündigen zu führen* "). If
Nature in our times has wrought a miracle of beauty in the
manly vocal organ, it is the tenor voice of *Tichatschek*,
which for forty years has retained its strength and roundness. Whoever heard him recently declaim in ' Lohengrin" the story of the Holy Grail, in noblest resonance and
most sublime simplicity, was touched and seized as by a
living wonder. Yet in Dresden many years ago I had to
strike out that passage from " Tannhäuser " after its first
performance, because Tichatschek, then in fullest possession of his vocal force and brilliance, was unable, owing to
the nature of his dramatic talent, to master the expression
of that passage as *an ecstasy of humiliation*, and positively
fell into physical exhaustion over a few high notes. Now
when I state that Schnorr not only delivered this passage
with the most heart-rending expression, but brought out
those same high notes of passionate grief with complete
fulness of tone and perfect beauty, I certainly have no idea
of ranking Schnorr's vocal organ above Tichatschek's,
in any sense as though it surpassed the latter in natural
power; but, as compared with this uncommon gift of
Nature, I claim for the voice of Schnorr just that aforesaid
tirelessness in service of the spiritual understanding.—

With the recognition of Schnorr's unspeakable import
for my own artistic labours, a new springtime of hope
had dawned upon my life. Now had been found the
immediate ligament, to link my work with the Present and
make it fruitful. Here one might both teach and learn;
the despaired-of, scoffed-at and reviled, it now could be
made an art-deed testifying of itself. The institution of a
German Style, for rendering and representing works of
German spirit, became our watchword. And now that I had
embraced this livening hope of a great, but gradual advance,
I openly declared myself against any speedy resumption of
" Tristan." With this performance, as with the work itself,
we had taken too vast, nay, wellnigh forlorn a leap across
to the New, that still remained to be first won; rents and

chasms yawned between, and they must be most diligently filled, to pave a highway for the needful comrades to escort us lonely ones to those far distant heights.—

So Schnorr was to become our own. The foundation of a Royal School for Music and Dramatic Art was resolved on. The difficulties in the way of releasing the artist from his Dresden contract suggested to us the peculiar character of the position which we ourselves must offer him, to make it once for all a worthy one. Schnorr should retire altogether from the Theatre and become teacher of our School, simply taking part in special, extraordinary stage-performances, in confirmation of our course of study. This project thus involved the liberation of an artist, whose soul burnt clear with noblest fire, from the common drudgery of the operatic repertoire ; and what it meant for him, to have to languish in that service, could be felt by none more keenly than myself. Have not the most inextricable, most torturing and most dishonouring molestations, cares and humiliations in my life proceeded from that one misunderstanding which, perforce of outer haps of life and outward semblance, held me up to the world, to every social and æsthetic relation contained therein, as just nothing but an "opera-composer" and "operatic Kapellmeister"? If this singular *quid pro quo* was bound to bring eternal confusion into all my relations with the world, and particularly into my demeanour toward its claims upon myself, one certainly cannot make light of the sufferings which the young, deep-souled and nobly earnest artist had to endure in his position of "opera-singer," in his subjection to a theatric code devised against refractory heroes of the wings, in his obedience to the orders of uncultured and overbearing official chiefs.—Nature meant Schnorr for a musician and poet ; like myself, he took up the special study of music after receiving a general education in the sciences ; and very probably he would already have followed a road both outwardly and inwardly akin to mine, had there not early developed in him that organ whose exhaustlessness was to serve for fulfilment of my most ideal wants, and thus to associate him directly with my life-career, as complemental counterpart of my own tendence. But behold! our modern Culture had nothing to offer him save theatrical engagements, the post of "tenor," in much the same way as *Liszt* became a "pianoforte-player."—

Now at last, protected by a Prince most graciously disposed to my ideal of German art, our Culture was to be grafted with the shoot* whose growth and fruitage would have fertilised the soil for genuinely German deeds of art; and truly it was time that rescue were afforded to the downcast spirit of my friend. Here lay the hidden worm that sapped the man and artist's buoyant life-force. This became plainer and plainer to me, as to my astonishment I remarked the passionate, nay, furious intensity with which he jibbed at misdemeanours in the traffic of the stage, things that are always happening in this blend of bureaucratic priggishness and comediantic want of conscience, and therefore are not felt at all by those concerned. Once he complained to me: " Ah! it's not my acting and singing, that take it out of me in 'Tristan,' but the provocations in between; my lying quietly upon the boards, after the sweating fever of excitement in the great scene of the last Act,—that's what kills me. In spite of all my complaints, I haven't been able to get them to screen the stage from the terrible draught that pours like ice across my rigid body and chills me to death, while the gentlemen behind the wings trot out the latest scandal of the town!" As we had noticed no symptoms of a catarrhal cold, he gloomily hinted that such chills had other, more dangerous results, with him. In the last days of his Munich stay his excitability took an ever darker tinge. Finally he appeared on the boards once more, as Eric in the " Flying Dutchman," and played that difficult episodic rôle to our highest admiration; nay, he positively made us shudder by the singular moody vehemence wherewith—in strict accordance with the wish I had expressed to him—he portrayed the sorrows of this young Norwegian hunter,

* The Music-school, of course.—Tr.

Q

making his hapless love break out in flames of lurid fire. Only, by a word or two he betrayed to me that night a deep dissatisfaction with all his surroundings. Moreover, he seemed suddenly invaded by doubts as to the feasibility of our cherished hopes and plans; he appeared unable to comprehend how, with this prosaic, utterly unsympathetic, nay, spitefully hostile environment that lay in ambush for us, one could entertain a serious thought of doing good work. And it was with bitter grudge, that he received pressing orders from Dresden to return by a given day, for a rehearsal of " Trovatore" or the " Huguenots."

From this dismal anxious mood, in which I shared at last myself, we were set free again by the last glorious evening we ever spent together. The King had a private audience in the Residenz-theatre, for which he had commanded the performance of various excerpts from my works. From each of " Tannhäuser," " Lohengrin," " Tristan," the " Rheingold," the " Walküre," " Siegfried," and finally the " Meistersinger," a characteristic piece was rendered by singers and full orchestra, under my personal direction. Schnorr, who here heard many a new thing of mine for the first time, and further sang " Siegmund's Liebeslied," " Siegfried's Schmiedelieder," " Loge " in the " Rheingold " morsel, and finally " Walther von Stolzing " in the larger fragment from the " Meistersinger," with entrancing power and beauty,—Schnorr felt as if lifted above all cares of life, upon his return from half-an-hour's interview to which he had been graciously invited by the King, who attended our performance quite alone. Boisterously he threw his arms around me : " God ! how thankful I am for this evening ! " he cried, " Eh ! now I know what makes your faith so firm ! Be sure, between this heavenly King and you, I too shall turn to something splendid ! "— —So again we bade good-bye to serious talk. We took tea together in an hotel ; tranquil gaiety, friendly faith, sure hope, were the mainsprings of our wellnigh purely joking conversation. " Well, well ! " the word went, " to-morrow, once more, to the ghastly masquerade ! Then soon set free for ever !" Our speedy au-revoir was a thing so certain in our minds, that we held it superfluous, nay, quite out of place, to even say farewell. We parted in the street, as at our customary good-night ; next morning my friend departed quietly for Dresden.—

About a week after our scarcely heeded parting, Schnorr's death was telegraphed to me. He had sung at one more stage-rehearsal, and had had to rebuke his colleagues for expressing their surprise that he really was left with any voice. Then a terrible rheumatism had seized his knee, leading to a fever that killed him in a very few days. Our preconcerted plans, the representation of " Siegfried," his anxiety lest folk should attribute his death to an over-exertion with " Tristan," these were the thoughts that had occupied his lucid, and at last his waning consciousness.— With Bülow, I hoped to reach Dresden in time for the interment of our beloved friend : in vain ; it had been necessary to commit his body to the earth a few hours before the time appointed ; we arrived too late. In brilliant July sunshine, be-bannered Dresden was shouting its welcome to the crowds streaming in for the General Festival of German Singers. The coachman, hotly urged by me to reach the house of death, had great difficulty in forcing his way through the throng, and told me that upwards of 20,000 singers had come together. " Ay !"— said I to myself—" *The* singer has but just gone !"

Post-haste we turned our backs on Dresden.

NOTICES.

Censuren.

Of the following group of articles, Nos. I. and II. seem to have originally appeared in the Süddeutsche Presse, *1867; they were reprinted in the* Musikalisches Wochenblatt *(by E. W. Fritzsch, publisher also of Wagner's* Ges. Schr.) *of March 22nd and May 3rd, 1872, with the announcement that they formed part of the forthcoming eighth volume of the* Gesammelte Schriften.—*The Introduction (or* "Vorbericht") *first appeared in the last-named journal, of April 19th 1872.—Number III. (" Rossini") appeared in the Augsburg* Allgemeine Zeitung *of December 17th 1868, and was dated, at its close, " Tribschen, near Lucerne, December 7th, 1868"; it was reprinted in the* Neue Zeitschrift für Musik *of Feb. 26, 1869, with an editorial note to the effect that the copy had been reproduced from the* Allg. Ztg. " *at the request of very many readers."—No. IV. appeared in 1869 as a pamphlet, entitled "* Herr E. Devrient und sein Styl," *under the pseudonym of "* Wilhelm Drach"; *this would be a few months later than the republication of* "Judaism in Music."—No. V. *consisted of the Appendix to the latter pamphlet, which I have already published in Volume III. of the present series.*

TRANSLATOR'S NOTE.

INTRODUCTION.

HE kindly reader will be none too pleased to find the following articles, of cheerlessly polemic nature, so closely shouldering the file of essays with which this volume opened, seeing that those essays—suggestively prefaced by a song of Homage—already breathed a comfortable hope, inspired by the fair assurance of authority to set immediate hand to helpful action. In fact the author himself, when making up the present volume of his Collected Writings, was plunged into dire perplexity by his observation of the said abrupt discrepance: as author, I gladly would have pieced nothing to those first essays but matter of like nature with themselves, matter in due harmony with the hopes awakened by the introductory poem. Were I a book-writer, that certainly is the course I should have chosen; but with this Collection I have something in mind more earnest than the writing of books: my desire is, to render my friends a true account of myself, so as to put them in possession of the clue to much that is hard to understand about me.

That sudden contrast in character, of the essays gathered in this volume, exactly corresponds with the character of the experiences I had to reap, and out of which arose my original obligation to publish the articles now following.

This latter character can scarcely escape the divination of those who have granted their attention to my preceding treatises on "German Art and German Policy" and "A Music-School for Munich," and may have thereby felt disposed to ask : What, then, was the practical outcome of those suggestions and proposals? A question to which, for the moment, I prefer to give a merely indirect answer,

247

pointing to the larger and smaller essays that follow here-
upon and close this volume; from these, and more particularly from my having been compelled to engage in this
kind of communication with certain factors of our modern
trade in Art and Culture, the well-informed reader will be
able to draw his own conclusions, in the most becoming
manner.

After my so auspicious summons to *Munich,* not for an
instant did it escape me that the soil on which I then was
placed, for the realisation of unusual artistic tendences,
could never belong to either myself or those tendences.
Yet for a brief time there seemed to have arrived a certain
expectant calm, a sort of armistice, in the humours that
opposed me. Observing this, it needs must occur to myself
that I, too, had best withhold my harshest views of many
a thing; not to drive folk needlessly to desperate measures,
where a good-natured acknowledgment of small, and even
doubtful,* merits might move the opposing interests, if not
to aid in execution of my plans, at least to leave such
execution unimpeded. That policy dictated the wording
of my Report on the Music-School, which the reader will
probably recognise as an utmost attempt, on my part, to
effect a compromise. However, a singularly eloquent
reserve shewed me that people did not deem needful to
enter on a compromise with me; which renewed, though
under very altered circumstances, an experience I had
already reaped at the place of my earlier labours, with the
reception accorded to my draft for a re-organisation of the
Dresden Court-theatre.†

Very soon my hopes had to repose on nothing but the
results of my practical activity. Of what importance, in
this regard, became the acquisition of *Ludwig Schnorr* and
my intimate alliance with him, I have stated plainly in the
preceding "Recollections." What I lost by his sudden
death is, in a certain sense, as immeasurable as the dowry
of that artist was inexhaustible. In him I lost, as I expressed myself at the time, the great block of granite

* See page 215.—TR.   † See *Gesammelte Schriften*, Vol. ii.—R. WAGNER.

needed for the erection of my building, in whose place I found myself directed to a load of bricks.

As this death produced a rent in my only solid piece of evidence, the art-work, so a rent occurred in my behaviour toward all those hostile interests which merely aired their theories the better to obstruct my practical path of work. I soon discovered that once more I must defend my one and only tendence against the perpetual attacks of men whose sole concern had always been to so mislead the judgment of the public—which can form a right one only in presence of the deed—that the resulting bewilderment should render it impossible for me to bring about the deed itself.

So for a while I thought I could do no better, than myself descend into this arena of the Daily Press, where impotence seeks to satisfy its spite by bidding-in the public to an exhibition of its horseplay. Disgust at the sort of company into which it inevitably threw me, soon damped my ardour; the immediately-succeeding articles are the scanty harvest gathered by me on this field. Nevertheless I remained henceforth determined to counteract my adversaries' hopes of success from their operations in the Press by at least exposing their selves and motives, haply too, their doings and their capabilities, with regardless candour to my friends. The fact that calumny was here opposed by the most plainspoken truthfulness, seems to have called forth mighty indignation, and with many a friend of mine even dismay. Both consequences betray a great disdain of the Press, in whose regard all parties are astonished that one doesn't leave it severely alone,—a course I also held most suitable till I found a wish arising in me, that all parties would really allow this so despised Press no influence over earnest and important projects. Here, again, I was always met by the doctrine of "necessary evil"; which I had then to try and put up with, to the best of my ability, by endeavouring to divert the necessary consequences of that evil from my self and efforts, and turn them on the Press itself. If the only power that can ever speed us to success in such attempts must reside in the *higher idea* we champion, I believe I may call my friends to witness that I took more thought for victory of my idea, than for damage to my foes, even in cases where the mere exposure of my adversary's emptiness sufficed to bring about that victory. And how shall the genuine be recognised, so long as the spurious is let usurp its place?

The most and most heterogeneous rejoinders I drew upon me through my renewed discussion of *Judaism in Music.** Only a very few—but by so much the more reputable— voices allowed that I had maintained an eminently objective attitude towards the question. My own conscience was so clear upon this point, that it preserved me from any chafing at the countless embroglios to which I had given rise: since it really did not touch myself at all, I quietly could let the tempest pass above my head. The only thing I actually regretted, were the misunderstandings of certain solicitous friends: they represented to me that it was precisely the Jews who applauded most at my operas and brought, in general, the last stir of life into our public art-world; whence I had to gather that people fancied I wanted above all to make a great *effect* in our theatres and cherished the delusion that the Jews were against that sort of thing. From other quarters I received most positive assurances as to the destination of the Jews : the Germanic Christians were quite played out, and the future belonged to the "Judaic Germans." Moreover in a report of the Berlin Victory-playwright, Julius Rodenberg,† in the Augsburg *Allgemeine Zeitung*, I lived to see that a "blond-bearded German" had already been upheld to the scorn of his readers, as it seems, for breaking a lance in my favour. From all these signs I could only conclude that I had not overrated the situation when, in publishing my

---

* In the original this "renewed discussion" forms No. V. of the present "Notices"; but it has already appeared, as Appendix to the main article, in Vol. III.—Tr.

† Rodenberg's original name was Levy; in 1874 he founded the *Deutsche Rundschau.*—Tr.

"explanations," I safeguarded myself against the assumption that I believed the great change which had come over our public life could now be anywise staved off,—whereas I simply pointed to the necessity of handling the problems in question with utmost candour.

One remarkable result of the enormous and, in itself, vexatious notice which this last-named publication roused, was that my art-writings were henceforth eagerly read, or at all events bought; which in Germany, unless an author has been admitted into one of the close-hedged literary rings, seems possible of attainment only through a scandal—as the present case shews—however unintended. From this I have reaped the advantage of being able to commit my more serious artistic thoughts to the press with better prospect of consideration than before; owing to which—as I learn through my publisher at least, albeit through no other organ of public opinion—I really am becoming heeded as a writer, too, on Art. Such a discovery would certainly be a trifle for the compilers of our numerous Histories of Art and Literature, which, let them be never so silly and dull to read, are bought nevertheless by our well-to-do shoemakers and tailors for the library-table of their cultured families, and hence are continually blossoming into new editions and magnificent reviews; but it is encouraging indeed for him who has always been forbidden access to those tables, forbidden with contempt, and, where that sufficed not, with absolute horror. For, in that traffic of our damaged literati with their public, it had not been foreseen that a working artist would one day get *his* word on Art. Wherever would the poor creatures be, if our great masters—whose works can now be twaddled over, because the public only knows them in defacement—had also provided for the public's arriving at a sound judgment of those works? That, however, is what *we* have to do, since our public art is in such evil hands. Wherefore if anyone like myself writes about Art, it is not to shew how Art is to be made, but how one ought to judge it; and this, naturally, with the simple object of making easier for the artist, if not his creative work, at anyrate its effect upon the laity. And the aptitude for this, which I have dared to feel within myself, perchance is not the meanest gift conferred on me by Fate, as way-penny for my journey through the world of nowadays as creative artist ; for without its aid, haply with but my lyre in hand, I could not possibly have held out so long. If "Tasso" comforts himself with the thought that a god had given him the power to say what he endured—by which he means his gift of poetry itself,—I venture to rejoice that it was granted me to also *write* thereon.

Whoso has correctly judged the character of our age, so totally averse to sterling Art, will never underrate the value of that gift, and therefore will not take it ill of me if I use it at my full discretion ; but I leave to each to form his own idea, whether it can afford me any sense of happiness or satisfaction.

I.

W. H. Riehl.*

("Neues Novellenbuch."

 NE consequence of the sad turning taken by
the policy of the major German Princes after
the rousing times of the War of Liberation, a
policy that fenced itself against every claim
of the resurrected German spirit, may be seen
in the strange survival of a ruin which still distinctly shews
the German essence of that age, but in features ever more
decayed and mutilated.   While everything that makes for
power and publicity is obeying more and more the laws of
an entirely un-German civilisation, that crushes out alike
all German earnestness and German cheerfulness,—rotting
unnoticed in the profound seclusion of private life, in petty
non-official posts, but chiefly in small university-towns, we
often meet most touching evidence of the placid, hope-
bereft survival of a typic national spirit, checked from any
unfolding of its nobler self.   Shut from all prospect of
furtherance or even recognition by the summits of society,
the eyes of this sphere are directed almost exclusively to
the lower regions of the equally neglected, unloving as
unloved, unbeautiful and crumbling Folk-life.   To this
direction, when followed with all the fervour and thoroughness of the German spirit, we owe the glorious enlivening
results of the newer researches into German language,
German sagas and German history ; and if one is to signal

* Further information as to W. H. Riehl will be found in *The Meister* of
this year (1895), Nos. XXIX to XXXI.—TR.

by a single name whatever has accrued to the honour and
solace of the German spirit since the extinction of our
great poetic period, that name is *Jakob Grimm.*

Modern stage-wit has pounced on the figures of this
Jakob and his faithful brother Wilhelm, of all others, to
shew the laughter-loving public how scholars such as these
may look when viewed quite close.   Though the skit is
reckoned for nothing but the guffaws of our happy theatre-
goers, yet the almost phenomenal helplessness, nay, utter
ineptitude of these two worthies as concerns real life, may
even tempt a good-humoured smile from the man of better
sense, upon whom they waft a wonder-breath of that German spirit rapt into the caverns of its primal birthplace.
For all that, one is deeply moved by the childlike gentleness, and guileless sweetness, in the dealings of these
mighty heroes of a science which owed to them its first
inception.—But this same ineptitude and helplessness cuts
a very different figure when, in life or positively in books,
we meet it naked and unashamed, without any deep background to excuse it, but pluming itself with a certain pride
on just its clumsiness and taking its own necessitously
narrow orbit for centre of the world, into which it would
force by hook or crook all there that lies outside.   To see
the attributes of great genius or grave misfortune assumed
by sheer vapidity, has something really laughable : yet to
none of our playwrights has it occurred to set before the
German of our days a mirth-provoking theme so close to
his own doors.   To mock at the sublime, at any rate seems
easier than to shew the fatuous in all its solemn ridicule !

Alas ! the latter figure also, when taken in the bulk, is
not without its highly explanatory and apologetic reason.
Characteristics innate in the German, and only to be given
the effect of merits by a very favourable development of
the *whole* of his propensities,—with the lamentable neglect
under which German nature has suffered for the last fifty
years, these characteristics inevitably develop their evil
side alone.   The sense of individual freedom, with whose
stirring apotheosis young Goethe in his "Götz von Berlich-

ingen " began his great career as poet, is the trait that most
distinguishes the spirit of the German peoples from that of
the Romanic : if the sad results of its degeneration confront
us in the history of the German Reich, they are no less
lamentably manifest in our modern period of Literature.
And yet the consequent mistakes are certainly the least of
our dangers ; through their exposure and rebuke one still
may hope to clear one ample source of German virtue :
whereas the real disease of the literature that flourishes
to-day is of so repulsive a kind, that any baring of the
natural roots of that peculiar-smelling bloom would bring
neither a German nor a Romanic, nor even an Oriental
virtue to light.

It is explicable and to be excused, that the German who
pines in petty circumstances, hindered from evolution to
any sort of power, and sees around him a flaring world
with which he feels no inner relationship,—it is explicable
that he should growl at everything, no matter what, that
glitters and obtrudes its power. To the gentle temper and
open mind, even when driven from helplessness to boorish-
ness, and squeezed into the narrowest sphere of burgher
action, it may amiably arrive to carve an idyll from the
only world it knows, and, often in touching variations,
announce that it is happy and has no desire to step beyond
its idyll. It has all the greater right to laud its idyll, as
from out its shade it looks upon a world wherein the sun,
to it, illumines naught but hollowness and nothingness ; it
can afford to laugh at the affectation, the spurious pathos,
which are meant to give the false dealings out there an air
of reality and serious life ; and, if it feels a true and urgent
call thereto, it may uplift its voice in warning and instruction of that world without. But it will beseem it ill
enough, if, waxing wroth on such occasions, it should want
to mount the hedgerow of its idyll and hurl its threats
upon the world. Quite a mad figure' would it cut, however, if, reduced by its wrath to incapability of distinguishing, it should confound the sterling with the counterfeit,
and run amuck at everything that will not just square with

its idyll. If, for instance, with beautiful German instinct it
has felt out for itself that, after all, there lurks in that butt
of our modern Civilisation, the German "Philistine," a
last and weighty remnant of the sterling forceful German
nature, it will excellently well become it to endeavour with
all love and diligence to bring that nature to understanding
by a Folk-spirit exposed to ever greater decadence :—but
how if an incarnation of all that the most propitious fortune could possibly develop from that remnant should step
before it, and, confounding it with the Devil there outside,
it should fight the apparition off in fury, and yell aloud :
"I want my Philistine, only my Philistine ; this creature
is a human being!"—Yes, it would cut a highly comical
figure, to the point where gravity sets in, and æsthetic
delirium passes into moral perversity. A sturdy (*bieder*)
German such as this, who sees the soil of the burgher
world all round him loamed with just his sturdiness,
might add to the old evils, from which we all are suffering, a ruinous horde of new. For if ye goad the pettiness and envy of the German Philistine much farther, ye
bar to those who have put their only hope in the tranquil
sense of freedom, ingrained in unspoilt German nature, the
last road to rescue of us all from common downfall.

The well-known author of the "New Book of Tales"
("*Neues Novellenbuch*"), Herr W. H. Riehl, may claim to
speak as an authority on the theme to which we have just
devoted our attention. True, as he hovers between poet
and critic, the subject doesn't seem to have fully reached
the objective region of his consciousness ; with a strong
dose of subjective feeling, he appears to be half-way
plunged in it himself. We say "half-way," to denote alike
the position he occupies not only between the German
erudite, whose noblest type we have in J. Grimm, and the
true German Folk's-poet whom we still are looking-for in
vain, but also—as regards his judgment and tendence—
between those extremes of character we have briefly
sketched above. He has not been at all times able to
keep aloof from a hazardous fanaticism for the Philistine ;

and it was this that once betrayed him into an over-estimate
of his own powers, for which, if we mistake not, he had to
pay a none too pleasant penalty. This "new book of
tales," however, appears to us an evidence of the noble
sanctuary Herr Riehl has found, in his true vocation,
against the less encouraging results of his labours on that
by-way. The apostles of the Idyll, of temperate self-
restraint, are irresistibly touching and attractive so long as
they address us in the tones of heartfelt modesty and
mildness : the effect of such an appeal, if it really comes
from a tender heart and lucid brain, instinctively reminds
us of a lost paradise ; and it thrusts the deeper as that
paradise lost is here the paradise of homely and yet so
pregnant German sense, that kernel of the noble German
majesty (*Herrlichkeit*) whose decay we moan. Real and
undissembled "harmlessness,"—ah ! what a fount of everything sublime ! Always to be more plentiful and deeper
than one seems, always to render more than one promises,
always to administer a more potent cordial than one had
let be hoped,—this is the reward of sterling harmlessness.
But how the virtue loses in force, so soon as ever it boasts
of itself, were it but the faintest shadow of a single time ;
ay, when it merely points to itself with ever so bashful a
finger ! If we find an outstretched hand, however, as on a
shop-sign, proclaiming it purveyor of great and special
dainties ; and if we positively remark that that hand is
stealthily doubling into a fist, to deal a blow at the first
"harmful" passer-by : then not only have we a ridiculous
spectacle before us, but we should find it impossible to
ward off a very justifiable doubt as to the nature of that
self-advertising productive "harmlessness." Now, as Herr
Riehl is not only poet, but also critic, we fancy this
dilemma of his own nature has occupied his mind, and, in
in our opinion, in a manner highly profitable to his development : already he knows how to treat it as poet,—at least,
his charming story "the Quartett" above all seems to us
to owe its inspiration and its fashioning to the poet's inner
occupation with the said dilemma.—Perhaps we might

express the wish that this purging of the inner man would
direct itself a little more fastidiously to the rank and value
of the poet's fancies, before he works them up : presumably
Herr Riehl would then find that the publication of a piece
like his "Abendfrieden," which he gives as preface to his
book, reposes on a misunderstanding of similar idylls,
built from the unlikeliest-looking stuff, that have won their
inexplicable and yet indisputable value from the hand of
truly great poets.   Herr Riehl, however, will always be
vastly engaging, and enrich the reader's store of happiness
with a fund of brand-new pictures—left quite unheeded in
everyday existence, but called into artistic life by the
magic of sincerity—when he directs his shaping-force so
definitely, so regardlessly and exclusively to the portrayal
of what he has beheld within, as in his original tale "the
High School of Humility."   A beautiful, a most suggestive title, which, we cannot help feeling, should have been
chosen as motto for the whole gracious book.

Unfortunately Herr Riehl has recently seen fit to play
truant from his Idyll refuge, adopted with such praiseworthy
decorum, and work all kinds of petty, but malignant
mischief.   Is it really his anxiety about our Culture—to
which the newspapers tell us he has devoted the minutest
study—, or is it a periodic annoyance at his failure as
public composer "for the house," that drives him from time
to time to the field of Music, albeit under cover of some
incident or other ?   Certain it is, that he appears unable to
cease firing from the school of musical humility, ever and
anon, an impertinence directed against that pride which
will not stoop to mate with impotence.   Thus, for instance,
he is distressed of late at the bandsmen having acquired
too great a mastery of their instruments, and deplores their
having finished by betraying so good a composer as
Beethoven—whose works as far as the C-minor Symphony
allowed of being played down to the Riehlish idyll—into
so difficult a style of writing that one no longer can settle

to his music "in the house" with pipe in mouth. With this remark he leaves us to imagine for ourselves a performance of that so simple C-minor Symphony in the musical Tobacco-parliament, and, should we find no particular edification in the attempt, he conducts us with great gusto through picture-galleries and reading-rooms; where, perforce of "harmless" comparisons and analogies, he keeps giving us the friendly counsel to be most mistrustful of everything great in Art—and for the matter of that, in Life. As for music, he has set his heart on naïvety, and mourns that the newer composers, from Weber onwards, have written *reflected* music; in which opinion he is quite at one with the renowned Vienna Doctor, Hanslick. He sets this "naïvety" in opposition to "reflection," but spares us any definition of the term; presumably since Schiller had already taken thought for that. But our Culture-researchers no longer read their Schiller; and thus it happens that their recollection of his famous treatise on "Naïve and Sentimental Poetry" is in so far erroneous as they pit the *naïve*, there defined in clear antithesis to the *sentimental*, against a confused idea of the *reflected* (haply after Hegel). Now, as it is well known that much can be done by Reflection, only no Art and above all no Music, our harmlessly-idyllic critics—relying on a premiss about as correct as it is single-minded—arrive at the conclusion so fatal to the newer music, that there can't possibly be anything in it. Further, Herr Riehl delivers himself of his personal demur before a public whose flesh creeps at bare mention of the word "reflection," since no one to this day has been able to convince people that Reflection is a form of *knowledge*, whose only possible antithesis is simply *the intuitive* (the apperceptive— "*anschauende*") mode of knowledge; wherefore that it is precisely as nonsensical to pit naïve art-production against a "reflective music-making," as it would be to contrast intuitive apperception with a "sentimental knowledge." Yet Herr Riehl holds public lectures on this basis, and much alarms those minds upon which the

word "reflection"—provided they don't confound it with
"resignation" — has the effect of a call to *meditation*
(Nachdenken): a thing they nowadays are wont to have
altogether spared them by a universally blooming
(*allgemein blühende*) Press and its organs.   Now, for the
public to be obliged to think that the music it hears played
in the Theatre—where harmless exhilaration can really be
the only aim!—had been brought about by meditation, is
for it to realise a dire calamity; and to have roused at
least suspicion thereof, must certainly be counted to the
great credit of Culture's famous student.

And yet, it seems that we are here in presence of a
mystery, close-veiled before.   Herr *Riehl* has really
brought music about by Reflection.   Since he grew aware
of the decay of German music through extinction of those
"Character-heads" of his studies,* he meditated earnestly,
and no joke about it, how to write a music which should
remedy the scandal,—and he wrote it.   But when he began
to have his doubts of its pleasing a single soul, he meditated on that in turn, and discovered that the earnestness
of his design had made him quite forget "naïvety."   So he
surely has good reason to urge the point upon his
followers : for, once bit, twice shy.

All honour to him, and—God help him !—

---

* "*Musikalische Charakterköpfe*," the title of a brochure by W. H. Riehl,
dealing with Astorga, Hasse, Pleyel, Gyrowetz, Kreutzer, Onslow, and
others.—Tr.

II.

Ferdinand Hiller.

("Aus dem Tonleben unserer Zeit.") *

E shall never rightly estimate the rank of great art-geniuses if we lose sight of the fact that the first foundation or ground-work of all artistic practice is nothing but a handicraft, which thousands may learn, attain dexterity in, and even mastership—precisely as with a trade—yet without approaching any essential affinity to the art-genius proper, nay, without so much as coming within earshot of genuine, ideal Art. This is quite peculiarly the case with the musician : to-day a nuisance, to-morrow by desire, he steps into the circle of the burgher's occupation or the burgher's pleasure, here welcomed, there kicked out; a loiterer, without soul for spiritual culture, with very feeble reasoning power (*Vernunft*), a scanty gift of under-standing, ay! amazing little phantasy, he leads a sort of semi-human existence which perceptibly shades off into the so pronouncedly musical nature-life of the Gipsies (*Zigeuner*) and loses itself hard on the borders of the human animal. That the demigod should have seized this semi-man, with him to call to life that most suprahuman of all the arts, divine Music, the world's second revelation, the unspeakable sounding mystery of Being,—strictly speaking, this has just as much and just as little to do with the intrinsic nature of that musician, as the great tragic poet with the comedian, upon whose pre-existence

* "From the Tone-life of our Time," or "The Musical World of To-day"; published, nominally 1868, really October or early November 1867.—TR.

he nevertheless had based the genesis of his work. But just as, favoured by the total anarchy of modern art-conditions, the mime has succeeded in making himself lord of the Theatre, so the common musician, profiting by a very different set of circumstances, has succeeded in placing himself top of the tree, flapping his trade-guild mastership in the face of the art-genius, and giving himself the airs of sole proprietor of Music. The difference between these two revolts lies in the diversity of the ground usurped : the mime was able to dominate the Theatre because he there could exercise a blindingly popular function, and directly lead astray the public's verdict on dramatic art ; the musician, of the kind to which we will devote our prompt attention, had to devise for himself the Concert-room, and assemble round him, no public proper, but a species of conventicle, in order to pass for an art-genius. Through what peculiar attribute of Music's it became possible to fool and misguide the various local conventicles of Concert-subscribers, belongs to a future special inquiry ; as we are concerned to-day with nothing but the musician's social physiognomy, so to speak, we will content ourselves with signalising the personal means he has employed for his end.

The selfsame gentry, musicians pure and simple, who had been equipped by Nature with a real talent for play-ing music on this or that instrument, mainly the piano-forte in latter days, became "geniuses" in their own right ; just like Haydn, Mozart and Beethoven, they composed everything that these had composed, but in recent times—since Mendelssohn supplied them with the model—more particularly oratorios and all manner of biblical psalms ; precisely as though they were the others, if not in degree perhaps, assuredly in kind at least. A motive for this wondrous aberration may well reside in the immemorial demands addressed to applicants for certain civic and royal posts, of Musikdirektor or Kapellmeister, where-according they have had to turn out suitable music-pieces for certain official episodes of joy or mourning.

From this modest-looking stipulation, which had its reasonable practical sense in earlier times (when even a hero like *Händel* himself would compile his hastily be-spoken cantatas from older pieces of his own or others'), there has sprung the foolish consequence that nowadays every Kapellmeister or Musikdirektor, instead of being simply chosen for his ability to conduct correct perform-ances of true musical artworks, must at least be also held by a few intimate acquaintances for a considerable com-poser, if he is to do requisite honour to his installation by the respective Committees or Intendants. What incalcul-able harm has been done to the spirit of performance of our genuine musical art-literature through thus entirely leaving out of sight the main requirement, that of plain conductors intelligently educated for their weighty task, we must likewise postpone to a special inquiry, and keep to the mere physiognomy of our musician of the present day. What helped to getting-on in life, to wit the utmost fame as a "composer," thus became our musician's main con-cern ; how to reach that fame, his partly flattering, partly torturing care. Composition itself, indeed, is easily and swiftly to be learnt in our year of grace : but so to compose that fame shall come quite easily and swiftly of itself, that is, and always will be, most abominably hard. Hence the majority content themselves with an abstemious local fame, and the confidential prefix "our" has generally to be swallowed with the "gifted master" and so forth.

But there cropped up a brand-new variety of musicians, whose means allowed of their playing the game a little higher : uncommon examples of success lay before them ; the fortune of the sainted Meyerbeer gave them no sleep o' nights. The labours of one such, to reap a passable renown at any cost, we could characterise with a few strokes of the pen : yet it might not be right to make merry over the comic details of his zigzag after fame,—and that would be unavoidable. From tenderest youth ' this musician has been driven on the road to fame, with the most watchful eye for every helpful chance that offered,

as may easily be gathered from the book before us, but
without ever bringing off a genuine success through any
public deed of art. At last, abandoning the larger theatre
of fame, of France and Italy, he fell back upon the
more modest expedient of his simpler German guild-
fellows. He became Music-director at Cologne on the
Rhine, especially for sake of the so widely-circulated and
much-read *Kölner Zeitung*, it seems ; as permanent
trumpeter in which he soon knew how to employ a particular friend, the since deceased Professor Bischoff, after
disclosing to him the value of his works.   In any case a
tedious job. So one day our musician fancied he might
give it up, to grow famous all at once : he obtained a call
to Paris, as conductor of the Italian Opera ; let Cologne,
music-school and concert-direction vanish into space ; and
believed he now could take the thing by storm.   Only,
whenever our musician played the big game, he had always
had ill luck : the Italian Opera in Paris was no exception.
Cologne must serve him once again : he returned, to see
whether his bishop could not make of him at least a
Nether-Rhenish pope.   He was on a fair way to it, when
he had to learn that the Nether-Rhine itself was not so
altogether sound and sure : the Committee of the Music-
Festival had come by the notion that it really would not
make its feasts a monopoly for local celebrities, and one
fine day it invited another man to take the lead.   Now, that
other was quite the most fatal opposite to our musician :
growing-famous had come so absurdly easily to him from
earliest youth, that the musician, who had toiled and
moiled for it in vain, must needs fall into a furious rage at
this intrusion, of all others.—Herr *Ferdinand Hiller*, author
of the book announced above, is he whose sorrows we have
just depicted : " the other," who toillessly had reached the
most delirious height of fame through the wilfulness of a
Nature that singled out precisely him for bestowal of her
amplest gifts, was *Franz Liszt*. The incident, whereof we
speak, happened in the Summer of 1857.   Into what
explosion of wrath Herr Hiller, else so mild and tractable

allowed himself to be betrayed on that occasion, we shall see upon looking through his book.

For the moment merely a word to Herr " M. H.," who has done us the service of drawing our attention to the Hillerian book by an article to be read in the weekly issue of the Augsburg *Allgemeine Zeitung* for November 15th of this year,* and, as we thence have derived some instructive hints, has earned our grateful notice. We will endeavour to repay the obligation by a few return lessons.—Alluding to a newspaper-article made public by Herr F. Hiller at the time, and now rescued from oblivion through its reprint in the book under mention, Herr M. H. delivers himself as follows :—

" The highest rank we assign to the author's Report on the Aachen [Aix la Chapelle] Music-Festival of 1857, for here he proved himself possessor of that courage which Marx denies to musicians. 'Tis no trifle, to take the field against a *clique* deified by the length and breadth of mediocrity, and mutually deifying itself, against an army of musicians who write more newspaper-notices than notes ; no trifle to tell the Corybantes, that they are merely making a noise to drown the voice of the child of the gods ; no trifle, to cast in the teeth of the Sect the truth that their Liszt knows nothing of conducting, and their music is music only now and then. The polemic, then commenced by Hiller, has to-day already borne its fruit ; and many of those who then would have been the first to stone him to-day are of his opinion." †

Anyone at all accurately acquainted with the physiognomy of the persons and circumstances in question can readily comprehend that statements such as this may pass in conversation between Messrs M. H. and F. Hiller, if perchance one wants to display oneself in a becomingly valorous light to a new pupil of the Cologne Music-school,

* 1867.—R. Wagner.

† Compare with this choice Philippic the letter of Liszt to Herbeck (*Letters of Franz Liszt*, Vol. I.) dated June 12th, 1857 : " The Aix-la-Chapelle Musical Festival may be considered successful on the whole, from the very fact that opponents do not conceal their dissatisfaction."—TR.

just arrived from California; that something of the sort should even get written down, in emboldening intercourse by letter, is also conceivable : but, that it should be publicly printed,—this we can only explain by these gentlemen hugging the reassuring knowledge that that "army of musicians who write more notices than notes" has not a shadow of existence. For, survived there but a feeble bobtail of that army vanquished by the Cologne Falstaff in his great battle of the Nether-Rhine, these gentlemen would surely go in proper terror of one of those "press-notices" which, according to their own confession (so obvious here), form their sole material source of joy and sorrow.   With much certainty we may assume that they will be very surprised by even the present lines, to hear a poor straggler from the rout of 1857 suddenly raising his voice : for, so safe did the gentlemen deem themselves in their tranquil public converse, that, astounded at the marvellous success of their heroic deeds, they really thought they must trace the deed which had worked such amazing results to at least the "courage" disallowed by the departed Marx to all musicians, and thus to himself as well.*   That Herr M. H. here uses *Wuth* (fury) and *Muth* (courage) as convertible terms, thus gains its meaning. One result was experienced by the gentry even at the time : the slaver (*Geifer*) churned so mighty soon from zeal (*Eifer*) in a mouth constructed for the needs of Semitic speech, is downright loathsome; one moves out of its reach, if only to protect one's clothing.

Yet for certain public ends, such as the illustration of modern musical life in Germany, it may be time to don a slaver-proof suit, and exchange a word with these gentry. So, for once in a way, we give Herr M. H. the following

---

* A. B. Marx (born 1799), one of the founders of Stern's Conservatorium, died in May 1866, as Musical Director of the Berlin University,—a post he had held for over a third of a century. His musical compositions were not generally successful, but his theoretical works passed through many editions, "*Die Lehre von der musikalischen Komposition* (in 4 vols., 1837) having reached its ninth edition by 1887, and his "*Allgemeine Musiklehre* (1839) its tenth in 1884.—TR.

items of advice. Firstly: when one has the Cologne and
Augsburg Allgemeine Zeitungs so completely at one's call
that any stray reports of the enemy's actual successes are
always at least accompanied by spiteful editorial notes,*
one shouldn't commit the folly of twitting that enemy
with a fame acquired through newspaper advertisement unless one can at like time shew what sheet, at least as widely
read as those two largest-circulated German journals (con-
siderately we mention *them* alone), has stood at his behest
for the last ten years and more. Secondly: one should
not allow one's adversary's abstention from the commerce
of the larger papers to tempt one into the imprudence of
writing about things one doesn't understand ; or, if what
one has to write is inspired by persons of whom it might
be supposed that they really knew something, one should
be on one's guard against expressions which leave the
realm of expert knowledge for that of personal favour :
we mean, one should behave like a man of sense, and not
a genius ; otherwise, upon the notoriously treacherous ice
of ignorance, one can't tell what may happen. Wherefore,
in all things a little more moderation ! Let Herr F. Hiller
be lauded for his amiability, his gentleness, his agreeable
conversation in society, his finished pianoforte-playing, the
regularity of his beat, his solid style of composition ; moreover it will interest many members of Singing-unions to
see that the works they once had sung in, the " Destruction
of Jerusalem," the " Psalms " &c., can afterwards be read
about in print : that pleasure one may well prepare for
both sides, without talking of "immortality" and big mouth-
fuls of the sort; for things like that are easily said, but
what is thought by those who read them ?   Also, Herr
M. H. should not embarrass his readers in respect of
their memory · for instance,

" Does the reader remember that in the author of these
essays he has before him a profound student and master of
his art ? "

Such a question propounds the dilemma, that one either

* For one such, see the Augsburg *Allg. Ztg.* of Feb. 8, 1868.—Tr.

does not know Herr Hiller at all, or, should one know him, mayhap one has no memory of what Herr M. H. implies. All these are damaging blunders in case such a compost as this should be subjected to minuter analysis,—an event the author can never have taken into his reckoning. But it happens once in a way, you see, and will happen again upon fresh provocation. Wherefore our final piece of advice shall be : should the need to praise Herr F. Hiller exist with all the cogence of a nature-necessity, it would really be best to do it *cum grano salis.* As we are acquainted with very many agreeable and excellent qualities of Herr F. Hiller's, Herr M. H. will always find us ready and willing to heartily support him in such a praise ; a closer scrutiny of the very book before us, as we hope, will yield us welcome instigation. Only—we have named the reason—let Herr M. H. avoid all fervour, parrot no untruths, not ride the high horse, and, above all, never mount to dithyrambs ; for "the child of the gods," with a tender side-glance at the Cologne friend in opposition to the tumultuously "corybantic" Liszt, can only make him look amazingly ridiculous. That kind of thing won't wash, even in our musical Germany of to-day.—And now to business, to the literary object !

On dipping deeper into this book of two volumes, we find it mere feuilleton-gossip about which we have no remarks to offer, though for many reasons we advise our readers to look through it. To Herr *W. H. Riehl* we commend it in·particular, as a Culture-historical study ; and that for reason of the divers choice cigars the author smokes, between its covers, with *Rossini.*—

III.

A Remembrance of Rossini.

N Paris early in 1860 I conducted several frag-
ments from my operas, mostly instrumental
pieces, in the form of a concert twice repeated. The daily press raised quite a stir
about it, for the most part hostile, and
presently a reputed bon-mot of *Rossini's* went the round
of the papers. His friend Mercadante, so the tale went,
had taken sides for my music; thereupon Rossini had
read him a lesson at dinner, helping him merely to the
sauce of a fish, with the remark: that the extras were
good enough for a man who set no value on the dish
itself, as upon melody in music.

I had been told many an uninviting story of Rossini's
questionable indulgence to the very motley company that
filled his salon every evening; so I took the anecdote,
which gave great joy to German journals in particular, as
not entirely without foundation. On no hand was it
mentioned save with laudings of the master's wit. When
it came to Rossini's ears, however, in a letter to the editor
of a certain newspaper he indignantly protested against
this "*mauvaise blague*," as he called it, declaring that he
should not presume to express an opinion about me, as
he had only chanced to once hear an orchestra at a
German watering-place play a march of my composition,
—which, for that matter, had pleased him very much;
further, that he had too much respect for an artist who
sought to enlarge the field of his art, to descend to jests
at his expense. By Rossini's desire this letter was made
public in the sheet in question; the other journals, however, religiously kept silence on the fact.

This attitude of Rossini's prompted me to call on him ; I was received as a friend and informed afresh, by word of mouth, of the annoyance caused the master by that offensive piece of fiction. In the ensuing lengthy con- versation I endeavoured to assure Rossini that, even when I believed the jest to have really emanated from himself, it had not pained me ; through partly ignorant, partly malevolent distortions of single expressions from my art- writings, I had grown quite accustomed to being the prey of misconceptions even on the part of well-intentioned persons, and could only hope to set them right by first- rate performances of my dramatic-musical works them- selves ; until I somewhere could succeed in this, I was patiently resigned to my curious fate, and bore no grudge against anyone who innocently became mixed up in it. Rossini seemed sorry to gather from my hints that I had reason to be discontented with musical affairs in Germany, for he prefaced a brief review of his own artistic career with the remark that he had always cherished the notion that he would have turned out all right, if born and educated in my country. "*J'avais de la faculté*," he said, "*et peut-être j'aurais pu arriver à quelque chose.*" But Italy in his time, he continued, was no longer the land where a more earnest purpose, particularly in the field of operatic music, could be either inculcated or entertained ; there all higher aims were forcibly suppressed, and the people consigned to a mere fool's paradise. Thus he, as well, had unconsciously passed his youth in service of that tendence, had been forced to stretch his hand to right and left for the wherewithal to live ; when time brought him easier circumstances, it was already too late; he would have had to undergo an amount of toil that would have come hard to a man of mature age. More serious minds should therefore judge him mildly ; he himself had no pretension to be numbered with the heroes ; but it was not indifferent to him, to be deemed so low as to rank among the empty scoffers at earnest efforts.

With these words, and the gay, yet seriously kindly tone in which he uttered them, Rossini gave me the impression of the first truly great and reverable man I had as yet encountered in the art-world.

Though I never set eyes on him after that visit, I have not quite exhausted my reminiscences.

For a French prose-translation of some of my opera-poems I wrote a preface,* summarising the ideas set forth in my various art-writings, particularly as regards the relation of Music to Poetry. Here my estimate of modern Italian Operatic music was guided largely by Rossini's graphic utterances, founded on his own experience, in our aforesaid conversation. That very part of my treatise was dragged against me by the Parisian musical press, and has been an unfailing source of agitation to the present day. I learned that the aged master was besieged in his house with reports and protestations against my imaginary attacks upon him. The result shewed that people did not succeed in driving him to the obviously desired denunciation of me ; whether he felt himself concerned by calumnies purveyed to him each day in my regard, I still am unaware. Friends begged me to visit Rossini and furnish him with the true particulars of that agitation. I declared that I would do nothing that might supply fresh fuel for misunderstandings ; if Rossini himself did not see through the thing, it would be impossible for me to provide him with the needful light. A little after the catastrophe that befell my " Tannhäuser " at its Paris production, in the spring of 1861, Liszt arrived in Paris and had many a friendly meeting with Rossini ; †

* " *The Music of the Future* " ; see Vol. III., p. 295.—Tr.

† In further amendment of the latest inventions about Rossini [died Nov. 13, 1868, at Passy—Tr.] I may incidentally relate what Liszt told me many years ago : once, after submitting to the master one of his earliest, highly eccentric youthful compositions, he had received the amusing encomium that his Chaos had turned out even better than Haydn's (*das Chaos sei ihm noch besser gelungen als Haydn*). Now, it shews but little veneration, and certainly a most uncultivated taste, to spoil this really witty saying of Rossini's, as has recently happened in this place, by turning it into the platitude : "he preferred the Haydn Chaos," and thus irreverently burdening the worshipped

he also begged me to call on the latter—saying that he
really had always behaved as a steadfast friend in face of
all my enemies' attacks—and dispel the last cloud that
might have been conjured in his mind regarding me. Even
then, I felt that it was no season for removing deeper-lying
evils by outer attestations ; in any case, I remained averse
to giving opportunity for erroneous interpretations, either
here or there. After Liszt's departure Rossini sent to me
from Passy, through an intimate acquaintance, the scores
my friend had left behind ; accompanying them with a
message that he gladly would have brought them personally, had his ill health not confined him to the house
for the time being. And even then I abode by my prior
resolve. I left Paris without having visited Rossini a
second time ; and thus I took it on myself to bear the
self-reproach of behaviour difficult to judge, towards a
man I honoured so sincerely.

Later I chanced to learn that about this time a German
music-sheet (" *Signale für Musik* ") had published an imaginary account of a last visit paid by me to Rossini, after the
fiasco of my "Tannhäuser", in the sense of a tardy "*pater pec-
cavi.*" In that tale, too, the aged master was provided with
a repartee ; namely, upon my assurance that I had no
manner of mind to pull down all the great men of the past,
Rossini had answered with a subtle smile : " But, dear Herr
Wagner, if you only *could* ! "

I had little prospect of seeing this fresh anecdote denied
by Rossini himself, for earlier experience had certainly
taught his entourage to keep such stories, when impli-
cating himself, from reaching his ears at all ; nevertheless
I have not till now felt called to take up arms for the

master with a repetition of the old and well-worn witticism, " *l'autre me plaît
d'avantage.*" Finally, the transplanting of the anecdote from Liszt's earliest
youth to his latest " Abbé "-time is one of those wanton injuries to the memory
of Rossini that, if allowed to pass unrighted, might easily give the honourable
master—who always treated Liszt with friendship and sincere esteem—the
appearance of having been guilty of a very questionable duplicity. — R.
Wagner.

slandered party, in my eyes patently Rossini. But as the master's recent death appears to have roused on all sides a passion for publishing biographic sketches of him; and as I observe with sorrow that these stories, against which the deceased can no longer protest, are mainly arranged with an eye to effect,—I believe I can no better prove my veneration for the departed, than by contributing to an historic valuation of the tales about Rossini my own experiences of their reliability.

Rossini, who for long had led a private life, and seems to have treated all sorts of men with the careless lenience of the cheerful sceptic,—Rossini can scarcely be handed to posterity in falser guise, than by stamping him as a hero of Art, on the one hand, and degrading him to a flippant wag on the other. It would be very mistaken to assign him, in the manner of our modern self-styled "impartial" criticism, a middle post between these two extremes. No: Rossini will never be judged aright, until someone attempts an intelligent history of the Culture of our current century; a history in which, instead of boasting of a general advance, for once one took in eye the actual downfall of an earlier refinement. Were this character of our age correctly drawn, it would then be possible to allot to Rossini also his true and fitting station in it. And that station would be no lowly one; for with the same title as Palestrina, Bach, Mozart, belonged to their age, belongs Rossini to his; if the era of those masters was one of hopeful effort and wholly individual new-fashioning, the era of Rossini must be rated somewhat after the master's own verdict, the remarks he made to those he credited with earnestness and truth, but very probably withheld when he knew himself surrounded by a gaping herd of parasites and punsters. Then, and not till then, will it be possible to estimate Rossini at his true and quite peculiar worth; for what fell short of full dignity would have to be accounted neither to his natural gifts nor his artistic conscience, but simply to his public and environment, which made it difficult for a man like him to raise himself above his age and thereby share the grandeur of the veritable art-heroes.

Until that competent historian is found, may contributions to an amendment of the ribald jests which nowadays are strewn upon the open grave of the departed, in lieu of flowers, at least not pass unheeded.

IV.

Eduard Devrient.

"Meine Erinnerungen an Felix Mendelssohn Bartholdy." *

 STRANGE book, which seems to owe its origin to a precipitate resolve; although the author's reminiscences of his departed friend come somewhat late, and certainly would have made a better Effect at the proper season.

For, had this elaboration appeared soon after the death of Mendelssohn, in the first shock of that blow the reader would have heeded nothing but the good will so unmistakably predominant in this composition, at least as regards its principal subject; whilst the workmanship of the book, as such, might easily have been overlooked, and its somewhat too strictly commercial German might not particularly have struck us. But after tender memories had been nursed for one-and-twenty years, they really ought to have been worded in a style a little more worth printing; and we therefore must conclude that some specially excitant cause determined the author to publish his "recollections" with a certain dash of suddenness. In the book itself we find no open hint of such a thing, however, and consequently are left to form all kinds of queer conjectures.

Perhaps we may derive a clue from the author's obvious

---

* "My Recollections of Felix Mendelssohn Bartholdy."—As most of the quotations drawn by Wagner from this book are merely instances of atrocious German, and as their interest is therefore confined to the student of that language, I have only occasionally added an explanation in English.—Tr.

effort to establish for his early cut-off friend, Mendelssohn, an eminent predestination for the career of dramatic composer; that being no easy matter, since Mendelssohn did not in fact arrive at the fulfilment of such a destiny, Herr Devrient comes forward with a happy string of recollections to shew that *he* himself was the real dramatic genius of his friend, to whom the latter always turned for counsel when tortured by the dramatic question. It is very instructive to see how, despite this ever ready counsel and that indisputable predestination, so fortunately distributed between the two friends, the ardently longed-for opera was doomed to never come about. As the whole account of this remarkably unproductive relation, however, was to prove the eminent calling of Mendelssohn, it is manifest that the feat could only be accomplished by a highly fascinating display of dialectics and an insinuating style; but Herr Devrient having denied himself any such employment of his intellectual forces, it remains for us to lay the blame on the obvious haste to which some passionate resolve or other must have urged him. What may have been the motive of this unmistakable precipitance in dressing up the present reminiscences—whether peevishness at Offenbach's successes, or something else *—we have no wish to here inquire, though we are unable to assume a great integrity of motive; on the other hand the simple, noble language of a correction written and published by Frau Therese Marx in defence of her dead husband's character, which she deems disfigured in these "recollections," at once inspired us with a firm assurance of her truthfulness and the purity of her grounds of action.

* The inner history of the relations between Wagner and Devrient has not yet been made public, but we may obtain some light on the above allusion from the fact that the article on " Schnorr " (in which E. D. is mentioned—cf. p. 227) was published in June 1868, and the second editon of *Oper und Drama* (which disputes Mendelssohn's dramatic talent) was issued at about the same time, whilst Devrient's preface is dated September, 1868. As to the pamphlet by Frau Marx ("*A. B. Marx' Verhältniss zu F. Mendelssohn-Bartholdy*"), it traverses Devrient's statements about her late husband at every point, and forms a far graver indictment than even the present article of Wagner's.—TR.

Accordingly we will merely express our regret that once again a book whose subject is sufficiently interesting to ensure its being largely read, particularly in Berlin, should have been written in so undignified a style ; for if the German tongue is to go on being mangled without anyone denouncing it—as has been permitted in the present case once more—we well may fear a scandalous and total collapse of our literature. Wherefore, instead of a criticism of these "remembrances" themselves, we feel bound to give a mere selection from the solecisms and defacements of the German language that we have noted in reading through a volume composed by the remembrancer in honour of his famous friend, and a volume compiled from recollections treasured up for one-and-twenty years.

At the first glance one sees that word-dockings, especially of verbs, which had spread from third-rate journals to our book-literature and at last are becoming quite usual, have made themselves a cosy home in Herr Devrient's "Recollections." "Vorragend" (p. 4, 94 *et passim*) instead of: hervorragend ; "üben, Übung," for: ausüben, einüben, Einübung &c. (p. 33, 48, 60, *et al.*); "fürchten" for: befürchten (p. 65 etc.); "drohen" for: androhen, bedrohen (48 etc.); "wirken" in place of: bewirken (42 etc.); "ändern" for: verändern (156 etc.);

Dringen" for: Andringen (212); "merklich" in lieu of: bemerklich (238, 266 etc.); "hindern, Hinderung," for: verhindern, Verhinderung or Hinderniss (p. 32 and many another); "geladen" for: eingeladen; but above all "sammeln" for: versammeln. All these are great favourites with the author; the last, for instance, is regularly employed whenever an orchestra (p. 13), a number ("Zahl," p. 19, for: Anzahl) of members, a chorus (227), or even a "funeral train" (287) assembles—"gesammelt werden" or "sich sammeln," according to Devrient's formula—and tempts us to anticipate either an access of devotion or something like a monetary collection.—As, however, the reading-public of these chatty artist-books, in especial, seems to notice nothing but what it understands already

of itself, the purely " Selbstverständlich," the havoc played
by such verbal mutilations will surely produce too little
impression for us to make Herr Devrient's " Recollections "
a first example. More instructive, in an estimate of style,
are the instances of senseless or utterly nonsensical use,
arrangement and combination, of words neither mutilated
nor preposterous in themselves ; for these bear witness to
the author's low degree of education, in general, and
obstruct the reader's normal, healthy understanding of what
is written, in particular.

(P. 5) The " Herausgabe . . . unternahm eine Ausdehnung."—(12) " Die Musik *war* . . . die komischen
Momente *benutzend*."—P. 14, " gemüthwarm," as though
one said : gehirnweich ["warm-minded " and soft-brained].
—(16) A " verpflichteter Einfluss."—(18) A " nichtsver-
lierendes Gedächtniss " for : ein Gedächtniss *aus* welchem
sich nichts verliert [a memory which nothing escapes].
On the same page : " mir machte sie seinen Beruf
überzeugend," instead of : sie überzeugte mich von seinem
Berufe.—(P. 29) " der verständnissvolle Ausdruck der
singenden Personen," instead of : der (? dramatische)
Verstand, welchen er in der Wahl des Ausdruckes für
die singenden Personen zeigte ; since " verständnissvoll "
can only be applied to the person who understands, and
not to the thing to be understood.—(P. 30) " bewahrens-
werthe Melodien." From what are they to be " preserved " ?—(33) " Recht von Herzen gefiel die Oper nicht."
One *loves a thing* from one's heart, but nothing can *please
us* from *its* heart. Compare p. 40 : this " machte ihn
Felix sehr *lieb* " (sempstress-German). On the same page :
" Ein sehr musikalisch begabter Student " ; why not
Austrian-wise at once : " Sehr ein musikalisch begabter
Student " ?—(35) " Offenbar zeigte dies Charakteristik den
klärenden Wendepunkt in Felix' Compositionsvermögen."
A power with a turning-point, and that a clarifying one ?
Downright counterjumper's German !—In the same place :
" Seine charakteristische Kraft " (probably meaning : his
powerful capacity for musical characterisation) " war in

einem gewaltigen Entwickelungs*sprunge* erstaunlich *gewa-chsen*!" Presumably: through a leap, which *he* took in his evolution, this capacity was strengthened? For, beyond the question of what is to be reached thereby, a leap can strengthen (the muscles, for instance) but not effect a general growth. Another time (p. 38) did "Felix' evolution come by a surprising jerk," in which moreover B. Marx "*Antheil* hatte" ["had his share"]. Presumably Marx had contributed (though share and contribution are not the same thing) to some favourable progress in that evolution, but certainly not to any "*Ruck*" (hodman's German) thereof; an evolution does not *jerk*, for the simple reason that it *e-volves.*—(35) "Das leise Gefühl" instead of: das zarte Gefühl. When we speak of a quick ear (*ein leises Gehör*), we mean that the ear is quick to catch low sounds.—(36) A "Durchbruch der Selbstständigkeit." Self-reliance "breaks" neither through nor forth (though the latter would certainly be better German), but *steps forth*, simply, without any breaking. The author is very fond of "Durchbruch," however, and repeatedly observes it in the case of Felix (e.g. page 190); he is quite right in preferring it to a "Durchfall" ["fall-through"], with which the word betrays a fatal kinship.—Ibidem: "Er suchte seinen Lehrer zu begüten," instead of: begütigen; somewhat as "beruhen" for: beruhigen.—(38) "Dieser Umgang *reichte* nicht in den Salon des Hauses." If an intercourse is to "reach" at all, at least we should have "*bis* in den salon." In any case we deem this verb more intelligibly employed in: "Reich' mir die Hand, mein Leben!"—(40) Professor Gans "dominirte mit seiner breiten Sprache das Gespräch." The keenness of another visitor "unterhielt die Unterhaltung" ["entertained the entertainment," or "conversed the conversation"].—(P. 42) "*entsteht* eine dramatische *Behandlung*," above all through the aid of "*einschlagender* Chöre"; and "diess Alles *wirkte* Staunen."—(46) "Ich war jung genug, *dass*," instead of "um"; followed by an amazingly constructed sentence, which needs some reading over.—(47) "In solchem Spass *gipfelte* bei ihm Zärtlichkeit,"

and so on. Ibidem: "Erfindungs*kraft* für den Eindruck" (?)
—(48) " Unsre Gesangs*übungen* " (surely solfeggi and the
like, under guidance of a singing - master ?—No) " der
Bach'schen Passion " (hm !) " nahmen " (what ?) " weiteren
Fortgang." (Culled, perchance, from the diary of the old
charwoman of the Singakademie). Ibidem : " ein so welt-
fremdes Werk." Less poetical, but more sensible, would
have been : a work so foreign to the spirit of our age.
But that's too circumstantial for the swing of Devrient's
pen. Again (p. 49): " das Berliner Herkommen aus den
Angeln heben " is at smallest to be taken Hamlet-fashion,
for it surely cannot have been borrowed from the car-
penter's shop—though even that is conceivable.—(P. 55)
" wo er auf einem Sopha *niedersass*," instead of : sich
niedersetzte.—(63) " Er hat in seinem Leben kein Meister-
stück der Direktion geliefert, *als* " (for : wie) " dieses "; it
needs but the word " allein," to add a little, presumably
unwelcome clearness to the author's verdict.—(P. 64) it is
" *vorausempfunden*, dass es nöthig ist, den Taktstock zu
gebrauchen."—(65) " Musik der Neuzeit," conjecturably
the analogue of an " Altzeit," as " Neustadt " of " Altstadt."
Ibidem : " der Stimm*klang* hochgebildeter Dilettanten."
Half-educated (*niedriggebildetes*) reporter's German!—
(67) " In dem *Bildungskreise* Berlins," much as : in der
Kleidungsherberge, instead of : Schneiderherberge. Also, a
"performance" was "crowded."—(68) "Mendelssohn *set* the
deepest of composers once more in living action." On the
same page, " to his father " he is said to have " shewn "
(*erweisen*)—his gratitude or the like ? Oh, no !—" that "
etc : meaning *be*weisen. " Erweisen " crops up again and
again (e.g. p. 94, et passim), and seems particularly to
charm the author.—(P. 69) " seine *notenmässige* Auffassung."
So ! he conceives note-wise ? — Ibidem : " *Zur* Stelle
nachspielen." He retrieves a certain passage which he
had forgotten to play ?—(72) The " relations had nourished
an obscure point." So the author knows of a food for
points ?—(73) " An expression that went *against his
streak* " (flyman's German) " would make him quite

averse." To what? To the "expression," or averse to things in general?—(76) "Gefallsames." Quite the latest; presumably meaning : reckoned for merely pleasing? One might coin for it an opposite : "Durchfallsames" perchance?—(91) "Mir *klang* der bedeutende dramatische *Beruf* des Komponisten aus jeder Note." A vocation cannot ring to anyone, not even ring out (*er*klingen) to Herr D.; perhaps, however, it was the call of Felix begging for an opera-text?—(93) "Er verlangte, ich sollte mich dispensiren lassen vom Hofkonzerte." Jew-German for : mich vom Hofkonzerte dispensiren lassen.—(94) A "von Freundestheilnahme *getragener Verlauf*," and "eines Festes" too!—(96) "Seine Pflichten *für* die Oper." Duty "for" something is quite a favourite (compare p. 228 and others).—(112) "Er lenkte nach Deutschland," not "ein" or "um"; but simply "er lenkte," pretty much as in the expression : "der Mensch denkt" and so on.—(144) "Ein *ausgedehntes* Personal"— probably "expanded" by the rack.—(145) Eine "Einrichtung" war "eingewöhnt" [an "arrangement" was "made feel itself at home"].—(164) "Mendelssohn-Briefe," as one might say : "Devrient-texts."—(215) "Unnachlassliche Energie" would seem to be an energy that was not discovered by Mendelssohn's executors.—(216) "Er versprach, über sein Vermögen zu" —what?—simply "thun" ["he promised to do above his powers"].—(217) "There was little to set up (*aufzustellen*) with him" (stage-scenery?)—Ibidem : "Felix war *mit der Farbe herausgegangen*" ["Felix had gone out with the colour,"—say "colours"]. This leads one to suppose a curious scene, of which we had not heard before.—(218) "Dichtwerk," after the analogy of *Machwerk* [shoddy].— Ibidem : the "Aufschubsabsichten Tieck's," a construction on the model of "Schubsmassregelung" [? "measurement of pitch," in bowls or skittles] ; but the author surely must mean "Aufschiebungsabsichten" ["postponement-intentions"] : a charming word in any case!—(P. 219) "die wörtliche Verständlichkeit." Presumably that attribute of a poem which is to make it understood literally, not allegorically? But it remains un-understandable, both literally and illiterately.—(222 and 224) "Verlebendigung," a suggestive combination of "Belebung" and "Veranschaulichung": its antithesis, "Versterblichung," however, we do not meet with.—(224) The author is set "in einen Rausch der Erhabenheit"; there is not much to be said against this, as we don't happen to know that state of mind, though Herr D. assures us he has personally experienced it.—(226) "Vornahmen des Winters," in lieu of: projects for the winter.—(243) Felix becomes "komplett berlinscheu,"—also "he *took* our troubles as his own." Where did he deposit them?—(244) The author "überkommt eine Überzeugung."—(253) "If one *overlooks* this importunacy for an opera-text." Willingly will we overlook it, not to be obliged to over*see* it, especially as set forth by the author.—(264) The author "traf ein Gewandhauskonzert"; we are not informed whether he hit it in a rifle-gallery or a lottery. Our only sorrow is for the "ninth symphony," which he "hit" at like time.—(266) "Obschon ich mich schon" is probably to be excused by the passionate precipitance of the recollecting author.—(P. 267) "komponibel." Peddler's German, clumsily modelled on "kompatibel." (276) "Wir sahen ihn viel in *unserem* Hause oder in *befreundeten*" (query: anderen Häusern?)— (277) "Die *Verkürzung* von zwei englischen Musikern" [strictly, "the shortening of two English musicians"] seems to point (as in the case of the "expanded personnel") to a gruesome deed of bodily disfigurement, of which we have heard nothing through the criminal annals. To this may be linked the very risky story of B. Marx' appearance in the Mendelssohnian house (38), where we read: "trotz des ungelenken Benehmens seiner untersetzten Gestalt, seiner kurzen Pantalons und grossen Schuhe."* Though it is surprising enough, to hear of a "figure" having a "demeanour," yet as regards the boots and pantaloons

---

* Strictly, "despite the awkward demeanour of his under-sized figure, his short trousers and large boots." The other meaning of "Benehmen" is the act of "taking away" or "removing."—TR.

we can only assume that the author employs the word "Benehmen" in an altogether different sense from what the epithet "ungelenk" might lead one at first to suppose. Upon our appearance in a strange house we may quite becomingly have our shyness, our embarrassment etc., *taken from* us, and one can conceive an act of "removing" that frame of mind; but such an interpretation of the startling word would make the sentence imply a most uncivil treatment of the departed Marx in the highly decorous mansion of the Mendelssohns. In any case it is fatal that the author of these "recollections" should have given ground for such double-meanings through his peculiar choice of terms, and affords another proof that it is not good for a Theatre-director to read nothing but theatrical journals inspired by himself; thereby his style acquires not even the soundness sufficient to describe the happenings in a rich Jew-banker's home.

But, if this selection of Devrientian flowers of speech has not already worried and wearied the reader past all bearing (and we certify that we have given a mere *selection* from our notes), let us finally turn to a bunch which shews the oddity and misunderstandableness of the author's whole construction of his sentences.—Here we will first remark that the difficulty of understanding this author's phrases, due to a wrong employment of individual words, is much exacerbated by his curious interpunctuation. The comma he uses very charily, the colon with great glee, but always in the wrong place. Thus, for instance, in the sentence (p. 229) "er hatte ihm die Ehre erzeigt: ihn in den Orden" etc. "anzunehmen."—Herr D. is also very fond of dropping his "und," especially where it is positively indispensable. For example (275): "Felix ging an den Rhein zu den Musikfesten" (and ?—no, simply:) "wieder zurück nach Leipzig, den Elias fertig zu machen, den er" etc.—But all the above-named quiddities of style combine their unsophisticated parts to form the following sentences, which we likewise cull at random from our many notes.

Page 189 : "Der Vorsatz, den jeder gutgeartete Mensch vom Grabe eines verehrten Todten mitnimmt : in seinem Sinne fortzuleben, musste bei Felix *um so* entschiedener in dem *Gedächtniss* seines Vaters" (so the dead have still a " memory " for things) " zur Herrschaft kommen, *und* " (the " um so " is consequently deprived of its companion " als ") " die Überzeugung, dass er nur durch Erfüllung des väterlichen Wunsches den neuen *gemüthlichen Anhalts-punkt* " (not a mainstay for his heart, — bad enough !— but a truly hearty mainstay ?) " für sein Leben gewinnen könne, kam in den zehn Tagen, die er noch im Trauerhaus weilte " (for : verweilte), " *bei* ihm " (in the region where the heart has its seat ?) " zum Durchbruch " ; where it " comes " to something twice in one sentence, namely once to " Herrschaft " and again to the old familiar " Durch-bruch."—This same page (on which Felix also " anwirbt " David, the friend of his youth, for the orchestra) gives us : " der *Verlauf* des Winters brachte dem Gewandhaus-publikum überraschende Kunstgenüsse, *in theils* dort noch nicht aufgeführten Werken, *theils in* neuer Auffassung und immer auf's Feinste ausgefeilter Aufführung schon bekannter." That art-delights should be brought in works, as ices in saucers, is not less novel than the preposition's chequered play is singularly graceful.—Again (192) : " Er *opferte* dafür einen *Reiseplan in* die Schweiz und das *Seebad* in Genua " (apparently : auf. Or simply as Abraham offered his son Isaac to the Lord ?). " Vergolten wurde ihm diess Opfer *nicht nur* durch den Erfolg seiner Bemühung um den Cäcilienverein und durch den, ihm sehr werthen Umgang mit Ferdinand Hiller, der eben wieder in seiner Vaterstadt verweilte," (surely we now shall get the " sondern," demanded by the " nicht nur" ?—No, F. Hiller's lingering at Frankfort, where he stayed per-chance beyond all bounds, would seem to have driven the " sondern " into oblivion ; for, after an unassuming comma, which he has not entirely despised for this once, the author continues :) " nein, er sollte hier die Erfüllung von seines Vaters Wunsche finden." And here it is

noteworthy that Felix "finds" for his father the "fulfilment" of a wish, which he really might have "brought
about" himself; but that would have made the clause
precise, and stolen its whole poetic nimbus.—Later (228) :
"Er gab ein letztes Konzert: *den* Lobgesang und
Klavierproduktionen."—(231) : "Moscheles trat noch für
Klavierspiel (,) und nach Polenz' Tod : " (a colon !) " Böhm
für Gesang ein," (followed by a simple comma) "und
andere Hilfslehrer." (Full stop. We have to fill up the
sense for ourselves, presumably to the effect that these
other assistants also "entered" somehow.)—(Page 240) :
"So konnten wir manche Sorge *austauschen*" (barter
them for one another, or among ourselves ?); immediately
thereafter : "manche Mäkelei an der scenischen Anord-
nung." This also is "bartered" : forcibly suggesting a
harangue between Hamburg ship-brokers (Schiffsmäklern).
—(71) : "Die Liebe zu seinen Schwestern war von der
zärtlichsten Vertraulichkeit, *was* in Beziehung auf seinen
Bruder jetzt noch der trennende Unterschied der Jahre
hinderte." (A most ambiguous sentence !)—(29) : "Der
Stoff der Oper—*im* Dorfbarbier schon benützt *und*"
(without a comma to precede it ; therefore also *in* the
Dorfbarbier) "sehr bekannt—eignet sich nur zu einer
komischen" (episode ? Oh dear no :) "Katastrophe."
Later we have a "verstellte Vergiftung"; so ! in the
fashion of a "simulated" friendship, where hate takes on
its mask. But what sort of condition is that, which
disguises itself as poisoning ?— — —You see the harm
it has done Herr D. to mix so long with no one but talent-
less actors, whose acquisition and retention he has deemed
the only requisite for maintaining the model character of
his theatre : even the utmost stickling for one's own
authority will not shield one from the effect of such
influences in the long run ; as we cannot but gather from
the language of these "Recollections," alive with crying
jargon of the wings.

Two further extracts in conclusion.—

(Page 66) : "Ich war mir bewusst, dass der Eindruck

den der Vortrag des Jesus hervorbringt, wesentlich über den Eindruck des ganzen Werkes entscheidet; *auch hier sind alle Dinge zu ihm geschaffen."* (? ?) " Mir galt *es* " (what?) "*die* grösste Aufgabe, die einem Sänger werden kann. Mich beruhigte (es ?), dass die Partie " etc. "und so konnte ich, getragen von dem *Total"* (quite a favourite!) "der Aufführung, aus voller Seele singen" (comma?) "und fühlte dass die andächtigen Schauer, die mich durch-*rieselten"* (taking a metaphor from the rain-shower?) "auch durch die Zuhörer " (trickled ?   No :) "*wehten."* (A shower of *wind* ?—Rather an excess of horrors for one time !)—Finally we find, or, to copy the author, simply "treffen," on page 25 : " Im neuen Hause trat Felix " (into his chamber, or the drawing-room ?—No !) " in sein Jüng-lingsalter "; and then he further "trod," all with *one* tread in favour of a simple " und," this time not grudged us, " in die Neigung*en* und Beschäftigung*en*, welche frischer angeregte Kraft " (for : fresh incentive to force) "*bringt."* — — —

And this all has actually been set and printed in Wigand's book-printery at Leipzig in the year 1868, corrected, revised, and finally reviewed and passed by all the world as quite in order !—

After furnishing these samples of his intellectual culture, Herr D. bewails the " Hamlettragik in Mendelssohn's Opernschicksal," (—on our part we bewail the fact that we seldom can quote three words of this author's without bringing down a solecism, even when by no means aiming at that side!—) and "how much the nation has lost" by the circumstance that Felix could not make up his mind to set music to an opera-text of his Eduard's, as we gather from the "total" of these souvenirs.   The book itself is nothing but a threnody thereon.   On the other hand we are given among the " recollections " a few letters of Men-delssohn's own, which, however thin and unimportant in themselves, refresh us by their simple, quite supportable German ; the very contrast leads us to suppose that Felix had his own good reasons for not expecting too much from his Eduard. That the brilliant musician nevertheless found himself always thrown on this one friend for fulfilment of his wish to procure a good opera-poem, gives us a disappointing idea of the atmosphere—in the author's eyes so uncommonly stimulant and intellectually alive—which surrounded Fortune's darling.—

We will not here discuss the causes of the " Hamlet-Mendelssohn opera-fate-tragedy"; enough, that Devrient was not the man to take a world all "out of joint " (according to Shakespeare) and " lift it to its angles " (according to himself). What drove the author so late and yet so hurriedly to pen and publish these "Recollections," we have already briefly questioned in the opening of our present criticism; having left the subject unexplored, as probably most unpleasant, we propose to abide by that arrangement. On the other hand the incredibly bungling style in which this book is written, as proved above in detail, brings us to a final consideration of very grave moment for our era and its state of culture.

We have evidence of the high esteem enjoyed by the author for a long while past.—*Mendelssohn* deemed him the only man capable of writing him a good opera-poem ; —*Paul Heyse*, son to one of the foremost teachers of the German language, and himself endowed with the highest qualifications for its use, clothes one of his poems with a dedication to the " Meister Devrient " ;—one of the *pattern Rulers* of our day, in firm conviction that he is thereby dealing an earnest and weighty stroke for culture, hands his Court-theatre over to this selfsame man, with a devolution of authority so full that nothing save belief in a great aim could have prompted it amid existing relations. This confidence increases, in its turn, the general reputation of the recipient of such distinguished and unwonted honours, and no one dares to seriously ask himself what the man has really done to deserve it all.

A book appears, like that before us, and everybody finds it excellent ; ay, it adds fresh laurels to the author's reputation. But we have viewed this book a little closer, and found to our amazement that never yet had we read such a thing, saving in the correspondence of the two Gymnasiasts, may be, which the " Kladderadatsch " serves out in serial parts. Now, it is impossible to suppose that a man of so neglected an education in his mother-tongue can have very much æsthetic culture. As the basis of his artistic training has been the Theatre, and it being known that he never evinced any particular talent for play-acting, the present question is : how, equipped with this utterly barbarous sense of the commonest propriety in diction, is he to afford his players any useful guidance, to supervise their doings ?—But, whatever is the man besides ? That as a "comedian," with Felix as a " Jew-youth " (p. 62), he got from Zelter and the members of the Berlin Singakademie a performance of Bach's Passion-music, testifies to his acting-talent *off* the stage ; and Felix acknowledged as much by his shout of glad astonishment : " you really are a devil of a fellow, an arch-jesuit " (p. 59). At any rate the acting-talent of Herr D., thus designated and admirably employed for once, can be no trifle ; it must even be rated pretty high ; for here, outside the theatre, he has won such great successes that he ranks quite universally as a somebody, though it would puzzle one to find a proof of his identity. For sure, a very notable phenomenon ! It reminds us of the "weeny thing called Cinnabar," of Hoffmann's fairy-tale. If Herr D. will undertake to work no mischief with the charm he owns so patently, in this sense, on our side we will promise to keep the secret of the single hair that holds it for him.

ABOUT CONDUCTING.

Über das Dirigiren
(1869).

Motto after Goethe:

" Fliegenschnauz' und Mückennas'	Nose of gnat and snout of fly,
Mit euren Anverwandten,	With all your kith and clansmen,
Frosch im Laub und Grill' im Gras,	Midge in grass and toad on high
Ihr seid mir Musikanten ! "	Be ye my chosen bandsmen !

Über das Dirigiren *was first published in the* Neue Zeitschrift für Musik, *of Nov. 26, Dec. 3, 10, 17, and 24, 1869, and Jan. 1, 7, 14 and 21, 1870 (and simultaneously in the "New Yorker Musik-Zeitung," according to C. F. Glasenapp). Immediately thereafter it appeared as a separate pamphlet, issued by the firm of C. F. Kahnt, Leipzig.*

I fancy I have somewhere seen its authorship assigned in part to Hans Richter, owing to a misunderstanding of the title of Maurice Kufferath's independent brochure : "L'Art de diriger l'orchestre. Richard Wagner et Hans Richter." *To make negative assurance doubly sure, I asked Dr Richter personally whether he had had any hand in the composition of Wagner's treatise ; his reply was a most emphatic " No."*

The " Motto after Goethe" is taken from the Walpurgisnachtstraum, Oberon and Titania's Golden Wedding, Faust I., a reference for which I am indebted, as also for information contained in some of the explanatory notes, to Mr Edward Dannreuther's excellent translation of the following treatise. In this motto Wagner has changed nothing save the last line, the original being : " Das sind die Musikanten." An apology is needed for the roughness of my English rendering of the somewhat catchy quatrain.

TRANSLATOR'S NOTE.

PROPOSE to relate my own experiences and judgment of a field of musical activity that has hitherto been left to routine for its practice, to ignorance for its criticism. To ratify my verdict I shall not appeal to conductors themselves, but to bandsmen and singers, as these alone have a right sense of whether they are being conducted well or badly; though they certainly can never decide the point until, for once in a most exceptional way, they really are well conducted. Moreover I shall make no attempt at setting up a system, but merely jot down a series of personal observations, reserving to myself the right of continuing the same as occasion offers.

Unquestionably the guise in which their works are brought to the public's ear can be no matter of indifference to composers; for the public, very naturally, can get the correct impression of a musical work from nothing save a good performance, but is unable to distinguish between the incorrect impression and the badness of the work's performance. Many a reader, on the other hand, will become aware how things stand with the generality of performances in Germany, not only of operas but also of concert-music, if he will lend his attention, and a modicum of knowledge, to my account of the elements of such performances.

The faults apparent to the expert in our German orchestras, faults alike of constitution and achievement, spring for the most part from the prejudicial attributes of their conductors, the Kapellmeisters, Musikdirektors and so forth. The choice and appointment of these officials, by the chief authorities of our art-institutes, has been executed the more ignorantly and perfunctorily in direct ratio as demands upon the orchestra itself have become harder and more exacting. When the highest problems for the orchestra were covered by a score of Mozart's, at its head still stood the veritable German Kapellmeister, a man of weighty reputation (locally at least), sound, sure, despotic, and above all gruff. The last specimen of this class, within my acquaintance, was Friedrich Schneider of Dessau ; Guhr of Frankfort was another. What excellent work, of its kind, these men and their like were able to do—though their attitude toward newer music had earned them the name of " pigtails " (" Zöpfe ")—I learnt some eight years back, through a performance of my " Lohen-grin " at Carlsruhe under the bâton of old Kapellmeister Strauss. This most estimable man stood up to my score with manifest dread and wonder : but his anxiety was also put into his leading of the orchestra, than which nothing more precise and forcible could be imagined ; one saw that all obeyed him as a man who understands no jokes and keeps his people well in hand. Strange to tell, this elderly gentleman was also the only noted conductor I have ever come across who owned real fire ; his tempi often were rather over-rushed than dragging, but always sinewy and cleanly taken.—A similar good impression I obtained from a like achievement of H. Esser's at Vienna.*

What was bound to make these conductors of the old school, when less gifted than those just named, unfit at last to cope with the more complicated style of modern orchestral music, was primarily their ancient usage as regards the manning of the orchestra itself ; a usage which had once seemed needful, or at least sufficient for the tasks in hand. I know of no instance in Germany where the constitution of an orchestra has been radically transformed to meet the claims of modern instrumentation. Now, as of yore, the bandsmen make their way to the top of the tree by right of seniority, and consequently never take the leading parts until their powers are failing, while younger and more capable musicians occupy the second desks ; an arrangement most markedly prejudicial to the 'wind.' Though we owe it to recent intelligent efforts, and in

* See Vol. III., p. 279.—Tr.

particular to the modesty of the executants concerned, that these evils are gradually diminishing, yet another custom has entailed persistent mischief, namely in the casting of the 'strings.' Here the second violin is constantly sacrificed without ado, to say nothing of the viola. This latter instrument is almost universally made over to invalided fiddlers, or even to worn-out wind-players if they have ever handled a member of the fiddle family in their lives ; at most one tries to set a really good viola-player at the first desk, chiefly for sake of the occasional soli ; nay, I have been at places where one made shift for even these with the leader of the first violins. In a certain grand orchestra, out of eight viola-players only one was named to me who could correctly execute the frequent ticklish passages in one of my later scores. This particular custom, pardonable on grounds of humanity, arose from the viola in earlier instrumentation having been merely used to fill up the accompaniment ; and to our day it has found justification enough in the unseemly mode of instrumenting common to Italian opera-composers, whose works indeed make out a favourite and substantial portion of the German operatic repertoire. As the Intendants of our larger theatres set great store by these operas, so dear to the august taste of their Courts, it also is no matter for wonder that requirements grounded on works utterly distasteful to these gentry should only have a chance of being met when the Kapellmeister is a man of real weight and assured repute, provided always he himself has an adequate knowledge of what is needed for a modern orchestra. But that is just where our older Kapellmeisters were for the most part deficient; above all, they lacked perception of the necessity of increasing the 'strings' proportionally to the great increase in number and employment of the 'wind'; for what has been doled out in this regard, now that the discrepance had become too glaring, has never sufficed to raise our far-famed German orchestras to a level with the French ; in power and excellence of the violins, and particularly of the violoncelli, they still lag far behind.

To recognise and carry out what had escaped those
Kapellmeisters of the old stamp, should have been the
first duty of the conductors of newer date and style.   Care
was taken, however, that these latter should not become
a thorn in the side of the Intendant, that the weight and
authority of the sturdy " Zöpfe " of olden times should not
pass on to them.

It is weighty and instructive to learn how this new
generation, representing now the whole of German music-
mongering, has reached its dignities and office.—As we
chiefly have to thank the great and small Court-theatres,
in fact the Theatre in general, for the maintenance of
orchestras, we must put up with the consequence that
the musicians who are to represent the spirit and dignity
of German Music in the eyes of the German nation,
and often for half - a - century through, are selected by
the authorities of those theatres.   The majority of these
patronised musicians must know how they came by their
distinction, for only with a minority of them can the un-
practised eye detect the services by which they reached
it.   The regular German musician mostly arrives at one
of these " good berths," as which alone they seem to be
regarded by their patrons, by a simple application of the
law of inertia : one works one's way up wedge-wise.   The
Berlin Court-orchestra, if I mistake not, has received most
of its conductors in this way.   Now and then, however,
the trick has been done at a leap : brand-new eminencies
have suddenly shot up, under protection of the lady-in-
waiting to a princess, and so forth.   The injury done by
these spiritless beings to the nature and development of
our very largest orchestras and operahouses, is impossible
to overestimate.   Entirely devoid of merit, they have only
been able to keep their footing by submissiveness towards
an ignorant chief, who usually thinks himself omniscient,
and fulsome lenience towards the inertia of the musicians
committed to their charge.   By throwing over all artistic
discipline, for whose maintenance they were utterly dis-
qualified, as also through a pliant obedience to every

senseless order from above, these masters have managed to even soar to universal popularity. Each knotty point of study has been got over at rehearsal, amid mutual smirkings, with an unctuous allusion to the "ancient fame of the Such - and - such Kapelle." Who has ever noticed that the doings of that famous institute were deteriorating year by year? Where were the true musicians, to deliver judgment? Certainly not among the reporters, who only bark when their mouth isn't stopped; and that stopping was fairly understood by all concerned.

But in still later times these conductorships are also getting filled by special summons: as the need or humour of the supreme control dictates, one imports a dashing routinier from somewhere; and this is for sake of grafting an "active force" upon the inertia of the home-grown Kapellmeister. These are the gentlemen who "bring out" an opera in a fortnight, are capital hands at "cutting," and write "cadenzas" for prime donne to interpolate in other people's scores. To such skilfulness as this the Dresden Hofkapelle owes one of its most vigorous conductors.*

Now and then, too, one flies at a veritable vocation: "musical big-wigs" shall be called in. The Theatre has none to shew: but the Sing-academies and Concert-establishments, if we are to trust the feuilletons of our great political journals, turn them out at the rate of one to every two or three years. These are our modern music-bankers, sprung from the school of Mendelssohn, or recommended to the world by his personal protection. At any rate it's quite another make of man, to the puling after-growth of our ancient Pigtails,—musicians not bred within the orchestra or on the stage, but decently brought up at the new-fangled Conservatoria, composers of oratorios and psalms, listeners to the rehearsals of Subscription-concerts. In conducting, as well, they had taken lessons, and crowned the whole with an elegant polish such as no musician had ever displayed before. Gruffness was no longer to be

* Julius Rietz?—TR.

thought of : and what with our poor native Kapellmeisters
had been anxious, self-distrustful modesty, with them took
on the aspect of good tone ; a thing to which they felt
bound the more by their somewhat uneasy feeling toward
our whole German-pigtailed plan of society.* I honestly
believe these people have exercised much good influence
upon our orchestras : a deal of rawness and loutishness has
disappeared, and many an elegant detail of rendering has
since been better heeded and brought out. They were
already more at home with the modern Orchestra, as it was
indebted in many respects to their master, Mendelssohn,
for a specially refined and delicate advance along that path
which Weber's glorious genius first had trod with new
inventive power.

But these gentry lacked one thing, above all needful for
the refashioning of our orchestras and allied institutes :—
Energy, that energy which nothing but a self-confidence
backed by genuine force of character can give. For
everything, alas ! was artificial here : calling, talent,
culture ; ay, faith, love and hope. Each one of them has
so much ado to maintain his artificial standing, that he has
no time left to think of generalities, of the coherent, the
consequent and re-organic ; and indeed these matters, to
tell the truth, are not his business. The gentlemen stepped
into the shoes of those old hard-grained German masters,
simply because the latter had sunk into too deep a decay
and become incapable of recognising the needs of the
newer age and its art-style ; and it seems as if they themselves were perfectly aware that they merely fill an
interregnum, for from the bottom of their souls they don't
know what to make of the German art-ideal—toward
which alone all noble things are struggling. Thus, when
faced with stiff requirements in the newer music, they fly
to the merest stopgap. Meyerbeer, for instance, was very
considerate (*delikat*) ; out of his own pocket he paid for a
new flautist in Paris, to blow him a certain passage. As
he was fully alive to the advantages of a good delivery,

* Obviously the Jews, again.—TR.

moreover rich and non-dependent, he could have done wonders for the Berlin orchestra when the King of Prussia called him to the post of Music-director in Chief. Mendelssohn was summoned at the same time, nor did he lack for quite unusual gifts and knowledge. True, they both were confronted with the selfsame obstacles that had always barred the way to any good in this department : but, those very obstacles were just their duty to remove, since they were amply armed for the bout as none besides. Why did their strength forsake them ? Apparently because they never had any. They left the thing in its rut: and now we have the "celebrated" Berlin orchestra with even the last traces of the Spontinian legend of precision worn away. And these were Meyerbeer and Mendelssohn ! What shall their natty silhouettes put right, elsewhere ?

From a survey of the attributes of the survivors from the old dispensation, as also of this newest species of Kapellmeister and Musikdirektor, it is clear that we can't expect much from *them* for the reformation of the Orchestra. No: the initial step toward such a thing has always come from the executants themselves ; which is plainly ascribable to the great advance in technical virtuosity. The boon conferred on our orchestras by the virtuosi of their various instruments is past all questioning ; it would have been complete if the conductors, particularly amid such circumstances, had only been what they should be. But with the pigtailed remnant of our old Kapellmeisterthum, the screwed-up beings in constant terror of their own authority, the pianoforte-teachers nominated by ladies-in-waiting, and so forth, the virtuoso of course shot high above their heads ; in the orchestra he played somewhat the same rôle as the prima donna on the boards. The "elegant" Kapellmeister of newest stripe, on the contrary, struck up an alliance with the virtuoso—a thing not without its uses in many respects, but conducive to a general prospering of the whole only in the event of the heart and soul of German Music having been grasped by these gentry.

The point of prime importance, however, is this : equally
with the Orchestra itself, they owed their standing to the
Theatre, and their chief duties and avocations were concerned with *Opera*. The Theatre, the Opera, it thus was
their business to understand, and to learn something
beyond their music pure and simple ; namely—much as
with the application of mathematics to astronomy—the
application of music to dramatic art. Had they rightly
understood dramatic singing and expression, that comprehension would have reflected a light upon orchestral
delivery, particularly with the works of newer German
instrumental-music. The best hints I ever had for the
tempo and phrasing of Beethoven's music were those I once
derived from the soulful, sure-accented singing of the great
Schröder-Devrient ; it since has been impossible for me to
allow e.g. the affecting cadenza for the oboe in the first
movement of the C-minor Symphony

to be draggled in the way I have always heard elsewhere.
Nay, harking back from this cadenza itself, I also found
the meaning and expression for that prolonged fermata of
the first violins in the same passage,

and the stirring impression I won from this pair of
insignificant-looking points gave me a new insight into the
life of the whole movement.—Merely citing this by the way,
my main object has been to suggest the finish that would
have been added to the conductor's higher education in
musical rendering, had he correctly understood his position
toward the Theatre, to which he strictly owes his whole
emoluments and office. But no, he treats the Opera as an

irksome daily task, to be got through with a sigh (to which he gains a mournful right from the havoc played with that art-genre at German theatres), and pins his honour to the Concert-room, his birthplace and his house of call. For, as already said, whenever a Theatre-Intendance is seized with the longing for a musician of renown, that musician has invariably to come from somewhere other than the Theatre.

To judge the stage-capabilities of such a quondam Concert and Sing-academy Conductor, we first must visit him in his habitual home, where his fame as "solid" German musician has been established. We must take a look at him as conductor of concerts.

———

A strange impression of discontent was made upon me in my earliest youth by the orchestral rendering of our classic instrumental - music, and has been recalled to memory whenever I have attended such performances in recent days. Things that had seemed to me so full of life and soul when reading the score, or at the piano-forte, I scarcely recognised in the form wherein they skimmed before the audience, for the most part quite unheeded. Above all was I astonished at the mawkish-ness of the Mozartian cantilena [cantabile ?], which I had imagined to be so full of charm and feeling. Not till later years did the reasons become clear to me; and as I have gone into them pretty closely in my "Report on a Music-school for Munich," * I will beg anyone, who wishes seriously to follow me, to refer there for that portion of the matter. I may say, however, that they reside primarily in the total lack of a true German Conservatorium for Music, in the strictest sense of the word : i.e. an institute in which the accurate tradition of the legitimate rendering for our classical music, as practised by our masters them-selves, should have been preserved and handed down alive ;

* Given earlier in the present volume.—R. Wagner.

which would naturally involve our presupposing those masters themselves to have arrived at performing their works there, and entirely to their liking. Both that proviso and its necessary consequence, alas! the German notion of Culture has altogether overlooked; and thus we are left to each several conductor's fancies as to the tempo or phrasing of a classical piece of music, for our only guide to its indwelling spirit.

At the famous Leipzig Gewandhaus-concerts in my youth these pieces were simply not conducted at all; they were led off by Matthäi, the first violin (*Konzertmeister*) of those days, somewhat as the overtures and entr'actes at the Play. Hence there was no trace of disturbance by the conductor's personality. Moreover those masterpieces of our classic instrumental-music which presented no great technical difficulties *in se* were got through regularly every winter: they went quite smoothly and precisely; one saw that the orchestra, knowing them all by heart, was glad to give the annual greeting to its favourites.

Only with *Beethoven's Ninth Symphony* things would not go at all; yet that, too, was a point of honour to perform each year.—Myself I had copied out the score of that Symphony, and made a pianoforte arrangement of it for two hands. Imagine my amazement to receive the most confused impressions from its performance at the Gewandhaus! ay, to feel at last so disheartened by them that I turned my back for a while on Beethoven, about whom I had been thrown into such utter doubt. It has also been very instructive to me, that my later genuine delight in *Mozart's* instrumental works was not kindled until I found occasion to conduct them, and thus to follow my own feeling of the animation demanded by Mozart's cantilena. My most thoroughgoing lesson, however, was a hearing of that despaired-of " Ninth Symphony " at Paris in the year 1839, played by the so-called Conservatoire-orchestra. 'Twas as if scales had fallen from my eyes in regard of its rendering, and I saw at once the secret of the problem's solving. For in every bar the orchestra had learnt to recognise the Beethovenian *melody*; which plainly had escaped our brave Leipzig bandsmen of the time. The orchestra *sang* that melody.

That was the secret. And it had been laid open by a conductor of no especial genius; Habeneck, to whom was due the credit of that great performance, had rehearsed this symphony for one whole winter without feeling anything beyond the impression of its unintelligibleness and ineffectiveness,—an impression as to which it would be difficult to decide whether German conductors have likewise deigned to feel it. Him it moved, however, to rehearse the symphony yet a second and a third year through, and not to rest till the new Beethovenian *melos* had dawned on every member of his band and been correctly reproduced by each; for these were bandsmen of true feeling for melodic phrasing. But Habeneck was at least a director of the good old stamp: he was master, and all his men obeyed him.

The beauty of that rendering of the Ninth Symphony I still am quite unable to describe. Yet, for a faint idea, I will select one passage from a host, to illustrate the difficulty of Beethoven's phrasing (*Vortrag*) and the scant success of German orchestras in coping with it.—Never have I succeeded in getting even the most distinguished orchestras to execute the following passage of the first movement:

so absolutely evenly as I heard it rendered (thirty years ago) by the musicians of the Paris Conservatoire-orchestra. This one passage, the oftener its remembrance has recurred to me in later life, the clearer has it shewn me the principles of orchestral delivery; for it holds within itself the law of *moving* and *abiding tone*, at like time with that of *dynamics.** That the Parisians were able to execute that passage *exactly* as it stands written,—in this was shewn their mastery. Neither in Dresden nor in London,† at both which places I since performed this symphony, could I get the instrumentists to make the change of bow-sweep and of string quite imperceptible in the ascending sequence; still less could I check an involuntary accentuation as the figure rises, for the ordinary musician is always prone to increase his force in ascending the scale and decrease it in descending. With the fourth bar we invariably had arrived at a *crescendo*; so that the sustained g-flat which enters with the fifth bar was involuntarily, nay, necessarily given a prematurely passionate accent, most detrimental to the peculiar tonic significance of that note in this connection. To the dull-of-feeling it is hard to convey the difference between the plainly expressed intention of the master, as indicated in the score, and the expression given to this passage when strummed in such a banal fashion: to be sure, even then it expresses discontent, unrest and longing; but the *manner* of these moods we never learn until we hear the passage executed as the master himself conceived it, and as I never yet have heard it realised save by those Paris bandsmen in the year 1839. On that occasion, I remember, the impression of dynamic monotony (if I may be allowed that apparently senseless expression for a phenomenon most difficult to define) in the uncommon, nay, eccentric intervals and convolutions of the ascending figure, with its final discharge on the infinitely softly held g-flat— answered by the just as softly sung g-natural,—seemed like a magic spell initiating me into the matchless mys-

* "An dieser einen Stelle ist es mir, bei oft in meinem späteren Leben erneueter Erinnerung, recht klar geworden, worauf es beim Orchestervortrag ankommt, weil sie die *Bewegung* und den *gehaltenen Ton*, zugleich mit dem Gesetze der *Dynamik* in sich schliesst."
† March 26, 1855.—TR.

teries of Spirit ; which thenceforth spake to me in language clear and understandable, without a mediator.

But leaving on one side that lofty revelation, I continue my practical experiences by asking : On what path was it possible for those Paris musicians so infallibly to solve this trying problem ? In the first place, obviously, by nothing but the most conscientious diligence ; a diligence only to be found among musicians who do not content themselves with mutual compliments, don't plume themselves on their "self-understanding," but feel awed in presence of the not directly understood, and seek to compass the Difficult from *that* side on which they are quite at home, to wit the side of technique. The French musician is in so far influenced by the Italian school, to which he primarily belongs, that music to him is unseizable except through Song : to play an instrument well, in his eyes, means to be able to make it sing. And (as already said) that glorious orchestra really *sang* this symphony. To be able to "sing" it correctly, however, the *right tempo* had to be found for its every beat : and that was the second point impressed upon my mind on this occasion. Old Habeneck had certainly no abstract-æsthetic 'inspiration' of the thing ; he was without all "Genialität": but *he found the proper tempo, while diligently leading on his orchestra to grasp the symphony's melos.*

But a correct conception of the melos alone can give the proper tempo : the two are indivisible ; one conditions the other. And if I do not scruple to declare that by far the most performances of our classic instrumental works are seriously inadequate, I propose to substantiate my verdict by pointing out *that our conductors know nothing of proper Tempo, because of their understanding nothing about Song.* I have never met a single German Kapellmeister or musical conductor who could really *sing* a melody, let his voice be good or bad ; no, Music to them is an abstraction, a cross between syntax, arithmetic and gymnastics ; so that one may well conceive its votaries making capital teachers at a conservatoire or musical gymnasium, but never imagine them breathing life and soul into a musical performance.

In my next I will take the liberty of relating some further experiences of my own upon this point.

To sum up in one word the question of a tone-work's right performance, so far as depends on the conductor, it is this: Has he given throughout the proper *tempo*? for his choice and dictation of that, tells us at once whether he has understood the piece or not. Upon closer acquaintance with the piece, the proper tempo will give the players almost of itself a clue to the proper rendering, whilst that tempo itself is direct evidence of the conductor's acquaintance with the latter. How far from easy it is to determine the proper tempo, however, is shewn by the fact that only through a knowledge of the correct rendering, in every respect, can that proper tempo itself be found.

Earlier musicians had so true a feeling of this, that Haydn and Mozart, for instance, mostly denoted their tempi in very general terms: " *allegro*," " *adagio* " and " *andante*," with the simplest qualifications, embrace well-nigh everything they thought needful in this regard. And going back to S. Bach, we find the tempo scarcely ever even indicated at all ; which, in a truly musical sense, is quite the most correct. Bach told himself something like this: Whoever does not understand my theme and figuration, does not divine their character and expression, what will it profit him to be given an Italian sign of tempo ?—To speak from my very own experience, I may state that I furnished my earlier operas—those played at the theatres —with downright eloquent directions for tempo, and fixed them past mistaking (as I thought) by metronomic cyphers. But whenever I heard of a foolish tempo in a performance of my " Tannhäuser," for instance, my recriminations were always parried by the plea that my metronomic marks had been followed most scrupulously. So I saw how uncertain

must be the value of mathematics in music, and thenceforth dispensed with the metronome ; contenting myself with quite general indications for even the principal time-measure, and devoting all my forethought to its *modifications*, since our conductors know as good as nothing of the latter. Now these generalisms, in their turn, have lately worried and confused conductors, as I hear, especially owing to their being couched in German ; for the gentlemen, accustomed to the old Italian labels, are all at sea as to what I mean by " Mässig " (" moderate ") for instance. This complaint was recently made me by a Kapellmeister whom I lately had to thank for spinning out the music of my " Rheingold "—which had lasted two hours and a half at the rehearsals under a conductor instructed by myself *
—to three full hours, according to the report in the Augsburg " Allgemeine Zeitung." Something similar was once told me in characterisation of a performance of my " Tannhäuser," namely that the overture, which lasted just twelve minutes under my own conduct in Dresden, had here [Munich] been spun to twenty. To be sure, I now am speaking of the thorough bunglers, people who have an uncommon dread of the *alla breve* beat and always abide by four strictly measured quarter-strokes per bar, apparently to keep awake their consciousness that they're conducting to some purpose. How these four-footed creatures ever jumped from their village-churches to our opera-houses, God only knows.

" Dragging," however, is not the forte of our strictly elegant conductors of latter days ; quite the contrary, they manifest a fatal love for scurrying and hunting down. Thereby hangs a tale wellnigh sufficient in itself to summarise the newest, the so extremely fashionable goings-on in music.

* Hans Richter, after the first dress-rehearsal in August 1868 (according to Glasenapp), very properly refused to conduct the " Rheingold " with " *such* an inscenation " as that provided by the Munich management. Although Wagner subsequently intervened, and obtained the promise of both parties that Richter should after all conduct, at the eventual production on September 22nd the bâton was wielded by Franz Wüllner !—Tr.

Robert Schumann once complained to me, at Dresden, that Mendelssohn had quite ruined his enjoyment of the Ninth Symphony by the rapid pace at which he took it, particularly in the first movement. Myself I once heard Mendelssohn conduct a symphony of Beethoven's, at a concert-rehearsal in Berlin : it was the Eighth (in F). I noticed that he would pick out a detail here and there—almost at random—and polish it up with a certain pertinacity ; which was of such excellent service to the detail, that I only wondered why he didn't pay the same attention to other nuances : for the rest, this so incomparably buoyant (*heitere*) symphony flowed down a vastly tame and chatty course. As to Conducting, he personally informed me once or twice that a too slow tempo was the devil, and for choice he would rather things were taken too fast ; a really good rendering was a rarity at any time ; with a little care, however, one might gloss things over ; and this could best be done by never dawdling, but covering the ground at a good stiff pace. Mendelssohn's actual pupils must have heard from the master a little more, and more in detail, to the same effect ; for it can hardly have been a maxim confided to my ear alone, as I later have had occasion to learn its consequences, and finally its grounds.

Of the former I had a lively experience with the orchestra of the Philharmonic Society *in London*. Mendelssohn had conducted that band for a considerable period, and the Mendelssohnian mode of rendering had confessedly been raised into a fixed tradition ; in fact it so well suited the customs and peculiarities of this society's concerts, that it almost seemed as if Mendelssohn had derived his mode of rendering from them. As a huge amount of music was consumed at those concerts, but only one rehearsal allowed for each performance, I myself was often obliged to leave the orchestra to its tradition, and thereby made acquaintance with a style of execution which forcibly reminded me at any rate of Mendelssohn's dictum to myself. The thing flowed on like water from a public fountain ; to attempt to check it was out of the question, and every Allegro ended as an indisputable Presto. The labour of intervention was painful enough ; for not until one had got the right and rightly-shaded tempo, did one discover the other sins of rendering that had lain swamped beneath the deluge. For one thing, the orchestra never played else but *mezzoforte* ; neither a genuine *forte*, nor a true *piano*, came about. In important cases, as far as possible, I at last insisted upon the rendering that I myself deemed right, as also on the suitable tempo. The good fellows had nothing against it, and expressed sincere delight; to the public, too, it plainly seemed the thing: but the reporters flew into a rage, and so alarmed the Committee that I once was actually asked to be so good as scurry the second movement of Mozart's Symphony in E-flat again, as one had always been accustomed to, and as Mendelssohn himself had done.

Finally the fatal maxim was put into so many words, when a very amiable elderly contrapuntist whose symphony I was to conduct, Mr Potter (if I mistake not), implored me from his heart to take his Andante right-down fast, since he had great fears of its proving wearisome. I pointed out that, let his Andante last as short as it might, it could not fail to weary if played without all finish and expression; whereas it might prove quite fascinating if its dainty, naïve theme were only rendered by the orchestra in somewhat the way I proceeded to hum it him, for that was surely what he meant when writing it. Mr Potter was visibly touched, agreed with me, and merely advanced the plea that he had lost all habit of counting on such a style of orchestral delivery. On the evening itself, just after this Andante, he pressed my hand for very joy.—

How scanty is the sense of our modern musicians for this proper grasp of tempo and expression, has set me in sincere amazement ; and unfortunately it is precisely with the Coryphæi of our present music-mongering that I have

reaped my worst experiences. Thus I found it impossible
to convey to Mendelssohn my feeling of the abomination
universally put upon the tempo of the *third movement* of
Beethoven's Symphony in F (No. 8). And this is one of
the instances I will select, from many others, to throw
light on a side of our musical art-sense into whose shocking
haziness we well may think fit to inquire.

We know how Haydn employed the *Menuet*-form as a
relief to the Adagio of his symphonies and a bridge
conducting to the final Allegro, particularly in his latest
masterpieces of that order, and how he arrived at a marked
acceleration of its tempo quite foreign to the character
of a genuine Menuet. Especially for its Trio, he even
pressed into this movement the " Ländler " * of his day ;
so that the designation " *Menuetto* " no longer really suited
it, above all in regard of tempo, and became a mere
traditional title. Nevertheless I believe that even the
Haydn Menuet is commonly taken too fast; and quite
certainly this is the case with Mozart's symphonies, as
everyone must feel after hearing *e.g.* the Menuet of the
G-minor Symphony, and still more emphatically this
master's Symphony in C, conducted at a slower rate.
The latter in especial acquires a very different expression,
graceful alike and firm, from what it has when scrambled
through almost at presto, making the Trio with its deftly

held 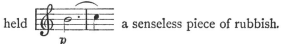 a senseless piece of rubbish.

Beethoven, however, as we shall also find in other of
his works, had a true Menuet in mind when writing his
Symphony in F : as a kind of supplemental contrast to
a preceding *Allegretto scherzando*, he placed it between
two larger Allegro movements ; and lest any doubt might
arise as to his intention in respect of its time, he marked
it, not " *Menuetto*," but " *Tempo di Menuetto*." Now, this
new and unusual characterisation of the two middle movements of a symphony has been wellnigh altogether over-

* An Austrian peasant-dance in ¾ time, prototype of the Waltz.—TR.

looked : the " Allegretto scherzando " has had to personate
the customary Andante, the " Tempo di Menuetto " the
equally accustomed Scherzo ; and since neither of them
would behave quite well in such a rôle, the whole wondrous
symphony, whose middle movements would lend themselves to none of the wonted Effects, has come to be
regarded by our musicians as a sort of bye-blow of the
Beethovenian Muse ; as if, after her exertions with the
Symphony in A, she had meant to take things easy for
a while. Thus everywhere, after the Allegretto scherzando
has been somewhat dragged, with unflagging obstinacy
the Tempo di Menuetto is made the best of as a re-
enlivening Ländler ; and when it's over, one hasn't the
remotest notion what one has heard. As a rule, however,
one is glad to have survived the tortures of that Trio.
For this most charming of all idylls becomes a positive
monstrosity under the habitual rapid beat, owing to the
triplet passages for the violoncelli : that accompaniment
accordingly has ranked as one of quite the hardest for the
'cellists, and they scamper through their skeltering *staccato*
as best they may, without producing aught beyond a
painful scraping. But this difficulty vanishes of itself
as soon as ever the right tempo is taken, in keeping with
the tender theme for horns and clarinet ; whereby, again,
these latter are released from all the hardships to which
the rapid beat exposes them—hardships so agonising to
the clarinet, that even the best performer goes in terror
of a so-called " squeak." * I shall not forget the sigh of
positive relief sent up by all the band when I let them
play this piece in its proper tempo moderato, whilst the
humorous *sforzando* for the basses and bassoon

made at once its understandable effect, the brief *crescendi*
grew distinct, the gentle *pp* close came by its own, and,

---

* " *Kicks* "—" quack," technically known in England as " goose."—TR.

to crown all, the principal section of the movement reached
a fit expression of its leisured gravity.

Well, I once was in Mendelssohn's company at a performance of this symphony in Dresden, conducted by the
now deceased Kapellmeister Reissiger, and spoke with
him about the said dilemma, telling him how—as I believed — I had arranged for its right solution by my
colleague of those days, since he had promised open-eyed
to take the tempo slower than of wont. Mendelssohn
quite agreed with me. We listened. The third movement began, and I was horrified to hear the old familiar
Ländler tempo once again. Before I could express my
wrath, however, Mendelssohn was rocking his head in
pleased approval, and smiled to me : " That's capital !
Bravo ! " So I fell from horror into stupefaction. Reissiger
was not so much to blame for his relapse into the ancient
tempo, for reasons which soon dawned upon me, as I
will presently explain ; but Mendelssohn's callousness
towards this curious artistic contretemps inspired me
with very natural doubts as to whether the thing presented
any difference at all to him. I fancied I was peering into
a veritable abyss of superficiality, an utter void.

Precisely the same experience as that with Reissiger,
and in the selfsame movement of the Eighth Symphony,
occurred to me soon after with another noted conductor,
one of Mendelssohn's successors in the direction of the
Leipzig concerts.*   He, too, had given his adherence to
my views of this *Tempo di Menuetto*, and promised to take
the proper slow time for the movement at a concert to
which he bade me. Marvellous were the terms of his
excuse for likewise not keeping his word : he laughingly
confessed that, distracted by all sorts of cares of management, he hadn't remembered his pledge until after the
piece had begun ; of course he couldn't make a sudden

* Ferdinand Hiller.—Tr.

change in the habitual tempo, once commenced; and so had been obliged to leave the thing for this while in its old, old groove. Vexing as this admission was, at least it pleased me to have at last found someone to ratify my view of the distinction, and someone who did not think it a matter of indifference which tempo was taken. Not that I believed I must tax the conductor in this latter case with the utter levity and thoughtlessness implied in his own excuse, of a "slip of memory"; but that the reason why he did not take a slower tempo, albeit an unconscious, was yet a quite legitimate one. To materially alter such a measure at hazard between rehearsal and performance, would certainly have betrayed the most reprehensible folly; from whose grievous consequences the conductor was saved for once by his lucky "slip of memory." With its customary interpretation of this piece, dictated by the faster pace, the orchestra would absolutely have lost its head on a sudden demand to take the more deliberate tempo; for which, of course, *a quite other rendering* must *also* be discovered.

It is here that lies the crucial point for our plain understanding, if we are ever to come to a profitable agreement on the so frequently neglected and vitiated rendering of our classic works of music. For the evil custom in respect of Tempo has a seeming right to its assumptions, since a certain harmony has been evolved between it and the mode of rendering: while concealing from its votaries the veritable ill, on the one hand, on the other that harmony makes it perilous, nay, mostly insupportable, to attempt a one-sided change of pace with the phrasing left to its old devices.

To make this clear by one simplest of all examples, I select the opening of the C-minor Symphony:

After quite a brief sojourn on the fermata of the second

bar, our conductors pass it by, and employ that halt almost solely for concentrating the band's attention upon a sharp attack on the figure in the third bar. The e-flat is habitually held no longer than the duration of an ordinary forte taken by a careless bow. Now let us suppose the voice of Beethoven to have cried from the grave to a conductor: "Hold thou my fermata long and terribly! I wrote no fermata for jest or from bepuzzlement, haply to think out my further move; but the same full tone I mean to be squeezed dry in my Adagio for utterance of sweltering emotion, I cast among the rushing figures of my passionate Allegro, if need be, a paroxysm of joy or horror. Then shall its life be drained to the last blood-drop; then do I part the waters of my ocean, and bare the depths of its abyss; or curb the flocking herd of clouds, dispel the whirling web of mist, and open up a glimpse into the pure blue firmament, the sun's irradiate eye. For this I set fermate in my Allegros, notes entering of a sudden, and long held out. And mark thou what a definite thematic aim I had with this sustained e-flat, after a storm of three short notes, and what I meant to say by all the like held notes that follow."—Now if, upon receipt of such a warning, this conductor should suddenly ask an orchestra to give to that fermata bar the significance, and *consequently* the length he thought needful in Beethoven's sense, what result would he obtain? A most deplorable. After the 'strings' had squandered the first impact of the bow, their tone would grow the thinner the longer they were made hold on to it, and fade away in a fogged piano: for—and here I touch one of the evil issues of our modern conductors' habits,—nothing has become more foreign to our orchestras than *even strength in holding a note*. I challenge the whole body of conductors to demand a full and equably sustained forte from any instrument of the orchestra, no matter which, just to give them a taste of the surprised amazement such a claim arouses, and what patient exercise it needs to bring about the right effect.

Yet this equably sustained tone is the basis of all

dynamics, as in Song, so in the Orchestra : only by making it our starting-point, can we arrive at all those modifications whose multifariousness determines the general character of execution. Without this foundation an orchestra puts forth much noise, but no power ; and herein lies a first token of the feebleness of most of our orchestral doings. But, since our modern conductors know as good as nothing of it, they plume themselves instead on an *over-hushed piano*. Now, this is attainable by the ' strings ' without much effort, but it costs a great deal to the 'wind,' and in particular the 'wood-wind.' From the latter, and above all the flautists—who have turned their once so gentle instruments into veritable tubes of violence,—a delicately sustained piano is hardly to be obtained any more ; save perhaps from French oboists, as they never transgress the pastoral character of their instrument, or from clarinetists when one asks them for the echo effect. This evil, to be encountered in our very best orchestras, suggests the question : If the wind-players are really incapable of a smooth piano, why doesn't one try at least to maintain a balance, and make the strings replace their often positively laughable contrast by a somewhat fuller body of tone ? But this disproportion plainly quite escapes the notice of our conductors. From another point of view, the fault is largely to be found in the character of the stringed instruments' piano itself : for just as we have no *true forte*, neither have we any *true piano* ; both lack all roundness of tone. And here, again, our string-players might take a lesson from the ' wind ' ; whereas it certainly is easy enough for the former to draw the bow quite loosely across the strings, and thus produce a mere buzzing whir, it requires great artistic control of the breath to make it stream forth evenly and low, upon a wind-instrument, and yet preserve clearness and purity of intona-tion. Wherefore our fiddlers should learn the true round-toned piano from first-class wind-players, providing the latter have deigned to adopt it themselves from firstrate singers.

Now, this hushed tone and˙ that aforesaid strong-held

tone are the two fixed poles of all orchestral Dynamics,
between which the Rendering has to move.   How stands
it with this Rendering, then, if neither the one nor the other
is firmly planted?   Of what kind can be its modifications,
when the extreme landmarks of dynamic energy are indistinct?   Beyond a doubt, so very faulty that the maxim
I quoted from Mendelssohn, of gliding over the ground,
becomes a right blessed expedient, and has therefore been
elevated by our conductors to an actual dogma.   And it is
just this dogma that rules to-day the whole church of our
conductors and their hangers-on, so that any attempt to
render our classical music correctly is hooted down by them
as rank heresy.—

To tarry yet a while with these conductors, I must keep
on coming back to *Tempo* for the present; for, as already
said, 'tis the point where the conductor has to shew himself worth his salt.

Manifestly, the correct speed for any piece of music can
only be determined by the special character of its phrasing
(Vortrag); to determine the former, we must have come
to terms about the latter.   The requirements of the phrasing, whether it leans chiefly toward legato tone (Song) or
more toward rhythmic motion (Figuration), are the points
that must determine the conductor as to which class of
tempo he has to make preponderate.

Now, *adagio* bears the same relation to *allegro* as legato
tone to figured motion.   The *legato tone* lays down the
law for the *tempo adagio*: here Rhythm dissolves into the
pure and self-sufficing, self-governing life of Tone.   In a
certain subtle sense one may say that the pure Adagio can
not be taken slow enough: here must reign a rapt confidence in the eloquent persuasiveness of tone-speech pure
and simple; here the *languor* of emotion becomes an
ecstasy; what the Allegro expressed by a change of
figuration, is spoken here by infinite variety of modulated
tone; the faintest change of harmony surprises us, the
most remote progressions are prepared for and awaited on
the tiptoe of suspense.

Not one of our conductors trusts himself to grant the Adagio a proper measure of this its attribute; they start by hunting for some figuration or other, and trim their tempo to its hypothetic speed. Perhaps I am the only conductor who has dared take the Adagio proper of the third movement of the Ninth Symphony at a pace in strict accordance with its character. This Adagio is first contrasted with an alternating Andante in triple time, as though to stamp its quite peculiar quality for anyone to see; but it doesn't restrain our conductors from so blotting out the character of each, that nothing remains save the rhythmic interchange of common and triple time. Finally this movement—one of the most instructive in the present connection—supplies with its richly-figured $^{12}/_8$ time the plainest example of a refraction (*Brechung*) of the pure Adagio-character by a more pointed rhythmicising of the figured accompaniment, now raised to self-dependence, while the cantilena still preserves its characteristic breadth. Here we have the focused image, so to speak, of an Adagio which had erewhile yearned to melt into infinity; and just as an unshackled freedom to revel in expression by Tone had earlier allowed the pace to oscillate between the gentlest laws, so now the firm-set Rhythm of the figured ornament supplies the new law of adherence to one definite rate of motion—a law whose ultimate corollaries will be our law for the *Allegro's* speed.*

As the held note with its various modifications of length is the basis of all musical delivery, so the Adagio—particularly through the logical development given it by Beethoven in this third movement of his Ninth Symphony —becomes the basis of all measurement of musical time. In a delicately discriminating sense, the Allegro may be

---

* " Hier erkennen wir das gleichsam fixirte Bild des zuvor nach unendlicher Ausdehnung verlangenden Adagio's, und wie dort eine ungeschränkte Freiheit für die Befriedigung des tonischen Ausdruckes das zwischen zartesten Gesetzen schwankende Maass der Bewegung angab, wird hier durch die feste Rhythmik der figurativ geschmückten Begleitung das neue Gesetz der Festhaltung einer bestimmten Bewegung gegeben, welches in seinen ausgebildeten Konsequenzen uns zum Gesetz für das Zeitmaass des *Allegro* wird."

regarded as ultimate outcome of the pure Adagio's refraction by a busier figuration.   If one takes a closer look at the ruling motives in the Allegro itself, one will always find them dominated by a singing quality derived from the Adagio.   Beethoven's most significant Allegro movements are mostly governed by a root-melody, belonging in a deeper sense to the character of the Adagio; and hereby they obtain that *sentimental* import which distinguishes them so explicitly from the earlier, *naïve* order.   Yet to the Beethovenian

the Mozartian

already bears no distant kinship, and neither with Mozart nor Beethoven does the Allegro's true distinctive character appear till Figuration entirely gains the upper hand of Song: that is to say, until the reaction of rhythmic motion against legato tone is thorough and complete.   This case is met the most frequently in closing movements modelled on the Rondeau, of which the finales of Mozart's E-flat major, and Beethoven's A-major Symphony are very speaking specimens.   Here purely rhythmic Motion celebrates its orgies, so to say, and hence this kind of Allegro cannot be taken sharp and brisk enough.   But whatever lies between those two extremes, is subject to the *laws of reciprocity*; and these laws can not be read with too much subtlety, for they are the same at bottom as those that modified legato Tone itself into every conceivable nuance. And now that I am about to deal more searchingly with this *Modification of Tempo*—a thing not merely quite unknown to our conductors, but doltishly proscribed by them for reason of that non-acquaintance—, the attentive reader will understand that we here are handling a positive life-principle of all our music.

In course of the preceding exposition I distinguished between two orders of Allegro, ascribing to the later, the true Beethovenian, a *sentimental* character : as against the earlier, pre-eminently Mozartian, to which I assigned a *naïve* character. With this distinction I had in mind the beautiful characterisation which Schiller gives us in his famous treatise on Naïve and Sentimental Poetry.

In view of my immediate object, I will not now dilate on the æsthetic problem here suggested ; merely I wish to define my meaning of the *naïve Allegro*, by stating that I find it most pronounced in the majority of Mozart's rapid *alla breve* movements. The most perfect of this kind are the Allegros of his opera-overtures ; above all, those to "Figaro" and "Don Juan." It is known that these could never be played fast enough to please Mozart ; once, when he had forced his bandsmen to a pitch of angry despera-tion which enabled them to succeed at last with the *presto* of his Figaro-overture, to their own surprise, he told them by way of encouragement : "Now that was splendid ! This evening, though, a trifle faster !"—Just so ! As I said that the pure Adagio could never be taken slow enough, in an ideal sense, so this pure, this unadulterated Allegro can never be given quick enough. As there the bounds of opulent array of Tone, so here the limits of figured Motion are ideal out-and-out ; and the only measure of the attainable is furnished by the law of beauty, which fixes for the opposite extremes, of completely curbed and entirely untrammelled motion, the boundary where yearning for resumption of the opposite becomes a sheer necessity.—It therefore testifies to a profound insight, that our masters planned the movements of their symphonies to lead from an Allegro to Adagio, and thence again, through intervention of a stricter dance-form (the Menuet or Scherzo), to the swiftest of all, the final Allegro. On the contrary it is just as sure an evidence of bankruptcy of all proper feeling, when composers of to-day attempt to relieve the tedium of their inspirations by furbishing up the ancient Suite-form,* whose irrational string of dance-types has long since been evolved elsewhere to greater multiplicity of form and richer blending.

What further stamps the Mozartian *absolute* Allegro as specifically belonging to the naïve order, is its simple play of *forte* and *piano*, on the side of dynamics, as also, in respect of formal structure, its random juxtaposition of certain stock melodic-rhythmic forms adapted to the piano or the forte method, in whose employment (as in the perpetual repetition of the selfsame thunderous half-closes) the master shews an almost more than startling unconstraint. Yet everything here, even the most heedless use of altogether banal phrases, explains itself by just the character of this Allegro : it has no desire to chain us by a cantilena, but to plunge us into a certain tumult through its restless motion. It is a profound trait in the Allegro of the Don Juan overture, that this commotion at last is cut short by an unmistakable turn towards the sentimental : upon reaching the extreme limit to which I have already referred, the reaction sets in, at like time with an obligation to modify the speed ; and thus the latter unobtrusively but definitely slackens down, in the rendering of these transitional bars, to the somewhat more moderate pace at which the succeeding first tempo of the opera itself should be taken—an *alla breve,* 'tis true, but at any rate less rapid than the main tempo of the overture.

That the last peculiarity of the Don Juan overture escapes the slovenly majority of our conductors, must not tempt us into premature reflections. I hope to have established one thing, however : namely that the character of this older, classic, or—as I have called it—naïve Allegro is separated by the breadth of heaven from that of the newer, sentimental, distinctively Beethovenian Allegro.

* Franz Lachner, according to Mr Dannreuther.—TR.

Mozart was the first to learn Crescendo and Diminuendo
in orchestral execution, and that from the Mannheim band,
in which it had been introduced as something new: till
then, as we may see by the old masters' mode of instrumenting, between the *forte* and *piano* sections of an Allegro
there was strewn nothing reckoned for a really emotional
rendering.

But how compares with this the genuine Beethovenian
Allegro?—To characterise Beethoven's unheard-of innovation by his boldest stroke of the kind, what figure will the
first movement of his Heroic Symphony cut when played-
off in the strict tempo of a Mozartian overture-Allegro?—
But does it ever occur to any of our conductors to take
this movement's tempo otherwise than straight ahead, in
one gulp from the first bar to the last? Should there be
talk of a "reading" of the tempo, on his part, we may take
it for certain that he will follow the Mendelssohnian "*chi
va presto, va sano*,"—providing, at least, he belong to the
"elegant" set. How bandsmen with any sense of expression are to make head or tail of the

or the wailing:

they then may find out for themselves. It's no concern of
their masters', for they are on "classical" ground, where
things are taken off-hand : *grande vitesse,* alike genteel and
lucrative ; in English : *time is music* [? money].—

In fact we now have reached the decisory point for a
verdict on our entire music-making of nowadays ; a point

I have approached, as probably will have been remarked, with a certain amount of circumspection. For my first care could only be to lay bare the dilemma itself, and make clear to the feeling of every reader that with Beethoven there arrived an intrinsic change in music's treatment and expression. What had earlier been held apart in single close-hedged forms, each leading a life of its own, here—as regards its innermost chief-motives at least—is brought together in the most opposed of forms, embraced in their totality, and evolved from their reciprocal reaction. Now, this naturally should find its counterpart in the Rendering; wherefore, above all things, the time-measure must be no less sensitively balanced (*von nicht minderer Zartlebigkeit*) than the thematic tissue which is to be thereby set in motion.

Let us start with the proposition that, as regards the said constant and effectual *modification* of the Tempo of a classical music-piece of newer style, we are faced with difficulties no smaller than those wherewith a proper under-standing of these revelations of sterling German genius has to contend in general.—In the preceding pages I have devoted special notice to a few experiences reaped from Music's foremost Coryphæi of our age, to spare myself the chaotic detail of recounting minor instances within my knowledge: if, taking all these facts together, I do not hesitate to say that in the mode wherein we hitherto have made his acquaintance the real true Beethoven remains with us a pure ·chimera, I now would fain support the negative side of that by no means mild assertion by a positive proof of what, in my opinion, is the proper mode-of·rendering for this Beethoven and his next of kin.

As the subject to me seems inexhaustible, even under this aspect, I will again confine myself to a few salient points of experience.—

One of the major forms of musical construction is that of a series of *variations* upon a preliminary theme.

Haydn at first and Beethoven at last have conferred artistic value on this intrinsically disconnected form, of a mere sequence of dissimilarities, not only by their brilliant inventiveness, but also by giving these dissimilarities *a reference to one another*. This is done the most felicitously by evolving them from out each other, and consequently affording us the grateful surprise of seeing one form of motion lead over to the next through the elaboration of what in it had merely been a hint, or the making good of what it lacked in. The real weakness of the variation style of structure, however, is bared whenever strongly contrasting parts are set side by side without a bridge or mediator. Yet from this, again, Beethoven knows to draw his profit, and in a sense precluding any supposition of the accidental or inept : arrived at what I have called the bounds of beauty, of infinitely extended tone (in the Adagio) as of unbridled motion (in the Allegro), with a seeming suddenness he satisfies our invincible yearning for the redeeming opposite, and lets the contrast enter as the only possible successor. This we learn from the master's great works in particular, and the last movement of the *Sinfonia eroica* forms one of the most instructive guides to such a lesson ; providing that movement is grasped as an infinitely magnified variation-section, and rendered, as such, with the most varied motivation. But to make oneself conscious master of the latter—with this, as with every movement like it—the aforesaid weakness of the variation-form must first be fully recognised, and its prejudicial effect upon the Feeling averted accordingly. For we find too frequently that variations have arisen one by one, each for itself, and merely been strung together in conformity with a certain purely external convention. The most disagreeable effect of this fortuitous concatenation we experience when upon the heels of a tranquil-breathing theme there follows an incomprehensibly sprightly first variation. The first variation of that peerless theme in the second movement of Beethoven's great A-major Sonata for pianoforte and violin [op. 47], since I have never heard it treated by virtuosi otherwise than as beseems one of those "first variations" just meant for nothing but gymnastic display,

X

has always set me in revolt against all further music-hearing. Wonderful to relate, though, whenever I protested, my pains were rewarded by nothing but a repetition of my experience with the *Tempo di Menuetto* of the Eighth Symphony. People agreed with me " on the whole," but had no detailed notion of what I wanted. Certain it is (to abide by the case just mentioned) that this first variation of the marvellously stately theme already bears a conspicuously animated character; it is impossible that the composer should have invented it in direct succession to, and thus in full connection with, the theme itself; he surely must have been unconsciously influenced by the formal segregation of parts in the variation-form. These parts, however, have to be rendered in immediate sequence. Now, from other of the master's movements modelled on the variation-form, but conceived as a connected whole (the second movement of the C-minor Symphony for instance, the Adagio of the great E-flat major Quartet, and above all the wondrous second movement of the great C-minor Sonata, op. 111), we know how delicate and full of feeling can be his treatment of the transitional points between the single variations. Wherefore the interpreter who aspires to the honour of fully becoming the master's mouthpiece in a case such as that of the so-called Kreutzer Sonata [op. 47] should make it his business at least to bring the entry of this first variation into some sort of connection with the *Stimmung* of the theme just ended ; one might suggest a certain initial restraint of the pace, a mere foreshadowing of the new character borne by this variation in the unalterable opinion of pianoforte and violin players. Were it done with true artistic taste, the first part of this variation itself might perhaps afford a gradually quickening introduction to the new, more lively tense ; and thus, quite apart from the inherent interest of this portion, it would acquire the additional charm of a coaxingly prepared, but at bottom not inconsiderable change of the main character laid down in the theme itself.—

As a still stronger case of like significance I may cite the entry of the first Allegro's ⁶/₈ time, after the lengthy opening Adagio-movement, in Beethoven's C-sharp minor Quartet [op. 131]. This is marked " *molto vivace*," which answers admirably to the character of the movement as a whole. In this quartet, however, Beethoven quite exceptionally allows the individual movements to follow one another without the usual break in execution ; nay—if we bring our wits to bear upon it—he lets them evolve from out each other by subtle laws of their own. Hence this Allegro movement follows *immediately* after an Adagio of such dreamy sadness as scarce another of the master's ; and we may interpret the new subject as a phantom rising from the depths of memory, a loveliest image seized as soon as recognised, and clasped with growing agitation. Here, then, it is obviously a question of the mode in which this radiant vision shall ascend, so to say, from the mournful torpor of the directly-preceding Adagio, not to wound our feelings by the abruptness of its entry. Quite appropriately too, the new theme appears at first in unbroken *pianissimo*, as one would expect from a tenuous, scarcely realised dream-image, and presently melts into a filmy *ritardando* ; whereafter it seems to be gathering strength to manifest its actuality, and passes through the crescendo into its own brisk sphere of motion. Plainly the duty of the executant is here to delicately modify the *tempo* of its first appearance, in keeping with the sufficiently-indicated character of this Allegro : taking his cue from the

closing notes of the Adagio  he should link

with them the following so unobtrus-

ively that at first no change of tempo may be remarked at all ; then, after the ritardando, he should gradually animate his rendering of the crescendo in such wise that the eventual faster tempo, prescribed by the master, may

appear to be a rhythmic consequence of the dynamic value
of that crescendo.—How it offends all sense of artistic
decency, when—as happens without exception at each performance of this quartet—that modification is not carried
out, and the impudent *Vivace* trips in as though the whole
thing were merely a joke and matters were now to take
their merry course! And that's what these gentry call
" classical."

But, seeing that the rendering of our classical music
depends so vastly on modifications of Tempo such as I
have shewn by a few detailed instances to be positively
indispensable, I now will take those instances as a text for
further needs of our classical music in the way of correct
execution ; and that at risk of telling our musicians and
Kapellmeisters—so careful of the classic line in music, and
so honoured for that care—a few home truths.—

I venture to hope I now have shewn what a problem is
involved in finding the Tempo for classical works of the
newer, the specifically German style, together with the
difficulties of its Modification ; difficulties neither cognisable nor superable by any but the more refined initiate.
For in what I have called the *sentimental* class of music,
raised by Beethoven to an eternal type of art, all the com-
ponents of the earlier pre-eminently naïve musical type
combine to form a material ever ready to the creative
master's hand, and employed by him at amplest will.
Sustained and broken tone, broad song and nimble figuration, no longer stand in formal opposition ; the con-
trarieties of a series of variations are here no longer merely
strung together, but have immediate reference to, and
shade into, each other. Certain it is (as I have already
shewn in detailed instances) that this new, so very complex tone-material must be set in motion with a corresponding ingenuity, if the whole symphonic movement is
not to appear in fact a sheer monstrosity. I well remember

how older musicians shook their heads over the "Eroica" in my youth: Dionys Weber, at Prague, spoke of it as an utter abortion. True enough: he knew no other Allegro than the Mozartian, which I have characterised before; he let the pupils of his conservatorium play the Allegro of the Eroica in the strict time of that; and whoever witnessed such a performance, must surely have agreed with Dionys. But no one played it otherwise; and if this symphony to-day is received with acclamation almost everywhere, the sufficient reason, to take the matter seriously, is that for some decads past this music has also been studied outside the concert-room, especially at the pianoforte, and thus has found all kinds of circuitous routes for the exercise of its irresistible force in its no less irresistible fashion. Had Fate not planned for it this path of rescue, but left it to the mercies of Messrs Kapellmeister and Co., our noblest music must needs have gone to ground.

To give such startling assertions a basis easy to be verified, I now will cite an instance whose popularity can scarce be matched throughout all Germany.

How often must not everyone have heard the *Overture to Der Freischütz* played by our orchestras?

Yet I know of only a few persons who are horrified to-day to think what untold times they have heard this wondrous musical poem done trivially to death without their wincing at it; those few consisting of the audience at a concert given in Vienna in the year 1864, in which I had been politely invited to take part, and whereat I conducted among other things this selfsame Freischütz-overture. At the rehearsal the orchestra of the Viennese Court-opera, one of the most excellent bands in the world, was quite put out of countenance by my demands for this overture's rendering. To start with, it transpired that the introductory Adagio had always been taken at the tempo of the "Alphorn" * and other pleasant compositions of the kind, that is to say, a comfortable Andante. That this was no special Viennese tradition, however, but had be-

* A popular song by Proch, according to Mr Dannreuther.—TR.

come a general rule, I had already learnt in Dresden on
the very spot where Weber himself once led his work.
Eighteen years after the master's death I conducted the
Freischütz for my first time at Dresden ; recking nothing
of the habits that had crept in under my older colleague,
Reissiger, I was taking the overture's introduction according to my own idea of its tempo, when a veteran from
Weber's days, the aged violoncellist Dotzauer, turned
solemnly to me and said : " Eh ! *that's* how Weber took it ;
at last I hear it right again." From Weber's widow, still
living then in Dresden, this earnest of my right feeling for her
deceased husband's music won me cordial wishes for my prospering in the post of Dresden Kapellmeister, since she now
might entertain the long-lost hope of once more hearing
that music correctly performed. This touching compli-
ment has remained for me a grateful memory, and I now
adduce it in comparison with divers other modes of judging
my artistic capability, even as conductor.—Inter alia, those
noble words encouraged me to insist on the last consequences of a purification of the method of performing the
Freischütz-overture at the aforesaid Viennese performance.
Though the orchestra knew the piece to weariness, they
studied it entirely afresh. Under the refined artistic lead
of R. Lewi, the cornists altogether changed their mode of
attack upon the dreamy forest-fantasie of the introduction ;
instead of braying it out like a swaggering piece of clap-
trap (*Effektstück*), they brought it into keeping with the
pianissimo of the string-accompaniment, as prescribed by
the score, thus shedding over their melody the intended
witching fragrance. Only once did they swell their tone
into a mezzoforte (also according to prescription), and then
let it die away, without the customary sforzando, upon the

scarcely   emphasised   [♪ notation]   .   Above   the

tremolo of the violins the 'celli likewise softened to the merest

sigh their usual violent assault upon the

thereby allowing to the fortissimo, which crowns at last the following crescendo, its due effect of horror and despair. After thus restoring to the introductory Adagio its dignity and mystery of awe, I gave free reign to the headlong passion of the Allegro; nor was I checked by any care about the phrasing of the gentler second theme, for I felt quite sure of being able *to gradually moderate the tempo* at the right moment to a speed appropriate to that theme.

And this is a characteristic of most, nay, wellnigh all the newer, more complex Allegro movements : they plainly consist of two radically different factors. As compared with the earlier more naïve, or less composite order, their wealth of structure lies in just this combination of the pure Allegro with the vocal attributes of the Adagio, in all its grades. The second principal theme of the Allegro of the overture to " Oberon " :

displays this contrasting quality in the most unmasked of fashions, for it absolutely ceases to belong to the character of an Allegro proper. Naturally, however, its technical form has been selected by the composer for the express purpose of interweaving with the main character of the piece, just as its inner substance was inspired by the prospect of that union. That is to say, this singing theme bears all the outward visible signs of the Allegro scheme ; but as soon as it is to speak its character aloud, it shews us *of what modification that scheme must be held capable, to serve the tone-poet equally for displaying both chief characters.*

Not to cause a longer break in my account of that Viennese performance of the Freischütz-overture, I must go on to state that, after working up the speed to fever-heat, I employed the long-drawn melody of the clarinet (borrowed wholly from the Adagio) :

to effect a gradual slowing of the tempo, since figured motion here dissolves into legato (or tremolo) tone ; so that, despite the brisker movement of the intermediate figure :

by the time we reached the cantilena in E-flat, so beautifully led up to, we had obtained the gentlest possible nuance of the main tempo without abandoning it. As for that theme itself,

I insisted on its being taken uniformly *piano*, without the habitual vulgar accentuation of its rising steps, and without any break in the phrasing : that is to say, not

And though I had to explain all this to the really admirable musicians, the result was so prompt and successful that I merely had to give the faintest hint of acceleration, with the pulsing

to find the whole orchestra on the alert for resuming the most energetic nuance of the main tempo with the subsequent fortissimo. It was not an altogether easy matter to give full value to the two so strongly opposing motives in the more succinct renewal of their contest, without sensibly affecting the main tempo itself ; for this contest is compressed into briefer and briefer periods, till the real

Allegro's culminating-point of desperate energy is reached
with the

Yet it was just here that the benefit of a continual adjust-
ment of speed at last was most apparent.—Again, after
those gloriously held chords of C and the mighty silences
that give them such a meaning, the band was highly astonished when I made it take the second theme (now raised to
a pæan) not at the rushing speed of the first Allegro-theme,
but in that gentler nuance of the tempo.

For of all our orchestral usages the most common is a
galloping of the principal theme at the close, so that one
often lacks nothing save the crack of the big whip for the
exact effect of a circus.   Increase of speed is frequently intended by composers in the closing section of an overture,
and it results quite of itself wherever the spirited Allegro-
theme proper at last usurps the field, as it were, and
celebrates its apotheosis ; whereof Beethoven's great Overture to " Leonora " affords a world-famed instance.   Only,
the effect of the entry of the presto (*des gesteigerten
Allegro's*) is here most frequently discounted by the conductor's not knowing how to modify the main tempo to
meet the various claims of earlier thematic combinations
(among other things, *to restrain it in due season*) and its
having already attained a velocity impossible to exceed,—
unless, indeed, the ' strings ' are to indulge in a wellnigh
phenomenal tour-de-force, as I have also witnessed in the
Vienna orchestra with much personal astonishment, but
little satisfaction ; since the necessity for this eccentric
effort proceeded from a serious blunder, that of hunting

the previous tempo to death, and consequently resulted in an excess to which no genuine artwork should ever be exposed, even though, in a certain crude sense, it be meant to picture such a thing.

How the close of the Freischütz-overture could have come to be galloped in such a fashion, remains an absolute enigma if one is to credit the Germans with any delicacy of feeling, though it gains some explanation from this second theme's having already been dragged into the trot of the main Allegro upon its first appearance. Here it cut somewhat the figure of a buxom damsel taken prisoner and tied to the horse-tail of a musketeer; in due accordance with poetic justice she finally gets lifted to the saddle, presumably after the caitiff rider has fallen off: and so the Kapellmeister winds the whole thing up as merrily as you please.—Whoever witnesses at each and every public performance of the Freischütz-overture, year in, year out, the indescribably repulsive effect of this utter trivialising— to put it mildly—of that motive which should breathe out all the fervent thankfulness of a devout and loving maiden's heart; whoever finds the thing quite as it should be, prates of the wonted vim and vigour of our bands, and appends his own peculiar notions of the art of Tone, as Herr Lobe has recently done on his jubilee: it singularly becomes him to warn us of "the absurdities of a spurious idealism, and direct to the sterling artistic and eternally true, as against all manner of half-crazy, half-quibbling doctrines and maxims."* As said, I once succeeded, naturally by dint of main force, in giving a number of Viennese friends of music a somewhat different notion of this poor polluted overture. Its success is not forgotten to this day. People declared they had never really known the overture before, and asked me what on earth I had done to it. In particular, some found it inexplicable by what means I had given the closing section its fascinating new effect, and would hardly believe me when I referred them to the more

---

* See: Eduard Bernsdorf, *Signale für die musikalische Welt*, No. 67, 1869.—R. Wagner.

moderate tempo. The gentlemen of the band, however, could divulge a something further—a veritable secret. This, to wit :—in the fourth bar of the splendidly and broadly played entrata :

I gave to the sign > (which looks like an accent gone astray in the score) the meaning obviously intended by the composer, namely of a *diminuendo*-mark ————, and thus obtained a dynamically gentler entry of the following thematic period

By letting its volume swell quite naturally into the renewed fortissimo I was able to give the whole sweet motive for this once, upon its sumptuous background, an expression of the utmost rapture.—

Our Messrs Kapellmeister are none too pleased to hear of a thing like this and its success. Herr Dessof, however, who had presently to conduct the "Freischütz" again at the Court Opera, thought best to leave the orchestra in undisturbed possession of its new style of rendering the overture ; smilingly he announced his intention as follows : "The overture, ahem ! we will take *Wagnerish*."

Ay, Wagnerish indeed !—Methinks a little more might be taken "Wagnerish" without much harm, dear Sirs !

Nevertheless this really seemed a *whole* concession on the part of the Vienna Kappellmeister, whereas my former colleague Reissiger (now deceased) once made me but a *half* one. While rehearsing at Dresden the last movement of Beethoven's Symphony in A, conducted many a time before by Reissiger, I lit upon a "*piano*" which the earlier conductor had interpolated in the orchestral parts entirely at his own good pleasure. It was in the stupendous con-

clusion of that final movement (Härtel's edition of the full
score, p. 86) where, after repeated chords of the seventh on
A, there comes the passage :

still in forte, and leads through "*sempre più forte*" to
wilder and yet wilder riot.   Annoyed by this, Reissiger
had ordered a sudden drop to *piano*, to make room for
working up a marked *crescendo*.   Naturally I had this
piano done away with, restored the most energetic of
fortes, and thereby sinned against the Lobe-Bernsdorf
"eternal laws" of the true and sterling, whereof Reissiger
also was presumably a guardian in his day.   But when
that A-major Symphony came to be played again under
Reissiger, after I had gone away from Dresden, the
wavering conductor halted at this spot, and bade the
orchestra play *mezzo*-forte.

Another time at Munich not so long ago I attended a
public performance of the Overture to "Egmont" no less
instructive to me than my discoveries in respect of the
Freischütz-overture.   In the Allegro of this overture the
terrific *Sostenuto* of the introduction :

is repeated in diminution as the first half of the second
theme, and answered by a gentle counter-motive :

Here, as elsewhere in the "classic" mode, this drastic
motive—a very epitome of terrible earnest and placid self-
reliance—was spun to and fro in the whirl of the Allegro

just like a withered leaf; whenever one chanced to catch it, one had at most the impression of a *pas de deux* where the couple 'sets' with the first two bars, and takes a brief turn, Ländler fashion, with the two that follow. Now, when Bülow had to conduct this music one fine day, in the absence of the honoured senior conductor,* I got him to read that phrase correctly: it produces an instant effect, laconic as the tone-poet meant it, if one ever so slightly curbs the passion of the tempo for a moment, giving the orchestra time to duly accent a thematic combination which alternates so rapidly between tremendous energy and tranquil ease. Since this combination obtains a broader treatment and critical importance toward the end of the 3/4 measure, the whole overture cannot fail of a new, and indeed the only proper understanding, through a simple observance of that needful modification.—As to the impression made by this correct performance, all I heard was that the Court-Theatre Intendance considered things were "turned inside out."!

The audience of the famous Munich Odeon-concerts was certainly spared all suppositions of the sort when, as part thereof, I once heard a performance of *Mozart's G-minor Symphony* presided over by that same time-honoured Classical conductor. In the rendering of the Andante, as in its reception, I experienced a thing I should have deemed incredible. What youngster has not laid enthusiastic hands on this ethereal piece, in his own fashion? In *what* fashion? No matter! Though the expression-marks give out, our Feeling, kindled by this composition's wondrous swing, steps in to fill the breach; and Phantasy dictates the mode of rendering in answer to that Feeling. Then it seems as if the master meant to leave us wellnigh free to choose, for he binds us with the scantiest indications. And free we were; thrilled with the boding tremours of the softly swelling quaver-figure; melted in the rising moonbeams of the violins:

* F. Lachner, again.—TR.

whose notes we imagined smoothly linked at least; felt as though fanned by wings of angels, with the tender whisperings of the

swooned before the fateful warnings of the questioning

(which assuredly we dreamed as executed in a fine crescendo); till the last bars hospitably closed around us with their tidings of the blessedness of death through Love.—All fancies of that sort, to be sure, had to vanish before a truly Classical performance of this movement under a renowned old-master * in the Munich Odeon: there things went solemnly enough to make one's flesh creep, as immediately before receiving sentence of eternal doom. The lightly-poised Andante became a cast-iron Largo, and not a hundredth fraction of one single quaver's length was spared us; stiff and grisly, like a brazen pigtail, swung the *battuta* of that Andante above our heads; the very feathers of the angels' wings were turned to buckram bobwigs from the Seven Years' War. As I had already begun to think myself under the recruiting footrule of the Prussian Guard in 1740, and was dying for someone to buy me off, imagine my horror when the old-master turned back the leaves and had the first section of the Larghett-ised Andante played all through again, merely because he had no intention of letting the traditional two dots and a double bar be graven in the score for nothing! I looked round for help;

---

* "Altmeister," a term ironically borrowed from Journalism.—TR.

but I then beheld the second wonder:—everybody was listening patiently, found it all in perfect order, and was convinced, at the close, of having had a pure, in any case an irreproachable delight, a genuine Mozartian "feast of hearing."—So I sank my head, and held my tongue.

Once I a little lost my patience. At a rehearsal of my "Tannhäuser" I later had to put up quietly with many things, among others the clerical tempo of my knightly march in the Second Act. It transpired, however, that the invincible old-master did not even know how to resolve a 4/4 beat into the corresponding 6/4, that is to say, two crotchets ♩ ♩ into the triplet ♩ ♩ ♩. This was in Tannhäuser's narration, where instead of a 4/4 :

we have the 6/4 :

This change of time came hard to the old-master: to squaring all the angles of the 4/4 beat he is used enough, in all conscience, but that stamp of conductor invariably treats the 6/4 after the pattern of the 6/8, that is to say *alla breve*, one—two; only in that Andante of the G-minor Symphony did I ever see the fractions of this measure beaten gravely and correctly out with 1, 2, 3—4, 5, 6. For my poor story of the Roman Pope, however, the conductor made shift with a timorous *alla breve*, as if to leave it to the bandsmen to do what they pleased with the crotchets. In consequence the time was taken exactly twice too fast, the proportion being as follows:

etc.

Now this was very interesting, musically, but it compelled the poor singer of "Tannhäuser" to make the best of his painful memories of Rome in a highly flippant, nay, a merrily tripping waltz-rhythm,—reminding me, in turn, of Lohengrin's narration of the Gral, which at Wiesbaden I once heard recited *scherzando* (as though it were about Queen Mab). However, as this time I had so glorious a representative of Tannhäuser as *L. Schnorr* by my side, for eternal justice' sake I was obliged to respectfully insist for once on my old-master's reinstating the proper tempo, —which caused some faint unpleasantness. I rather think it led in time to "martyrdoms," and moved a cold-blooded critic of the Gospels * himself to hymn them in a pair of sonnets. So we now have real live martyrs of pure Classical Music ; a matter into which I will permit myself to look a little closer.

———————

As I have mentioned again and again in the preceding, all attempts at Modification of Tempo in behalf of the rendering of classical, and particularly of Beethovenian music, have been received with displeasure by the Conductor-guild of our times. I have given circumstantial proofs that a one-sided modification of Tempo, without a corresponding modification of Tone-production itself, affords *primâ facie* ground for objections ; on the other hand I have exposed the deeper-lying cause of this one-sidedness, and thus have left those objections with nothing to fall back on save the incapacity and general unfitness of our conductors themselves. It certainly is a valid argu-

* David Strauss.—Tr.

ment, that nothing could do more harm to the pieces I have instanced than a wilful introduction of random nuances of tempo, which must at once throw wide the door to the fantastic whims of every empty or conceited time-beater aiming at effect, and in time would make our classical music-literature completely unrecognisable. To this, of course, there is no reply, save that our music is in a very sad plight when such fears can arise ; since it is as good as saying that one has no faith in the good sense of our artistic public, against which those quips and quiddities would break in vain. Consequently this objection also—sound enough on one side, but seldom honestly meant—is reduced to an admission of the general incapacity of our conductors : for, if the bunglers are not to be allowed a free hand, why have our most eminent and respected musicians not set the right example ? And why have they, above all others, led the execution of our classical music into such a rut of triviality and utter disfigurement, that it grates on every sensitive ear ?

Thus it also comes about that this objection, albeit valid in itself, is used as pretext for all manner of opposition to every effort in the sense I mean ; while the reason and motive of that opposition remain nothing but personal incapacity and mental inertia, kindling under circumstances into aggressive action, as the incapable and inert are in so immense a majority.

Seeing that most of our classical works were first introduced to us in a very halting fashion (one has only to read of the conditions under which Beethoven's most difficult symphonies came to a first performance !), whilst much has been set before the German public in total defacement from the first (*vide* my article on Gluck's Overture to " Iphigenia in Aulis " in the fifth volume of these Collected Writings and Poems *), we may judge the state in which these works are ardently " conserved " under the régime of that inertia and incapacity, if we simply ponder, without fear or favour, how even a master like *Mendelssohn* went to

* Volume III. of the present series.—Tr.

work on their conducting! We surely cannot expect far
lesser musical magnates to arrive of themselves at an
understanding denied to their master, there being but *one*
guide for smaller men—*example*; and this they never could
hope to meet on their chosen path. The cheerless thing,
however, is that this leaderless path has been trodden so
broad that no room remains for those who might strew-
in a chance example. And therefore it is, that I propose to submit to a sharper scrutiny the pietistic opposition offered to that spirit which I have called the proper
one for rendering our great music, to expose that opposition's curious paltriness, and above all to rob its reni-
tent spirit of the halo wherewith it loves to adorn itself
as "Spirit of Chaste German Art." For it is this last-
named spirit that checks all upward motion in our musical world, holds back each freshening breeze from mingling
with its atmosphere, and in time may really blanch our
glorious German Music to a hueless, ay, a jibbering ghost.

To me it seems of weight to meet this spirit face to
face, and tell it to its teeth from whence it springs,—to
wit, emphatically *not* from the spirit of German Music.
Into *the latter* there will be no need to inquire to-day.
To appraise the positive worth of the newer music, the
music of Beethoven, is no light task; its weight is heavy,
and for any attempt to weigh it we must await more
leisure and happier days than our modern musical fudge
allows us. For the present we will merely make a preparatory study in the negative, laying bare the worthless-
ness of the music-mongering that struts just now as Classical and Beethovenian.—

There is one preliminary remark to make: namely that
the said Opposition, noisy enough in the scribblings of its
totally uneducated followers in the Press, takes a more
reticent and sullen form with its real immediate chiefs.
("It would never do, you see, for him to speak his mind
out"—said a lady once to me, with a significant glance,
about one of these well-behaved musicians.) The fate of
German Music, the utter recklessness of German art-

officials, has made over the conduct of our higher musical affairs to the hands of these gentry: they feel safe and snug in their posts and dignities.—As I noticed at starting, this Areopagus consists of two radically dissimilar tribes: that of the setting German 'musicianer' (*Musikant*) of olden style, which has kept its head far longer above water in more naïve Southern Germany; and that of the rising 'elegant' musician of newer style, chiefly to be found in Northern Germany, and sprung from the school of Mendelssohn. To certain quite recent disturbances of their equilibrium we owe it that these two varieties—none too impressed by each other's worth before—have joined in mutual recognition, and the Mendelssohnian school, with its appendages, at last is no less fancied and favoured in Southern Germany than the prototype of South-German unproductiveness is welcomed in North Germany with sudden veneration: a piece of good fortune the lamented *Lindpaintner* did not survive to see. Both parties thus clasp hands in guarantee of common quiet. Perchance the first variety, that of the pure-bred German musicianer, as I have dubbed it, has had to overcome a certain inward squeamishness at this alliance: but it is assisted over the difficulty by a not particularly laudable trait in the German character, namely jealousy linked with want of spirit. This attribute had already betrayed one of the most notable musicians of recent times (as I have shewn elsewhere *) into denial of his own nature, into subjection to the new anti-German law of the elegant second variety. As for the opposition of inferior craftsmen, it had little other meaning than: We can't get on, we don't want others to get on, and we're vexed when they do. Here all is honest narrowness, only becoming dishonest when crossed.

Things are different in the newer camp, where the strangest medley of personal, class, and national interests has given birth to the most intricate code of behaviour. Without embarking on a catalogue of these manifold

* Robert Schumann—cf. Vol. III., p. 117.—Tr.

interests, I will merely cite their chief maxim, that *much must be hidden, much placed in the shade*. In a certain sense one even does one's best to keep the "musician" in the background : and that with reason.

With the true German musician it formerly was hard to consort. As in France and England, so in Germany the musician had ever been a social pariah ; here wellnigh none but Italian musicians were held by princes and the world of rank for human beings, and the humiliating fashion in which they were preferred above the Germans we may learn, for example, from Mozart's treatment by the Imperial Court in Vienna. With us the musician stayed nothing but an odd, half wild, half childish creature, entertained as such by his wagepayers. The culture of our greatest musical geniuses has borne the marks of this exclusion from all finer or even more intellectual company : witness Beethoven's encounter with Goethe at Teplitz. With the musician proper, one presupposed an organism totally inaccessible to higher culture. Seeing me engaged in active efforts to raise the spirit of the Dresden Kapelle in 1848, *H. Marschner* once took the greatest pains to warn me off, saying that I really should remember the Musician was clean incapable of understanding me.—Certain it is (as I began by stating) that our higher and highest musical posts have been filled for the most part by "musicians" who had risen from the ranks,—which in a good workaday sense had many advantages. In an orchestral patriarchate of such a kind there developed a certain family-spirit, not lacking in cordiality, but needing just an occasional puff of more bracing air ; and that breeze would pretty soon have kindled a fair fire, were it but more warming than illuminating, in the singularly intelligent heart of such a body.

But just as the Jews have stood aloof from our manual work, so our newer musical conductors have none of them risen from the ranks of musical craftsmen, for sheer reason of their dislike of real hard labour. No : this new style of Conductor forthwith planted himself atop of the musical confraternity, somewhat as the Banker on top of our world of work. For this he had to bring something ready in his pocket, something the step-by-step musician did not own, or found most hard to come by, and seldom in sufficience: as the banker his Capital, this gentleman brought his Polish (*Gebildetheit*). Advisedly I say *polish*, not culture (*Bildung*); for whoso owns this last in truth, can be no target for our scoffs: he towers above all others. But the possessor of Polish is fair enough game.

No instance has come to my knowledge in which the fruit of veritable culture, freedom of spirit, Freedom in general, had crowned the happiest cultivation of this Polish. Mendelssohn himself, for all his manifold and diligently-tended gifts, shewed plainly he had never reached that freedom; he never overcame that peculiar sense of constraint which, in the eyes of the earnest observer, kept him outside our German art-life in spite of all his merited successes, nay, perchance became a gnawing inward pain that led to his so incomprehensibly early death. And the reason is just this: there is no spontaneousness at bottom of such a thirst for culture, but it issues rather from the obligation to cloak a part of one's own nature than from any impulse to unfold it. The resultant culture can therefore only be a pseudo-culture: in certain directions the brain may acquire a high degree of keenness; but the point where all directions meet, can never be the true clear-seeing Intellect itself.—Now, if it wellnigh cuts us to the heart to trace this inner process in a remarkably gifted and high-strung individual, it soon disgusts us to observe its course and products in the case of lesser and more trivial natures. Here Polish meets us with nothing but its fatuous smile, and if we have no stomach for smiling back at this grimace, as the superficial students of our Culture are mostly wont to do, we probably fall into actual gloom at the sight. And the German musician has good grounds for such a feeling when he sees, as see to-day he must, that this vapid Polish is setting up a claim to judge the spirit and the value of our glorious music.

It is one main characteristic of this Polish, never to dwell strongly upon anything, to plunge deep into nothing, or, as the saying goes, not to make much account. Item : the greatest, sublimest and most arcane, is dubbed a thing of course, quite "self-intelligible," at every man's disposal at all hours, to learn or even imitate its trick. So no time must be wasted on the prodigious, the dæmonic, the divine, for simple reason that there's nothing at all imitable to be found therein. Wherefore this Polish is mighty glib with the terms "excrescence," "exaggeration" and the like ; whence, again, has sprung a new school of Æsthetics, pretending above all to take its stand on *Goethe*,—as he too, you know, had a dislike of all monstrosities, and replaced them by so fair and equable a clarity. Then "harmlessness" is praised as Art; *Schiller*, quite too impulsive here and there, is treated with a certain spice of contempt ; and so in wise agreement with our modern Philistine an altogether new idea of "Classicity" is built, to buttress which, in wider spheres of art, the Greeks are called upon at last, —the Greeks with whom transparent gaiety was so very much at home. And this sickly shuffling-off the earnestness and awe of Being is raised into a whole system of latest World-philosophy (*Weltanschauung*), in whose completed midst our "cultured" music-heroes take their undisputed easy-chairs of honour.

How they have behaved to our great German tone-works, I have shewn by a few striking examples. It only remains to find the cheerful-Grecian secret of that "gliding through the piece" so pressingly recommended by Mendelssohn. This we shall learn the plainest from his hangers-on and followers. Mendelssohn's maxim was to hide the unavoidable weaknesses of the execution—perchance of the to-be-executed too, under circumstances ; these gentry add to it their own peculiar motto : Hide everything and make no fuss. The reason is almost purely physiologic, and was made quite clear to me by an experience whose analogy may at first sight seem far-fetched. For the performance of my "Tannhäuser" in Paris I had re-written the first scene in the Venusberg, and carried out the merely fugitive hints of the original on a more extensive scale; so I explained to the ballet-master what a ludicrous contrast the wretched little tripping *pas* of his Mænads and Bacchantes presented with my music, and begged him to devise something answering to the Bacchanalian groups on famous antique reliefs, something bold and savagely sublime. The man whistled through his fingers, and said : " Oh, I quite understand ; but it would need a corps of première danseuses. Were I to tell my people a word of it, and ask them to strike the attitudes you mean, we should have the cancan on the spot, and all be ruined."—Well, precisely the same feeling that led my Paris ballet-master to adhere to the most meaningless dance-step for his Mænads and Bacchantes, forbids our music-conductors of the elegant new style to slip the reins of their Polish for one moment : they know it easily may end in an Offenbachian scandal. They have taken warning from the example of *Meyerbeer*, whom the Paris Opéra betrayed into certain Semitic accentuations in music so alarming that the "cultivated" have never yet regained their nerve.

A considerable part of their culture has since consisted in paying studious heed to their own demeanour, just as the victim of a congenital lisp or stammer must shun all utterance of passion, not to fall into the most unseemly stuttering and spluttering. Now this constant keeping-watch-on-oneself has certainly had the agreeable result of stopping much distastefulness from coming to too harsh a show, and the general mixture of races has gone on far less startlingly ; which in turn has had the good effect for all of us, that our native element, a little stiff and undeveloped on many a side, has reaped much incitation to unbend : as I mentioned at first, our musicians have moderated their gruffness, neatness of detail-work in the execution &c., &c., have more become the order of the day. But it is another matter when this necessity for restraint and smoothing-down of certain objectionable personal attributes is to create an axiom for the treatment of our native art itself. The German is angular and clumsy when he takes on airs and manners; *but he's sublime and tops all others when he catches fire.* And we are to put out *that* for love of these gentry?

Indeed it has a look of it to-day.—At the time when I came into closer contact with a young musician * who had been in Mendelssohn's company, I was perpetually told of the master's one piece of advice: In composing never think of making a sensation or effect, and avoid everything likely to lead to it. That sounded beautiful and right enough, and in fact not a single faithful pupil of the master's has ever chanced to produce a sensation or effect. Only, there seemed to me a deal too much negation in the doctrine, and its positive results were not particularly ample. I fancy all the teachings of the Leipzig Conservatorium are founded on that negative maxim, for I have heard that the young folk there are plagued to death with its warning, whilst the most promising talents can gain them no favour with their teachers unless they forswear all taste for music not in strict accordance with the Psalms.

The first outcome of this negative maxim, and the most important for our present inquiry, has shewn itself in the rendering of our classical music itself. Here the guiding principle has been a fear of falling into the Drastic. Never yet have I been able to ascertain, for instance, that those pianoforte-compositions of Beethoven's which exhibit the master's own peculiar style at its ripest have really been studied and played by the professors of that creed. It long remained my dearest wish, to find someone who might treat me to a hearing of the great B-flat Sonata; at last it was fulfilled me, but by someone from a very different camp from that where the Mendelssohnian drill is practised. 'Twas *great Franz Liszt* himself, who moreover fulfilled my longing to hear *Bach* at last. Bach, to be sure, has been cultivated with predilection in that camp too; for here, where there can be no possible talk of modern Effect, or even Beethovenian Drastic, it seemed

* Query—Raff?—Tr.

the very place to introduce the saving smoothness of a purely unseasoned rendering. Once I begged one of the most reputed older musicians and comrades of Mendelssohn (I have already referred to him in connection with the *Tempo di Menuetto* of the Eighth Symphony) to play me the Eighth Prelude and Fugue (in E-flat minor) from the first part of the Wohltemperirte Klavier, as that piece had always had such a magical attraction for me; I must admit that seldom have I felt so great a shock as that experienced from his friendly compliance. At any rate there then was no question of gloomy German Gothic, or tomfoolery of that sort; under the hands of my friend the piece flowed over the keyboard with such a " Grecian gaiety" that its " harmlessness " quite bore me off, and involuntarily I saw myself seated in a neo-Hellenic synagogue, from whose musical rites every trace of Old-Testament accentuation had been decently purged away. That singular reading was still ringing in my ears, when one day I begged Liszt to cleanse my musical feelings from the painful impression : he played me the Fourth Prelude and Fugue (C-sharp minor). Now, I knew what to expect from Liszt at the pianoforte; but from Bach himself, much as I had studied him, I never expected what I learnt that day. For then I saw the difference between study and revelation; through his rendering of this single fugue Liszt revealed the whole of Bach to me, so that I now know of a surety where I am with him, can take his every bearing from this point, and conquer all perplexity and every doubt by power of strong faith. But I also know that those self-constituted guardians know *nothing* of their Bach ; and if anyone doubts it, I have only to say : Let them play him to you !

Further, I challenge the firstcomer from that pietistic Musical-Temperance Union—which I will view a little closer in a moment—if he has ever heard Beethoven's great B-flat Sonata played by *Liszt*, to tell me honestly whether he really knew and understood this work before. At least I can name one such, who felt driven by sincere emotion to

confirm the unalterable verdict of all present at that wonderful event.   And who is it, to come to to-day, who really
renders Bach and the true great Beethoven in public, and
wins from every audience a like rejoiced avowal?   Is it a
pupil of the school of Abstinence?   No!   'Tis none other
than Liszt's own follower pre-elect, *Hans von Bülow.*

Let this suffice for the present.

Returning from these superb revelations, it needs must
interest us to note the further bearing of those gentlemen
with whom our immediate business lies.

Their political successes, in so far as the foes of "sensation" usurp the field of action in our German musical
community, shall not trouble us just now ; whereas their
sectarian evolution is of some religious interest.   In this
connection, the earlier maxim "Before all no Effect!"—
engendered rather by embarrassment and doubt of self—has
been raised from an almost too fastidious counsel of pru-
dence to a positively aggressive dogma, whose professors
turn away their eyes with canting prudery (*mit muckerischer
Scheu*) when confronted with a whole-limbed male, as though
they detected something quite improper. This prudery,
originally a simple cloak for personal impotence, has now
become a screed against all potence, and wins its operative
force from slander and insinuation.   And the soil, from
which all this derives its nurture, is just the starveling
spirit of German Philistinedom, of plain sense spoilt by
pettiest cares : a category which includes, as we have seen,
our working musicians themselves.

The main ingredient, however, is a certain judicial
attitude toward what one cannot do oneself, with disparagement of what one would only be too glad to.   It is
supremely sad that people should have succeeded in
entangling so sound a nature as that of *Robert Schumann*
in this litter, ay, and making his memory at last an oriflamme for the new communion.   The misfortune was,
that Schumann attempted a thing he was unfit for, and it
was just that feeble side of his artistic work which could be
turned into a specious door-sign for this latest Guild of

Music. The field where Schumann was positively charming, and whose fruits were consequently nursed and noised abroad with finer care by us (I here am proud to number myself with *Liszt* and his henchmen) than by his own adherents,—that field has been studiously neglected by them, perhaps because it shewed a true productiveness, perhaps for simple reason that they lacked the proper style of rendering. On the other hand, where Schumann bared the limit of his powers, to wit his efforts on the bolder, grander scalé,—those works are diligently marshalled out to-day. If the public exhibits no genuine liking for them, it is promptly told there is a peculiar beauty in making no " effect " ; and finally these people have even gone the length of a comparison with the Beethoven of the last period, who still remains so very unintelligible under *their* hands. It was a brilliant thought, to cast the turgidly uninteresting Robert Schumann (so easy to be mastered by them, through his demanding nothing save a smooth half-heartedness) into one pot with Beethoven, to shew that, even when matched with the most stupendous daring, their ideal is strictly on all fours with the profoundest depths of the German Spirit. So Schumann's shallow turgidness at last is ranked as one and the same with Beethoven's ineffable depth ; yet with the reservation, that drastic eccentricity is strictly unallowable and the nothing-saying neutral the correct and decent thing : a point whereon the rightly-rendered Schumann may at any rate be measured quite supportably against the wrongly-rendered Beethoven.

These singular guarders of musical chastity thus fall into the position, toward our great classical music, of eunuchs in a Sultan's harem ; and this is probably the reason why our spirit of Philistia so cheerfully entrusts them with the watch over music's somewhat perilous influence upon the Family, for one thinks oneself secure against all danger from such a body-guard itself.

But what becomes of our great, unutterably glorious German Music ?

What is done with our musical treasures, is after all

our only business with these gentry. After a whole
golden century of the most marvellous productivity, we
might proudly rest content to choke our grief that nothing
remarkable has been produced within a certain period.
But that precisely these people are treating themselves, and
striving to get others to treat them, as keepers and guardians of the sterling "German" spirit of that glorious
heritage of ours,—this makes us deem them dangerous.

Looked at *per se*, there is little to object to in these
musicians; most of them compose quite well.   Herr
Johannes Brahms was once so kind as to play me a piece
of his own with serious variations; it shewed me that he
understands no jokes, and in itself I thought it excellent.
I also heard him play other men's compositions on the
pianoforte at a concert, which certainly gave me less
delight; in fact I could only deem it an impertinence of
this gentleman's entourage to ascribe to Liszt and his
school "a by all means extraordinary technique," and
nothing further, whereas the woodenness and primness of
Herr Brahms's rendering so much distressed me that I
would have given anything to see his technique moistened
with a little of the oil of that school : an oil which appears
not to exude from the keyboard itself, but to be dropped
from at least a more ethereal sphere than that of simple
"technique."   Taken all in all, however, it presented quite
a respectable figure, about which the only enigma was how
it could be mistaken for the figure, if not of the Saviour
himself, at least of his best-beloved disciple; unless,
indeed, a craze for medieval carvings should have misled
us into taking those angular wooden images for the beau
ideal of churchly Sainthood.   Nevertheless we ought at
smallest to defend ourselves from having our great live
Beethoven set before us in the garment of that Sanctity,
for sake mayhap of placing him, the un-understood and
mangled, by side of Schumann the un-understandable for
the most natural of reasons; as though, where *these* men
know not how to mark a difference, there really were no
difference to mark.

How things stand at present with this Sanctity in detail, I have already pointed out. To investigate its aspirations will bring us to another field, but a field to which the whole course of our inquiries "About Conducting" was eventually to lead us from the first.—

Not long ago a South-German newspaper-editor discovered "*muckerisch*"* tendencies in my art-theories: plainly the man didn't know what he was saying; he was merely at loss for an opprobrious word. From what I have gathered of the nature of *Muckerei*, however, the peculiar tenet of this odious sect appears to have been a sedulous pursuit of the incentive and alluring, with intent to exercise one's power of resistance of temptation through their final overcoming. But the true scandal of the thing came out in the exposure of its highest adepts, who had so reversed the ostensible tenet of this sect that resistance of temptation merely served in their case as a whet to crass indulgence.—Applied to Art, one thus would not be talking nonsense if one accused that singular Musical-Temperance Union of "*Muckerei.*" For if the lower orders of that school plod on between the allurement offered in especial by the art of music and the abstinence imposed upon them by a, maxim now become a dogma, one may prove with little trouble that its higher orders hanker after nothing but the indulgence forbidden to their inferiors. The "Liebeslieder-Walzer" of Saint Johannes, however odd their name may sound, might still be classed among the religious exercises of the lower grade: but the higher and highest grades of Abstinents are unmistakably distinguished by an ardent yearning for the "Opera," which devours all their spiritual devotion in the long run. If only once a true felicitous embrace of "Opera" could be attained, presumably the whole school would be broken up. The solitary fact of constant failure has kept the school together; for every abortive attempt can always be given the look of voluntary abstention, in the sense of

* See Vol. III., p. 115; also my note on the Königsberg "Muckers" of 1835, Vol. II., p. 114.—Tr.

those ritualistic exercises of the lower grades, and Opera,
never happily wooed and won, can figure again and again
as mere symbol of a lure to be resisted finally; so that
the authors of operatic failures may rank as Saints par
excellence.—

But in sober earnest, how do these Messrs Musicians
stand toward "Opera"?—Having sought them in the
concert-room, their starting-point, it is here that we have
to complete our inquiry into their "Conducting."—

Herr Eduard Devrient has reminded us of his friend
Mendelssohn's "*Opernnoth*," i.e. his hunger for an opera,
in a book of "Recollections" dedicated to that composer a
short while back.   Thence we also learn the particular
nature of the hungry master's craving, namely that the
opera predestined him by Fate should be right "German";
for this the material was to be specially procured him,—
which unfortunately refused to come about.   I presume
this latter had its natural grounds.   Much may be made
to order: but "Germanity" and that "nobly limpid"
("*edel heitre*") opera which loomed before Mendelssohn's
supercilious ambition are things that just can not be made,
their recipe occurring in neither the Old Testament nor
the New.—Nevertheless what stayed beyond the master's
reach has never seriously been given up by his comrades
and disciples.   Herr *Hiller* believed he might wrest the
prize in time by cheerful perseverance, for it after all
appeared a simple question of "a lucky hit," which—in
his opinion—fell to the lot of others under his very eyes,
and with due endurance, as at any game of chance, must
really fall to *his* at last.   But the wheel of Fortune was as
obdurate as ever.   It stopped for no one: not even for
poor Schumann; and many as have been the higher and
lower members of the Church of Abstinence who "chaste
and harmlessly" have stretched forth operatic hands to the
longed-for sound success, after a brief but toilsome spell of
illusion the lucky hit has—failed them.

Such experiences embitter even the most harmless, and
are the more vexing as the political constitution of the

Music-State in Germany, upon the other hand, involves the binding of our Kapellmeisters and Musikdirektors to the Theatre, for the principal exercise of their functions, and these gentlemen have in consequence to devote their energies to a field of musical action on which they are clean incapable of producing aught themselves. The ground of their sterility can scarcely be a qualification for presiding over the operatic system, i.e. for being a good opera-conductor: and yet the peculiar fate of our art-affairs, as described by me at the commencement, has led to these gentlemen, who cannot even conduct our German concert-music, being entrusted with the control of so very complicated a thing as Opera. Any man of penetration may imagine the result!— —

Circumstantially as I have gone to work with the exposure of their shortcomings on that field where they really ought to feel at home, I may be just as succinct in respect of these Messrs Conductors' dealings in the *sphere of Opera*; for here it is simply a case of "Lord forgive them! they know not what they do." To properly denote their shameful dealings in this sphere I should have to resort to a positive demonstration of the good and important work which could be done, and that might lead me too far from the goal I have set before me ; so I will defer that demonstration to another time. In its stead I merely offer the following contribution to their portraiture as Opera-conductors.—

In the domain of Concert-music, from which these gentry take their start, they seem to think it mannerly to don as serious a mien as possible ; here in Opera, however, they deem it fitter to shew from the first the sprightly mien of the flippant sceptic. With a smile they admit they're not particularly at home here, and don't profess to know much of things they don't think much of. Hence, upon principle, a gallant complaisance toward singers male and female, whom they are always only too delighted to oblige : they take the tempo, introduce fermate, ritardandi, accelerandi, transpositions, and above all "cuts," wherever and howsoever those persons wish. What arguments have they to prove the absurdity of a single proposition addressed them from that side ? Nay, if it ever occurs to a pedantically-inclined conductor to insist on this or that, as a rule he is in the wrong. For, especially according to these gentle-men's contemptuous view of Opera, those singers are thoroughly at home here, and know to a nicety how and what they can do ; so that if anything at all acceptable ever comes to light in Opera, one really owes it solely to the singers and their artistic instinct, just as wellnigh all the credit for a similar thing in the Orchestra belongs of right to the good sense of the bandsmen.—On the other hand one has only to examine an orchestral part of the kind, of " Norma " for instance, to judge what a curious changeling has come of such a harmless sheet of notes : the mere chain of transpositions, where an aria's Adagio is played in F-sharp, its Allegro in F-natural, and the bridge between them in E-flat (for sake of the military brass), affords a truly horrifying picture of the music to which such an esteemed Kapellmeister merrily beats the time. Only at an outlying theatre of Turin (in Italy, observe) have I chanced to hear the " Barber of Seville " given entire and really correctly ; it is too much trouble to our own Kapellmeisters to render justice even to so innocent a score, for they never dream that the least considerable opera, if unimpeachably presented, can make a relatively quite satisfying impression on the cultured mind for very reason of that correctness. The shallowest theatrical patch-work upon the smallest Paris stages has an agreeable, nay, an æsthetically detaching effect on us, because it is never rendered else than surely and correctly in its every part. So great in fact is the power of the Artistic principle, that, if rightly applied and thoroughly carried out in but one of its parts, we straightway obtain an æsthetic effect; what we have here, is genuine art, albeit on one of quite its lower steps. But we in Germany know nothing of that sort of effect, except from a *ballet-performance* in Vienna or Berlin. Here every-thing is gathered in *one* hand, and that the hand of a man who understands his business: the ballet-master. He fortunately also lays down the law to the orchestra, for expression as for tempo; not like the singer with his personal caprice, in Opera, but with a view to ensemble, to the co-ordination of the whole. And behold! of a sudden we find the orchestra playing quite rightly,—a feeling of supreme relief which must have come to everyone who, after the torture of an opera-performance in those cities, has witnessed such a ballet. In Opera the Regisseur might contribute to a like agreement; but strange to say, we abide by the fiction that Opera belongs to Absolute Music, despite the proven ignorance — known to every singer—of the musical chief; so that if a performance has really turned out well for once, through the artistic instinct of talented singers and a company and band inspired by the work itself, we always find Herr Kapellmeister regarded as the backbone of the whole affair, called up, applauded, and distinguished as you will. How he ever got there, must be a puzzle to himself; and then he well may join in the prayer: "Forgive them, Lord! they know not what they do."—

But, as I only meant to speak of Conducting proper, and have no desire to lose myself in a general discussion of Opera, I now have merely to confess that with this chapter I have reached the close. 'Tis not for me to squabble about our Kapellmeisters' conducting in Opera. That must be left to singers who have to complain of one conductor that he doesn't give way to them enough, of another, that he doesn't prompt them with sufficient heed; in short, upon a basis of the commonest journeyman-work, which is all the matter comes to, some sort of dispute may be raised. From the higher standpoint of true artistic work, however, this kind of conducting deserves not a moment's notice. Upon this the word does fall to me, and to me alone among all living Germans; wherefore I will conclude by setting forth a little more minutely the grounds of that dismissal.

Upon reviewing my experiences, it remains impossible

Z

for me to decide as to which of the said attributes of our conductors' I myself have to do with in the performances of my operas. Is it the spirit in which our great music is performed at concerts, or that in which Opera is handled at the theatre? I have an uncomfortable idea that these two spirits join hands in the treatment of my operas, to supplement each other's action in a manner not particularly cheering. Where the first—the spirit presiding over our classical concert-music—has free play, as in the instrumental introductions of my operas, I can discover nothing but the most dejecting consequences of that method which I have fully discussed above. In this connection I need speak of nothing save the Tempo, which, contrary to all sense, is either rushed (as years ago by Mendelssohn himself at a Leipzig concert, where my Tannhäuser-overture was made a deterrent example) or dragged (as at Berlin, and nearly everywhere else, with my Lohengrin-prelude), or rushed and dragged * alike (as of late my prelude to the "Meistersinger" at Dresden and other places),—but never treated with that intelligent Modification upon which I must reckon no less determinedly than on the playing of the proper notes.

To give an idea of the last-named mode of havoc, I will confine myself to the usual procedure with my *Prelude to the "Meistersinger."*—

The main-tempo of this piece was inscribed by me as "sehr mässig bewegt," meaning something the same as *Allegro maestoso* in the older style of signature. No tempo stands more in need of modification than this, when maintained for any length, and especially when the thematic subjects are treated strongly episodically. It also is a favourite for the varied combination of motives of different types, because the broad symmetry of its 4/4 beat lends itself with great facility to the modifications required by such a treatment. Moreover, this medium 'common time' is the most comprehensive of all; beaten in vigorous (*kräftig "bewegten"*) crotchets, it can represent a true alert

* "Verschleppt und verschludert zugleich."

Allegro,—and this is the real main-tempo here meant by me, appearing at its swiftest in the eight bars leading from the March to the E-major:

or it can be treated as a half-period composed of two 2/4 beats, and will then assume the character of a brisk Scherzando, as at the entry of the theme in diminution:

or, again, it may even be interpreted as an *Alla-breve* (2/2), and then express the older sedate *Andante* proper (particularly employed in Church-music), which rightly should be marked by two moderately slow beats. In this last sense I have used it from the eighth bar after re-entry of C-major for combining the principal March-theme, now borne by the basses, with the second principal theme now sung in flowing rhythmic duplication by the violins and 'celli:

This second theme made its first appearance 'diminished' and in pure 4/4 time:

There with the greatest softness in delivery it combines a passionate, almost a hasty character (somewhat of a clandestinely whispered declaration of love); since the

passionate haste is sufficiently expressed by a greater
mobility of figuration, to preserve the theme's chief characteristic, that of tenderness, the pace must necessarily be
a little slackened, dropping to the utmost shade of gravity
whereof the 4/4 beat is capable; and to bring this imper-
ceptibly about (i.e. without really effacing the fundamental
character of the main-tempo) a bar of "*poco rallentando*"
introduces the phrase. Through the more restless nuance
of this theme, which gains at last the upper hand,

and which I have also marked expressly with "more
passionate," it was easy for me to lead the tempo back to
its original swifter motion; and this in turn was convertible
into the aforesaid *Andante alla breve*, for which I had only
to resume a nuance of the main-tempo already developed
in the first exposition. The first development of the staid
March-theme, to wit, had terminated in a longish coda of
cantabile character, which could be given proper breadth
only if taken at that *Tempo andante alla breve*. As this
full-toned cantabile:

was preceded by a Fanfare in massive crotchets:

that change of tempo had obviously to enter with the
cessation of the pure crotchet-movement, that is to say,
with the sustained dominant chord that introduces the
cantabile. Now, as the broader minim-movement is here
worked out to a long and animated climax, particularly as
regards the modulation, I believed I could safely leave the
pace to the conductor's common-sense, since the mere

execution of such passages will of itself put more fire into the tempo if only one yields to the natural feeling of the bandsmen ; so surely did I count on this, as a conductor of some experience, that I thought it needless to indicate anything but the place where the original 4/4 beat is resumed, as suggested to every musical ear by the return of the crotchet motion in the harmonies. In the conclusion of the Prelude this broader 4/4 beat is just as obviously called for by the re-entry of that sturdy march-like Fanfare, with which the doubling of the figured ornament combines to close the movement in precisely the same tempo as it had begun.—

This Prelude was first performed at a private concert given in Leipzig, under my personal lead ; and, in exact accord with the above directions, it was so splendidly played by the orchestra that the tiny audience, consisting almost exclusively of non-local friends of my music, vociferously demanded an encore,—a wish the band, apparently of like opinion with their hearers, fulfilled with great alacrity. So favourable a report would seem to have spread abroad, that people thought good to give the real town-public a hearing of my new prelude at a Gewandhaus Concert. This time it was conducted by Herr Kapellmeister *Reinecke*, who had been present at the performance conducted by myself ; under his lead the very same musicians executed it in such a way as to get it soundly hissed by the audience. Whether this result was solely due to the 'sturdiness' of those concerned, i.e. to intentional disfigurement, I will not ask too curiously, for simple reason that the wholly unassumed ineptitude of our Conductors is only too well known to me : enough, that I learnt from very reliable ear-witnesses *what beat* the Herr Kapellmeister had given my prelude ; that sufficed me.

For, should a conductor of this stamp desire to shew his public or his Herr Direktor, and so forth, what wretched stuff my " Meistersinger " is, he has merely to beat its prelude in the fashion in which he is wont to handle Beethoven, Mozart and Bach, and which may not be at

all amiss for Schumann; no one then will have any difficulty in convincing himself that this music is highly disagreeable. Only imagine a thing so full of life, and yet so
delicately shaded, as the tempo I have instanced with this
prelude, suddenly packed into the Procrustes'-bed of one
of these Classical time-beaters! It's a case of: "Lay
yourself in here; and what's too long of you, I'll chop it
off; and what's too short, I'll stretch it!" And up strikes
the music, to drown the victim's moans!—

Thus safely bedded, the Dresden public—which once
had heard many a living piece from me—made acquaintance with this Prelude to the "Meistersinger"; ay, as the
following will shew, with the whole work itself (so much
of it, at least, as had not been cut in advance). To speak
with technical exactitude again, the conductor's services
consisted in demurely squaring out the whole work by his
own four-crotchety conception of the main-tempo, and
taking the very broadest nuance of that tempo as an
unalterable standard. One of the consequences was as
follows. The conclusion of this prelude—the combination
of the two principal themes in an ideal *tempo andante alla
breve*, as already described—serves me to bring the work
itself to a gay but thoughtful close, after the pattern of an
ancient popular refrain: on top of this suggestive combination, which I have here expanded in a different manner
and employed in some sense as a mere accompaniment,
Hans Sachs has to sing his kindly praises of the "Mastersingers," concluding with his words of comfort for German
Art itself. Despite all earnestness of its content, this
closing apostrophe was meant to have an inspiriting effect,
for which I trusted chiefly to the heartiness of that thematic
combination, whose rhythm should not take on a broader,
more solemn character till just towards the end, where the
chorus enters. With a very conscious purpose, readily
comprehensible by everyone who knows my general views,
I here pass over any deeper meaning of my dramatic
work, and from pure respect for naïve "Opera" I abide by
mere conducting and the beating of time. Well, the

necessity of modifying to an *Andante alla breve* a tempo reckoned at first for the breadth of a pompous processional march having already been totally unheeded in the prelude, it was felt just as little in the opera's closing song, which has no longer any direct connection with that march; and the tempo bungled there became here a binding rule, in pursuance whereof the conductor harnessed the sympathetic (*lebendig fühlenden*) singer of Hans Sachs to the primmest 4/4 beat, inexorably forcing him to drawl this closing speech as stiffly and woodenly as possible. By parties most concerned I was begged to sacrifice this close, and allow a "cut," as its effect was really too depressing. I declined. Soon the cries grew dumb. At last I learnt the reason : the Herr Kapellmeister had come to the rescue of the self-willed composer, and, acting on his own artistic judgment (naturally to do the work a service), had—"cut" that final apostrophe.

"Cut! Cut!"—behold the *ultima ratio* of our Herren Kapellmeister ; whereby they strike an unfailingly happy mean between their incapacity and the artistic problems they never can properly solve. Their motto is : "Where ignorance is bliss, 'tis folly to be wise" (" *Was ich nicht weiss, macht mich nicht heiss*") ; and the public, after all, must share their way of thinking. For myself, however, what am I to think of a performance of my work so hedged between a radically faulty alpha and a mangled omega ? Outwardly the thing looks well enough : an audience uncommonly roused, to the point of calling out the Kapellmeister at the finish, and the Father of my native land returning to the front of his box to join in the applause. But the tell-tale reports that gradually leak out, of constant shortenings, cuts, and alterations ! whilst there lingers in my mind the memory of a completely undocked, but at any rate completely correct performance in *Munich*, and I therefore cannot possibly persuade myself to give in my adhesion to the mutilators. This sorry plight, which appears unalterable since very few can even gauge the evil, is certainly alleviated by one thing : the comforting knowledge that, in spite of all the unintelligence of its treatment, the work's effective power can not be broken,—that fatal power of effect which is the bugbear of the Leipzig Conservatorium, and which, in retribution, one cannot even get at to destroy ! If the author needs must deem this all the greater wonder as he cannot bring himself to attend another performance of his works—for instance, that recent one of his " Meistersinger " at Dresden—yet their proved, their almost incomprehensible success supplies him, wondrously enough, with a peculiarly consoling answer to the question of these same Conductors' effect on our great classical music. Despite all mangling at their hands, that music lives with ever waxing power of warmth, because they have not strength to slay it : and this miraculous conviction seems to have become a comfortable dogma to the German genius, giving it alike the peace of perfect faith and the courage to pursue its path unflinching.—

But one more question remains : These wonderful conductors with the famous names, what is to be said of them as *musicians*? Remembering their absolute consentience, one might almost be led to the conclusion that they really knew their business, and, despite the shock to one's own feelings, that theirs was after all the Classic way. The assumption of their excellence stands so firm, that the whole musical community of Germany never hesitates an instant as to who shall beat time when the nation wants something played to it (at Grand Music-Festivals and such-like). That, of course, can only be Herr *Hiller*, Herr *Rietz*, or Herr *Lachner*. Beethoven's centenary could downright not be celebrated, if these three gentlemen were suddenly to sprain their wrists. I, on the other hand, don't know a soul whom I could safely trust to take a single tempo of my operas ; at least, no soul upon the General Staff of our time-beating army. Here and there I have come across a poor devil who shewed real taste and talent for conducting : but they promptly spoil their chance of getting on, not merely by seeing through the ineptitude of our Kapellmeister bigwigs, but also by indiscreetly speaking of it. A man, for instance, who discovers the most atrocious mistakes in the orchestral parts of " Figaro " from which such a General has allowed that opera to be played—God knows how often !—does not, of course, commend' himself to favour. So these poor gifted stalwarts come to grief, just like the heretics of old.

This being the universal order of the day, there is nothing for us but to keep on demanding its secret. We have the strongest reason to doubt these gentlemen's being *true* musicians, as they betray not a spark of *musical feeling*; but they really have a very accurate ear (mathematically accurate, if not ideally: the fatality with the false orchestral parts does not, be it said, befall each one of them); they have a quick eye, read and play from notes (at least a good number of them); in short, they prove themselves true professionals. Again, their culture—such as it is—is just of the kind one permits to none but a musician ; so that if one robbed them of that title, nothing would remain over, and least of all an intellectual human being. No, no! Indeed they *are* musicians, and most able musicians, who know and can quite everything that pertains to music. And yet ? When they come to music-ing they turn everything higgledy-piggledy, and feel safe with nothing but " Ewig, selig," or, if it be the grand style, " Gott Zebaot!" To be sure, our great music confuses them outright only by what makes it great, and what certainly is no easier to express in words than in cyphers. But is it not music, and nothing but music ? Whence then comes that aridness, that chill, that total inability to thaw under Music's influence, to forget one's worries, jealousies, one's fixed ideas? —Can *Mozart* perchance explain the thing, through his enormous gift of Arithmetic ? It seems that in him, whose nerves were so supersensitive to dissonance, whose heart beat with such ebullient kindness, the ideal extremes of Music met in direct contact and fused to form so marvellous a being. *Beethoven's* naïve method of doing his sums is equally well known ; arithmetical problems undoubtedly entered no conceivable relation with his musical drafts. Compared with Mozart he seems a *monstrum per excessum* on the Emotional side, unbalanced by an intellectual counterpoise on the side of Arithmetic ; and we can only conceive him saved from premature death by an abnormally robust, nay, rugged constitution. His music also ceases to be measurable by cyphers, whereas with Mozart (as mentioned incidentally before) many a quite banal regularity may be explained by the naïve blending of those two extremes of musical perception. The musicians of our present survey, on the contrary, appear to be monstrosities on the side of sheer arithmetic,*—and that, unlike the Beethovenian temperament, can jog along most comfortably with a very ordinary set of nerves. Therefore, if our famed and unfamed Sirs Conductors have been born in the House of Musical Arithmetic, and that alone, 't were devoutly to be wished that some new school or other should expound to them by rule-of-three the proper tempo of our music ; to bring this knowledge to them on the simple path of musical Feeling, appears to be a hopeless task. So once more I may say, my close is reached.

Yet stay ! There is some hope that the school I have just expressed so great a wish for is really on the point of opening. Under the auspices of the Royal Academy of Arts and Sciences in Berlin, as I hear, a " *High School of Music*" has been founded, and the supreme control already confided to the famous violinist, Herr *Joachim*. To have founded such a school without Herr Joachim, his services being available, must at any rate have seemed a woeful blunder. What inspires me with hopes of him is that, from all I have heard about his playing, this virtuoso knows and exactly carries out the mode of rendering I demand for our great music ; he consequently serves me as the only musician, apart from *Liszt* and his school, to whom I can point as proof and example of my previous assertions. Whether it annoys Herr Joachim, as I am told, to be mentioned in such company, makes no differ-

* Cf. p. 303, antea.—Tr.

ence to my argument; for in any serious question of what we can do, the point is not what we profess, but what is true. Should Herr Joachim deem it advantageous to give out that he has matured so fine a style in his intercourse with Herr Hiller or R. Schumann, he is welcome to do so, provided he will go on playing in such a way that one recognises the good effect of many intimate years with Liszt. I also think it a matter for congratulation, that the first thing people did for this " High School of Music " was to cast eyes upon a distinguished artist of *style* (des *Vortrages*): if to-day I had to give a stage-Kapellmeister an inkling of how to conduct, I certainly would rather send him to Frau *Lucca* than to the lamented Cantor *Hauptmann* of Leipzig, even were the latter still alive. On this point I am quite at one with the most naïve public, nay, with the taste of our fashionable friends of Opera themselves, as I hold by the man who gives us something from his heart and makes it really touch our ear and feeling. Yet it would alarm me to see Herr Joachim mounted on the curule stool of the academy with nothing but his fiddle in hand, as my own taste in the way of fiddlers is that of Mephistopheles with the " fair," whom he catalogues " once and for all in the plural." The baton is said to have not become him; composition, too, seems to have given more bitters to himself than sweets to others. And how the " High School " is to be conducted from nothing but the high stool of the first fiddler, is beyond my comprehension. Socrates, at least, was not of opinion that Themistocles, Cimon and Pericles were qualified to lead the State to paths of pleasantness by their eminence as generals and orators; for he was able to prove by results, alas! that this State-governing turned out very badly for themselves. Perhaps, though, it is different with Music.—But I have a second ground of alarm. They tell me Herr *Joachim*, whose friend *J. Brahms* is anticipating all sorts of good things from a return to the ballad-melody of Schubert, is personally awaiting a *new Messiah* for Music at large.

Had he not better leave this expectation to those who have made him High-Schoolmaster? For my part I will bid him: Cheerily on! Should it happen that he himself is that Messiah, at least he may hope not to be crucified by the Jews.—

THREE POEMS.

Drei Gedichte.

Of these " three poems," the first appears to have been written in 1868 (vide p. 305, antea) ; the second would seem, from its last two lines, to have been composed for King Ludwig's twenty-fifth birthday, August 25, 1869 ; the third, of course, is in celebration of the succeeding anniversary, together with the re-uniting of Germany,—Richard Wagner's fondest wish through all his previous life, as evidenced by the earlier pages of this volume.

TRANSLATOR'S NOTE.

I.

RHEINGOLD.

PLAY on, ye dwarves of darkness, with the Ring;
well may it serve your huckst'ring pranks of old!
Yet have a care: its hoop may prove a sling;
ye know the Curse: see if 'twas lightly told!
The Curse has said, the work to life shall spring
with him alone who *fearless* guards the Gold;
but you, your niggling play with paste and pap
shall soon be curtained by the Niblung's cap!

II.

UPON THE COMPLETION OF
"SIEGFRIED."

BRÜNNHILDE wakes, who many a year had slumbered,
fulfilled is now All-father's silent law;
whom she had loved or e'er his birth was numbered,
whom shielded she or e'er day's light he saw,
for whom her lot with wrath of gods was cumbered—
behold him now the veil of sleep withdraw.
To her through circling fire his steps were driven,
who but to mate her love to youth had thriven.

A wonder! Yet I scarce can call it wonder,
that here a stripling grows to strength of youth:
when time's great wheel is joyous in its thunder
full blithely might he scour the woods, in sooth.
This, this I needs must deem a greater wonder:
when manhood's strength has felt that wheel's sharp tooth,
that one should find his force by years replenished
to bring to issue tasks in youth unfinished.

And for thy friend this deed has come to bringing :
what years eleven had locked in sleep of fate,
at length has woken into life of singing ;
to Brynhild new-aroused is joined her mate.
Yet stay—how were this reveil set a-ringing,
did not thy warm young heart its strains dictate ?
I'm warned by wonder of the day whereon I send it,
that but for thee I never could have penned it.

III.

AUGUST 25TH, 1870.

Decreed has been the kingly word
    and Deutschland new awoken,
the nation's bright ancestral Hoard
    its shaming bonds has broken ;
what statesmen's craft could never speed
one regal word has brought to deed :
    that German word once spoken,
each German heart resounds accord.

And I—that word of sense profound
    as few have grasped its setting,
bore it our Folk glad vict'ry's sound,
    to me it gave Forgetting :
then buried I full many a smart
that long had rankled in my heart,
    and years of weary fretting
at Germany in sloth around.

Thou too, the sense that in it lay
    thou hadst no need to borrow :
who served the noble Hoard alway,
    was partner in my sorrow.
The raven sped by Wotan's fear
has found him tidings of good cheer :
    aglow is manhood's morrow—
come lift thy dawn, thou gods' to-day !

SUMMARY.

POEM. *To the Kingly Friend* (2).

STATE AND RELIGION.

Written at the King's request. A definite utterance on these subjects more difficult the older and more experienced one grows. Schiller's saying: "Life is earnest, Art is gay." I had taken Art in earnest, and Life avenged itself. Political confusions and social problems; idea of Occupation *versus* Labour; a gladsome world wherein to set my earnest artwork. The purer I imagined that world, the more it departed from the political tendencies of the day: where Socialists and Politicians came to end, should *we* commence. A spiritual intoxication, soon sobered down. The poet's intuition ripens sooner than his abstract thought; the *Ring* and Denial of the Will (8).

The artist's "kingdom" also is "not of this world," yet he stands within a careworn world that seeks for mere dissipation in art. Futility of the noblest attempts to better the world, when made by single thinkers; incredible pettiness of the average human intellect, blind to all but the moment's need; success of the violent and passionate. The State expresses the human Will's necessity of establishing a compact between the myriad blindly-grasping individuals into which it is divided: as in Nature-religions a portion is offered in propitiation to the Gods, so the unit offers up a fraction of his egoism to insure its major bulk (11). *Stability* the State's intrinsic object: only to be ensured when it is the interest of *all* parties. The King above all party-interests, and thus the State's ideal; the reverence accorded him by the average citizen a form of *Wahn*. Illustration of Wahn by animal instinct, as of bees and ants in providing for future of species at cost of individual (14). Wahn as Patriotism; a strain that cannot endure for long, and really tinctured with egoism; requires a symbol, somewhat like the flag—this symbol the King. Though Patriotism may sharpen the citizen's eyes to interests of State, it leaves him blind to the larger interests of mankind; injustice and violence to other States, with violent reaction on internal affairs (17). The difficulty of bringing true Reason into the joint resolves of men is increased by machinations of ambitious individuals, who employ the Wahn of "Public Opinion" to serve their personal ends; its self-styled organ the Press. Each several journalist may represent nothing but a carrière manqué, but all together they form this illusory "Public Opinion" that betrays to-day what it dubbed sacred yesterday. Invention of Printing; its final ruin of memory and judgment; people more incapable each day of sympathy with truly great ideas. The narrowness and injustice of this so-called Public Opinion most obvious in its dealings with the

King and his peculiar interests; it steps up to him with the boast of being identical in kind (21). In the State the King alone is in a position to make purely-human considerations his rule of conduct, yet has to sacrifice them for "reasons of State." The tragedy of human life nowhere more manifest; up to the King a clearance of all State-obstacles to the human Will is possible; but the kingly King desires justice and humanity, and these are irrealisable ideals : to be bound to strive for them notwithstanding, is to be condemned to a life of misery. The King's only succour is in Religion; for him it is what Patriotism is to the burgher (23).

True Religion is radically divergent from the State, and in itself upheaves it. Primitive Nature-religion a mere bond of tribal solidarity [Ancestor-worship— Tr.]; later replaced by Patriotism. True Religion reverses all the aspirations which built the State, and strikes an opposite path. What is the other world? As different as our mode of cognisance thereof must differ from the practical mode of everyday. The *divine* Wahn, prompting free-willed suffering and renunciation; the sublimity of its source a necessary inference from this supernatural effect. Christianity no egoistic compact; he who chooses suffering and renunciation is already raised above all notions bound by Time and Space. The World-overcomer must be our teacher of the nature of this Wahn (26). Philosophy shews the nullity of the present world, Religion the true world beyond; but the Religious can communicate his vision only in allegorical terms—like a dream told in daylight; upon these lines is Dogma formed. Disputes of the Church and the Rationalists; the Church *lowered* to an institution of State (29). Religion's dwellingplace the inmost chamber of the world-fleeing heart; its evidence by *deed and example*. The Saints as mediators for the Folk; the English grocer and his prayer-book. The King's ideal : unflinching Justice, ever ready Mercy—trysting-place of State and Religion (31).

How shall the King endure? The most trivial incident reveals to the truly great mind the terrible earnestness of life and the world; at every moment such an one is faced with what often drives the common man to suicide. A periodical distraction therefore a necessity : supplied by Art. Here the Wahn is conscious; by shewing us Life as a game of play, it lifts us above it, and comforts our distress. The counterpart of Religion in the serenity of Art (34).

GERMAN ART AND GERMAN POLICY.

1.—C. Frantz, the European Balance of Power and the Napoleonic propaganda. French "Civilisation" an incubus on Europe; the best French minds despair of their nation's mounting from materialism to spiritual beauty. Splendour and power *versus* true Art : France has done nothing to equal Spain in poetry or Italy in art. Louis XIV. and the laws of the beautiful; grace turned to etiquette (39). Frederick the Great's contempt for things German; French Civilisation as deadening and levelling as that of ancient Rome. As German folk-blood regenerated Europe then, so must its Spirit now; contrast between the Renaissance and the rebirth of German art. Napoleon I. kidnapping German Princes; his policy to "*dépayser*" the German Spirit. If German Princes help French Civilisation to triumph over that Spirit, their doom is sealed (42).

2.—The German Spirit of three centuries ago and its effects on European civilisation : e.g. in costume ; Dürer *v.* Leibnitz. Winckelmann, Lessing, Goethe and Schiller reaching back to the olden days, and across to Greece. The German "Jüngling" and the Princes' treachery ; they had lost all sense of solidarity through the heterogeneousness of the "Holy Roman Empire"; the Kaiser's sons had to learn 4 different languages, to be able to converse with his subjects ; the *Reich* like an inn where the guests make out the bill ; Vienna in the Romo-Spanish rut. Berlin's idea of Art, a French ballet or Italian opera. Goethe and Schiller only rescued by a *lesser* prince, the Weimar wonder. But the German "Jüngling" was not the man to need the "smiles of Princes" ; ousting the French despot (45). The Princes hug the leading-strings of France once more, and treat the German youth as "demagogues" and regicides. Founding of the *Burschenschaft* ; its high ideals for soul and body ; suppressed by frightened princes. Sole survival of German Spirit the Prussian Landwehr : Battle of Königgrätz ; French alarm. The Prussian victor over Austria has only to speak one word [i.e. unification of Germany] and a new power stands erect in history (49).

3.—A nation's artistic genius both dependent and non-dependent on its political life : the birth of great art-geniuses a mystery of Nature, but the *receptivity* of the nation lessened in times of lethargy. Goethe and Schiller were far in advance of the theatric technique of their time, but it was our duty to rightly study and digest their works, and thus prepare the field for Nature to sow afresh. The Princes gagged the Theatre, and bound it to French ballet and Italian opera : Weber punished for his songs of freedom. The most calculating wickedness could have done no worse, and no less horrible is the supposition that it sprang from mere trivial love of pleasure (52). Mdme de Stael found stamped on Germany the impress of Kant's philosophy ; what will the modern Frenchman find ? A philosophy of superficiality, bickerings and calumny, and a public fed by ignorant journalists who thrust materialism down its throat (54). German art to-day a mere hankering after Effect ; Literature, where not translated from the French, a trading on Germany's former great-ness : 'tis so easy, this "German." The Theatre and its disfigurement of our great poets—statues erected to Schiller to have done with him ; drawling recitation, from difficulty of following the prompter ; the "now-time" and "local" skits ; German gaucherie and imported cancan-dancers ; a Prussian nobleman and art-patron driving off with "Mdlle Rigolboche." Our blood-relations, Swedes, Danes and Dutch, turning to Paris for the originals of our counterfeits. The French visitor needs must sigh for home again (57).

4.—The Germans letting foreigners 'discover' their men of genius : a true German Policy would seek them out. The Federal spirit and its present make-believe of action : Turnvereins, Chambers of Deputies, and their impotence ; soon we shall have "*Deutschthum*" floated as a company, and a bourse-speculation on "German sturdiness" (60). No amount of Associa-tion can bring forth a genius, but it might make the nation acquainted with the works of genius ; that it does not now, is proved by present neglect of works of German masters of the past. One step from the region of power could alter this : as Prussia organised her army, so could German Princes give the lead to organisations in furtherance of Art. The universal aptitudes of the

German people only need an example, to unite them in the ennobling of public life; the Princes, in turn, need an example set them by one of themselves (63).

5.—Example set by Bavarian Kings: Ludwig I. and the plastic arts—Munich masters summoned to adorn the capitals of other princes; but a broader culture of the people was still lacking, and therefore this revival soon died down. Maximilian II., longing for the re-unification of Germany, took the first step toward that end by the encouragement of learning and literature; his noblest task, the Maximilianeum—a unique school for teaching the teachers *comprehensive* culture, and thus preparing the people's mind for *receiving* Art —left unachieved (65). Maximilian recognised the onesidedness of bestowing all one's favour on the plastic arts and leaving the Folk uncultured, but he passed over the *drama*, the Folk's true cultivator. He furthered belles lettres and literary poetry; but his great-hearted efforts were here doomed to plainest failure, since the chain of gifted epigones had come to end with Platen's death; nothing remained but imitators of Heine's cynicism, apostles of " harmlessness," and copiers of Byron (68).

6.—No branch of art can truly flourish till the Theatre's all-powerful aid shall have been recognised : a dæmonic abyss of possibilities, the highest as the lowest; the whole man set in terrifying nakedness before himself, here *living* what lies beyond all possibility of his personal experience. Different nations' treatment of the Theatre; the wizards of Tone pouring balm of heaven's melody into the gaping wounds of man. Banish the kindly spirits and ye leave the field, where Gods had wandered, to the filthiest spawn of Hell (71). This Theatre despised, save for a gala-show, and ye wonder that Art will not advance ! Yet great poets have always done their greatest in the Drama. To crown the work begun by two noble princes, we invoke the example of their august heir, Ludwig II. (73).

7.—Reason for retaining title " German Art and German Policy " for remaining chapters. Two chief epochs in European art. Plastic art as influenced by the Theatre; Phidias the junior contemporary of Æschylus. Italian Renaissance and Italian Music. Drama reborn elsewhere from Spirit of the Folk; Calderon and Shakespeare. Its urging toward the Theatre was the sole true progress in all the evolutionary march of reborn Art ; now that all the artistic possibilities for a higher drama are won, would ye keep the Theatre an idle pastime ? (75). Histrionic art, the bent-to-*imitation* and bent-to-*interpretation*; artists and their models; the poet crystallising abstractions; artistic illusion and laws of technique. The Mime as the model set in action ; the mere machinery sets the crowd agape. The "theatrical" passing into every department of art, of life, of manners (79).

8.—Mime to Poet as monkey to man [in Darwinian sense]. Nature's secret in preferring ape to elephant or dog, for her last step in evolution : from pedant no poet—from Russian privy-councillor no ballerina. States and Religions crumble, but Art eternally resurgent. Realism and Idealism both founded on Nature : the poet selects one principal attribute of the object, it being impossible to shew its every facet ; matter-of-fact-ness of the mime, but he is Nature's link through which that absolutely realistic Mother of all Being incites the Ideal within us; the realistic mime revealing undreamt possibilities to the idealistic poet (82). Realism of the French stage and Voltaire's definition of his countrymen as a cross between ape and tiger; Richelieu dancing before the French Queen; his vengeance on her laughter. Life conventionalised in France, and every Frenchman a good comedian; but no stage-piece of ideal trend in all their drama. Versailles, Louis XIV., and God addressed with courtier's *Vous* (83). Only through a glance at the Ideal does man outstep the circle drawn by Nature. But the "tiger" could rebel; French Revolution; Marat the tiger, and Napoleon the tiger-tamer. French army-discipline and theatrical *Gloire* (84). The French character has no less natural disposition to culture of the Purely-human than other nations, but its vanity and light-mindedness fostered by this theatrical display (85).

9.—Schiller and the "Gallic spring": the German tempo the *Andante*, the walk. Thus Goethe, from Götz, reached Egmont: strength and grace combined. Were Religion to vanish from this earth, Goethe's "Ever-womanly" would suffice to keep alive its memory. Goethe as much an idealist as Schiller. Never has a friend of man done for a neglected people what Schiller did for the German Theatre, teaching it to advance through realism of the burgher-play to realms of the Idea (88). *Don Carlos* and the Sublime; in what language of the world shall we find such noble thoughts so humanly expressed? Schiller had reached the swing of the *Allegro*; but he and Goethe let their players practise first a few orthodox French pieces, to teach them the benefit of artistic Culture too, before steering to the German Theatre's ideal haven (90.) A passion for the theatre seized and ennobled every class, age and youth. But the worm of Reaction already gnawing both at Politics and Art. Kotzebue, annoyed by the glory of the gods, imports melodrama, the Abject and the "suggestive." His murder by Sand, a student in the old-German gown, for being a "corrupter of German youth." But the German Theatre belongs to Kotzebue's spiritual heirs (93).

10.—Former good deeds of German princes and nobles, in furtherance of the Theatre: strolling players taken into pay of Courts; Joseph II., the Duke of Weimar, Goethe and Iffland. But Kotzebue had been murdered: "away with the German lumber"; a royal page installed as Intendant, ruling Dresden theatre for quarter of a century. Here everything was Instinct. One fed the mime with sugarplums, and let the poet starve: all the actor's bad propensities fostered; latest stage-fashions imported from Paris; unwieldiness of repertoire, and daily performances (96). Court-theatres, finance, and spectre of the subscribers. A foreign ambassador, or the monarch, wishing to taste the Classics; so Sophocles & Co. are added to the list; Schiller and Goethe, too; but they're not easy to 'play to the prompter.' The 'wings' reserved for the aristocracy, but their scandal the chief topic of the town (98). Goethe deplored the improvement of the universities, as it reduced the supply of partly *educated* recruits for the stage: were he alive, he would never allow *Faust* to be even printed. Two summits of German genius: *Tell* and *Faust*; their operatic parodies (101).

11.—Balzac and the ghastly details cloaked by French Culture; Germans concealing their sterling character beneath theatrical trappings borrowed from Paris. Plastic artists without a living model; literature-poets *condescending* to the stage with bad counterfeits of French goods, and demanding protective duties ; musicians doing ditto ; the public taste corrupted (105). And how stands the School to the Theatre ? Fruitful relations in time of Lessing and the Humanists ; Goethe and his praises of Hans Sachs ; importance of the Classics ; *Bride of Messina,* teachers and pupils. Then was shewn what *German* is—the thing one does for its own sake and no personal end : none but a great nation, confiding with tranquil stateliness in its unshakable might, can mature this principle and bring it into application for good of all the world (108).

12.—The Church upbraids the State for its utilitarian education of the people ; the State replies by accusing the Church of merely trying to found a hierarchy and throw a helpless population on the State for shelter and support. Polytechnic and Folk-Schools ; classical education tabooed and left to the well-to-do. Good work done in schools by Jesuits, down to French Revolution (110). A German art-revival must needs benefit the Church by its effect on the *shape* in which she appeals to the burgher's senses : Michael Angelo, Palestrina, Goethe's Mater Gloriosa, Schiller's last Act of *Maria Stuart,* and the tinsel rites of modern Church. *Wilhelm Meister* and mysteries of the Sanctuary of Sorrow : here is a lesson for both School and Church. Re-unification of Christian creeds, as against a Germany finally divided into Protestant Prussia and Catholic Austria (114).

13.—The State cannot be brought directly into play for Art, for the State represents the law of Expedience, of utilitarianism. The blunder in this Expedience was the attempt to organise it from *above,* as in Prussia : Frederick the Great and his State-ideal ; officialdom grown so rigid that it is regarded by Throne and Folk as the State itself. But signs of awakening in almost every German land, and when the State is finally built up from *below,* the King-hood will form its fitting crown (116). The King's sphere the ideal, the State's the realistic ; King alone has positive, active freedom, and exercises it in his Grace and prerogative of Pardon—a safeguard against miscarriage of human equity. This freedom can dwell in none but a legitimate prince, the usurper being always in anxiety for his hard-fought personal interests (119). The King draws into his sphere of Grace the citizen whose merits are beyond the normal duty to State. The conferring of an order on a soldier ennobles his whole regiment : these orders should be fused into one comprehensive Order, as in France, but with the vitality of an active fellowship pledged to the highest ends. Thus the King would be surrounded by a body of like-minded men, Emeriti, set free from law of expedience, to fulfil his ideal aims for raising of the desolated spirit of Art (122).

14.—The corruption of the Theatre has proceeded from the Princes' and nobles' error, a misunderstanding of the German Spirit. The nobles, having gradually lost their political privileges, should set an example to justify the esteem in which the burgher still regards their social station : a league of honour, recruited by fresh members raised by the King to his sphere of Grace, to devote themselves to ends beyond the common law of utility (125). How-ever much State-organisations may remove all human distress and restore the world to moral order, a field will always stay open to the energy of these Exempt. The burgher has no time to devote to Literature and Art, and seeks an easy entertainment—at the theatre : let that Theatre be raised from the need of speculating on the public's curiosity, make it the meeting-place of the spiritual and moral forces of a people and of its leading minds, and this sphere of Grace will have found one principal sphere of action (128).

15.—To bring these various forces into harmonious play the stimulus must come from the King, the Royal example. The pursuit of the Beautiful should proceed side by side with the Useful, not wait till that is perfected, i.e. for ever : the one the care of the King and his peers, the other the care of State and municipal bodies ; illustration of the aqueduct and art-building. Court-theatres foreshadow this relation of the King to his Folk, but their manage-ment is largely commercial : the Civil List and endowment of the Theatre (131). Improve the character of performances, reduce their number, still there will remain the need of a theatre *beyond the common*, uninfluenced by industrial considerations, a true 'model' for standardising German Style, where the works of great German masters may be rendered in perfect harmony with their spirit (133). Influence of this *example* on German Art, Poetry, Life itself.—Prussia now claims a " German calling " : what is Bavaria's ? To become a model *German* State, recognising that beyond all ends of utility there lies a high Ideal. This is the German Spirit ; an example to the world (135).

APPENDICES TO "GERMAN ART AND GERMAN POLICY":—

(*a*) *Vaterlandsverein Speech.*—The drift of our Republican efforts : Extinc-tion of aristocratism, useless court-offices and court-parade ; *one* Chamber ; manhood suffrage ; Landwehr ; one free Folk. Then shall we begin in earnest : liberation from bondage to Money, division of labour and exchange of products ; *not* Communism and equal division of property and earnings ; give no *alms*, but acknowledge rights of Man ; found colonies, beget and bring up " children like the gods " ; German freedom and gentleness shall light and warm the world (140). Let the King be the first and truest Republican of all ; it would be no *sacrifice* to so noble a prince, to lose the tinsel of a Court and ensure his people's love. Abolish Monarchy, but emancipate the Kinghood. No other King in Europe so fit as ours to effect this reconciliation : that is the Man of Providence (143). Let the King declare Saxony a Free State ; let us, in turn, invest the House of Wettin in perpetuity with the highest executive power : that oath would never be broken, since we had sworn it freely. Constitutional Monarchy a contradiction in terms : let the King be First of his Folk, Freest of the Free ! Thus would the historic cycle of Germanic Kinghood's evolution have rounded back upon itself. One signature alone required, to such a petition—the King's (145).

(*b*) *Letter to von Lüttichau.*—The right accorded nowadays to even the most uneducated to debate questions of State : the more need for educated men to do so. Reasons for joining the political Club, and delivering speech. According to present notions, no crime in saying that Republic is best form of State : were the Court-survivals of an earlier age done away with, the discontent now fastening on the King's own person would disappear. Enthusiasm that greeted my eulogy of the King's virtues ; but even this has won me enemies. That might well be indifferent to me, but not that the

King himself should misunderstand me, however unpractical he may think my suggestion. An evil time is approaching. If my step has *only* wounded, not helped to reconcile, I heartily crave forgiveness (148).

WHAT IS GERMAN?

History of M.S. for the article.—Meaning of "deutsch"; applies to those peoples who remained faithful to the fatherland and mother-tongue (152). Curiously enough, the memory of German glory is always attached to a period fatal to the German nature, when the Germans ruled over non-Germanic peoples; with the fall of outer political might began the real development of genuine German qualities (154). The Reformation contrasted with German evaluation of the Antique: had Germany's ruler, Charles V., been guided by the German Spirit, the Christian Church might then have been strengthened and re-knit; none but a universal religion is Religion in truth (157). Owing to the German's phlegma and fantasticism, gradual invasion of the Jew, usurping whole range of German public life and travestying the German spirit (159). Characteristics of genuine German Spirit: its openmindedness and introspection, conservatism and assimilation, love of intellectual liberty and refusal to trim its sails to worldly profit (161). Thirty Years' War decimated the nation, and dressed the remnant in French costume, but the German spirit survived: its sanctuary was Music; Bach as forerunner of Goethe. The *Beautiful and Noble not for profit, nor even Fame*—that is German, and alone can lead to German greatness (163). Let its Princes shew the German Folk they belong to it in this sense: it is high time, for fear the German spirit vanish again from the world, out of sheer inertia, and yield place to the Judaic. Franco-Judaico-German demagogues and Revolution of 1848: the genuine German represented by a race of men quite alien to him. German nation now being taught by blatant mediocrities to imagine it *is* already something great and does not need to first *become* it (167).

Experiences since 1865: the Franco-German War, courage of Bismarck and the army; Liedertafel songs. Return of the victorious troops. I offer to compose music in celebration of our fallen heroes; "upon so joyful an occasion we desire no painful impressions." *Kaisermarsch* proposed for the march past: declined; let it fit the *concert-room* as best it may. New Coinage, Free Trade, and "Reichs-broker"; I surrender my "lease of the German Spirit," for I no longer (1878) can read the meaning of the new German Reich. Will some political writer enlighten us (169).

A MUSIC-SCHOOL FOR MUNICH.

By the King's desire. "Conservatorium" means an institution for "conserving" the classic *style* of a ripe stage in Art's development; Naples, Milan, Paris; such a style unknown at German art-institutes. Pride in our great masters not justified by the manner in which we perform their works: Italian Opera imported *en bloc*, French Opera mangled by our singers; in our opera-houses we badly copy and distort the Foreign (175). Oh, we perform Gluck and Mozart, too; but how? Those works require the old Italian style of singing, lost even in Italy itself; we Germans have, nowadays at least, no

Style at all; nowhere a *correct* performance, and Concert attempts to improve the public's taste always undone by the corrupting influence of haphazard Opera. In desperate situations abstract theory not of the slightest use; a practical example needed—model performances of *original* German works (178). The King's consent to a provisional theatre being built for the *Ring*, and commission to choose an exceptional company from best singers at German opera-houses; but choice is so limited that for most of the rôles in that drama the proper artists cannot possibly be found (180). Necessity of founding an efficient Singing-school: restore Munich Conservatorium to its original basis, and don't extend its functions till it can teach Dramatic singing. The German's difficulty arises chiefly from nature of his speech: we must practise Italian singing, to acquire euphony, but must discover for ourselves a mode to suit peculiarities of our native tongue, a tongue so fitted for *dramatic* art. The German, his 'reflective' culture and power of assimilating the best of what is foreign (184). The singer must also be a sound *musician* : study of Harmony and analysis of Composition. Elocution and applied gymnastics indispensable ; hitherto quite neglected, the German singer himself not knowing what he is saying ; one's dealings with him often a positively sickening pain (186). The musician, whether composer or what not, should have elementary instruction in singing, as Human Voice the basis of all music ; he also should take part in, and be taught to *judge*, good performances : the theory of Composition to be relegated to private tuition. Instruction at our Munich Music-school must be practical : the workshop of the master is the true school for the chosen pupil (188).

German instrumental executants far better than our singers. Instl technique not to be taught in classes : the 'rendering' is our business. How stands this in Concert-world ? Origin of Subscription-concerts ; their crowded halls and family-gatherings ; a docile audience. Hypocrisy of our Classical cult : where is the authentic tradition of these pietists ? Does it come to our conductors of itself? (192). Mozart's hurried scoring of his symphonies, scanty marks of expression supplemented by his *vivâ voce* instructions at rehearsal ; *singing* quality of his themes ; played sleekly, how much of the true Mozart do we get? A soulless pen-music, nothing more (194). Beethoven's scores certainly more minutely notated than Mozart's, but his thematism far more complex, and his orchestration, owing to his deafness, does not fully represent his thought : the closest, most careful study required at rehearsal—Paris Conservatoire and Ninth Symphony. But, not content with leaving these nearest problems unsolved, our German conductors attempt the works of Bach, that most stupendous riddle of all time : here no tradition could possibly avail, for Bach was never given the means for an adequate performance of his concerted works ; their correct rendering will be the last outcome of a true artistic culture (196).

The School to merely lay down lines of instruction, leaving technique to private tuition : the higher mode of *Rendering* will best be taught at the pfte —this to be at the School itself ; relation of Sonata to Symphony. This higher pfte course both to train private teachers, thus advancing art in the home, and to train future orchestral and choral conductors to judge form and spirit of larger works (199). To crown our purely-musical efforts we must have concerted rehearsals by the pupils : selection and sequence of the programme a matter for earnest thought—medley at our best-famed concerts; a graduated progress needed from earlier to more recent works. Finally public performances by the School; the public's instinctive Feeling will teach us whether our choice and execution are right (202).

Not to have our work undone by the opera-houses, we should have to exert an influence on the Theatre: decline of the recited Play in Germany since Goethe and Schiller; their dramas were in advance of German actor's evolution; a Stage-school is needed; the public, already having classical works set before it, would certainly prefer them *correctly* rendered. Difficulties in way of possessing ourselves of this influence (206).

From theory to practice.—A Royal Commission to overcome personal obstacles in way of administrative changes.—Technical laws for learning every instrument have been perfected, but technique of human voice as yet a positive enigma; therefore not till we have succeeded in establishing a sound school of Singing can we advance to further developments. When this effected the master of dramatic declamation might be made Director of Stage-school, with a really cultured staff to teach pianoforte *expression*—no special *classes* needed for other instruments (209). Private teachers to be affiliated with School; the Director of any particular department to hand over the pupil to private teachers, periodically examining their proficiency, and correcting mode of tuition if need be; this to be supplemented by rehearsals of larger works in common. Four Directors: of Song, Stage, Pfte-playing, and Orchestra, each with an under-master (212). Our School, "conserving" classic style of rendering for works of the past, would offer stimulus and media to creative artists of the present; absence of these media has always been a drag on German genius. In *something* each German is akin to our great masters; this something needs to be developed and enlightened; masterworks accepted on Authority—as with conversion of the heathen—to be brought home to the nation's heart by lifelike rendering, as in Paris, and then the heritage of our great masters will bear fruit for future of art (217). A journal to be founded by School, to counteract influence of flippant journalistic criticism and form a channel between artists and public (218). The School and works of new composers: ephemeral works, of mannerism etc., we must leave alone; from the Folk's-theatre we may borrow many a refreshing hint; but new *original* works by national creative masters are what we need. For these a prize to be offered and kept perpetually open: that prize the work's performance at proposed model Festival-theatre; an example to the world, a monument to German Art. *This* is what the King desires (222).

The author's previous suggestions of reform: Dresden, Zurich, Weimar, Vienna; all unheeded. The unknown "German Prince"; so far as present means permit, the present broader plan is secured fulfilment by that longed-for Prince's patronage (224).

LUDWIG SCHNORR OF CAROLSFELD.

Reports of Schnorr's talent in 1856 etc.; reluctance to meet him, lest his obesity should destroy artistic illusion. *Tristan* projects at Carlsruhe fall through; secret visit to *Lohengrin* there; the "youthful Hercules" the God-sent hero of the legend: instantaneous impression, as with Schröder-Devrient.

Interview; scarcely a serious word needed. Biebrich on the Rhine: home recitals of *Ring* and *Tristan* with Schnorr and Bülow; Schnorr's one doubt, as to meaning of a passage, really a mere question of tempo; the physical exertion he made light of, for spiritual understanding gave strength to overcome material difficulty (230). Schnorr engaged for *Tristan* at Munich in 1865; preliminary "guest"-rôle as Tannhäuser: that character's *utmost energy, of transport alike and despair*; prompting Schnorr on the boards; the Venus-scene and magic trance in act i. His acting opened new insight into my own creation: that fills one with a certain awe, and prescribes, in place of praise, a reverent silence (232). Neither Kean nor Ludwig Devrient in *Lear* could have exceeded Schnorr's power in act iii.: dæmonic energy; the audience overwhelmed, but mostly stupefied; a friend's verdict, "no right to get Tannhäuser performed my way, as the public is quite satisfied with the old" (233). Working together for an artistic deed: *Tristan* rehearsals at Munich; Schnorr seizes each nuance, every hidden allusion at once; never was there such complete accord between author and performer. Act iii.: motionless upon my chair, with eyes averted; my ideal fulfilled; no after-discussion, save in jest. The complex *score* will make clear this fleeting miracle of histrionic art; the orchestra seemed part and parcel of the singer. To enrol this achievement in ordinary repertoire appeared a sacrilege (236). Only *before* the performances was Schnorr in agitation; after each fresh success his carriage more vigorous than ever—thus silencing charge of "overtaxing the voice." With Beethoven a new era of musical declamation began; our singing-masters must adopt new methods of voice-training to fulfil its demands; a *spiritual mastery of the task*; to be taught by example. Here one might both teach and learn (239). Our isolation: chasm between this New and the old, to be bridged by patient effort to pave a highway for the needful comrades in our art. Schnorr to be freed from drudgery of Opera and become master of our School. My own humiliations as "opera composer" &c., Schnorr's as "tenor," Liszt's as "pianoforte-player." Schnorr's complaints of Munich stage-management; stage-draughts and last act of *Tristan*. As Eric in *Dutchman* (241). Prosaic and hostile surroundings. Last glorious evening, extracts from *Ring* &c. as concert for King: "between this heavenly King and you, I too shall turn to something splendid." Not farewell, but simply good-night. Death after brief illness; be-bannered Dresden and the German Singers' Festival, but "*the* singer has gone" (243).

NOTICES.

INTRODUCTION.—Polemical nature of following articles a cheerless contrast; but the fact of being compelled to write them supplies answer to question of the practical outcome of foregoing proposals. Hostility at Munich forced me into arena of Daily Press; disgust at the company in which I found myself there; indignation of foes, dismay of friends (249). Yet I took more thought for victory of my *idea* than for damaging my foes. *Judaism in Music* and heterogeneous rejoinders: "the Jews applaud my operas"; "Germanic Christians' day is over, and future belongs to Judaic Germans." Notice into which the pamphlet unintentionally brought my other writings; a creative

artist getting *his* word on Art ; this perhaps not the least serviceable gift conferred on me by Fate (252).

I.—W. H. RIEHL.—Survivals of the old German spirit, and thoroughgoing
research ; Jakob and Wilhelm Grimm turned into laughing-stocks at theatre,
while the fatuous pedant is left unmocked ! (254). The German in petty
circumstances carving his idyll from the only world he knows ; so far so good,
but if he waxes wroth and threatens ? Ridiculous indeed. "I want my Philistine": Riehl's hazardous partiality for that genus (256). Critic as "poet":
virtues of "harmlessness," but not if it stealthily doubles its self-advertising
fist; the "High School of Humility," an excellent title which should have been
given to Riehl's whole book (258). But Riehl has recently played truant and
worked all kinds of paltry mischief: Beethoven's C-minor and the musical
Tobacco Parliament ; counsel to be most mistrustful of all great things !
"Naivety" versus "Reflection"; Schiller opposed it to the "Sentimental."
Lectures on the new basis, terrifying an innocent public. "Composer for the
house," but he forgot his "naivety" in the task : God help him (260).

II.—FERDINAND HILLER.—Gulf between genius and craftsman : the demigod and the semi-man ; these second-rate musicians deem themselves sole
proprietors of Music. One reason lies in peculiar selection by Committees and
Intendants of their Kapellmeisters &c.—local "fame" a *sine qua non* (263).
Hiller's zigzag after Fame on grander scale ; Cologne Music-school and newspaper ; Prof. Bischoff and a would-be Nether-Rhenish pope ; local mono-
polists' fury at Liszt's being chosen to conduct Aachen Festival of 1857 ; Herr
M. H. and "rout of the Corybantes" (265). One may say these things entre
nous, even write them in private intercourse by letter ; but to publish them !
Fury evidently mistaken by the Jews for Courage. Advice to the Cologne
Falstaff and his followers : parrot no untruths, behave as men of sense, not
geniuses ; let Hiller be praised for his playing, agreeable ways &c.; but "immortality"! Hiller's book mere feuilleton-gossip ; choice brands smoked with
Rossini (268).

III.—ROSSINI.—Reported witticism "sauce without the fish" as applied to
Wagner's music ; Rossini's public letter of denial, suppressed by every other
journal. Visit to him : "*J'avais de la faculté,*" but Italy in his youth was no
place for earnestness (270). Fresh attempts of R.'s motley entourage to breed
discord between us two ; Liszt suggests a second visit, but "I remained averse
to giving occasion for erroneous interpretations"; the *Signale* publishes
imaginary account of such a visit, with a second repartee (272). Rossini
himself the slandered party ; nothing falser than to brand him as a flippant
wag, on one hand, and raise him to rank of art's heroes on the other ;
influence of environment upon the artist. "My veneration for the departed
master" ; the "recollection"-hunters strewing ribald jests, in lieu of flowers,
upon an open grave (274).

IV.—E. DEVRIENT.—"*Recollections of Mendelssohn.*" Twenty-one years
late, yet hurriedly prepared ! The reason ? Will not too curiously inquire.
Eagerness to prove Mendelssohn's gift for *dramatic* composition and E. D.'s
predestination as his librettist. Marx traduced, his widow's dignified rejoinder
(276). The book's literary style : word-dockings, improper use of terms,
"sempstress and hodman's" German ; an "expanded personnel," "Felix

went out with the colour," an "energy" not discovered by Mendelssohn's executors, "shortening of two English Musicians," Marx's "awkwardly-behaved boots and pantaloons." Ill results of a Theatre-director reading nothing but theatrical journals inspired by himself (283). Commas, colons, "and" &c. And this all has been printed and issued by a publisher of standing, reviewed and passed by all the world! Contrast of Mendelssohn's own letters in the book, a simple, quite supportable German; that the brilliant musician could find no better author for a long-proposed libretto gives a disappointing idea of the vaunted atmosphere surrounding Fortune's darling. Lesson as to our general state of culture; the "Meister Devrient"; a good actor *off* the stage; the "weeny thing called Cinnabar" and the single hair that holds D.'s magic (288).

ABOUT CONDUCTING.

Not a "system," but a mere record of some personal experiences. Importance to composer of his work being *correctly* set before the public. Who and what are our Conductors? Carelessness in their selection has increased in direct ratio with difficulty of their task. Old style of Kapellmeister, sound, sure, despotic and gruff; but the ancient usage in manning of orchestra was bound at last to unfit them for dealing with modern complex music; bandsmen advancing by seniority to first desks, too few 'strings' for 'wind,' second violins, violas and 'celli neglected (293). New style, (a) appointed by personal favour, lady-in-waiting to a princess &c.—utterly unable to keep their men in hand; (b) appointed by special summons, to wake up the regular home-grown Kapellmeister and bring out an opera in a fortnight; (c) "big-wigs" drawn from the Concert-room—this includes the "elegant" variety, from school of Mendelssohn—they have really done much good in attending to *details* of rendering, but no energy, no sense of the *whole*, out of touch with the *German* art-ideal, and consciously filling an interregnum (296). Meyerbeer and Mendelssohn faced with obstacles, but those were just their duty to remove; they had everything in their favour, save force of character. What shall their natty silhouettes set right? No hope from that quarter: striking an alliance with the virtuoso, who, again, has really done much to improve orchestral technique. Had both but had the one thing lacking! But they dislike the stage, though it was a great dramatic singer, Schröder-Devrient, who gave me my best hints for rendering of Beethoven's instrumental music; bred in Concert-room, they abide by its traditions (299).

Youthful recollections: scores that seemed so full of life when reading or at the pfte, I scarce recognised when publicly performed by orchestra; Gewandhaus Concerts at last drove me away from Beethoven for a while; Paris Conservatoire's inimitable playing of Ninth Symphony removed the scales from my eyes in '39. Yet Habeneck no genius: by patient rehearsals for three years he and his band had learned to recognise Beethoven's *melos*, and his orchestra *sang* it—that was the secret; H. a conductor of good old style, he was master and his men obeyed him (301). Contrast with Dresden and Philharmonic orchestras; initiation into mysteries of Spirit; these musicians solved the problem by diligence and *technique*, and found the tempo through rightly seizing the melos—the two are inseparable. Our conductors know nothing of Song ; their idea of music a cross between syntax, arithmetic and gymnastics (303).

Conductor's choice of *tempo* tells us whether he understands the piece ; earlier masters gave merest general indications in their scores, and metronomic signs have not saved my own earlier operas from total bungling—I gave them up, but German notation confuses these conductors just as much ! How did these four-footed beings jump from their village-churches to opera-house ? Dragging not the fault of modern "elegants" ; Mendelssohn's maxim of "gliding over the ground," its consequences with Philh. orchestra in London, the sins of Rendering swamped beneath the deluge ; Mr. Potter's timidity, and gratitude for his Andante (307). Lack of feeling for right tempo illustrated by *Menuetto* of Eighth Sym., its difference from Haydn's, generally scampered and becomes a torture ; a Dresden incident and Mendelssohn's blissful ignorance (310).

Hiller and this *Tempo di Menuetto* : a " slip of memory," but it would have been rank folly to alter tempo between rehearsal and performance, as the *mode of rendering* must also be altered. Voice of Beethoven from the grave : " Hold my fermate long and terribly " ; how is this to be done with our present style of forte ? We have neither a *true forte* nor a *true piano*, no balance in power of wind and strings, no *even strength of tone* ; this to be learnt from first-rate singers (313). Hushed and strong-held tone the poles of orchestral dynamics. The preponderance of legato Tone or figured motion determines the tempo ; Adagio the embodiment of legato tone and unit of all measurement of musical time ; Andante and Allegro its gradual refraction into Rhythmic motion—illustration from third movement of Ninth Sym. (316).

Distinction between Mozart's 'naïve' and Beethoven's 'sentimental' Allegro. *Figaro* and *Don Juan* overtures ; as the pure Adagio can never be taken slow enough, so this unadulterated Allegro can scarcely be taken fast enough ; simple play of forte and piano, stock phrases etc.—for it has no desire to chain us by a cantilena, but to plunge us into tumult by its rapid motion (318). How ever could first movement of Eroica be played in strict tempo of a Mozartian overture-Allegro ? Yet our " classical " conductors do it, since they know nothing about *modifying* tempo (320). Proper mode of rendering music of Beethoven, and his next of kin, illustrated by examples : variation-form and its dissimilar parts welded into a whole in last movement of Eroica—needing most varied interpretation ; Kreutzer Sonata ; Quartet op. 131 and its radiant vision rising from depths of brooding memory, but "classical" performers treat it as a joke and take their merry way (324).

Older musicians once shook their heads at Eroica, and it has won most of its present popularity through private study, chiefly at pfte : its irresistible force. Had Fate but left it to the mercies of our Kapellmeisters ! (325). *Freischütz*-overture played oftener than any work in Germany, but always done trivially to death. Invited to conduct it at Vienna, I surprise the band by total change of rendering—support of a veteran 'cellist and Weber's widow, at Dresden : introductory adagio *not* an Andante, its horns must *not* bray out the dreamy forest-fantasie ; free rein to headlong passion of Allegro's first theme, but tempo *moderated* for gentler second theme—analogy of *Oberon*-overture; resumption of velocity with subsequent fortissimo, and difficulty of adjusting tempo to the more succinct renewal of contest between the two chief themes; gloriously held chords of C and mighty silences; second theme now raised to a pæan, but still subdued in tempo; vulgarity of circus-like galloping of close of overtures, though intended in some works as *Leonora*-overture—but here the effect is mostly discounted by our conductors, unless the band is to indulge in an excess to which no genuine work of art should ever be exposed (330). Success of performance, people said they never really knew the overture before; the Vienna Kapellmeister taking it "Wagnerish." Yet this a *whole* concession, a *half* once made by Reissiger with a mezzoforte in last movement of Seventh Sym.; the Lobe-Bernsdorf "eternal laws of truth." *Egmont*-overture at Munich, its customary *pas de deux*; Bülow's restoration and its effect on the Intendance, "things turned inside out" (333). Andante of Mozart's G-minor Sym. at Odeon-concerts; angels' wings become bobwigs, and bâton a brazen pigtail; oh for some one to buy me off!—but everyone delighted with the "Mozartian treat." *Tannhäuser* at Munich, poor Schnorr compelled to give his 'narration' in waltz-time; my protest, unpleasantness; martyrs of pure Classical Music and a gospel-critic's sonnets (336).

Possible objection to *modification of tempo* that it opens a door to whims of every self-conceited time-beater; but this only testifies to incapacity of our leading musicians, for why have they not set the right *example* to lesser men? Secret of opposition lies deeper: mere laziness, kindling under circumstances to aggressive action. Halo of "Chaste German Art," and alliance between conductors of old and new style to stave off change (339). These *new* conductors of a different tribe to the old, they bring their Polish in their pockets as the banker his Capital; as the Jews have always held aloof from our manual work, so these new conductors have never risen from the ranks; sheer dislike of hard labour. Even Mendelssohn shewed a certain constraint in presence of our German art-life; no spontaneousness at bottom of this pseudo-culture; cloaking one's nature instead of unfolding it (341). "Polish" never goes deep into anything, and takes the most stupendous as a thing of course; its "classicity" a sickly shuffling-off the earnestness and awe of Being. Analogy of Tannhäuser-ballet in Paris—a code of behaviour dictated by dread of betraying the Semitic accent; objectionable racial attributes studiously put out of sight (343). And the German's *fire* is to be put out for sake of these gentry? So it seems at our Conservatories; fear of falling into the Drastic; "above all no Effect." Hiller's pretty playing of a fugue of Bach's, then Liszt revealing the whole Bach by one fugue; difference between study and revelation. Liszt and Bülow alone can play the true great Beethoven, for this Musical Temperance-Union is shocked by a whole-limbed male (346). How they entangled Schumann and finally made his weakest side an oriflamme for the new communion; if the public doesn't like it, it is told there's a peculiar beauty in the neutral, and the adequately-rendered Schumann is ranked with the inadequately-rendered Beethoven. Eunuchs of musical Chastity. Most of them compose quite well; Brahms the respectable figure of a wooden Saint (348). Musical "*Muckers*," their grades and religious exercises; temptation wooed to be resisted, and authors of operatic failures ranking as

Saints par excellence; a prudish School of Abstinence (350). Their sterility can scarcely be a qualification for presiding over so complex a thing as Opera; "forgive them! they know not what they do "; solemn concert-conductors affecting a sprightly mien in Opera. If ever an operatic performance turns out well, it is due entirely to artistic instinct of singers and band; yet the Kapell-meister invariably regarded as backbone of the whole, applauded and distin-guished (353). My right to criticise this Conducting: the two spirits, of Concert-room and Opera ineptitude, join hands in treatment of my operas; preludes and their tempo dragged or rushed, or both. Illustration, *Die Meistersinger* prelude: elasticity of 4/4 time, its modification to suit diverse themes and combinations; first performance at Leipzig privately, the same bandsmen under Reinecke get it hissed by Gewandhaus audience—when told *what beat* he took, the thing was clear to me (357). Demurely squaring out the prelude in four crotchets, applying this principle to the whole work itself; mutilation and cuts; applause and outward success, but no more will I attend a performance of my works (360). The fatality with false orchestral parts of *Figaro*: are these conductors musicians? If not, what *are* they? Arithmetic, but no musical feeling. Let them have a school to teach them by rule-of-three (362). Such a "High School for Music" seems already under way; luckily a master of (Liszt's) *style*, Joachim, chosen for its chief; I hold by the man who gives us something from his heart. But how is the High School to be conducted from the high stool of the first fiddler? Like Mephistopheles with "the fair," I prefer fiddlers "in the plural." Joachim awaiting a new Messiah of Music; he may hope not to be crucified by the *Jews* (364).

THREE POEMS:

Rheingold.—On the Completion of Siegfried.—August 25th 1870.—(368).

INDEX

As in previous volumes, the figures denoting tens and hundreds are not *epeated* for one and the same reference unless the numbers run into a fresh line of type. Certain references will be found enclosed in brackets, the object being to distinguish my own footnotes &c. from the author's text.—W. A. E.

A.

Aachen, 265.
Abject, the, 92, 4, 7, 100, 2.
Abnormal, 362.
Above and Below, 40, 115, 6, 7, 35, 295.
Abraham offering up Isaac, 284.
Absolute Music, 353.
Abstinence, School of, 346, 9, 50.
Abstract Reason, 8.
Abstractions, 76, 8, 178, 97, 303; crystallising, 77.
Absurdity, 233, 352. See Ridiculous.
Abyss, a dæmonic, 69-71.
Academy of Arts and Sciences, Berlin, 362. See French, Sing.
Accelerando, 322, 8, 9; relation to crescendo, 324.
Accent : Melodic, 193, 333; Reciting, 89; Singing, 182, 298.
Accentuation : Semitic, 343; Vulgar, 328.
Accidental, the, 76, 80, 160, 321.
Acoustics, 179.
Acting, its importance for Singers, 180, 5, 209, 39.
Acting off the stage, 83, 288.
Actors prattling about Art, 81, 98; social standing of, 93, 5, 8. See German, Mime &c.
Actress and her lover, 98, cf. 57.
Actuality, 33, 323.
Acumen, critical, xi.
Adagio, 304, 8, 12, 4, 25; refraction of, 315, 6. See Allegro.
Adaptations, German, 56, 160, 5.
Advice, a piece of, 267-8.
(Æginetan marbles, 74).
Æschylus, 70, 4, 5, 204.

Æsthetes, 87, 98, 119, 201, 17, 303, 342 ; delirium of, 256.
Æsthetics, 76, 81, 6, 107, 11, 3, 28, 155, 6, 63, 200, 317, 52.
Affectation, 255.
Aggressive mediocrities, 337, 46.
Agitators, alien, 166.
Aim, artistic, 232 ; aims, ix, 5, see Tendence.
Aimfulness, see *Zweckmässigkeit*.
Airs and graces, 101, 62, 344.
Akin, 34, 43, 213, 8.
Alexandrines (metre), 70.
Aliens, see Foreign element.
Alla breve, 305, 17, 8, 35, 55, 8, 9.
Allegory, 282 ; sacred, 27.
Allegretto scherzando, 308, 9.
Allegro, 304, 16-7 ; and Adagio, 308, 312, 4, 6, 21, 3, 7 ; and Andante, 89, 355 ; Beethovenian, 318-9, 323, 9 ; Maëstoso, 354 ; Mozartian, 318, 25 ; Passionate, 327 ; Presto, 307, 17, 8, 29.
Allgemeine Zeitung (viii et seq), 68, (150), 163, (246), 250, 60, 5, 7, 305.
Alliance, artistic, 237, 97 ; a distasteful, 339.
" Allons enfants de la patrie," 168.
Alpha and omega, 359.
" Alphorn " (a song), 325.
Alps, the, 152.
Alsace, 154.
" Altmeister," 334, 5, 6.
Altruism, 10.
Amateurs, musical, 198-9, 200, 2.
Ambassador, a foreign, 97 ; the pianoforte as Music's, 198.
Ambition, 18, 22, 156, 350; the burgher's, 124.
Ambushed enemies, 242, 338.

CONDUCTOR—*continued*—
Lessons, taking, 295.
Liszt as, 265.
Mendelssohn as, 280, 95, 6, 306-8, 310, 37.
Mozart as, 192, 317, 9.
as Musician, 360-2.
New style, 294, 340. See Eleg.
Old style, 292-4, 6, 301, 25, 35, 9, 340.
Opera, contempt for, 298-9, 350-3.
Patronised, 294, 5, 7, 305.
Selection and appointment of, 262-263, 91, 4, 338-9, 51 ; by special summons, 295, 9.
unable to sing, 303 ; cf. 192, 307, 313.
Wagner as, 240, 2, 300, 2, 5, 9, 15, 325-32, 57, 8.
Young and talented, 360.
See Beat, Classical, Concert, Tempo.
Confessions (relig.), 156, 7.
Conflict : social, 117 ; of soul, 231.
Connexion in music, 320, 1, 2, 4, 7.
Conqueror, the, 22, 6, 45.
Conscientiousness, 230, 41, 303.
Conscription, 49, 62.
Conservatism, 123, 30, 1, 60, 4, 212, 218.
Conservatorium and "conserving," 173-6, 81, 9, 93, 5, 202, 12, 99, 337.
Consonants, 182.
Conspiracy, 92, cf. 47.
Constant, Benj., 53, 5, 90, 1, 103.
Constitutionalism, 12, 32, 127, 31, 5, 142, 4.
Constraint, 117, 8 ; feeling of, 341, 3, 346.
Construction : of Sentences, 278, 83 ; Verse, 185. See Musical.
Content : musical, 197 ; poetic, 185.
Contradictions, 19, 29, 38, 61, 144.
Contrapuntist, an amiable, 307.
Contrast, musical, 308, 17, 21, 3, 7, 328, 33.
Controversy, relig., 30. See Disput.
Conventicles, musical, 262. See Saints.
Convention : artistic, 76, 82, 321 ; in Life, theatrical, 83, 4 ; symbolic, 74.
Conventional, the, 83, 8, 9, *vid. sup.*
Conversation, agreeable, 267, 79.
Conversion of the Heathen, 139, 215.
Convictions, 138, 43, 5, 7, 8.
Copy of reality, 83, 4. See Imitation, Naturalism.

Copying the foreigner, 175, 7. See Civilisation.
Cornelius, Peter (painter), 54.
(Corps Saxonia, the, 47.)
Correctness of Performance, 175-8, 187, 92, 200, 1, 6, 12, 6, 8, 20, 63, 270, 91, 304, 7, 14, 24, 6, 47, 52, 9.
Corybantes, 265, 8.
Coryphœi, 307, 20.
Cosmopolitanism, 54, 5.
Cossacks, 46, 140.
Costume, old German, 43, 6, 154.
Coulisses, 85. See Wings.
Counterfeits, 57, 104, 255.
Counterjumpers and Goethe, 99.
Counterpoint, exercises in, 188.
Courage, 44, 62, 141, 3, 67, 8, 265, 6, 360.
Court-Theatres, 52, 6, 78, 94, 6-8, 131, 77-8, 287, 93, 4, 333.
Courts and courtiers, (vii), 41, 83, 9, 137, 46, 61, 3.
Craftsmen, artistic, 93, 261, 339, 40, 353.
Creative faculty, 58, 74, 162. See Genius.
Crédit Mobilier, 111.
Credo and *Agnus*, 112.
Crescendo and diminuendo, 302, 19, 323, 7, 31, 2, 4.
Criminal courts, ix, 48, 282.
Critic as poet, 256, 7.
Criticism : modern, 217, 91, 342 ; scientific, 155, 268, 83. See Journalism, Theatre.
Critics, Wagner-, ix, xiii, 249, 69, 271, 326, 38.
Croats, 46.
Cross, the, 112.
Crowded halls, 191.
Crowded off the path, 338.
Crown of the State, 117, 8, 31, 5, cf. 146, 7.
Crucified by the Jews, 364.
Culture, 54, 114, 66, 261, 87, 340, 61 ; artistic, 76, 90, 176, 83, 96, 202, 4, 215, 28 ; literary, 66, 7, 99, 109, 26 ; national, 37, 54, 60, 2, 5, 9, 74, 106-8, 66, 90, 204 ; *versus* Polish, 296, 341 ; so-called, 84, 102, 241, 248, 300, 42, 3. See also Folk.
Cultured men, 7, 72, 91, 128, 45, 86, 352.
Culture-folks, 40, 58, 153.
Culture-historian, 48, 67, 85, 103, 251, 8, 9, 60, 8, 73, 341.
Curiosities, literary, 160.
Curiosity, 201 ; prurient, 92.

392

INDEX.

Domestic life, ix, xiv, 7, 98, 198, 9,
  283, 347.
Don Carlos, 88-9.
Don Juan Overture, 317-8.
Dotzauer ('cellist), 326.
Double meanings, 283.   See Sug-
  gestive.
Doubt, 300, 45 ; of self, 346.
Dragging and drawling, 56.   See
  Tempo.
DRAMA, 66, 74 :—
  Burgher, 88, 9, 203.
  French, 83.   See Theatre.
  German, 94, 127, 33 ; higher, 204.
    See G.
  Historical, 83.
  Literary, 69, 103.
  Rebirth of, 74, 5, 88.
  Romantic, 97.
  Sensational, 88, 91.
Dramatic : Action, 76 ; Dialogue and
  Declamation, 88, 9, 203, 5, 8-9.
  See Histrionic, Portrayal, Theatre.
Drastic, 88, 219, 332, 44, 7.
Draughty stage, 241.
Dream : and Day, 27 ; -Image, 323 ;
  the World a, 24.
Dreamers, a nation of, 53.
Dreamy sadness in music, 323, 6.
Dresden, 148, 223, 39, 43, 332 ;
  Orchestra, 302, 5, 10, 26, 40 ;
  Theatre, 95, (136), 228, 36, 40, 2, 3,
  248, 95, 331, 58, 60.
  (*Dresdner Anzeiger,* 136.)
Dull reading, 251.
DUMAS, A., 55, 6.
Dummies, 166.
Duping, artistic, 78, cf. 33.
DÜRER, ALBERT, 43.
Dutch, the, 57, 86.
Duty, 120.
Dynamics, instrumental, 302, 13-4,
  318, 24, 31 ; "monotony," 302.
Dynasties, 12, 59, 143, 53, 62, 4 ;
  intrigues, 38 ; policy, 44.

E.

Ear, musical, 357, 61 ; and heart, 363.
Ear and Eye, 231.
Earnestness, 5, 30, 42, 53, 68, 79,
  151, 60, 247, 53, 73 ; in Art, x, xiii,
  5, 9, 54, 178, 90, 240, 9, 60, 70,
  358 ; terrible, 332.   See Life.
Earth, the soil of, 139.
Ease, Royal, 49, 59.
Easy-chairs of honour, 342.

Easy-goingness, 20, 165, 6, 309.
Echo-effect (clarinet), 313.
Ecstasy, 100, 231, 314, 31.
Editions, twelfth &c., 68, 251.
Editors, xi, xiv, 217, 67, 9.
Education : Artistic, 65, 184, 5, 8,
  240—assisted, 189, 98 ; National,
  x, 108-14, 6, 40.
Effect : "avoid all," 344, 6, 7, 60 ;
  Dramatic, 219, 52 ; Musical, 214,
  309, 33 ; -Pieces, 104, 326, see
  Sensat. ; Running after, 53, 5, 250,
  273, 5, 337 ; Theatrical, 60, 78,
  83, 9, 101, 12.
Effeminacy of taste, 233.
Egmont, Goethe's, 86.   See Beeth.
Egoism, 11, 4, 5, 8, 25.
Eighteenth Century, 43, 50, 63, 71,
  135, 74, 204.
Elegance, 39, 155.   See Polish.
Elephant, the, 79.
Elocution, 182, 5, 208.
Emancipation, 117, 39, 40 ; of Artist,
  240, 3 ; of King, 144, cf. 119.
Emeriti, 122, 5, 7, 8.
Emotional expression, 88 ; nature,
  362.
Emperor, see Kaiser, Napol.
Emphasis, over-, 89.   See Accent.
Encore, an, 357.   See Applause.
Encouragement, 251.
End unto itself, 107, 17, 24, 7, 67.
Endurance, phys., 62, 229, 37, 8.
Enemies, my, 147, 267, 72.
Energy, (xvii), 66, 88, 230, 1, 8, 41,
  281, 92, 6, 329 ; and Ease, 333 ;
  and Initiative, 63.
England, 151, 340 ; Oratorio in, 190.
  See Britain.
English : Comedianism, 87 ; Musi-
  cians, the two "shortened," 282 ;
  Parliament, 60 ; Shilling, 169 ;
  Shopkeeper, 30, 140 ; Theatre, 70,
  86.
Enjoyment, artistic, 126, 32, 83, 90,
  202, 6, 335.
Enlightened times, our, 30.
Ennobling, 91, 116, 8, 26, 7 ; taste,
  114, 31, 77, 206.
Ennui, 186.
Entertainment, 33, 190 ; harmless,
  191 ; home, 198 ; necessary, 127,
  130, 77, 219 ; sensuous, 217.
Entr'acte-music, 300.
Environment, see Surrounding.
Envy, xiv, see Jealousy.
Ephemeral works, 219.
Epigones, 68.

Episodic : rôle, 241 ; themes, 354.
Equable tone, 312-3.
Equity, 12, 7, 20, 31, 118, 43.
Eric, in *Holländer*, 241.
Erinnyes and Eumenides, 70.
Error : the German's, 176 ; Princes',
123 ; Singing-masters', 237-8.
Erwin's cathedral (Strassburg), 107.
Esprit de corps, 340.
Esser, H. (Viennese cond.), 292.
Established Churches, 28, 9, 157.
Estates of the Realm, 115.
Eternal bliss for finite pain, 25.
Eternal doom, sentence of, 334.
" Eternal laws," 330, 2.
Eternal type of art, an, 324.
Ethics, 51, 69. See Moral, Theatre.
Etiquette, 83, 169.
Eunuchs, 347.
Euphony, 182-4, 361.
Euripides, 156.
European Balance, 17, 37 ; Family,
85, 144, 52, 4, 8.
Evangel of the stage, an, 101.
Every age and country, Germans per-
forming the works of, 177, 83, 4, 9,
195, 200, 3, 4, 5.
Evolution, 279 ; of Art, 73, 5, 173,
180, 2, 4, 204, 17 ; Artist, 203, 13,
257 ; Human, 20, 79-80 ; .King-
hood, 144 ; National, 154, 5, 61, 4,
254 ; Religion, 23, 156 ; Social, 48,
121, 3, 39-40 ; Spiritual, 11 ; Style,
176.
Evolving from each other, 320, 1, 3, 4.
" Ewig, selig," 361.
Exacting, Wagner, 234.
Exaggeration, 90, 342.
Examination of pupils, 208, 11, 2.
Example, 30, 1, 125, 32, 4, 79, 213,
214, 9, 22, 32, 7, 40, 337, 8, 63 ;
Royal, 63-4, 7, 9, 72, 3, 94, 102, 58.
Exceptional and excellent, 32, 97,
132, 3, 78, 9, 240, 91, 353.
Excess, 145 ; in Art, 330.
Exchange, Rate of, 169.
Excuse, a lame, 310-1.
Exempt, 134, see Emeriti.
Exertion, over-, 229, 36, 43.
Exile, 223, 7.
Existing, The, 124, 31, 42, 7, 210, 1, 8.
Expedience, 114-22, 9 ; ideal, 118.
Experience, 5, 14, 178, 206 ; personal,
70, 282 ; Wagner's, x, 73, 151, 68,
177, 88, 236-9, 47-8, 73, 91, 303,
304, 6, 8, 20, 2, 42, 5, 53, 60.
Experts, xiv, 95, 206, 253, 7.
Expiation, 50.

Exploitation, 58, 158, 202.
Exposure, 249, 50, 5, 338.
Expression, 217, 9 ; Dramatic, 233, 9,
298 ; Executant, 188, 97, 209, 12,
307, 19 ; Marks, 192, 333. See
Rendering, Scores.
Externals, mere, 32, 146, 60.
Eye, 228, 35 ; with half-closed, 234 ;
a quick, 361. See Ear.

F.

Failure canonised, 350.
" Fair " in the plural, the, 363.
Faith : in Art, 1, 242, 345, 60 ;
Religious, 24, 6, 8, 30, 156, 214.
Faith, Love and Hope, 2, 296.
Falsetto, 238.
Falstaff of Cologne, 266.
Fame, 163, 263, 7, 362 ; " ancient,"
295, 7 ; fanciful, 153 ; Hall of,
90, cf. 342 ; imperishable, 222, 4.
Familiar, the, 152, 5, 231, 3.
Family, the, 347 ; Archives, 137 ;
Parties, 191 ; Spirit, 340.
Fancy-picture, 33, cf. 81.
Fanfare (*Meistersinger*), 356, 7.
Fantasticism, xiv, 158, 64, 6.
Farces, 91, 9.
Farewell and Goodnight, 243.
Fashions, see Paris.
Fastidious, 258 ; too, 346, 50.
Fate, 23, 223, 52, 325, 34, 8, 50.
Father and dead child, 81.
Father of my country, 359.
Father of his Folk, 67, 137, 42.
Fatherland, xiii, 16, (47), 61, 4, 138,
159.
Faust, 43, 64, 87, 99-101, 12, 214,
289, 363 ; Gounod's, 101, 214.
" Favourite," a Royal, x, xv.
Favourites, stage, 99, 104, 81, 219,
262.
Fear *v.* Love, 46, cf. 367.
" Feast of hearing," 335.
Federation, 59. See Assoc.
FEELING :—
Addressing the, 192, 363.
Artistic, 93.
German, 52.
Instinctive, 124, 202.
Musical, 194, 299, 301, 21, 37, 45,
357, 60, 1, 2 ; dull of, 302, 8, 10,
318, 30.
and Resolution, 231.
Understanding by, 155, 91, 6, 206.
Fellowship, 11, 8, 121.

Machinations, (vii, 172), 242.
Madness, 29, 140, 2, 8, 233, 55, 330.
Mænads (*Tannh.*), 343.
Magic, 228, 33, 58, 88, 302, 26, 45; mantle, Helena's, 87.
Majesty, mantle of, 78.
Majority, the inert, 337.
Make-believe, 60, 1, 77.
Making *v.* creating, 78, 261.
Male, a whole, 346, cf. 256.
Man crown of Creation, 138.
Manhood, redemption into, 23, 99, 140.
Mannerism, 73, 8, 104, 204, 6, 15, 219.
Mannheim band and Mozart, 319.
Manual work and Jews, 340.
Marat the tiger, 84.
Marble palaces (Goethe), 86.
March past (troops), 168.
"Maria!", 231, 3.
(Maria de Medici, 82.)
Maria Stuart, 99, 112.
Marionnettes, 89.
Marschner, H., 340.
Martyrs, 30, 214; of music, 336.
Marx, A. B., 265, 6, 79, 82, 3; his widow, 276.
Masquerade, ghastly, 242.
Masses, the, 146, 8, 65-6, 219; marvel of, 77, 127, 233.
Mässig (moderato), 305, 54.
Masters, Great, 107-8, 67: and pupils, 188; works and performance, 87, 173-4, 89-96, 200, 2, 13, 7, 8, 22, 251, 99-303, 37, 57.
Mastersingers, the, 107.
Mastery of one's task, 207, 302.
Mater gloriosa, 112.
Materialism, 29, 108, 26, 238; French, 37, 8, 54, 8.
Mathematics, applied, 298. See Arith.
Matthäi, of Leipzig, 300.
"*Mauvaise blague*," a, 269.
Maximilian II., 64-9, 113.
Maximilianeum, 65-7, 116.
Maxims, see Mendelssohn.
Means and media, artistic, 174, 83, 7, 196, 213, 8, 21, 3.
Mechanics, 84, 109, 237.
Mechanism of pfte, 197.
Mediators with God, 30.
Medieval wood-carvings, 348.
Mediocrities, 101, 65, 261, 5. See Little.
Meditation, 64, 164, 260.

Medley of styles, 200, 4, 15.
(*Meister, The*, 48, 253.)
"Meister" Devrient, 287.
MEISTERSINGER, DIE, (x, xvii, 26, 43, 159, 64, 202, 15); excerpts at Munich, 242; final scene, 358-9; march, 354, 6, 9; Prelude, 354-8, first perf., 357.
Meistersinger-perfnces: Dresden, 295, 354, 8-60; Munich, 359.
Melodrama, birth of, 91.
Melody: alleged abolition of, 269; Beethoven's, 216, 301, 3, 16; Mozart's, 44, 71; Weber's, 52.
Memory, 20, 267, 84, 311, 23; committing to, 56, 98; a mournful, 72, 257, 99; national, 153, 61; a pleasant, 326, 59.
MENDELSSOHN, 262, 75-6, 8, 9, 80, 283, 4, 8 :—
as Dramatic composer, 276, 81, 2, 286-7, 350.
and German art-life, 341.
Letters of, 286.
Maxim and school, 295, 306, 7, 14, 319, 39-40, 2, 4, 5, 6, 9, 50. See Conductor.
Orchestration, 296.
and *Tannh.*-overture, 354.
Menuetto, 317; in Eighth Sym., 308-10, 22, 45.
Mephistopheles, 87, 363.
Mercadante, 269.
Mercenaries, besotted, 48.
Mercy, 31, see Pity.
Merit and distinction, 120, 294, 353; acknowledging small, 219, 48.
Merovingians, the, (xvii), 153.
Merry Andrews, 74, cf. 126.
"Messiah of Music," a, 363-4.
Metronome, 304-5. See Tempo.
Metternich, Prince, 165.
MEYERBEER, 112, 242, 63; at Berlin, 297; and his flautist, 296.
Mezzoforte, 307, 26, 32.
MICHAEL ANGELO, 111.
Middle Ages, 38, 154, 82, 348.
Milan Opera and Cons., 174.
Military bravado, 85; distinctions, 120. See Soldiers.
Mime, the, 56, 76-83, 127, 262. See Poet.
Miracle, 192, 232; of musico-mimetic art, 235; of voice, 239.
Mirror, image in, 81, 159.
Mischief-making, 258, cf. 249, 70, 288.
Miser, the, 81.

2 C

408   INDEX.

414 INDEX.